REGIONAL
FINANCIAL
COOPERATION

REGIONAL FINANCIAL COOPERATION

JOSÉ ANTONIO OCAMPO

Editor

UNITED NATIONS
Economic Commission for
Latin America and the Caribbean

BROOKINGS INSTITUTION PRESS
Washington, D.C.

Copyright © 2006

UNITED NATIONS ECONOMIC COMMISSION
FOR LATIN AMERICA AND THE CARIBBEAN

Regional Financial Cooperation may be ordered from:
BROOKINGS INSTITUTION PRESS
c/o HFS, P.O. Box 50370, Baltimore, MD 21211-4370
Tel.: 800/537-5487; 410/516-6956; Fax: 410/516-6998
Internet: www.brookings.edu

Library of Congress Cataloging-in-Publication data

Regional financial cooperation / José Antonio Ocampo, editor.
    p.   cm.
Summary: "Assesses how regional financial institutions can help developing countries, often at a disadvantage within the global financial framework, finance their investment needs, counteract the volatility of private capital flows, and make their voices heard"— Provided by publisher.
Includes bibliographical references and index.
ISBN-13: 978-0-8157-6419-9 (pbk. : alk. paper)
ISBN-10: 0-8157-6419-7 (pbk. : alk. paper)
  1. Developing countries—Economic integration. 2. Regionalism—Developing countries. 3. Developing countries—Foreign economic relations. 4. International economic relations. I. Ocampo, José Antonio. II. Title.
HC59.7.R369 2006
332'.042—dc22   2006027658

9 8 7 6 5 4 3 2 1
The paper used in this publication meets minimum requirements of the American National Standard for Information Sciences—Permanence of Paper for Printed Library Materials: ANSI Z39.48-1992.

Typeset in Adobe Garamond

Composition by Circle Graphics
Columbia, Maryland

Printed by R. R. Donnelley
Harrisonburg, Virginia

Contents

v

Foreword

The Monterrey Consensus, adopted by the 2002 International Conference on Financing for Development, highlighted in its paragraph 45
"the vital role that multilateral and regional development banks continue to
play in serving the development needs of developing countries and countries
with economies in transition." It went on to note, "They should contribute
to providing an adequate supply of finance to countries that are challenged
by poverty, follow sound economic policies and may lack adequate access to
capital markets. They should also mitigate the impact of excessive volatility
of financial markets. Strengthened regional development banks and subregional financial institutions add flexible financial support to national and
regional development efforts, enhancing ownership and overall efficiency.
They also serve as a vital source of knowledge and expertise on economic
growth and development for their developing member countries." Despite
this call, however, relatively little progress has been made since Monterrey in
enhancing the role that regional financial arrangements play in the international financial system.

The failure to devote attention to this issue is attested to by the absence of
any book or report providing a comparative evaluation of the experience

with regional financial cooperation in different parts of the world. This book seeks to fill this serious gap in the existing literature. Experiences in this area can be clustered into two groups: development financing; and mechanisms for macroeconomic cooperation and related financial arrangements (liquidity financing during balance-of-payments crises). Although our central aim is to explore the ways in which regional cooperation can promote the interests of developing countries, we will use Western Europe's experiences with regional financial cooperation as a benchmark for that exploration.

The experiences reviewed in this book indicate that regional cooperation can be a very effective means of surmounting the difficulties posed by the shortfall in the financial services provided by the current international financial architecture. Nonetheless, the scope of these institutions' operations is still limited and they have yet to be recognized as central elements in the international financial architecture. We hope that this book will spark a broader interest in initiatives in this area and indeed bring them to the center of the current discussion on South-South cooperation.

We are deeply grateful to the Ford Foundation for providing the United Nations Economic Commission for Latin America and the Caribbean with the support it needed to undertake this project.

JOSÉ LUIS MACHINEA
Executive Secretary
Economic Commission for
Latin America and the Caribbean

JOSÉ ANTONIO OCAMPO
Under-Secretary-General for
Economic and Social Affairs
of the United Nations

1

Regional Financial Cooperation: Experiences and Challenges

JOSÉ ANTONIO OCAMPO

The period following the 1997 Asian crisis generated an extensive discussion on the international financial architecture. The debate made clear that there is an undersupply of services by international financial institutions that has become more glaring as a result of the growing economic linkages created by the current globalization process. The associated "global public goods" that are being undersupplied include adequate mechanisms for preventing and managing financial crises, as well as for guaranteeing global macroeconomic and financial stability. The debate also underscored the fact that private international capital markets provide finance to developing countries in a highly procyclical way, effectively reducing the room for maneuver of developing countries to undertake countercyclical macroeconomic policies. Finally, the debate emphasized that international capital markets squeeze out many developing countries, particularly the poorest among them, from private global capital markets.

The possible role of regional institutions in providing these services was underestimated in the debate on how to improve global financial arrangements.

I would like to thank Roy Culpeper, Stephany Griffith-Jones, Jomo K. S., Ann Orr, José Luis Machinea, Ejeviome Otobo, María Angela Parra, Esteban Pérez, Francisco Sagasti, and Lance Taylor for their comments on a prior version of this chapter.

I

It was, indeed, absent in major northern reports[1] and from the views of international financial reform coming from the Bretton Woods institutions (for example, in the reports on international reform presented by the International Monetary Fund [IMF] to the Interim Committee and its successor, the International Monetary and Financial Committee). It was also given at best a passing reference in major academic analyses of reforms of the international financial architecture.[2] There was even open opposition to regional arrangements, particularly to the 1997 Japanese proposal to create an Asian Monetary Fund, although this idea was revived in 2000 in the form of the Chiang Mai Initiative among the Association of Southeast Asian Nations (ASEAN) countries, plus China, Japan, and the Republic of Korea.

There were obviously exceptions to this rule. Among the many reports, that of the United Nations stands out for its defense of the potential role of regional financial arrangements in an improved international financial architecture.[3] Strong defenses of regional financial arrangements were also made by Percy Mistry, José Antonio Ocampo, and the Emerging Markets Eminent Persons Group convened by the Ford Foundation.[4] Regional and subregional development banks have been given greater attention.[5] As already pointed out, after the crisis Asia took the most important steps forward,[6] while the Economic Commission for Latin America and the Caribbean (ECLAC) provided a strong defense of the role of regional financial arrangements in Latin America and the Caribbean.[7]

The lack of adequate attention to regional financial arrangements was surprising in at least three ways. First, it is evident to all observers that the new wave of globalization is also one of "open regionalism." Second, postwar Western Europe is widely recognized as a successful example of regional financial cooperation, which in the financial area encompasses a history that extends from the creation of the European Payments Union and the European Investment Bank (EIB) in the 1950s to a series of arrangements for macroeconomic coordination and cooperation that eventually led to the current monetary union among most members of the European Union. Third, regional development banks have been recognized as an important part of the world institutional land-

1. See, for example, Council on Foreign Relations (1999) and Meltzer and others (2000).
2. Eichengreen (1999); Kenen (2001).
3. United Nations (1999).
4. See Mistry (1999); Ocampo (1999, 2002, 2003); and Ford Foundation (2001).
5. See Bezanson and Sagasti (2000); Culpeper (1997); Birdsall (2001); and Sagasti, Bezanson, and Prada (2005).
6. See Park and Wang (2000).
7. See United Nations, ECLAC (2002a) and Agosin (2001)

scape since the 1960s. In the developing world, there are also several experiences with "developing-country-owned" multilateral development banks,[8] regional payments agreements, at least one successful reserve fund, and a few monetary unions. These experiences coincide in several ways with those of regional and subregional trade agreements, with undoubtedly a mixed history in both cases.[9]

Reflecting the lack of adequate attention to this issue, there is no book or report that makes a comparative evaluation of experience with regional financial arrangements. This book aims to fill this important gap. The different forms of financial cooperation are clustered into two groups: (1) development financing, the area where there is more extensive experience, including novel ideas, such as the Asian initiatives to strengthen regional bond markets, and (2) mechanisms for macroeconomic and related financial cooperation (liquidity financing during balance-of-payments crises), which include mechanisms of policy dialogue and peer review, and more elaborate systems of macroeconomic surveillance and policy consultation or coordination; reserve funds and swap arrangements among central banks; and, in the most developed form, monetary unions. Two additional forms of cooperation that belong to the second cluster are regional payments agreements and cooperation in the area of prudential regulation and supervision of domestic financial systems. This study makes only passing reference to them. It should be emphasized that, although our central aim is to explore the potential service that regional financial cooperation can make to developing countries, the experience with such cooperation in Western Europe is used as a benchmark.

This chapter provides an overview of a set of relevant experiences with both forms of regional cooperation and links the comparative evaluation of these experiences with the broader debate on international financial reform. In this regard, it looks not only at the advantages of regional financial cooperation in comparison with global arrangements, but also at its revealed shortfalls and, equally important, at the possible complementarities between regional and global institutions. The chapter is organized into six sections, the first of which is this introduction. The next two sections provide the case for regional financial arrangements and analyze some of the challenges they face. The fourth and fifth sections look at major experiences with regional cooperation in the areas of development financing and macroeconomic cooperation respectively. The last draws some conclusions.

8. This chapter uses the term "developing-country-owned" to denote multilateral development banks that do not have any capital from industrialized countries (although they may have capital from relatively rich oil-producing countries).

9. See the analysis of the different experiences of regional cooperation in the series of books published by the Forum on Debt and Development (FONDAD) in the 1990s. See, in particular, Mistry (1996) and Teunissen (1998).

The Case for Regional Financial Institutions

Several arguments can be made for a more active use of regional financial arrangements to strengthen the international financial architecture. This chapter groups them into four major arguments.[10] The first relates to the fact that, as already pointed out, the current globalization process is also one of open regionalism. Intraregional trade and investment flows have deepened as a result of both policy and market-driven processes of regional integration.[11] This process is, of course, uneven, being clearly stronger in Western Europe, East Asia, and North America and much weaker in other parts of the world, particularly South Asia. However, even in regions that have lagged behind, a web of regional initiatives has played an important role in reshaping the world economic system since the early 1990s. In addition, since the 1980s the contagion effects of financial crises have also had important regional dimensions. As a result of all these processes, macroeconomic linkages among countries and the externalities generated by national macroeconomic policies on neighbors have increased.

A stronger case can thus be made than in the past for policies and institutions that build regional defenses against financial crises and explicitly internalize the effects of domestic macroeconomic and financial policies on regional partners. In this regard, regional reserve funds and swap arrangements can serve as a first line of defense against crises. In turn, macroeconomic dialogue or stronger forms of regional surveillance and policy consultation could internalize, at least partially, the externalities that national macroeconomic policies have on regional partners. Furthermore, the effectiveness of national macroeconomic policies may be enhanced (or reduced) by the credibility generated by the willingness (or refusal) of regional partners to support a specific country.[12] A complementary argument is that, in a world where the room for maneuver of national macroeconomic policies has become more limited, the regional arena has become crucial for exercising what remains of macroeconomic policy autonomy. On the contrary, macroeconomic policies that take into account only domestic considerations (as has been traditional in IMF programs) may be said to contribute to

---

10. See complementary arguments in Culpeper's contribution to this volume. He differentiates between cooperative motives and the need to remedy the incomplete set of international institutions.

11. The first refers to the web of regional, subregional, and bilateral trade agreements that have generated the "spaghetti bowl" of current trade agreements. The second is used in the analysis of East Asia to refer to a process that was largely driven by investment and trade in intermediate goods for the production of manufactures for the world market—following the "flying geese" pattern that has been reshaped in recent decades by the irruption of China into global markets.

12. Mistry (1999).

the contraction of regional trade and to encourage competitive devaluations that effectively compound contagion.

Growing regional linkages also mean that there is a role for regional development banks or other mechanisms to support investments in regional infrastructure and other "regional public goods." Indeed, the limited financing for "regional public goods" in current development cooperation has led Birdsall to claim that the underfunding of regionalism is one of the major problems of current international arrangements.[13] Classical risk-pooling arguments also enhance the potential role of regional and subregional development banks. An advantage of all these mechanisms is that information asymmetries may be smaller at the regional level, and that the mix of peer pressure and the strong sense of ownership of regional institutions may reduce the risks that these development banks face, and have positive effects on investment and the financial development of members of a regional club.

Similar arguments can be made for cooperation in developing the financial infrastructure to support domestic financial development and to expand regional capital markets. Regional mechanisms can also play a role in supporting national systems for the prudential regulation and supervision of domestic financial systems, including the adaptation of international standards to regional conditions, or even in setting special regional norms (for example, in the developing world, on maturity and currency mismatches in the portfolios of financial institutions). In all of these areas, regional cooperation can help to reduce learning costs and help countries share the experience of institutional development.

According to the second argument, the heterogeneity of the international community implies that world and regional institutions can play complementary roles, following the principle of subsidiarity that has been central to European integration. The need to fill the gaps in the world's current highly incomplete international financial architecture makes this role even more important, as Roy Culpeper argues in this volume.[14] Furthermore, some of the services provided by international institutions may be subject to diseconomies of scale, and it is unclear whether others have large enough economies of scale to justify single international institutions in specific areas. In particular, regional and subregional institutions may be better placed to capture and respond to specific regional needs and demands. The diverse portfolios of existing multilateral development banks are tailored to the specific needs of countries in the regions

13. See Birdsall (2006).
14. See also Sakakibara (2003).

where they operate, and they are also capable of operating successfully on very different scales.

In the same vein, macroeconomic surveillance and consultation at the world level are necessary to guarantee policy coherence among major countries, but they are inefficient for managing the externalities generated by macroeconomic policies on neighbors in the developing world (or even within Western Europe). Thus, while the IMF should play a central role in macroeconomic policy coordination at the global level,[15] there is plenty of room for regional and subregional processes of a similar nature. Also, although regional and international contagion implies that the role of the IMF should be to manage the largest balance-of-payments crises, regional funds could actually provide full support to small and medium-sized countries during crises.[16] Indeed, the rising concentration of balance-of-payments support on a few countries indicates that there may be biases in the response of global financial institutions according to the size of countries.[17] Thus, an argument can be made for a division of labor in the provision of financing between world and regional organizations, with the latter assuming a greater role in the support of smaller countries.

The third is an argument for competition, particularly in the supply of services to small and medium-sized countries. Owing to their small size, the power of these countries to negotiate with large organizations is very limited, and their most important defense is therefore competition in the provision of financial services. For these countries, access to a broader menu of alternatives with which to finance development or to manage a crisis may be relatively more important than the "global public goods" that the largest international organizations provide (such as global macroeconomic stability). Furthermore, since they can assume they have little or no influence on the provision of those "global public goods," they are prone to take the attitude of "free riders" toward them. This implies that, aside from the case for complementarity between global and regional financial institutions, competition between the two sets of organizations in the provision of development bank services, liquidity financing, or technical support is the best arrangement for small and medium-sized countries.

The final argument in favor of regional arrangements is of a political economy order, and may be called the "federalist" argument. In this regard the essential issue is that regional and subregional institutions enjoy a greater sense of ownership because member states feel that they have a stronger voice in these organizations.

15. See United Nations (2005).
16. See, for example, the estimates of Agosin (2001) for Latin America.
17. See Griffith-Jones, Ocampo, and Cailloux (1999); and Ocampo (2002).

This creates a special relationship between them and member countries, which in the case of financial institutions may generate a strong "preferred-creditor status." The preferred-creditor status may, in turn, reduce the risks that regional and subregional development banks and reserve funds face, further encouraging the virtues of risk pooling.

One element of this argument is that, no matter what arrangements are adopted at the world level, the voice of small and medium-sized countries in global institutions is unlikely to be strong. The inadequate representation of developing countries in existing financial arrangements, an issue that was underscored at the International Conference on Financing for Development, held in Monterrey, Mexico, in 2002,[18] and the even greater informal concentration of power in international financial institutions, contributes to this view. This means that, within the global order, the smaller countries will be able to make their voice heard (or heard much more clearly) only if it takes the form of a regional voice. In fact, a paradox of the global system is that global rules are most important for small countries, even though it is precisely they that have the least influence over the formulation and defense of such rules. This problem can only be solved if the smaller countries organize themselves and if regional institutions are truly made part of a broader international order.

The foregoing discussion implies that, although there is a strong case for greater international macroeconomic and financial cooperation, it is unclear whether the increasing supply of services from the associated institutions should come from a few world organizations. Rather, in some cases the organizational structure should be one of networks of institutions providing the required services on a complementary basis, and in others it should function as a system of competitive organizations. The provision of services required for financial crisis prevention and resolution should probably be closer to the first model, whereas in the realm of development finance, competition should be the basic rule (and in fact should include competition with private agents as well). But purity in the model's structure is probably not the more desirable characteristic: it may be better for parts of the networks to compete against one another (for example, regional reserve funds or swap arrangements versus the IMF in the provision of liquidity financing) and for rival organizations to cooperate in other cases.

This implies that the International Monetary Fund of the future should be better viewed as the apex of a network of regional and subregional reserve funds and swap arrangements.[19] Indeed, such a structure would be more akin to that

18. United Nations (2002).
19. See United Nations (1999); and Ocampo (1999, 2002, 2003).

of the European Central Bank or the United States Federal Reserve system than to its current centralized structure. To encourage the development of regional reserve funds, incentives could be created giving them automatic access to IMF financing or a share in the allocation of special drawing rights (SDRs) proportional to their paid-in resources, or both—in other words, contributions to common reserve funds could be treated as equivalent to IMF quotas. As already noted, regional reserve funds or swap arrangements could provide not only most of the exceptional financing for smaller countries within a region, but also part of the financing for larger countries, and they could also serve to deter (at least partly) would-be speculators from attacking the currencies of individual countries within a region.

This model should be extended to the provision of macroeconomic surveillance and consultation, as well as to the surveillance of national systems of prudential regulation and supervision, and to developing the infrastructure for domestic and regional capital markets. This would complement, rather than replace, regular IMF surveillance and IMF/World Bank support to financial development. In the area of development financing, subregional development banks can play a significant role as a mechanism for pooling the risks of groups of developing countries, also allowing them to make more aggressive use of opportunities provided by private capital markets.

An institutional framework such as this would have two positive features. First, it would bring more stability to the world economy by providing essential services that can hardly be provided by a few international institutions, owing both to the heterogeneity of the international community and to the dynamic processes of open regionalism that are under way. Second, from the point of view of the equilibrium of world relations, it could be more balanced than a system based on a few world organizations. It could also increase the commitment of small countries to abide by rules that contribute to world and regional stability.

The Challenges Facing Regional Arrangements

Regional financial cooperation also faces significant challenges, which must not be underestimated. They relate to the viability and long-term sustainability of the arrangements that are created, and involve three major issues: the capacity of a given group of developing countries to supply the relevant financial services; the need to guarantee that strong regional institutions are developed; and an equitable distribution of the benefits of regional integration.

Culpeper's contribution to this volume poses the first of these issues as the need to match the demands from developing countries with their capacity to supply the associated financial services. In this regard, he argues that the presence of industrial or emerging-market economies within a region is crucial for successful financial cooperation, as they provide a rapidly growing pool of savings and greater creditworthiness. In this sense, regional cooperation may be unable, by itself, to meet the resource needs of the poorest countries, whether they are of a short- or long-term nature. This is particularly true when such funds must be provided with a larger, or even a full, grant component to avoid building an unsustainable debt dynamic, as has been underscored in recent years. However, not all the potential services of regional financial institutions require additional funding (some forms of macroeconomic cooperation do not), and some may actually reduce the need for external funds (reserve pooling) or allow countries to reduce the costs of accessing private capital markets (risk pooling).

In any case, for large-scale funding, partnerships with donor countries seem to be inescapable for low-income countries for the foreseeable future. The term of the partnership must be adequate, however, and could include channeling cooperation through regional institutions in ways that do not undermine developing countries' "ownership" of the regional arrangement. Indeed, this was the experience of Western Europe during the years of postwar reconstruction characterized by a "dollar shortage."[20] The channeling of Marshall Plan aid through the European Payments Union is a successful example of external financial support channeled through a regional institution.

For middle-income or "emerging" countries, the demand for regional financial cooperation will depend, in part, on how deep regional trade and financial integration are. The constraints on supplying effective services may also be important, but will differ in nature from those faced by low-income countries. The main problem lies in providing short-term liquidity financing to cope with capital account shocks, particularly if external funds are supplied in a procyclical manner to all countries in a region and there are significant factors of "regional contagion." However, cooperation from neighbors during crises may actually be highly effective, as evidenced by the successful support of France by Germany during the European currency crisis of 1992, or China's support for Hong Kong SAR during the Asian crisis.[21] Although of a more limited nature, the successful experience of the Latin American Reserve Fund (which, despite its name, continues to be essentially an Andean arrangement, with Costa Rica as the additional member) in supporting member countries during the Latin American debt crisis of the 1980s, and during the Asian crisis of the late 1990s, shows that, despite

20. Triffin (1957).
21. Mistry (1999).

contagion, all members of a region can benefit from the supply of liquidity financing by regional institutions (see Daniel Titelman's contribution to this volume). As the experience of the Latin American Reserve Fund indicates, the demand for funds by different countries does not coincide exactly in time. This facilitates the functioning of reserve funds and helps them to mitigate contagion. On the contrary, lack of support or, worse still, an explicit attempt by other countries in a region to differentiate themselves from a regional partner undergoing crisis, may reduce the effectiveness of any adjustment policies that this country undertakes and end up increasing contagion.

Although "ownership" provides a strong case for regional arrangements, it also has its downside. The essential problem is that regional and subregional institutions may be weak in the face of pressures from some of their individual members, particularly the more powerful among them. Therefore, the virtues of ownership can only be realized when matched by strong institution building, which is ultimately what will determine the effectiveness of regional cooperation arrangements. Political considerations play the dominant role in the process of institution building—and indeed, regional integration is always a political process and its weakness a sign of a lack of political will to build strong regional institutions.[22]

The history of European cooperation provides a clue about the long-term nature and complexities of this process. According to Charles Wyplosz (in this volume), since regional integration involves continuous erosion of national sovereignty—or, put in a more positive way, a transfer of sovereignty from the nation-state to regional institutions—it requires building confidence in regional institutions, which takes place only gradually. Each step in this process implies an uneasy compromise between integrationist and nationalist forces, and the latter may lead to reversals in the road to integration, implying that it is not a linear process.[23] Although it is essential to have clear vision and objectives, a master plan is neither necessary nor useful. To quote Wyplosz: "Integration has always been characterized by a process of muddling through, taking two steps forward and one step back, with deep and lingering divergences as to what the end objective should be. But each integration step has made the next one more likely. Success in one area emboldened political leaders to contemplate another even bolder project in another area. More crucially perhaps, each important step has been matched by some additional institutional buildup, which has provided

---

22. Teunissen (1998).

23. The associated complexities have recently manifested themselves, among other areas, in the Stability and Growth Pact. In this case, however, as recent debates have underscored, the inappropriateness of the Maastricht rules are a key part of the problem.

the backbone for further moves. It is difficult to overestimate the importance of the early creation of institutions to support the integration process, no matter how imperfect those institutions are."

Powerful countries may prefer weak regional institutions, to allow them to exercise more influence over them. The struggle for regional influence among major regional powers may also become an obstacle to strong institution building. This seems to have underlain some of the problems facing the design of strong regional macroeconomic arrangements in East Asia in recent years, and is evident in other processes, such as the Southern Common Market (Mercosur). The way a power struggle among major players is settled, and whether it results in strong or weak regional institutions, will be critical for smaller members of a regional or subregional club, which clearly benefit from strong regional institutions in their relations with large regional players.

Historical and cultural affinity may help institution building, as Culpeper argues in his chapter, but the story is mixed in this regard. European integration took place despite diversity, whereas Latin American integration has advanced slowly regardless of affinity. Political motivations are obviously behind the integration efforts in these two regions, and clearly have been stronger in Western Europe, as well as in building up the network of Arab and Islamic financial institutions and in the history of regional development banks. The breakdown of the regional arrangements inherited from the colonial past is quite a common historical phenomenon, as evidenced by both Spanish America in the nineteenth century and the end of colonialism in Africa and Asia in the second half of the twentieth century. It can perhaps be argued that national institution-building almost always comes at the cost of regional integration, and in many cases involves confrontation with neighbors. Some arrangements that have survived decolonization have sometimes had a troubled history, even when supported by an industrial country, as macroeconomic cooperation among the francophone countries in West Africa indicates.

The distribution of the benefits of integration is one of the crucial issues in the design of institutions appropriate for a given integration process. Owing to agglomeration economies, the benefits from trade integration may accrue disproportionately to larger and higher-income countries. So there is no presumption that trade integration will facilitate convergence in real incomes within regions.[24]

Most integration processes include provisions to facilitate an equitable distribution of their benefits. In trade integration, they commonly include preferential rules of varying types: slower liberalization, the possibility of maintaining

---

24. Mistry (1996).

higher levels of protection or subsidies, and exceptions to some rules. This practice has been extended to World Trade Organization (WTO) agreements and,
to a lesser extent, to bilateral trade agreements. In more elaborate integration
processes, they also include special development financing facilities and, in a few
instances, fiscal transfers to the weaker countries or regions. Western Europe
again represents the best model in both areas. In the past, some integration
processes in Africa and Latin America also included industry-sharing agreements, under which weaker partners were allocated certain industries, but these
arrangements usually failed and were abandoned. Freer labor mobility may also
be seen as an adjustment mechanism that allows weaker countries or regions to
adapt to the effects of integration. However, although it is generally seen as an
essential element of full integration, it is unlikely to be considered a rule for the
equitable sharing of its benefits.

In sum, the development of a dense institutional network of regional and
subregional institutions in development finance and macroeconomic cooperation faces three major challenges: matching demand with supply capacities; a
clear long-term commitment to institution building; and an equitable distribution of the benefits of integration. These issues are interrelated: supply capacities
are not exogenously given, as they are largely created through a gradual process
of institution building; and strong institutions are unlikely to be accepted by
weaker partners unless they perceive that there is an equitable distribution of the
benefits of integration.

Development Financing

Regional development financing arrangements have followed three basic models. The oldest and best-developed model is multilateral development banks and
related multilateral financial institutions. These institutions are present in all
regions, although with different coverage, structures, and priorities. A second
model, which is mainly used by the European Union, is fiscal transfers with
explicit redistributive regional objectives. A third and more novel model is the
development of regional bond markets; the most important initiatives in this
regard have come from East Asia.

The regional development banks (discussed by Francisco Sagasti and Fernando
Prada in this volume) are the oldest of the first group of institutions: the Inter-
American Development Bank (IDB); the Asian Development Bank (AsDB); the
African Development Bank (AfDB); and the European Investment Bank (EIB).
Strong political motivations led to their creation in the 1950s and 1960s. The first
two institutions may be viewed as the result of cold war politics, while the third is

the daughter of decolonization. EIB was born, in turn, out of two basic objectives of European integration: to support lagging regions and thus an equitable integration process; and to finance the investment in the infrastructure of integration—"regional public goods" in current terminology (see in this regard the chapter by Stephany Griffith-Jones, Alfred Steinherr, and Ana Teresa Fuzzo de Lima in this volume). To these we should add the European Bank for Reconstruction and Development (EBRD), which was established in 1991 and is the daughter of post–cold war politics.

With the exception of the EIB, which is made up entirely of industrial-country members, all of which can borrow from the institution, the regional banks include a division between developing country borrowers and nonborrowing industrial-country members. Borrowing members are a majority in AfDB and slightly over half of the capital of IDB, but are a minority in AsDB and particularly in EBRD. This structure was adopted only late (in 1982) by the African Development Bank, which was initially a strictly African institution, but was forced to converge with the structure of other regional development banks because of its financial difficulties.

This capital structure allows developing countries to benefit from the excellent credit rating of the industrial-country members. It is amplified by the practice of maintaining a large ratio of subscribed to paid-in capital, which may be seen as a huge guarantee fund for the credit operations of these institutions. This may be understood as a cross-subsidy from countries with good to weaker credit ratings. It may also be seen, however, as a correction of a market failure: the overestimation of risk in private capital markets, particularly during periods of bust in private financing. The better lending conditions, as well as the willingness of these institutions to finance countries under difficult circumstances—that is, during crises—tend to reinforce their preferred-creditor status. This becomes a "self-fulfilling prophecy" in terms of portfolio quality, and in this sense can also be considered a correction of market failures: low risk margins are justified by the fact that loan losses are minimal, but this reinforces the willingness of debtors to keep a good credit history with these institutions. The requirement that first-class guarantees be maintained (from governments or private banks) further reinforces credit quality, whereas the lack of retail services reduces the staff required and thus intermediation costs.[25]

The most elaborate system of multilateral financial institutions that are strictly "developing-country-owned" is that of the Arab and Islamic world. As Georges Corm describes in this volume, the origin of these institutions lies in

25. For a further analysis of these issues, see the two chapters by Sagasti and Prada and Griffith-Jones, Steinherr, and Fuzzo de Lima in this volume. See also Birdsall (2001).

the regional solidarity generated by the Arab-Israeli war of 1967 and, in economic terms, in the sudden increase in resources of Arab oil-exporting countries in the 1970s. Most of these institutions started to operate in the 1970s, although one of them, the Arab Fund for Economic and Social Development (AFESD), had been created in 1968. With the partial exception of the Islamic Development Bank, which includes some major non-oil-exporting countries as shareholders, these institutions essentially operate as mechanisms for transferring resources from the oil-rich countries of the region to poorer regional members, as well as to other developing countries, particularly in the Islamic world and Africa. Thus they complement the specific national cooperation extended by the oil-rich countries. This feature also implies that lending by these institutions is highly dependent on the oil price. This reduces the countercyclical role that financing by multilateral development banks should play.[26] The sharp upturn in oil prices since 2000 has led, however, to a small increase in funding, relative to the oil boom of the 1970s; thus financing by these institutions remains today significantly below the levels reached in the second half of the 1970s and early 1980s. They have also made suboptimal use of the opportunities to tap global or national capital markets.

The largest of these multilateral institutions in terms of cumulative commitments is the Islamic Development Bank, which also has the largest membership and the largest interregional coverage of its lending operations. It is followed by the Arab Fund for Economic and Social Development, which provides soft lending operations for Arab League countries, largely for infrastructure projects. In turn, the Arab Monetary Fund focuses its activities on financing inter-Arab trade. Although smaller in size, the Arab Fund for the Development of Africa channels funds to the African continent. Other institutions provide equity capital and insurance coverage for inter-Arab investment. The main beneficiaries of this network of institutions are the middle- and low-income Arab countries, which have received on average about three-fifths of the financing that has been available from the institutions since 1970. Indeed, some of these countries, particularly in the Middle East, have received more funds from these institutions than from countries in the Development Assistance Committee of the Organization for Economic Cooperation and Development (DAC/OECD).

Integration efforts in sub-Saharan Africa have also led to the design of some development banks and other financial institutions. These institutions were set up by the Economic Community of West African States (ECOWAS) and the failed (but now revived) East African Community—although its financial

---

26. See Ocampo (2002); and United Nations (2005, chap. 5).

branch, the East African Development Bank, survived that process. To these must be added the trade financing facilities set up more recently by the Common Market for Eastern and Southern Africa (COMESA). However, as Culpeper argues in this volume, their performance has been modest at best. Nonetheless, their existence creates the possibility of using them more actively in the future as instruments of regional development.[27]

Latin America and the Caribbean undoubtedly provide the best example of a well-developed network of subregional financial institutions, which include three major banks: the Andean Development Corporation (CAF, Corporación Andina de Fomento), the Central American Bank for Economic Integration (CABEI), and the Caribbean Development Bank (CDB) (see the chapter by Titelman in this volume).[28] These institutions were created in the 1960s to support the subregional integration processes and thus service the small and medium-sized countries of the region, which are the main participants in those integration processes. The Central American and Caribbean banks have the same structure as the regional development banks, and thus include both borrowing and nonborrowing countries; nevertheless, some of the nonborrowing countries are the larger Latin American countries in the vicinity of Central America, which are also part of the Caribbean basin.

The Andean Development Corporation is unique in being exclusively owned by developing countries (Spain joined in recent years, but is also a potential borrower). It is the most dynamic of all these institutions, and in recent years its loans to the Andean countries have actually surpassed joint lending to these countries by the IDB and the World Bank. Its membership has also gradually increased to near that of a regional development bank. This dynamic institution is, indeed, the best example of risk pooling in the developing world: it holds investment-grade status, regardless of the fact that none of the Andean countries does. The meager loan losses experienced by the Andean Development Corporation, despite the troubled macroeconomic history of most of its members, also demonstrate the strong preferred-creditor status of this institution with its members. The Caribbean Development Bank is a smaller but also very dynamic institution in the subregion. The history of the Central American Bank for Economic Integration is more mixed. It experienced a severe crisis in the 1980s as a

27. See a full inventory of these institutions in United Nations, Economic Commission for Africa (ECA) (2004, chap. 6). Some of these institutions have cofinancing arrangements with the African and the Islamic development banks.

28. A fourth small institution, FONPLATA (Fondo Financiero para el Desarrollo de la Cuenca del Plata), finances projects for the development of the Plata River basin.

result of the arrears of one of its members, Nicaragua, but recovered in the latter part of that decade and has expanded again since the 1990s.

There are crucial regional differences in the roles played by different types of multilateral development banks in the various regions (see table 1-1). As discussed, the expansion of regional development banks has focused primarily on the middle-income countries, where their combined net flows surpass those of the World Bank. In the Middle East and North Africa, the Arab and Islamic institutions are also an important financing source. In Latin America and the Caribbean, IDB lending surpasses the World Bank's by a large margin, and the subregional banks also play an important role where they operate. Indeed, as table 1-1 indicates, the subregional banks make the largest contribution, relative to gross domestic product (GDP), in the small and medium-sized countries of Latin America and the Caribbean, followed by the Middle East and North Africa. Sub-Saharan Africa and South Asia are highly dependent on the World Bank/IDA (International Development Association). East Asia falls somewhere in between, with the World Bank lending slightly more than the AsDB and, as in South Asia, with a relative absence of developing-country-owned financial institutions. The EIB is the dominant institution in Europe, even when we leave aside the old members of the European Union (EU-15 in the table). In the transition economies, however, both the World Bank and the EBRD play an important role.

The greater weight of poorer borrowing members in different regions, and the support provided through different financial institutions by nonborrowing industrial countries, is also reflected in the relative share of concessional lending and grants. Thus concessional lending is particularly important for AfDB (44 percent of total lending), the World Bank/IDA (40 percent), and the AsDB (27 percent); the IDB also has a concessional fund for special operations that amounts to 7 percent of total lending.[29]

Given the fact that only limited concessional lending can be provided by institutions entirely owned by developing countries, poor countries are likely to continue to be dependent on official development assistance (ODA) provided by industrial countries and to a certain extent intermediated by multilateral development banks. This coincides with the arguments put forward by Culpeper and the above analysis of the constraints on regional cooperation in the poorest countries. The strong presence of developing country–owned financial institutions in the Arab and Islamic countries and in several subregions of sub-Saharan Africa, as well as in Latin America and the Caribbean, reflects a mix of cultural affinity

---

29. World Bank and IMF (2005, box 6.1).

Table 1-1. *Multilateral Development Banks: Outstanding Loans, 2004*[a]
Millions of current U.S. dollars

| | | | Middle East and North Africa | Asia | | | Europe | | Latin America and the Caribbean | Rest of Latin America and the Caribbean |
| | | | | East Asia and Pacific | South Asia | Central Asia | EU-15 | Rest of Europe | Argentina, Brazil, Mexico | |
Institution	Outstanding loans	Africa								
World Bank group										
International Bank for Reconstruction and Development (IBRD)[b]	104,401	4,484	8,655	25,981	10,354	4,183		15,117	24,523	11,103
International Development Association (IDA)[b]	120,907	48,120	3,561	15,643	43,804	2,654		2,521		4,604
Regional development banks										
European Investment Bank[c]	656,578						597,486	45,960		
Inter-American Development Bank (IDB)[d]	49,800								28,138	21,661
Fund for Special Operations[d]	7,000								1,131	5,869
African Development Bank Group (AfDB + AfDF + NTF)[e]	8,511	6,724	1,787							
Asian Development Bank (AsDB)	24,159			15,112	9,047					
Asian Development Fund (AsDF)	27,216			17,025	10,192					
European Bank for Reconstruction and Development (EBRD)[f]	18,434					3,781	7,961	6,693		

(continued)

Table 1-1. *(continued)*
Millions of current U.S. dollars

Institution	Outstanding loans	Africa	Middle East and North Africa	Asia East Asia and Pacific	Asia South Asia	Asia Central Asia	Europe EU-15	Europe Rest of Europe	Latin America and the Caribbean Argentina, Brazil, Mexico	Latin America and the Caribbean Rest of Latin America and the Caribbean
Subregional development banks										
Nordic Investment Bank (NIB)[g]	14,125	424[h]		847[i]			11,300	989	565[j]	
Nordic Development Fund (NDF)[k]	528	240[h]		181[i]					108[j]	
Central American Bank for Economic Integration (CABEI)[l]	2,789									2,789
Caribbean Development Bank (CDB)[m]	2,484									2,484
Andean Development Corporation (ADC)	7,216								433	6,783
FONPLATA[n]	378								94	284
North American Development Bank (NADB)[o]	43								22	
East African Development Bank (EADB)[p]	111	111								
West African Development Bank (BOAD)	545	545								
Islamic Development Bank Group (IsDB + ICD)[q]	17,929	1,793	8,845	1,076	4,124	239		1,853		

	Total									
Arab Bank for Economic Development in Africa (ABEDA)	606	606								
Arab Fund for Economic and Social Development (AFESD)	11,982		11,982							
Arab Monetary Fund	1,297		1,297							
Total	1,077,050	63,047	36,138	75,865	77,519	10,857	616,747	73,133	54,341	56,251
Total without World Bank group	851,742	10,442	23,922	34,241	23,362	4,020	616,747	55,495	30,491	39,871
GDPr	511,818	622,396	3,016,618	878,785	645,548	12,167,879	1,154,722	1,432,854	564,519	

Sources: Data compiled from the official web pages of each institution. Where available, data were obtained from the annual reports of each institution for 2004.

a. Regions: Japan is not included in the figures for East Asia. Gulf Cooperation Council members (Saudi Arabia, Bahrain, Kuwait, Oman, Qatar, United Arab Emirates) are not included in total GDP for the Middle East and North Africa.

b. Country distribution by cumulative IBRD and IDA lending. Data from 2005.

c. Also reports credits to ACP (1 percent) and Asia and Latin America (1 percent) without any further disaggregation (not included in the table). Country distribution by 2004 loan approvals. Data from 2005.

d. Country distribution by approved loans (1961–2006).

e. Country distribution by debt outstanding.

f. Country distribution by total project value of EBRD investments.

g. Some relatively small credits go to the Russian Federation (Central Asia), without further disaggregation. Country distribution by 2004 loan portfolios. Data from 2005.

h. Includes North Africa.

i. Total for all regions of Asia.

j. Total for Latin America and the Caribbean.

k. Country distribution by project portfolios.

l. Reported as gross loan portfolio.

m. Reported as net total financing.

n. As reported. Not specific whether figures represent cumulative lending, outstanding lending, or lending for a specific year.

o. Country distribution for Mexico (50 percent) and United States (50 percent, not included in the table) by loan portfolios.

p. Data from 2003.

q. Country distribution by IsDB net approved operations sheet. Data from 1425H (2004–05).

r. GDP data from World Bank, World Development Indicators (online) database.

and political motivation, while their absence in South and East Asia reflects the lack of these factors.[30]

The difference in the portfolios of the various multilateral development banks reflects not only their specific strategies, but also their adaptation to the diversity of demands and financial needs of the developing world and the transition economies. Thus while the IDB has focused increasingly on social spending, subregional banks in Latin America and the Caribbean give greater weight to infrastructure and production sector lending.[31] Both the AfDB and the AsDB give more emphasis to infrastructure than the IDB does. The heavy focus on infrastructure lending is also typical of Arab institutions. Financing intraregional trade is also a mandate of some institutions, particularly the Arab Monetary Fund. Although many institutions have private sector lending facilities, which have tended to grow over time, this is the focus of EBRD activities (see the contributions of Corm, Sagasti and Prada, and Titelman in this volume). According to Sagasti and Prada, this diversity in the portfolios of these institutions is "in line with the general idea behind the creation of regional and subregional institutions: they play specific and localized roles, which are not always covered adequately by global or even by regional institutions."

The combination of collective-action problems in regional processes, in the absence of supranational institutions, indicates how important the regional and subregional development banks can be in supporting regional strategies. They can provide a coordination mechanism for member countries to plan and finance the provision of regional infrastructure. This is an incipient activity in most of the developing world but one that has been receiving increasing attention from some regional and subregional banks.[32] These institutions also have the ability to provide a regional public good essential for development: the transmission and utilization of region-specific knowledge. That ability puts them in a position to help countries in their respective regions to design specific policies

---

30. Nonetheless, South Asia set up a modest development fund in 1991. See United Nations Economic and Social Commission for Asia and the Pacific (United Nations, ESCAP) (2004, chap. 6), which provides a full inventory of regional cooperation mechanisms in South and East Asia. United Nations, ESCAP (2005) also proposed the creation of an Asian Investment Bank.

31. As Sagasti and Prada argue in this volume, the trend in lending by regional development banks has involved reduced support for the productive sector through state-owned financial institutions, but has been partially offset by operations with private banks and the development of domestic capital markets, which are classified as "financial infrastructure."

32. This is the case with the Initiative for the Integration of Regional Infrastructure in South America (Iniciativa para la Integración de la Infraestructura Regional Suramericana, IIRSA) and the Plan Puebla-Panama (involving Mexico and Central America).

appropriate to the countries' economic needs and political constraints.[33] Nonetheless, there is still very little financing of "regional public goods" in most of the institutions serving developing countries (1 percent or less for the AfDB, AsDB, and IDB), as well as in ODA in general.[34] This is in sharp contrast with the experience of the European Investment Bank, which has had regional infrastructure as one of its major mandates since its creation.

Indeed, as was pointed out at the beginning of this section, the EIB, the largest multilateral development bank in the world, is probably the best example of an institution designed to help compensate for regional disparities and to support the development of regional infrastructure. In recent decades, it has also been increasingly used for major extraregional initiatives of the European Union, such as projects in the African, Caribbean, and Pacific (ACP) countries and the Mediterranean region, as well as the liberalization processes of the former socialist countries of Central and Eastern Europe. Another reason for creating this institution in the 1950s was to correct market failures, since currencies were not fully convertible and international private capital markets had not fully recovered from the collapse of the 1930s, but it has continued to grow in recent decades, despite full capital account convertibility and booming global financial markets.

The chapter by Stephany Griffith-Jones, Alfred Steinherr and Ana Teresa Fuzzo de Lima in this volume provides some clues about the strengths of this institution in a region with significant financial development. Some of the reasons are: (1) the implicit subsidy and better access to finance by poorer countries in the region, which fulfills one of its historical mandates; (2) its signaling role to private lenders, which helps to correct another type of market failure (information asymmetries) and may be particularly important for infrastructure investment, one of its major lending activities; (3) the capacity to internalize the risks of offering long-term lending at fixed rates (which, nonetheless, as the authors argue, can be more costly to a borrower than floating interest rate loans of similar maturity); and (4) its capacity to be very competitive in its pricing, which makes it a desirable source of borrowing even by large private banks in the case of "global loans" for financing small and medium-sized enterprises. On the contrary, correcting market failures associated with large risks in innovative sectors has not been one of the main activities of the EIB. In the recent past, this has led to the creation of the European Investment Fund—of which it is the largest shareholder—to provide guarantees, take equity participation, and support venture

---

33. See Birdsall and Rojas-Suarez (2004).
34. See Birdsall (2006).

capital funds. However, on the whole, this institution continues to be risk averse, which is indeed a salient feature of multilateral development banks.

The creation of EIB as an instrument of European integration was matched from the beginning by fiscal transfers to poorer regions and specific sectors (particularly agriculture). This implied an explicit acknowledgment that integration would not achieve the aim of helping different parts of an integrating region to converge in their development levels, in the absence of an explicit policy to achieve this purpose—a policy that came to be labeled "cohesion policy." The focus on lagging regions rather than countries has also provided a source of support from major countries to this policy, because even rich countries may have lagging regions. These fiscal redistributive mechanisms (structural and cohesion funds) were further reinforced at every major step in the history of European integration. So they were extended as a result of the northern expansion of the European Community in the 1970s, particularly when the relatively poorer Southern European countries were incorporated in the 1980s. The 1990s saw, in turn, the design of more generous pre-accession funding for Central European countries. Although regional and even global trade integration processes have generally recognized the asymmetries of its member states, fiscal transfers have rarely been tried outside Europe; in fact, they were only used, rather unsuccessfully, in the early postcolonial experience of the East African Community.

The historical dearth of regional financial cooperation in South and East Asia has been amply compensated for in recent years by a series of initiatives in the area of development financing, as well as in monetary cooperation. The major reason was the traumatic experience of the 1997 East Asian financial crisis. These initiatives also reflect a sense of frustration with the slow speed and even, in many areas, the international financial system's complete lack of reform to enable it to face the problems that became evident during the Asian crisis, as well as a critical view of the policies implemented by the global financial institutions for managing the crisis.[35]

Although there have been proposals to create an Asian Investment Bank along the lines of the EIB,[36] the major initiatives under implementation relate to support for the development of national and regional bond markets. The basic rationale for these initiatives is the sense that over-reliance on short-term foreign currency loans was a major factor in the East Asian crisis. Since the crisis, another important factor has been the large current account surpluses and international reserves accumulated by economies in the region. International

35. Park and Wang (2000); Sakakibara (2003).
36. See United Nations, ESCAP (2005).

reserves, as well as private funds, are to a large extent invested in the deeper bond markets of the industrialized countries, some of which are recycled back into the region by foreign financial intermediaries. According to this view, the development of deeper national and regional bond markets would help to short-circuit this intermediation through world financial centers outside Asia. Therefore, the development of bond markets will be both a development and a crisis-prevention instrument, helping in the latter case to reduce the maturity and currency mismatches in the portfolios of private agents that were at the heart of the East Asian crisis.

The various initiatives, reviewed by Yung Chul Park, Jae Ha Park, Julia Leung, and Kanit Sangsubhan in their contribution to this volume, have taken place in different regional forums and are of two different types.[37] The first are of an institutional nature and aim to develop appropriate infrastructure for the functioning of either national or regional bond markets, particularly for bonds denominated in the local currencies of the economies of the region. This includes the Asia Pacific Economic Cooperation (APEC) initiative for developing securitization and credit-guarantee markets by means of policy dialogue and the provision of expert advice and panel visits to the economies concerned. In a similar vein, the ASEAN+3 (China, Japan, and the Republic of Korea) initiative focuses on facilitating market access by several public and private sector agents, and on improving the institutional infrastructure, including regional clearing and settlement mechanisms, credit-guarantee and hedging facilities, the development of national and regional credit rating agencies, and the dissemination of information on Asian bond markets. In a complementary manner, the various working groups convened under this initiative will aim to improve the harmonization of financial standards, regulatory systems, and tax treatment of financial assets throughout the region.

The second type of initiative, launched by the eleven members of the Executives' Meeting of East Asia–Pacific Central Banks (EMEAP), has focused on developing specific funds, the Asian Bond Funds (ABFs).[38] ABF 1, announced in June 2003, was composed of U.S. dollar-denominated bonds issued by sovereign and quasi-sovereign issuers of the eight emerging economies of EMEAP. Although this first action represented a milestone in central bank cooperation, it was limited in size (to U.S.$1 billion), and more particularly, it did not support the development of local-currency-denominated bonds. So a second fund (ABF 2)

37. See also United Nations, ESCAP (2004, 2005).
38. The eleven members of EMEAP are Australia, China, Hong Kong SAR, Indonesia, Japan, Republic of Korea, Malaysia, New Zealand, the Philippines, Singapore, and Thailand.

was launched in December 2004, with an initial amount of U.S.$2 billion, to invest in local-currency-denominated bonds of the EMEAP emerging economies, and to help create a convenient and cost-effective instrument fund and a new asset class for regional and institutional investors. As argued by Yung Chul Park and his coauthors, this new initiative has helped to introduce a new asset class (exchange-traded bond funds) and a new family of bond indexes; it has helped to remove some of the barriers to cross-border capital flows; and it has contributed to the adoption of new standards and to greater market transparency. All these effects, which largely relate to developing the associated regional financial infrastructure, indicate that this initiative is complementary to the above-mentioned approach that focuses directly on developing the regional financial infrastructure.

Macroeconomic Cooperation

Contrary to the rich historical experience in the area of development financing, particularly with multilateral development banks, there is a dearth of experiences in the area of macroeconomic cooperation in the developing world. However, several initiatives have been launched in this area in recent years. They sometimes match regional trade initiatives that have resulted from the dynamic process of "open regionalism" currently under way, and attempt to replicate in some ways the experience of European monetary integration. Some of the existing arrangements, as well as new initiatives, show the potentialities of this form of cooperation in the developing world, but also their limitations. As the attempts to replicate European trade integration in the past have had mixed success in the developing world, the more recent attempts to replicate European macroeconomic cooperation follow a similar mixed pattern. Furthermore, regional trade integration is more limited in the developing world than in Europe—although it has been growing rapidly in some regions, particularly in East Asia. There are, however, two additional rationales for macroeconomic cooperation in the developing world, particularly in emerging economies: to build stronger walls of defense against financial crises; and to avoid distorting competition among export-oriented economies.[39]

The links between trade and macroeconomic cooperation are, of course, at the heart of the formation of the European Union. As Wyplosz argues in this volume, this feature has been accompanied by two other major characteristics. The first is the emphasis on building strong institutions, albeit in a gradual and pragmatic way. The second is the clear subordination of macroeconomic coop-

39. See Sakakibara (2003).

eration to the objective of trade integration. The major objective of macro-economic cooperation has thus been exchange rate stability, which has been seen as the only way to create a level playing field for intraregional trade. In particular, *real* exchange rate stability has been the implicit target of such cooperation.

Since the breakdown of the Bretton Woods parities, this has implied the negotiation of regional arrangements (the snake, followed by the European Monetary System) to stabilize exchange rate parities, which finally led to European Monetary Union (EMU). Until the launch of EMU, these arrangements not only left room for limited flexibility (variable over time), but also involved a large number of nominal exchange rate adjustments, which used purchasing power parity criteria to determine the level of adjustment for achieving a desirable real target. These readjustments were fully symmetrical, thus involving both strong and weaker currencies at different moments. The choice of bilateral parities was collective, and was in fact based on consensus. Although the deutschmark gradually emerged as the anchor/central currency, this feature was not part of the system of cooperation to stabilize the exchange rates, and indeed was only consolidated de facto in the late 1980s. In turn, the defense of agreed parities implied the unprecedented commitment, if necessary, to defend the agreed parities with unlimited interventions by both countries whose bilateral rates were pushed to the declared margin of fluctuation. This rule implied that no explicit reserve pooling was necessary.

The commitment to exchange rate stability implied that capital mobility was entirely subordinated to that objective. This meant that capital controls were in place for decades, and were reestablished when necessary. Therefore, whereas current account convertibility came early (in 1958, coinciding with the launch of the Common Market), capital account liberalization came late, and was part of a gradual process that did not culminate in the collective removal of capital controls until 1990. This was soon followed by a major crisis in 1992. It thus became clear that exchange rate stability required a full-fledged movement toward monetary union. This was combined with the Stability and Growth Pact, which established explicit fiscal rules and convergence criteria. Although the principle that monetary integration must be accompanied by fiscal discipline is widely accepted, the rationale of the specific rules adopted in the Maastricht Treaty (which target the current fiscal deficit rather than a structural deficit or, better still, debt sustainability), as well as the mechanisms of enforcement (which are intrusive into national sovereignty, but for the same reason weak in practice), have become a subject of heated debate in recent years.

Wyplosz's summary of the sequence followed by the European Union and its implications for similar arrangements in the developing world today is sharp and simple: "Regional trade integration, exchange rate stability and institution-building came first, capital mobility and monetary union came later. A key question is whether this sequencing can be modified and whether the pace can be accelerated. The answer is that both are quite unlikely." This answer is, of course, critical, and refers both to the potential benefits of macroeconomic cooperation and to current debates on capital account liberalization.

Indeed, the classical case for optimum currency areas assumes not only a similarity among participating countries, but also a high level of economic integration among participating countries.[40] Accordingly, one of the major benefits of currency union is that it encourages intraregional trade by eliminating one of the "taxes" on trade: the uncertainties associated with exchange rate volatility. An additional argument is that it acts as an external disciplining agent on individual members and, to the extent that one of the members is a strong economy, it allows others to "borrow credibility."

Capital account liberalization continues to be a topic of heated debate. Its costs in terms of macroeconomic volatility are by now widely recognized.[41] On this basis, many analysts claim that capital account liberalization is undesirable for the developing world, and that some form of capital account controls or regulations should be the rule rather than the exception.[42] In terms of the debate on regional cooperation, this means that capital account liberalization should be, at best, the end rather than the beginning of a process of macroeconomic cooperation. This was, in fact, the route followed by the European Union—a long route indeed, taking more than three decades to complete the transition. It is also the sequence between trade and capital account liberalization recommended by McKinnon.[43] However, given the pervasiveness of global capital markets and related financial innovations, and the fact that several countries have already liberalized their capital accounts, new questions arise about the appropriateness of classical sequencing issues and even about the rationale for currency unions. In particular, and following the defense of polar exchange rate regimes, it has been argued that a developing country with full capital account liberalization that is not willing to adopt a fully flexible exchange rate may find

40. See Mundell (1961); and McKinnon (1963). The classical criteria proposed by Mundell and McKinnon include a large share of intraregional trade and synchronized business cycles, which assume a substantial degree of economic integration. They also indicate that a common currency area is more attractive for smaller countries and when factor markets are more flexible.

41. See, for example, Prasad and others (2003).

42. See, for example, Stiglitz and others (2006).

43. McKinnon (1979).

it more desirable to dollarize or euroize than to form a currency union with other developing countries.

Although the developing world's experience with monetary unions has been neither abundant nor successful, European monetary integration has sparked some initiatives for forming monetary unions in the developing world. The initiative taken by the members of the Gulf Cooperation Council stands out in this regard.[44] The members of the Caribbean Community are also formally committed to a monetary union but have not made much progress in that direction. As with other developing countries where independence was not gained until after World War II, the formation of a monetary union among these countries would in a sense be a return to the monetary arrangements of the past, where these countries shared a common currency (in the Caribbean, until the early 1960s), although they are now managed by the countries themselves and perhaps do not have the strict currency-board characteristics of the colonial arrangements.

Even more than monetary unions, the European experience has encouraged looser forms of macroeconomic dialogue or more elaborate consultations in the developing countries, including the adoption of Maastricht-type criteria in the context of several integration processes.[45] However, unless the adoption of these criteria leads to regular surveillance, as well as to consultation processes that help to internalize the effects of macroeconomic policies on regional partners, their credibility and rationale may be totally lost. In the developing world it is also necessary to strike a balance between targets and a certain degree of policy flexibility, which is essential for economies subject to large shocks. However, the right balance is difficult to achieve.

As discussed, the 1997 crisis led, in East Asia, to the adoption of the Chiang Mai Initiative, aimed at building a strong pillar of regional balance-of-payments support as a crisis-prevention device. Preexisting arrangements in this area were the Latin American Reserve Fund and the ASEAN Swap Arrangement.

One way to view these different initiatives is that they break up macroeconomic cooperation into its basic components: macroeconomic policy dialogue and eventual policy surveillance and consultation; liquidity support during crises; and exchange rate coordination. Furthermore, given the frequency of shocks faced by developing countries, they generally eliminate (or, at least, significantly postpone in time) the desirability of the third component—which, as we

---

44. International Monetary Fund (1973).

45. See, for example, United Nations, ECA (2004, chap. 6) in relation to sub-Saharan Africa, and United Nations, ECLAC (2002b, chap. 5) in relation to Latin America and the Caribbean.

have seen, was the major objective of European macroeconomic cooperation. It should be added that clearinghouses for intraregional trade are a weaker form of macroeconomic cooperation, which is closely tied to trade integration. They also bring specific benefits during crises: by reducing the need for foreign exchange to settle intraregional transactions they may help to mitigate the effects of crises on intraregional trade and the multiplier effects on macroeconomic activity. There are several experiences of this type in the developing world, some of which have been functioning for several decades; a few have faced difficulties owing to the accumulation of arrears by some members during balance-of-payments crises.[46] However, we shall not examine their experience here.

The history of common currency areas in sub-Saharan Africa shows how difficult these arrangements can be in the developing world, even when they have the strong backing of an industrial country.[47] The monetary arrangements among the former British colonies collapsed soon after independence, but a franc zone survived in Western Africa with strong French backing. It is organized into two currency unions: the West African Economic and Monetary Union (WAEMU), and the Central African Economic and Monetary Union.[48] The larger Economic Community of West African States, comprising the first group of countries plus some others, set an agenda that adopted a monetary cooperation program, aimed at a single currency, but its achievements have been limited to improving intraregional payments.[49] In 2000, five of its members agreed to create a West African Monetary Zone, and to merge this zone with the West African Economic and Monetary Union.[50] However, the convergence process has been slow and the deadline for merging this zone with the existing monetary union (December 2005) was postponed until December 2009. In recent decades, initiatives in East and South Africa have focused on

46. In Central America, for example, Nicaraguan arrears led, in the early 1980s, to the accumulation of large debts with other countries in the subregion, as well as to the suspension of lending by the Central American Monetary Stabilization Fund of the Central American Bank for Economic Integration.

47. See the chapters by Ernest Aryeetey and Roy Culpeper in this volume, as well as Honohan and Lane (2000).

48. The first includes Benin, Burkina-Faso, Côte d'Ivoire, Guinea-Bissau, Mali, Niger, Togo, and Senegal. The second encompasses Cameroon, the Central African Republic, Chad, the Republic of Congo, Equatorial Guinea, and Gabon. Guinea dropped out of the franc zone upon independence, and Mali dropped out for a while. Guinea-Bissau and Equatorial Guinea are new members that joined the corresponding arrangement in 1997 and 1985, respectively.

49. The other members are Cape Verde, Gambia, Ghana, Guinea, Liberia, Mauritania, Niger, Nigeria, and Sierra Leone.

50. The members are Gambia, Ghana, Guinea, Nigeria, and Sierra Leone.

trade integration and shied away from establishing major initiatives in the area of macroeconomic cooperation. To these we should add the Rand Monetary Area, which dates back to 1910 and was established formally as a monetary area in 1974 and a common monetary area in 1986.[51]

The former franc (now euro) zone captured for its member states some of the classical benefits of a monetary union. In particular, price stability has been greater for these countries than for neighbors in their region. However, the monetary union worked as a weak external mechanism of restraint. Although the central banks were freed by statute from fiscal pressure, they were forced to support commercial banks that had lent to fiscal authorities. This factor, together with other domestic and external factors, led to a banking crisis in the 1980s. Many of the institutions involved were joint ventures between national governments and major French-based banks. The recapitalization of these banks led to the eventual collapse of the system, which was formally recognized in the 50 percent devaluation of the CFA franc in January 1994.[52] The devaluation was matched by other reforms to strengthen the monetary union and deepen financial cooperation. Although the devaluation facilitated the recovery of economic growth in the following years, the political crisis of the largest member of WAEMU, Côte d'Ivoire, generated fresh macroeconomic problems in the early 2000s; the crisis was compounded by a broader lack of compliance with the agreed fiscal targets by members of the monetary union.[53]

This story showed the limits not only of monetary union as a mechanism of restraint, but also of the benefits of rules-based macroeconomic policy.[54] Also, as Culpeper claims in this volume, the hard peg of the CFA franc to the French franc, and now to the euro, reduces the zone's capacity to absorb external shocks and effectively externalizes authority for short-term financing to the French Treasury. The fluctuations of the exchange rate of, first, the French franc and, in recent years, the euro, have also been transmitted to these countries and, in fact, the strength of the French franc was a factor behind the conditions that led to the 1994 devaluation.

51. The Rand Monetary Area encompasses South Africa, Lesotho, and Swaziland. Botswana withdrew in 1974 before the monetary area was formed. There is also the very ambitious (and probably unrealistic) project of forming a single continental currency area by 2025, which is enshrined in the African Monetary Cooperation Program.

52. The CFA franc is the common currency of fourteen African countries that are members of the franc zone.

53. See Boogaerde and Tsangarides (2005).

54. See Honohan and Lane (2000).

In light of this experience and other problems facing sub-Saharan Africa, Ernest Aryeetey and Honohan and Lane suggest that the focus of cooperation among these countries should probably shift to the development of financial markets, aimed at overcoming the thinness and illiquidity of African capital markets, including possibly the regionalization of banking and capital-market development.[55] Other arrangements, such as liquidity financing to avoid regional contagion, seem less important in sub-Saharan Africa, given the absence of significant contagion in the region during past crises, but may become more important in the future.

In Latin America and the Caribbean, the Eastern Caribbean Currency Union (ECCU) may be considered one of the few success stories of its kind in the developing world.[56] It involves very small economies with a well-developed domestic banking system and an important offshore financial sector. Its history goes back to the British Caribbean Currency Board and operates as a quasi-currency board with large effective reserve cover. Its peg to the British pound was shifted to the U.S. dollar in 1976. However, it has faced some challenges associated with the rapid growth of public sector debts during the slowdown of the early 2000s, poor compliance with the agreed fiscal rules, and some weakness in its banking, regulatory, and supervisory framework.[57]

As previously mentioned, in 1990 members of the broader Caribbean Community made a commitment to create a monetary union as part of the development of a single market and economy. However, no concrete steps have been taken in that direction (and, it should be added, the commitment to build a single market and economy has also been postponed on several occasions).[58] In fact, divergence among the exchange rate regimes and deviation from the agreed convergence criteria continue to characterize this subregion.

Latin America has shied away from similar efforts but, in the 1990s, adopted mechanisms for macroeconomic policy dialogue in the context of its three major integration processes: Mercosur, the Andean Community, and the Central American Common Market.[59] Maastricht-type criteria for economic conver-

---

55. See the chapter by Aryeetey in this volume, and Honohan and Lane (2000).

56. This currency union includes Antigua and Barbuda, Dominica, Grenada, St. Kitts and Nevis, St. Lucia, and St. Vincent and the Grenadines, as well as two dependent territories of the United Kingdom (Anguilla and Montserrat).

57. IMF (2004).

58. It can be argued that, given the very different commodity shocks that these countries face, the Caribbean Community (Caricom) may not even be an optimal currency area. Worrel (2003) advocates a currency union, but based on arguments that justify fixed exchange rates rather than a common currency.

59. United Nations, ECLAC (2002b, chap. 5).

gence have been agreed for these processes. In their contribution to this volume, José Luis Machinea and Guillermo Rozenwurcel analyze the rationale for these efforts. Although intraregional trade is still limited and integration of domestic financial markets is virtually nil, macroeconomic linkages associated with global financial shocks have been significant during the past quarter-century. They have been reflected in macroeconomic adjustments that have had major spillovers onto neighbors, either through the contractionary effects of adjustment policies or through exchange rate variations. This creates a strong case for policy dialogue and eventual coordination of macroeconomic policies. A major incentive for such coordination is, however, absent: the ability to "borrow credibility" from neighbors. Rather, the attempt of neighbors to differentiate themselves from countries facing a crisis, as was typical of Mercosur in the late 1990s and early 2000s, contributed to the further loss of credibility by the authorities.

Based on the European and Latin American experience, Machinea and Rozenwurcel argue that the exchange of information and periodic technical meetings involved in integration processes help to build knowledge and mutual trust.[60] Nonetheless, the transition to more explicit coordination mechanisms, which would help to internalize the effects of macroeconomic policies on neighbors, is a difficult task in the Latin American context. These authors argue, furthermore, that in developing countries the agreed macroeconomic convergence criteria should include, in addition to fiscal objectives (the fiscal deficit, preferably set as the structural stance, and the public sector debt ratio), external sector targets, particularly for the current account deficit and the short-term external debt. Striking a balance between compliance with explicit targets and the degree of policy flexibility that is required in economies subject to large shocks is, however, an important challenge. Some degree of exchange rate stabilization would be desirable, particularly smoothing short-term swings, which may require active use of capital account regulations, particularly on short-term capital flows. In this area, according to these authors, at least two further objectives should be agreed: the harmonization of the exchange rate *regimes,* and the principle that countries should consult with one another concerning possible courses of action to follow in crisis situations.

The existence of regional reserve funds can serve as an important incentive for macroeconomic coordination. In this regard, the experience of the Latin American Reserve Fund, analyzed by Daniel Titelman in this volume, demonstrates the possibilities of using this type of mechanism, which has been widely underutilized in the developing world. It shows that even a modest fund can

60. See also Ghymers (2005).

make essential contributions to the balance-of-payments financing of developing countries. Since 1978 this fund has provided such financing to member states, equivalent to 60 percent of that of the IMF, benefiting in particular its smallest members, Bolivia and Ecuador. Its financing was clearly countercyclical, and its preferred-creditor status has been reflected in its healthy portfolio, even in the face of two major crises in the region, when some member countries accumulated arrears in their public sector obligations. It also shows that the fear that "soft conditionality" would result in major losses by an institution providing emergency liquidity financing is exaggerated. Such funds can help manage trade shocks and even, to a limited extent, abrupt reversals of capital flows. Indeed, Agosin has estimated that, during recent decades, even a relatively modest fund, equivalent to 15 percent of Latin America's international reserves, could have provided financing to cope with capital outflows equivalent to the entire short-term debts of all the countries except Mexico.[61]

The most ambitious project of this kind is the Chiang Mai Initiative, agreed in 2000 by the ASEAN countries plus China, Japan, and the Republic of Korea. The agreed mechanism is the negotiation of bilateral swap arrangements among the central banks of the member countries. To do this, it built on the modest ASEAN Swap Arrangement, which had been created in 1977. Aside from liquidity financing, the mechanism has provided an instrument of policy dialogue, and an appropriate surveillance mechanism is currently being designed. Strong regional monitoring and surveillance is deemed essential by net contributors to liquidity financing to guarantee that its lending is protected; this condition is deemed particularly important by Japan.

As Yung Chul Park argues in his contribution to this volume, this arrangement builds on two essential lessons from the Asian crisis: that in the face of capital account crises, policy coordination, or at least a regional policy dialogue, is essential in preventing contagion, and that the countries need ample access to liquidity to thwart the speculative attacks that characterize contemporary capital account crises. The capacity of regional partners to provide such financing is reflected in the fact that the funds provided by the IMF to Indonesia, the Republic of Korea, and Thailand during the crisis (U.S.$111.7 billion) were only a fraction of the international reserves held by the members of the Chiang Mai Initiative at the time (about U.S.$700 billion), and a very small fraction of the reserves accumulated by these countries since the Asian crisis (U.S.$2.5 trillion at the end of 2005). As noted above, this initiative is also a sign of East Asia's frustration with the speed of reform of the international financial system.

61. Agosin (2001).

The mechanism entitles countries to a disbursement of up to 20 percent of the maximum amount of drawings from the bilateral swaps without an IMF program. This limit, agreed to in May 2005, was an increase over the 10 percent originally set. When this limit is reached, the country would thus be placed under an IMF program. This implies that regional liquidity financing is complementary to that of the IMF in a more explicit way than in the case of the Latin American Reserve Fund. These bilateral arrangements, which added up to U.S.$71.5 billion in February 2006, could eventually be multilateralized. Indeed, a step in that direction was also agreed in May 2005, when it was decided that the swap activation would be based on a collective decisionmaking process, the details of which must be agreed. The mechanism has not yet been utilized, and indeed, the buoyant conditions of the member countries in recent years, including the accumulation of record levels of "self-defense" in the form of large international reserves, may have slowed the pace of action. According to Park, the major stumbling blocks in the process seem to be the weak institutional arrangements that have been established and the unsettled leadership among the two major economic powers in the region.

The recent decision to multilateralize the swap arrangement could lead to some form of reserve pooling, which could be used to back a common reserve currency. If a strong surveillance mechanism is put in place, using this mechanism of liquidity, financing could be detached from an IMF program. Also, the policy dialogue could eventually evolve into a more formal system of policy coordination, including the establishment of mechanisms to stabilize the bilateral exchange rates of the member countries, even though the members of the initiative have not yet expressed their desire to do so. If these steps are taken, and the membership of the initiative is expanded to include other countries that have requested membership (including India), the system could eventually evolve into a full-fledged Asian monetary system.[62] It must be added that this is more likely if the issue of the Asian countries' voice and participation in the IMF is not solved in an acceptable manner.

As the previous discussion indicates, designing an adequate monitoring and surveillance process is key to ambitious efforts in macroeconomic cooperation. In this area, four mechanisms have been agreed in Asia since the 1997 crisis. One of these was abandoned (the Manila Framework Group, adopted in the context of APEC), and another is still in its infancy (the South Asian process). The ASEAN Surveillance Process, adopted in 1998, is the most advanced. It has put in place a peer review mechanism for national policies, based on a Surveillance

62. Rana (2005).

Report prepared by the ASEAN Secretariat, and the ASEAN Economic Out-look, prepared by the Asian Development Bank. However, neither this mecha-nism nor the less structured ASEAN+3 Economic Review and Policy Dialogue (which is now integrated into the Chiang Mai Initiative) qualifies as an effective surveillance process. This has been attributed to the overemphasis on consensus and noninterference in the peer review, at the expense of frank and in-depth pol-icy discussions. So, although there is now an adequate supply of forums for pol-icy dialogue (those mentioned above, plus the dialogues among central banks), a full-fledged monitoring and surveillance process is still not in place.[63]

Conclusions

This chapter argues that the international financial architecture would be strengthened if it were to rely not on a few specialized world organizations, but rather on a *network* of institutions that provide the services expected from such an architecture (liquidity and development financing, macroeconomic surveil-lance and consultation, peer review of prudential regulation). An institutional framework such as this would have two positive features. First, it might help to bring more stability to the world economy by providing essential services that can hardly be provided by a few international institutions, particularly in the face of a dynamic process of open regionalism. Second, from the point of view of the equilibrium of world relations, it would be more balanced than a system based on a few world organizations.

The chapter sets out four arguments in favor of a strong role for regional and subregional cooperation in the international financial system: the growing link-ages generated by the open regionalism characterizing the current globalization process; the complementary role that world and regional institutions play in a heterogeneous international community, and in a world that still lacks a fully developed international financial architecture; the case for competition in the supply of services to small and medium-sized countries; and the strong sense of ownership that regional institutions have, and their capacity to serve as channels for better articulating the voice of smaller countries. At the same time, it is argued that such arrangements face three major challenges: developing the capac-ity to match the demand for financial support with their supply capacities, which restricts the capacity of the poorer developing countries to create viable regional financial institutions; making a strong long-term commitment to institution building, a basic lesson of European cooperation in this area; and putting

63. See, for example, Kuroda and Kawai (2004).

together arrangements that would guarantee an equitable distribution of the benefits of integration. These issues are interrelated, since supply capacities and equitable integration are not exogenously given because they are largely created through a gradual process of institution building.

The experiences of regional financial cooperation are clustered in two groups: development financing; and mechanisms for macroeconomic cooperation and related financial arrangements (liquidity financing during balance-of-payments crises).

The best-developed form of cooperation is that of multilateral development banks. The network of regional and subregional institutions of this type has shown the advantages of diversity, particularly in their capacity to adapt to the demands of specific regions. However, they have advanced only marginally outside Europe, to support the provision of "regional public goods." Whereas the most developed network is that of the regional development banks, the most elaborate set of "developing-country-owned" financial institutions is that of the Arab and Islamic world, with the network of subregional development banks in the Latin American and Caribbean region coming next. At least one institution, the Andean Development Corporation, shows that it is possible for a set of non-investment-grade developing countries to build an investment-grade institution. Most institutions of this type have a very strong financial structure, which is associated, at least partially, with their preferred-creditor status. Only a few have faced difficulties throughout their history (the African Development Bank and the Central American Bank for Economic Integration). The history of the African Development Bank shows, however, how hard it is to create dynamic development financing institutions for the poorest countries without backing from industrial nations—and, even with such backing, demonstrates the difficulties faced by these institutions in building strong loan portfolios in structurally weak development contexts. The Arab institutions have a different sort of problem: excessive dependence of available finance on oil prices, which reduces their capacity to operate as a countercyclical device.

Two other mechanisms of development financing have been available in a few regional processes. Fiscal transfers to the poorer members of a regional group are used exclusively by the European Union, having been tried unsuccessfully in only one integration process in the developing world. In recent years, East Asia has launched a third model of cooperation in the area of development finance, which focuses on bond markets. This novel form of cooperation aims to deepen local and regional financial development through joint actions to design the appropriate financial infrastructure and by launching specific bond funds that become investment vehicles for central banks in the region.

Contrary to the rich historical experience in the area of development financing, there is a dearth of experiences in the area of macroeconomic cooperation in the developing world. This is, however, an area where several initiatives have been launched in recent years, in many cases aiming to replicate European arrangements. The links between trade and macroeconomic cooperation are, of course, at the heart of the formation of the European Union. Certainly trade links are weaker in the developing world—although they have been growing rapidly in some regions, particularly in East Asia. However, two additional rationales for macroeconomic cooperation are present in the developing world: building stronger walls of defense against global financial shocks, and avoiding distorting competition among export-oriented economies. Aside from the role of the links between intraregional trade and macroeconomic cooperation, European integration brings two additional lessons for the developing world: the emphasis on building strong institutions in a gradual and pragmatic way, and the subordination of capital mobility to other macroeconomic objectives of regional cooperation.

The experience with macroeconomic cooperation in the developing world generally breaks up such cooperation into its different components: policy dialogue, monitoring, and surveillance; liquidity support during crises; and exchange rate coordination. The third objective, which has, of course, been central to European cooperation, is generally left aside, except in the few experiences with monetary unions, which have not usually been very successful. The most common recent initiatives have thus taken the form of macroeconomic dialogue and consultations based on Maastricht-type convergence criteria; and, even in the best example of its kind—the ASEAN surveillance arrangement—they have not evolved into effective surveillance processes. However, unless the adoption of convergence criteria and dialogue among authorities evolve into regular consultations, and eventually into effective coordination processes, their credibility and rationale may be lost. Furthermore, for the developing world, the balance between targets and a certain degree of policy flexibility required in economies subject to shocks is a difficult one to strike.

In the area of liquidity financing, the experience of the Latin American Reserve Fund illustrates the possibilities of using such mechanisms, which have been widely underutilized in the developing world. It shows that even a modest fund can make essential contributions to balance-of-payments financing of developing countries. In turn, the 1997 crisis led in Asia to the adoption of the Chiang Mai Initiative, aimed at building a strong pillar of regional balance-of-payments support as a crisis-prevention device. The recent multilateralization of bilateral swap arrangements could eventually lead to some form of reserve pooling. The basic weakness of the Chiang Mai Initiative has been its slowness to take strong institutional shape.

All in all, these experiences indicate that regional cooperation can be very effective in reducing the inadequate supply of financial services that the current international financial architecture provides. Nonetheless, these institutions remain limited in scope and are not recognized as central to the international financial architecture. In this regard, we argue that the International Monetary Fund of the future should be viewed as the apex of a network of regional and subregional reserve funds and swap arrangements—that is, a structure more akin to that of the European Central Bank or the United States Federal Reserve system than to its current centralized structure. In turn, competition among global, regional, and subregional institutions is probably the best arrangement in this area. And above all, in an era when developing countries have made a call for greater South-South cooperation, financial cooperation should be placed at the top of the agenda.

References

Agosin, Manuel. 2001. "Strengthening Regional Financial Cooperation." *CEPAL Review* 73 (April). Santiago, Chile: Economic Commission of Latin America and the Caribbean (ECLAC).

Bezanson, Keith, and Francisco Sagasti. 2000. *A Foresight and Policy Study of Multilateral Development Banks.* Institute of Development Studies, Sussex University/Ministry of Foreign Affairs, Stockholm.

Birdsall, Nancy. 2001. *The Role of the Multilateral Development Banks in Emerging Market Economies.* Report of the Commission on the Role of the MDBs in the EMEs, José Angel Gurría and Paul Volcker, cochairs. Washington: Carnegie Endowment for International Peace.

———. 2006. "Overcoming Coordination and Attribution Problems: Meeting the Challenge of Underfunded Regionalism." In *The New Public Finance,* edited by I. Kaul and P. Conceição, pp. 391–410. Oxford University Press.

Birdsall, Nancy, and Liliana Rojas-Suarez, eds. 2004. *Financing Development: The Power of Regionalism.* Washington: Center for Global Development.

Boogaerde, Pierre van den, and Charalambos Tsangarides. 2005. "Ten Years after the CFA Franc Devaluation: Toward Regional Integration in the WAEMU." Working Paper 05/145. Washington: International Monetary Fund (July).

Council on Foreign Relations. 1999. *Safeguarding Prosperity in a Global Financial System: The Future International Financial Architecture.* Task Force Report, C. A. Hills and P. G. Peterson (chairs), M. Goldstein (Project Director). Washington: Institute for International Economics.

Culpeper, Roy. 1997. *The Multilateral Development Banks: Titans or Behemoths?* Boulder, Colo.: Lynne Rienner and The North-South Institute.

Eichengreen, Barry. 1999. *Toward a New International Financial Architecture: A Practical Post-Asian Agenda.* Washington: Institute for International Economics.

Ford Foundation. 2001. *Rebuilding the International Financial Architecture*. Emerging Markets Eminent Persons Group, Final Draft Report, Seoul (September 24).

Ghymers, Christian. 2005. *Fomentar la coordinación de las políticas económicas en América Latina: El método REDIMA para salir del dilema del prisionero*. Libros de la CEPAL 82. Santiago: ECLAC and European Commission.

Griffith-Jones, Stephany, and José Antonio Ocampo, with Jacques Cailloux. 1999. *The Poorest Countries and the Emerging International Financial Architecture*. Stockholm: Expert Group on Development Issues (EGDI).

Honohan, Patrick, and Philip R. Lane. 2000. "Will the Euro Trigger More Monetary Union in Africa?" Policy Research Working Paper 2393. Washington: World Bank (July).

International Monetary Fund (IMF). 2003. "Monetary Union among Member Countries of the Gulf Cooperation Council." Occasional Paper 223. Washington.

———. 2004. "Eastern Caribbean Currency Union: Financial System Stability Assessment." IMF Country Report 04/293. Washington (September).

Kenen, Peter B. 2001. *The International Financial Architecture: What's New? What's Missing?* Washington: Institute for International Economics.

Kuroda, Haruhiko, and Masahiro Kawai. 2004. "Strengthening Regional Financial Cooperation in East Asia." In *Financial Governance in East Asia: Policy Dialogues, Surveillance and Cooperation,* edited by G. de Brouwer and J. Wang. London: Routledge.

McKinnon, Ronald I. 1963. "Optimum Currency Areas." *American Economic Review* 53: 717–24.

———. 1979. *Money in International Exchange, The Convertible Currency System*. Oxford University Press.

Meltzer, Allan H., and others. 2000. *Report to the U.S. Congress of the International Financial Advisory Commission*. Washington (March).

Mistry, Percy S. 1996. *Regional Integration Arrangements in Economic Development*. The Hague: Forum on Debt and Development (FONDAD).

———. 1999. "Coping with Financial Crises: Are Regional Arrangements the Missing Link?" In *International Monetary and Financial Issues for the 1990s*. Vol. 10. Geneva: United Nations Conference on Trade and Development (UNCTAD).

Mundell, Robert A. 1961. "A Theory of Optimum Currency Areas." *American Economic Review* 51: 657–64.

Ocampo, José Antonio. 1999. *La reforma financiera internacional: un debate en marcha*. Santiago, Chile: ECLAC/Fondo de Cultura Económica.

———. 2002. "Recasting the International Financial Agenda." In *International Capital Markets: Systems in Transition,* edited by John Eatwell and Lance Taylor. Oxford University Press.

———. 2003. "International Asymmetries and the Design of the International Financial System." In *Critical Issues in International Financial Reform: A View from the South,* edited by A. Berry and G. Indart, pp. 45–73. New Brunswick, N.J.: Transaction.

Park, Yung Chul, and Yunjong Wang. 2000. "Reforming the International Financial System and Prospects for Regional Financial Cooperation in East Asia." In *Reforming the International Financial System,* edited by J. J. Teunissen. The Hague: FONDAD.

Prasad, Eswar S., Kenneth Rogoff, Shang-Jin Wei, and M. Ayhan Kose. 2003. "Effects of Financial Globalization on Developing Countries: Some Empirical Evidence." Occasional Paper 220. Washington: International Monetary Fund.

Rana, Pradumna B. 2005. "Economic Integration in East Asia: Trends, Prospects, and a Possible Roadmap." Paper presented at the Third High-Level Conference on Building a New Asia: Towards an Asian Economic Community. Taiyuan, China, September 15–16, 2005.

Sagasti, Francisco, Keith Bezanson, and Fernando Prada. 2005. *The Future of Development Financing: Challenges, Scenarios and Strategic Choices.* Hampshire, United Kingdom: Palgrave/Macmillan.

Sakakibara, Eisuke. 2003. "Asian Cooperation and the End of Pax Americana." In *Financial Stability and Growth in Emerging Economies,* edited by J. J. Teunissen and M. Teunissen, pp. 227–40. The Hague: FONDAD.

Stiglitz, Joseph E., José Antonio Ocampo, Shari Spiegel, Ricardo Ffrench-Davis, and Deepak Nayyar. 2006. *Stability with Growth: Macroeconomics for Development.* Oxford University Press.

Teunissen, Jan Joost. 1998. *Regional Integration and Multilateral Cooperation in the Global Economy.* The Hague: FONDAD.

Triffin, Robert. 1957. *Europe and the Money Muddle: From Bilateralism to Near-Convertibility, 1947–1956.* Yale University Press.

United Nations. 2002. *Monterrey Consensus.* International Conference on Financing for Development. (www.un.org).

———. 2005. *World Economic and Social Survey: Financing for Development.* New York.

United Nations, Economic and Social Commission for Asia and the Pacific (ESCAP). 2004. *Meeting the Challenges in an Era of Globalization by Strengthening Regional Development Cooperation.* New York: United Nations.

———. 2005. *Implementing the Monterrey Consensus in the Asian and Pacific Region: Achieving Coherence and Consistency.* New York: United Nations.

United Nations, Economic Commission for Africa (ECA). 2004. *Assessing Regional Integration in Africa.* Addis Ababa, Ethiopia.

United Nations, Economic Commission for Latin America and the Caribbean (ECLAC). 2002a. *Growth with Stability: Financing for Development in the New International Context.* Santiago, Chile.

———. 2002b. *Latin America and the Caribbean in the World Economy.* Santiago, Chile.

United Nations, Executive Committee on Economic and Social Affairs. 1999. *Towards a New International Financial Architecture.* Santiago: ECLAC.

World Bank and International Monetary Fund. 2005. *Global Monitoring Report.* Washington.

Worrel, DeLisle. 2003. "A Currency Union for the Caribbean." Working Paper 03/35. Washington: International Monetary Fund (February).

2

Reforming the Global Financial Architecture: The Potential of Regional Institutions

ROY CULPEPER

The international financial crises of the 1990s and early years of the twenty-first century initiated the beginnings of reform to the global financial system. These focused principally on remedying the financial fragility of emerging market economies, the principal victims of financial instability. In contrast, there have been no real reforms aimed at preventing or constraining financial instability at its core, for example by fundamentally restructuring the Bretton Woods institutions, or by rewriting the rules of the game for global financial markets. In the meantime, the urge to reform has lost political impetus among the G-7, the key players on the reform agenda, with the recovery from the global financial turmoil of 1997–98, which had significantly abated by 1999.

The ensuing financial crises in Turkey and Argentina remained fairly contained to those countries. The absence of contagion seemed to signal that the international financial system, at least for the time being, had become more resilient, vindicating those who advocated a minimalist reform agenda limited to the vulnerable financial periphery, rather than the center of the global system. This was little comfort to Turkey or Argentina, or to other developing countries that, for whatever reason, might encounter crippling financial shocks in the future.

I am grateful for comments on an earlier draft by Gerry Helleiner and Rodney Schmidt.

Meanwhile, official development assistance (ODA) continues to be inadequate, although there has been a significant turnaround since the cutbacks of the 1990s. At the time of this writing, projections by the OECD Development Assistance Committee (DAC) indicate that ODA from OECD donors will increase from a little under U.S.$80 billion in 2004 to almost U.S.$130 billion by 2010. Aid to Africa in this period is forecast to double from U.S.$25 billion to U.S.$50 billion. Moreover, a number of donors outside the DAC are increasing their aid volumes—for example, the ten new members of the European Union and China (China announced a U.S.$10 billion program for infrastructure, technical cooperation, and debt relief at the United Nations Summit in 2005). The projected expansion in ODA is the largest since the formation of the DAC in 1960, although as a proportion of gross national income the level of 0.36 percent projected for 2010 is only slightly above the 0.33 percent recorded in the early 1990s and well below the record levels of 0.5 percent in the 1960s. These figures need to be treated with caution, since increasing pressures on public budgets in OECD countries may make rapid increases in aid spending difficult to sustain. Last but not least, in the Paris Declaration on Aid Effectiveness in March 2005, the major donors committed to improving the way aid is delivered.[1]

If restructuring the global financial architecture has been ruled out for the foreseeable future, it is important to seek alternatives. Some experts, including the Emerging Markets Eminent Persons' Group, recommend building or reinforcing regional institutions mandated with preventing or mitigating crises for countries in their regions.[2] To this objective could be added the achievement of longer-term development objectives. That is the focus of this chapter. Drawing on the relevant precedents in both the developed and the developing world, as well as on the shortcomings of the current system for developing countries, the chapter addresses the following questions:

—What organizational and institutional characteristics contribute to regional financial organizations' playing an effective role?

—What are the key financial constraints faced by different groups of developing countries with respect to short-term financing and longer-term financing?

—To what extent can regional organizations play a key role in financial crisis prevention and management?

—How can regional financial organizations help bridge the large resource gap required for longer-term growth and development?

1. Manning (2005).
2. Emerging Markets Eminent Persons' Group (2001).

The next section provides some historical context, particularly for developing countries' experience with regional financial cooperation. The third section examines the rationale for regional financial cooperation, relating it to the rationale of broader or deeper regional economic cooperation and to reforming the global financial architecture. The fourth section undertakes a brief survey of regional organizations in two continents—Latin America and the Caribbean, and Africa—to draw some lessons about the extent to which such organizations can help to meet the financial needs of developing countries. The final section examines the potential and pitfalls of regional financial cooperation in the broader agenda of reforming the global financial architecture.

Background

Regional financial cooperation among developing countries is not new. However, until very recently such cooperation was primarily aimed at longer-term economic objectives of growth, development, and integration and was best exemplified by a number of regional and subregional development banks.[3] It is worth noting that, in at least one instance, the aspiration to such long-term regional development cooperation predates both Bretton Woods and Europe's postwar initiatives on regional economic cooperation. The earliest attempt to create an inter-American bank took place at the Inter-American Conference in Washington, D.C., in 1890, when Latin American countries attempted, but failed, to persuade the United States to participate in their project for regional cooperation. Fifty years later, a convention to establish an inter-American bank was actually signed by the United Sates but abandoned during World War II. The latter proposal, four years before the Bretton Woods conference, was developed in part by U.S. officials such as economist Harry Dexter White, and helped shape the subsequent creation of the World Bank.[4]

The Inter-American Development Bank was ultimately born in 1959. Along with the Asian Development Bank (whose operations began in 1966), and the much later European Bank for Reconstruction and Development (EBRD), which came into being in 1991, the creation of these regional development banks (RDBs) owed much to the cold war. The first two came into being largely because the United States saw in them an economic bulwark against the spread

---

3. Several subregional banks, such as the Caribbean Development Bank and the Central American Bank for Economic Integration, are discussed further below. Here the discussion is restricted to the continental regional banks.

4. Culpeper (1997).

of communism in Latin America and Asia, while the EBRD quickly material-
ized after the fall of the Berlin Wall to assist Soviet bloc countries of Europe and
Central Asia in their transition to capitalist democracies. In contrast, the African
Development Bank (created at almost the same time as its Asian counterpart)
illustrated a fundamentally different history and political dynamic, discussed
further below.

Here, two aspects of the RDBs as vehicles for regional cooperation are
emphasized. First, notwithstanding their strong identification with, and ownership by, their developing-country members, until recently the membership of
nonborrowing countries has remained critical to their capacities as financial
intermediaries. Second, in practice, regional cooperation has meant cooperating to promote the overall flow of resources to individual regional member
countries, rather than fostering greater economic integration in the region.

Regional Ownership versus Nonregional Control

The fundamental purpose of the RDBs, much like that of the World Bank, was
to foster long-term economic and social development through investment in
infrastructure, the productive sectors, and the social sectors. The United States
and other leading industrial nations accepted some overlap in the mandates of the
RDBs and the World Bank, reflecting an acknowledgment that the overall supply
of long-term development finance was inadequate. But it also reflected their
acceptance that new regional institutions could give their developing-country
members what the World Bank would likely never give because of the permanent
voting majority OECD members enjoy at the bank: a greater sense of developing-
country ownership and control. This consideration, although never explicit, was a
key factor in the Western powers' political struggle against communism.

Greater ownership of RDBs by regional developing-country members has not,
however, led to radically different policies, operational programs, or conditionality from those of the World Bank.[5] Notwithstanding the voting majority held
collectively by the Latin American borrowing members of the Inter-American
Development Bank (IDB), *effective* control over major policy issues has been
exercised by its largest minority shareholder, the United States. And at the Asian
Development Bank, developing-country members never did have a formal voting majority.[6] In any event, effective control by industrial-country members in
the RDBs springs not from their voting position but from the fact that their

5. Kapur and Webb (1994).

6. A voting majority was held by *regional* member countries, which included Japan, Australia, and New Zealand (Kappagoda, 1996).

cooperation is vital to ensure resource mobilization through successive capital increases and replenishments, without which the RDBs would enjoy no growth in their lending program.[7]

The history of the African Development Bank (AfDB) illustrates how critical industrial-country membership can be to a regional bank's ability to mobilize resources. Unlike the other RDBs, the AfDB was not a by-product of cold-war power politics. On the contrary, it was the manifestation of African countries, newly independent from colonialism, seeking to be free of alignment with the cold-war superpowers. Without explicit sponsorship by the industrial countries, the AfDB reflected African countries' aspirations to blaze a specifically African path to development. For almost two decades, maintaining the "African character" of the bank required that eligibility for membership be restricted to African countries. By 1980 it became apparent that the bank's ability to mobilize resources was highly limited by this formula. Nonconcessional lending by multilateral development banks is heavily dependent on their access to key capital markets in the North, which in turn is secured by the capital subscriptions of highly creditworthy members—in other words, by the membership of industrial countries.[8] And concessional lending has always been wholly dependent on funds provided by donor countries.

The AfDB was in fact able to establish a concessional lending affiliate, the African Development Fund (AfDF), in 1973, without any formal donor-country membership in the bank per se. Moreover, an attempt was made to preserve the bank's "African character" in the fund as well, by insisting on voting parity between donors and African members. However, the magnitude of the concessional resources raised by the AfDF paled in comparison with the concessional affiliates of the Inter-American and Asian Development Banks, in which it was clear from the outset that donor members were in control. After much debate, the African bank's membership was ultimately "opened" in 1982 to nonregional—that is, developed-country—members in Europe and North America. However, the principle of maintaining an African voting majority in the bank (and parity in the fund) persisted, although in the case of the bank the African majority has subsequently drifted down through successive capital replenishment negotiations, at the insistence of the nonregional members.[9]

---

7. Culpeper (1997).

8. By the 1990s this had changed—the Andean Development Corporation (Corporación Andina de Fomento, CAF) illustrated that a regional bank whose membership was exclusive to developing-country borrowers could mobilize its resources solely on the strength of its borrowing members. The experience of the CAF is elaborated below.

9. English and Mule (1996).

Regional Integration

The RDBs were all created with support for regional integration as an objective, which was reaffirmed over the decade of the 1990s. Despite this fact, they have tended to operationalize this part of their mandate only to a negligible extent if the proportion of their lending portfolio allocated to regional integration projects is taken as the key indicator. For example, at the IDB, loans for regional integration constitute only 2 percent of authorizations, which amount to $8 billion annually, while regional technical cooperation amounts to only $12 million annually.[10] However, this indicator may not fully capture the RDBs' efforts to facilitate greater regional integration and cooperation. The IDB was extremely active in the 1990s, along with the Organization of American States (OAS) and the United Nations Economic Commission for Latin America and the Caribbean (ECLAC), in the Hemispheric Summit Process, providing technical and financial support for the Free Trade Area of the Americas (FTAA) negotiations. For its part, the AsDB has become involved in regional economic and financial surveillance, to complement surveillance at national and global levels. And the AfDB, analogously to its counterpart in the Americas, is centrally involved with the Organization of African Unity (OAU) and the United Nations Economic Commission for Africa (ECA) in pan-African cooperation initiatives such as the New Partnership for Africa's Development (NEPAD) and the creation of the African Union.[11]

To conclude, the RDBs should be viewed as highly successful regional cooperation initiatives in mobilizing financial resources for their members' national development efforts. However, this judgment must be qualified by the fact that, until recently, industrial-country membership has been vital to augmenting their lending capacity, and the fact that, again until recently, they have not been particularly successful at enhancing cooperation among members, either by means of economic integration initiatives or coordinating development strategies. In the latter case, change has been facilitated by a new approach to regionalism.

Put bluntly, the "old regionalism" of the 1950s and 1960s (the RDBs being exemplars) was characterized by groups of countries looking inward, motivated by a desire to substitute for the lack of multilateral liberalization or to facilitate holding aloof from what liberalization there was (such as the proposal for a Latin American free-trade area), or both. The "new regionalism," in contrast, is outward-looking, motivated by a desire to facilitate entrance into a more globally liberalized multilateral trading and investment system. Such regionalism is

---

10. The AsDB, however, has allocated a more considerable part of its lending portfolio to multicountry regional projects such as the Greater Mekong Subregion Initiative.

11. Devlin and Castro (2002).

characterized by greater liberalization on the part of smaller than larger coun-tries and by the quest for "deep integration," whereby participating countries go well beyond border measures to harmonize or adjust various economic policies (the European Union, the Canada–United States Free Trade Agreement, and the North American Free Trade Agreement [NAFTA] are examples).[12]

After the Asian financial crisis of 1997–98, however, the promise of the new outward-looking regionalism became a little tarnished. Capital account liberalization—particularly when adopted prematurely, as it was in many coun-tries, as part of a wider package of economic liberalization measures—left many vulnerable to massive financial shocks. The benefits of greater access to goods and long-term capital markets were dramatically offset, at least in the short run, by massive, crisis-induced capital flight and the domestic instability it precipitated. Furthermore, remedial measures implemented by the international financial insti-tutions (IFIs) (and supported by the G-7 countries) came under considerable criti-cism for being procyclical,[13] and for making a bad situation significantly worse.[14]

Asian countries themselves were particularly critical both of the diagnosis and of the prescriptions applied by the G-7 and the IFIs to the region. Accordingly, soon after the outbreak of the Asian financial crisis in 1997 there were proposals from Japan for a regional monetary fund that received a positive response from a number of East Asian countries. At the time, the idea was opposed by the United States, European countries, and the International Monetary Fund.[15] However, the idea resurfaced in May 2000 at the Asian Development Bank meetings held in Chiang Mai, Thailand. This gave birth to the Chiang Mai Initiative among the ASEAN+3 countries (the ASEAN nations plus China, Japan, and the Repub-lic of Korea). While this initiative began essentially as a network of bilateral swap arrangements, with informal surveillance arrangements, further discussion among the participants may lead to a multilateralization of the arrangements and the cre-ation of a regional monetary fund.

The Rationale for Regional Financial Cooperation

Regional financial cooperation can be motivated by larger political objectives as well as by narrower economic goals. Such political motives range from the

---

12. Ethier (1998). As Bhagwati (1998) pointed out, however, a regional trade agreement on the lines of NAFTA was *not* an aspect of the "East Asian miracle," or necessary to its emphasis of out-ward orientation through export promotion.

13. See Ocampo (2003).

14. See, for example, Stiglitz (2002).

15. See Park (2001).

need to facilitate conflict resolution or avoidance or mitigation between neighboring states, to aspirations for greater political integration or even union. The European Union, the preeminent example of politically motivated regional cooperation, has traveled from one end of this spectrum, in the search for a durable peace at the end of World War II, to the other end today, with monetary union and closely coordinated economic and social policies. Ever-increasing financial cooperation in the European Union project is just a part of a much larger agenda of economic and political harmonization and integration and, after half a century, it is still a work in progress. The deeper motives of political integration may be present in other parts of the world to the same degree as in Europe, but if they are, most are at a much earlier stage in the process. However, proposals for a Free Trade Agreement of the Americas, an African Union, and cooperative arrangements such as ASEAN and the South Asian Association for Regional Cooperation (SAARC) in Asia are all suggestive of regional projects in which political motivations are indeed present. Conceivably, over time (and bearing in mind the evolution of the European Union over five decades) the political objectives associated with such initiatives could become more ambitious.

Moreover, political and economic motives are often intertwined and difficult to separate. Purely economic motives are no doubt undermined by historical enmity, mistrust, or political grievances among neighboring countries, simply because the transaction costs involved in negotiation and cooperation are likely to be higher in such circumstances. Put positively, economic motives are likely to be reinforced where political relationships between regional members are already strong and the desire for even closer relationships is growing.

That being said, there are several economic reasons for greater regional financial cooperation. There would seem to be two broad rationales: *cooperative* or *self-help* motives, and the need to remedy *incomplete international institutions*.

The cooperative rationale is straightforward. When countries of a region cooperate financially, they help to fill gaps caused by incomplete markets; increase external financing for various purposes; meet external development financing resource gaps generally; and exploit economies of scale. There are a number of ways they can do this:

—By pooling their risks, they can gain access on better terms to capital markets or donors than if they attempted to approach markets and donors separately. Regional or subregional development banks, in effect, play this role through financial intermediation.

—By forming trade payments settlement systems, they can reduce the transaction costs of regional trade.

—By pooling foreign exchange reserves, they can reduce their individual reserve holdings and associated quasi-fiscal costs.

—By harmonizing policies and institutions in the financial sector and creating regional institutions, and instituting regional monitoring and surveillance to provide early warnings of countries likely to experience financial trouble, they can deepen regional capital markets, attract more foreign direct investment or attract it on better terms, and reduce the threat of regional contagion.

The "incomplete institutions" rationale deserves somewhat more explanation. As mentioned, global institutions such as the World Bank and the International Monetary Fund tend to be most responsive to the demands of their major shareholders—the G-7 countries—and also to the needs of the largest developing countries, which have significant voice and voting power in the institutions and constitute an important part of their lending portfolio (and hence their balance sheets) and greater systemic importance with respect to global financial crises. The global institutions do not serve the world's smaller and poorer countries particularly well, and this group of countries has a marginal role in the global institutions' governance.[16] Regional arrangements therefore help to complete the global financial architecture in the following ways:

—By providing an institutional space, complementary to the global institutions, in which the voice and voting power of smaller and poorer countries is greater, along with a greater sense of regional ownership.

—By taking a more efficacious approach to conditionality. Global institutions are more inclined to impose conditionality; regional organizations in contrast are more able to rely on peer pressure to adopt policy reforms.

—At the same time, by providing some competition to the global institutions, generating more attention to the problems of the smaller and poorer countries.

—By focusing on providing international public goods that are regional rather than global in nature; and consistent with the principle of subsidiarity, by basing the arrangement in the region concerned with regional members as key players.

—By providing a source of countercyclical financing, to offset the procyclicality of private financing and official financing from the global institutions.

There is clearly a rationale for greater regional financial cooperation in general terms. But as a practical matter, different developing countries and regions face vastly differing needs, opportunities, and constraints. Therefore it is useful to distinguish among groups of developing countries in order to discern the potential benefits from regional financial cooperation for different groups and regions.

16. Ocampo (2002).

Per capita income provides one basis for differentiating among groups of developing countries. Another basis is the degree of access to international capital markets. It seems useful to distinguish between two groups at opposite ends of the income spectrum—the poorest and the emerging market countries. The former could be identified with the least-developed countries (as defined by the United Nations)—countries that are extremely poor and are heavily dependent on foreign assistance on grant or concessional terms. Hereinafter, this group is referred to as the least developed countries (LDCs). The second group consists of emerging market and transition countries in Asia, Eastern Europe, and Latin America. This group consists predominantly of middle-income countries, but would also include India (a low-income country with growing access to capital markets), as well as China. This group is referred to below as emerging market economies (EMEs). Between these two is a group of small low- and middle-income countries (SMCs), which are neither among the poorest nor among the emerging market countries, since they have limited access to international capital markets.

These groups differ in their financing needs, whether for short-term financing or medium- to long-term financing. Short-term financing is required to meet emergencies and respond to crises; medium- to long-term financing is required for investment, capacity building, and other constituents of sustainable development. Income levels also determine creditworthiness. Combined with the classification of developing countries by income group, this yields a "financing needs matrix" (see table 2-1).

Least developed countries' short-term financing needs reflect their aid and commodity dependence and their greater vulnerability to natural disasters. Many of these needs are largely unmet, particularly in failed states. This group is generally not creditworthy for commercial financing on market terms. That is why they tend to be heavily dependent on the grant or concessional ODA from bilateral and multilateral aid agencies. Traditionally, such agencies have rendered project assistance and technical cooperation to support infrastructure, social investment, and productive sector investment. Recently, some agencies have begun a transition to program-based assistance in the form of sector or budget support.

However, there is considerable evidence that ODA and other official flows are procyclical, or serve to reinforce rather than dampen external shocks; therefore LDCs have unmet needs for countercyclical support.[17] Debt restructuring is a medium- to long-term need because the underlying problem is debt sustainability (that is, reducing debt overhangs to levels compatible with growth and development) rather than short-term liquidity financing. Finally, while on a

17. UNCTAD (2000, Part II, chap. 5).

Table 2-1. *Financing Needs of LDCs, SMCs, and EMEs*[a]

	LDCs	SMCs	EMEs
Short-term needs	Compensatory balance-of-payments (BOP) financing caused by commodity, financial, and aid shocks Relief for natural disasters, post-conflict assistance, and humanitarian emergencies (such as famine)	Compensatory BOP financing due to commodity and aid shocks Relief for natural disasters and post-conflict assistance Trade finance	Liquidity financing to prevent/mitigate financial panics, contagion Debt restructuring Trade finance
Medium- and long-term needs	Financing for infrastructure and for social and productive sector investment Debt restructuring Budgetary and sector support Capacity building Financing for countercyclical macroeconomic policy	Financing for infrastructure and for social and productive sector investment Debt restructuring Capacity building Financing for countercyclical macroeconomic policy	Financing for infrastructure and productive sector investment Financing for countercyclical macroeconomic policy
Creditworthiness	Grants and concessional lending FDI	Semi-concessional lending Some forms of private financing	Market-based official lending All forms of private financing

a. LDCs: less-developed countries; SMCs: small low- and middle-income countries; EMEs: emerging market economies.

global basis most private foreign direct investment (FDI) flows to middle-income countries, it is also true that the FDI that has flowed to a number of least-developed countries is very significant as a proportion of GDP and in its domestic impact. The likelihood is that such FDI will constitute a growing proportion of net resource inflows for such countries in the future. The fact is, however, that few LDCs have the monitoring or management capability even to maintain up-to-date, detailed data on the size and nature of such inflows.[18]

18. See Martin and Rose-Innes (2004).

In contrast, emerging market countries' short-term needs arise more from their integration into, and shocks emanating from, international capital markets. (Some countries still suffer from commodity price shocks but, given a far lower level of dependence on commodity exports and greater degree of export diversification, the effects are far less devastating than those felt by the poorest countries.) Since the Asian financial crisis, much of the debate about short-term crisis prevention and mitigation, along with the argument that more could be done through regional cooperation, has been focused on this group. Debt restructuring is generally a short-term liquidity issue rather than a longer-term sustainability issue for this group. Finally, there is also an unmet need for trade finance to put this group of countries at less of a disadvantage to their industrial-country competitors.

With regard to longer-term needs, emerging market countries have much in common with the poorest countries but face more choices in meeting them. There is greater scope for domestic resource mobilization through financial intermediation, taxation, duty collection, and public sector borrowing, and for a significant portion of investment, particularly for the productive sectors, to take place through private markets. However, particularly in those countries where domestic savings rates are low, investment needs must be met by accessing international capital markets. In particularly short supply (as in least developed countries) is medium-term countercyclical financing, since available financing (official as well as private) tends to be procyclical.

Between these two groups are the smaller low- and middle-income countries, which tend to have many of the same financing needs as the poorest countries and some of the capabilities of emerging market countries. Thus they are able to absorb some semi-concessional financing and more forms of private foreign investment than LDCs. Some countries in this group are eligible for heavily indebted poor-country (HIPC) debt relief (such as Bolivia, Nicaragua, and Honduras) and require medium-term debt restructuring.

Finally, casual observation suggests that the least developed countries face the greatest unmet needs, and that short-term needs tend to be more unmet than longer-term needs. In table 2-1, the greatest unmet needs are listed in the top left-hand corner. Moving down and to the right in the table, rising per capita income and greater access to capital markets gives middle-income and emerging markets more choices, either through official financing or through the markets.

This taxonomy of developing-country categories and their needs must now be applied to the geographic, historical, and cultural realities of the developing world. By definition, the membership of regional organizations is determined by geography. A large majority of the LDCs are in Africa; and a large majority of African countries are LDCs. It follows that regional organizations in Africa must inevitably contend with the challenges and demands of LDCs, which are among the most difficult in the developing world.

There are also important cultural and linguistic differences between the predominantly Arab states of the north and those of sub-Saharan Africa; and in sub-Saharan Africa, between those in which French, English, or Portuguese is an official language. There is, in addition, considerable diversity among indigenous languages both between and within countries. Other sources of cultural heterogeneity are rooted in religion. It is important to note that such diversity is not an obstacle to regional cooperation, as the case of European integration demonstrates. However, it does represent an important challenge to cooperation at a number of levels, from the negotiation of cooperation agreements to the structure and functioning of regional organizations: where they are located, their working languages, and so on.

In contrast to Africa, LDCs are virtually nonexistent in Latin America (with the exception of Haiti). Accordingly, in Latin America the demands faced by regional organizations are principally those of the EMEs and SMCs. Without minimizing those demands, it is fair to consider them more tractable than those of the LDCs, so that the regional organizations in Latin America face less formidable challenges than their counterparts in Africa.

Moreover, culturally and linguistically, as the descriptor "Latin" suggests, the region is less heterogeneous than other parts of the developing world (this may explain why some of the earliest attempts at regional cooperation were made in Latin America). Spanish is the official language of most countries and the lingua franca of the region: this undoubtedly facilitates cooperation at a practical level.

In Asia, LDCs are more numerous (they include Afghanistan, Bangladesh, Bhutan, Cambodia, Lao PDR, Myanmar, Nepal, and Yemen, plus several Pacific and Indian Ocean island states) but constitute a small portion of the region's total population, which is heavily weighted by China and India. There are as well a number of SMCs in Asia. At the same time, Asia is also home to Japan, the world's second largest developed economy, and other countries or city-states that are either developed (Singapore and Hong Kong SAR; plus Australia and New Zealand if these are considered part of Asia) or advanced middle-income countries (the Republic of Korea, Taiwan Province of China, and Malaysia). More generally, the Asian continent's size, huge population, and enormous cultural diversity, not to mention historical frictions going back many centuries, have militated against regional cooperation until very recently.

In contrast to Africa, however, it may be said that Asia's diversity also offers crucial strengths. In particular, the presence of industrial and emerging market countries provides the region with a rapidly growing pool of savings and greater creditworthiness. For obvious reasons, this is a significant advantage for regional financial cooperation. In Africa, there are no countries similar to Japan, Australia, the Republic of Korea, or Taiwan Province of China, with capital surpluses, deep financial markets, or large foreign exchange reserves.

The last point suggests that the rationale of regional financial cooperation viewed from the demand side, that is, with the needs of ultimate beneficiaries in mind, should be complemented by a "supply-side" perspective. Unless regional organizations are viable and sustainable over the long term, it is at best hypothetical to argue that there should be more of them, or that the emphasis on improving the international architecture should be on strengthening existing regional organizations rather than the global institutions.

One way of assessing the potential viability of regional financial organizations stems from the relationship between their balance sheets and the financial capacity of regional member states. For nonconcessional lending, a healthy balance sheet implies, on the liability side, a strong net equity position, and on the asset side, loans that are well-performing (or few nonperforming or doubtful loans). In turn, a strong net equity position typically means that the organization's membership includes a number of very creditworthy countries (or creditors with protracted current account surpluses), while a portfolio of well-performing loans usually implies that borrowers service their loans fully and on schedule. For concessional lending, there should be some aid donors able to provide low-interest repayable credits, or grants, to eligible members.

In Africa, "very creditworthy countries" able to provide either a strong equity position or concessional development resources are conspicuously absent. Asia, in contrast, includes a number of very creditworthy countries, and among these, some significant aid donors. In the first decade of the twenty-first century, Latin America is an intermediate case, in that the region features no significant aid donors or capital surplus countries. However, notwithstanding Argentina's default and subsequent restructuring of its international obligations, Latin American emerging market countries are increasingly creditworthy as international borrowers, a fact that provides strength to the asset portfolios of lenders to the region.

Table 2-2 summarizes the opportunities and challenges facing the three major continental regions of the developing world. It suggests that in Africa the challenges confronting regional financial cooperation are the greatest, on both the demand and the supply side. Asia has considerable advantages on the supply side in its accumulation of a growing share of the world's savings. Latin America does not face the exigencies of Africa on the demand side, but neither does it have Asia's advantages on the supply side. However, cultural affinities in Latin

Table 2-2. *Financial Opportunities and Challenges by Region*

	Africa	*Latin America/Caribbean*	*Asia/Pacific*
Regional characteristics	Predominantly LDCs	Predominantly SMCs and EMEs	LDCs, SMCs, and EMEs
Cultural affinities	Considerable diversity	Some cultural similarities, including regional importance of Spanish	Considerable diversity
Financial capacities	No highly credit-worthy countries or aid donors	No significant aid donors or lenders, but increasingly credit-worthy borrowers	Some significant aid donors, lenders, and creditworthy borrowers

America likely provide more "political glue" to the project of regional financial cooperation than exists on the other two continents.

Regional Financial Cooperation: Lessons from Current Experience

If the above is accepted as a useful conceptual framework, what lessons can be drawn from the experience of regional financial organizations, going beyond the regional development banks? What role do they play in meeting the needs of the three groups of countries? This question is addressed here via a brief survey of regional institutions on two continents—Africa and Latin America and the Caribbean.

Africa

Thirty-four, or almost three-quarters, of the world's forty-eight least-developed countries are in sub-Saharan Africa, which can be thought of as a least-developed region or a group of such regions. The African Development Bank Group (particularly its concessional affiliate, the African Development Fund) is the principal regional institution providing medium- to long-term development finance. However, the mandate of the African Development Bank Group covers the whole continent, including the countries of North Africa and the Republic of South Africa. There are a number of subregional organizations, including the following. The Economic Community of West African States (ECOWAS), comprising sixteen members in West Africa, was created in 1975 to promote intraregional trade.[19] The ECOWAS treaty also calls for joint infrastructural

19. Its members are Benin, Burkina Faso, Cape Verde, Côte d'Ivoire, Gambia, Ghana, Guinea, Guinea-Bissau, Liberia, Mali, Mauritania, Togo, Niger, Nigeria, Senegal, and Sierra Leone.

development, harmonized approaches to industrialization, and the improvement of regional competitiveness; these are the objectives of its affiliated financial organizations, the ECOWAS Bank for Investment and Development, the ECOWAS Regional Investment Bank, and the ECOWAS Fund for Cooperation, Compensation and Development. The fund has agreements with the African Development Bank and the Islamic Development Bank to cofinance projects. There is also a private regional investment bank, Ecobank Transnational Inc., based in Togo. Achievements in all these areas have been modest, although there has been some progress in infrastructure.[20] In December 2000, five countries (Gambia, Ghana, Guinea, Nigeria, and Sierra Leone) agreed to create the West African Monetary Zone with a common currency and central bank and to merge this zone with the Western African Economic and Monetary Union by the year 2005. However, this timetable did not prove feasible. In May 2005, heads of state and government of the five countries reaffirmed their commitment to a second monetary zone and to full West African monetary union, but agreed to postpone the date of attainment until December 2009. To that end, they also agreed to an implementation plan that included the formation of a customs union and a single economic space among the five countries to express political commitment to the regional monetary integration process.

The CFA franc zone (CFAF zone) is the longest-standing example of regional financial cooperation among a group of LDCs, dating back to 1948. The CFA franc is a common currency fixed via a "hard peg" to the euro (before 1999, to the French franc), which effectively externalizes authority for short-term financing to the French Treasury. Moreover, the hard peg reduces the zone's capacity to absorb external shocks, which is further complicated by the substantially different needs and capacities of its fourteen members in its two zones in West and Central Africa.[21] Therefore because of the nature of its external peg and other features, the regional common currency per se cannot be said to have resolved the zone's needs for short-term financing to meet commodity price fluctuations or natural disasters such as drought and desertification, or financing for longer-term development. Indeed, it could even be argued that, rather than leveraging

---

20. Rwegasira (1996).

21. The two zones are the West African Economic and Monetary Union (WAEMU), comprising Benin, Burkina Faso, Guinea-Bissau, Côte d'Ivoire, Mali, Niger, Senegal, and Togo; and the Central African Economic and Monetary Community (CAEMU), comprising Cameroon, the Central African Republic, Congo, Chad, Equatorial Guinea, and Gabon. Most observers would agree that the CFA franc zone is so large and heterogeneous that it does not constitute an optimal currency area in Mundell's sense. De Macedo, Cohen, and Reisen (2001) argue that regional cooperation is actually easier between countries with partly flexible, "intermediate" exchange rate regimes rather than "corner regimes" of hard pegs or complete flexibility.

additional resources for regional members, the rigidities of the CFAF zone (including the recent adoption of a Convergence, Stability, Growth, and Solidarity Pact modeled on that of the Eurozone) hamper its flexibility. However, its proponents argue that the requirements of an externally backed common currency have resulted in monetary and fiscal discipline, which in turn have served to strengthen the region's growth performance. In addition, members have agreed to a single banking supervisory authority (a "Banking Commission") in each of the two subregions, as well as setting up common accounting and prudential standards throughout the zone, which may contribute to making the region more attractive to foreign investment, reducing the problems of information asymmetry, and with it the threat of financial contagion.[22] Members of the West African Economic and Monetary Union (WAEMU or, in French, Union Économique et Monétaire Ouest Africaine, UEMOA) adopted a customs union and common external tariff in 2000. Progress toward regional integration in the Central African Economic and Monetary Union (CAEMU or, in French, Communauté Économique et Monétaire de l'Afrique Centrale, CEMAC) has been slower.[23]

The Southern African Development Community (SADC) is an association of fourteen states of central and southern Africa.[24] Before 1992, when South Africa joined what was previously the Southern African Development Coordination Conference (SADCC), its main objective was to promote regional integration through investment and sector coordination driven primarily by donor funding. This group now provides a forum and a framework within which to coordinate policies and facilitate greater regional integration (on political issues such as security and defense, and the strengthening of democracy and human rights, as well as on the regional economy). SADC is phasing in a free-trade area in 2008.

The Common Market for Eastern and Southern Africa (COMESA, formerly the Preferential Trading Area, or PTA) comprises seventeen members including many members of SADC.[25] Its fundamental objective is to promote intraregional trade through trade liberalization. It established a free-trade area among nine members in 2000 and is working toward a customs union in 2008. (A subgroup, the East African Community, comprising Kenya, Tanzania, and Uganda, formed a customs union with a common external tariff that came into effect in

22. Strauss-Kahn (2003).
23. International Monetary Fund (2002).
24. Angola, Botswana, Democratic Republic of the Congo, Lesotho, Malawi, Mauritius, Mozambique, Namibia, Seychelles, South Africa, Swaziland, Tanzania, Zambia, and Zimbabwe.
25. Angola, Burundi, Comoros, the Democratic Republic of the Congo, Eritrea, Ethiopia, Kenya, Lesotho, Malawi, Mauritius, Rwanda, Sudan, Swaziland, Tanzania, Uganda, Zambia, and Zimbabwe.

2005.) As part of this larger objective, COMESA has established three financial facilities, the Eastern and Southern African Trade and Development Bank (PTA Bank), created to establish a trade financing window, unique in sub-Saharan Africa; the COMESA Clearing House to facilitate the settlement of trade payments among members; and the PTA Reinsurance Company (ZEP-RE), established to develop the insurance and reinsurance industry in the region. Strengthening macroeconomic coordination is also an objective of the COMESA treaty, but little has been done in this regard.[26]

Certain features stand out from this brief survey of African regional organizations. First, apart from the CFA franc zone, regional trade is the principal objective rather than financial cooperation. To a lesser extent, regional integration through investment has been a motivation. In the case of the CFAF zone, regional trade and integration, including financial and macroeconomic harmonization, have been by-products facilitated by the common currency. Second, achievements have generally been modest, reflecting the stark challenges facing all member countries and the difficulties of coordinating policies in such circumstances. The level of intraregional trade is somewhat higher in the CFAF zone than in other regional blocs, but is still far from dominating the direction of trade as a whole, which continues to be strongly oriented toward Europe. This outcome is not surprising, given the low degree of complementarity in the region's trade and production structure. Third, notwithstanding some innovative attempts at financial cooperation (such as the PTA Bank in COMESA to facilitate trade financing), it is clear that such initiatives have not gone far in sub-Saharan Africa toward meeting the region's needs for short- and longer-term finance. Finally, criticisms of the CFAF zone suggest that regional economic cooperation may be a two-edged sword. While it may be intended to increase the interest and confidence of outside investors, an unintended consequence of overly stringent standards of harmonization may be to hamper growth. Such criticisms are important given various proposals for new common currencies (see below).

Perhaps it is the limited success of such regional efforts that led African leaders in 2002 to launch the New Partnership for African Development, an initiative that explicitly invited donors to support African-led efforts, whether for infrastructure investment, regional security, or the transition to democracy.[27] However, at the same time African leaders also agreed to a timetable for the creation of the African Union (AU) to replace the Organization for African Unity.

---

26. Rwegasira (1996); IMF (2002).

27. Mistry (1996), explaining the failure of structural reforms in Africa, argued for a more regional approach to investment coordination and cooperation, trade integration, and institutional development.

The AU, which came into force in 2001, will ultimately have power over economic, political, social, and judicial issues on the continent. It will eventually develop a common currency, a continental parliament, and a court of justice and is modeled on the European Union rather than on NAFTA or FTAA. These developments, which have occasioned both optimism and skepticism, reaffirm the importance of political factors underlying regional cooperation.

Latin America and the Caribbean

The Latin America and Caribbean (LAC) region includes groups of both EME and SMC subregions (the only LDC in the hemisphere being Haiti). Two examples of regional financial cooperation among SMCs and one among a heterogeneous group of EMEs and SMCs serve to illustrate some potentials and pitfalls.

The Central American Bank for Economic Integration (CABEI), established in 1960, is a subregional bank based in Honduras, serving that country and four others—Guatemala, El Salvador, Nicaragua, and Costa Rica, which in the framework of this paper all constitute SMCs. There are also four nonborrowing "regional" members, Argentina, Colombia, Mexico, and Taiwan Province of China, all of which are EMEs. Its mission is to promote the progress and the integration of the isthmus by fostering equitable, environmentally friendly economic growth. To that end, it supports public and private programs and projects that generate productive employment and contribute to improving productivity and competitiveness, as well as to raising the human development indexes of the region. Over the four decades of its existence, CABEI has proved itself to be a useful regional nonconcessional financial intermediary for both public sector investment and, increasingly over the past decade, private sector investment, including investment in small and medium-sized enterprises. However, it encountered financial problems because of the accumulation of high external debt and arrears by Nicaragua in the 1980s, part of which were due to its neighbors and to CABEI itself. This issue was compounded by the HIPC debt-relief initiative in the late 1990s, because two of its borrowing members (Nicaragua and Honduras) became eligible for relief. Without adequate compensation (for example through donor trust funds established under HIPC), the prescribed debt relief could have impaired one-half of the net worth of CABEI.

The Caribbean Development Bank (CDB) was established in 1970 to promote economic growth and integration among the countries of the Commonwealth Caribbean, particularly the less-developed members. It currently has twenty-five members, including three nonborrowing regional members (Colombia, Mexico, and the Bolivarian Republic of Venezuela) and five nonregionals (Canada, China, Germany, Italy, and the United Kingdom). Like CABEI, it has acted as a financial intermediary to mobilize nonconcessional financing. Unlike CABEI, it also has a concessional window supported by a small group of bilateral donors. A review of CDB undertaken in 1995 concluded that CDB is a highly effective lender to smaller countries (many of which are island micro-states), based on its portfolio of successful project loans and sound management practices. Its success, relative to CABEI, rests in part on its ability to access concessional funds for its lenders, which cannot sustain high levels of debt. An innovative agreement between CDB and the World Bank in 1990 resulted in CDB's "retailing" World Bank concessional funds to the micro-states of the eastern Caribbean.[28]

The Andean Development Corporation (Corporación Andina de Fomento, or CAF) began its operations in 1970 in Caracas. Its principal shareholders are members of the Andean community: Bolivia, Colombia, Ecuador, Peru, and the Bolivarian Republic of Venezuela. It also has seven extraregional shareholders (Brazil, Chile, Jamaica, Mexico, Panama, Paraguay, and Trinidad and Tobago), as well as twenty-two private banks from the Andean region (a unique characteristic of subregional development banks). Thus CAF membership comprises both EMEs (Brazil, Chile, Colombia, Mexico, and the Bolivarian Republic of Venezuela) and SMCs, all exclusively from the LAC region. (Spain also became a member in recent years, with a small share and the same standing as other members, and thus with the ability to borrow from CAF). Its mission is to promote sustainable development and regional integration in both the public and private sectors of Latin America and the Caribbean. CAF approvals to its five Andean members (U.S.$18.7 billion, 1990–99) considerably exceed those of the IDB ($14.4 billion) and the World Bank ($10.2 billion) and, while its bond rating is lower than those of the IDB and World Bank (S&P: AAA), it is higher than any other Latin American issuer (for example, Chile's S&P rating is "A–" while that of CAF is "A").[29] Its lending portfolio is concentrated in its Andean members, and 72 percent consists of infrastructure projects. CAF performance is all the more remarkable because one of its Andean borrowers, Bolivia, is a debt-distressed HIPC country, while another, Ecuador, experienced severe financial distress in 2003 and, like CABEI (but in contrast to CDB), it does not have a concessional lending window.

The experience of CAF proves that it is possible for a subregional financial institution to operate very successfully, without any industrial-country shareholders

---

28. Hardy (1995).
29. Financially its return on assets (1.9 percent) and equity (7.0 percent) outperforms the IDB (1.0 percent and 5.0 percent, respectively) and World Bank (0.7 percent and 5.6 percent). See Quintela (2000).

and without recourse to concessional funding. Indeed, it has done so on a scale comparable to that of the world's principal IFIs, despite the serious economic problems afflicting some of its key borrowing members—problems that have caused serious difficulties for CABEI. Factors explaining the comparative success of CAF likely include judicious management and the sectoral composition of the borrowing portfolio, with its heavy emphasis on public sector infrastructure. All three organizations include regional integration among their principal objectives but, like their IFI peers, this does not seem to translate into a significant portion of their lending portfolios. Finally, while all three meet some their respective regions' needs for long-term capital, none of them are particularly well placed to meet needs for short-term assistance—for example, in the face of natural disasters.

Other regional organizations worth mentioning briefly include:[30] (1) the Reciprocal Payments and Credits Agreement of the Latin American Integration Association (ALADI), an arrangement dating back to the 1960 Montevideo Treaty, to settle trade-related payments among Latin American countries. After growing rapidly in the 1980s to the point of processing 90 percent of intraregional import payments, the proportion processed by ALADI dwindled to 10 percent by 1999, partly because of the development of financial technology, de facto dollarization, and more flexible exchange rates, which reduced the advantages of the ALADI settlement system;[31] and (2) the Latin American Reserve Fund (Fondo Latinoamericano de Reservas, FLAR), a reserve-pooling arrangement initiated by the Andean countries in 1978 (Costa Rica has subsequently joined). FLAR current subscribed capital is U.S.$2.1 billion; its fundamental objective is to support the balance of payments of member countries by granting or guaranteeing loans. The ability to play this role effectively may be circumscribed both by relatively limited FLAR resources and by its (thus far) limited membership (the five Andean countries plus Costa Rica).[32] In the event of regional contagion spreading from a particular member's financial crisis, there would be simultaneous demands for balance-of-payments support that FLAR could not meet.[33]

Compared to Africa (and perhaps Asia as well, which is not surveyed here), the Latin American and Caribbean region seems well served by subregional organizations, despite the setbacks suffered by CABEI on account of the Nicaraguan arrears and the HIPC initiative. In large part this is due to the greater economic strength of countries in LAC, which include several EMEs. The CAF has broken

---

30. The list could also include FONPLATA, a subregional bank.

31. Chang (2000).

32. FLAR capital of $2.1 billion is clearly meager in comparison with the bilateral swap arrangements under the Chiang Mai Initiative of $32.5 billion.

33. Chang (2000).

new ground among regional financial institutions by virtue of both the overall volume of its operations and its success on a number of indicators. And the FLAR predates the Chiang Mai Initiative (CMI) as a regional monetary fund, even if its resources are still modest. The FLAR and CMI initiatives could well learn from each other—for example, FLAR could supplement its resources with bilateral swap agreements,[34] and the CMI could learn from the FLAR experience with reserve pooling. Finally, the "retailing" arrangement between the World Bank and CDB could be replicated in a number of other subregional banks as a way of efficiently channeling resources to the world's smaller and poorer countries.

Conclusion: Regional Organizations in the Global Financial Architecture

Notwithstanding the important and innovative financial contributions of regional organizations such as CAF, the fact remains that a number of key financial needs of their developing-country members likely remain unmet. This is particularly the case for *all* the financing requirements of the poorest countries and some smaller and lower-income countries, and for the *shorter-term* financing requirements of poorer and emerging countries alike. These are discussed in turn, with a mind to the role of regional organizations in filling the gap.

Longer-Term Resource Needs of the Poorest Countries

Following the pledges of the international community made at the 2002 International Financing for Development Conference in Monterrey and during 2005, the year of the Millennium Review Summit, it seems that there could be significant increases of about $50 billion in ODA in the years up to 2010. While welcome, this will still fall short of the amount required to help meet the millennium development goals (MDGs), which would require an ODA/GNI ratio of 0.44 percent in 2006, rather than the 0.30 percent currently projected for that year; even the 0.36 percent projected for 2010 falls short.[35] Moreover, calculations by the United Nations Millennium Project suggest that an ODA/gross national income (GNI) ratio of at least 0.54 percent would be necessary to help meet the MDGs. Given that backdrop, what can regional organizations or initiatives do to fill the gap?

---

34. Economic Commission for Latin America and the Caribbean (2002).

35. Report to the Secretary-General of the High-Level Panel on Financing for Development (United Nations A/55/1000, June 26, 2001); United Nations General Assembly, "Implementation of and follow-up to commitments and agreements made at the International Conference on Financing for Development" (United Nations A/58/216, August 5, 2003), paragraphs 115–21. See also Manning (2005), and the United Nations Millennium Project, "Why 0.7 percent matters for the Millennium Development Goals" (www.unmillenniumproject.org/involved/action07.htm).

There are two possible answers. The first looks *outward,* principally to donors for resources, by facilitating aid flows through collective regional efforts. The obvious example here is NEPAD, an initiative of African leaders aimed at catalyzing aid and other resource flows to Africa. Through collective commitments to undertake economic and governance reforms, monitored through an African peer-review system, the objective is to increase the confidence of donors and private foreign investors that the economic and political climate is conducive to development, and therefore that aid will be more effective and private investment more productive and profitable.

An offshoot of the NEPAD initiative involves the United Nations Economic Commission for Africa (ECA) and the OECD Development Assistance Committee's own peer-review system, through ECA participation in the reviews scheduled regularly for each donor member of DAC. Indeed, there is a paucity of mechanisms in the aid architecture to ensure that donors meet their pledges and stated commitments, in contrast to the host of mechanisms to ensure that developing-country recipients meet theirs.[36] While a few recipient countries are developing mechanisms to monitor the commitments and behavior of their entire family of donors, perhaps regional organizations (for example, the East African Community) could collectively arrange for independent monitoring and review of donors. The aim would be to identify and build on best practice as well as to remedy unacceptable practices of those donors.

The second answer to meeting the needs of the poorest countries looks *inward,* to the possibility of mobilizing more resources domestically. Regional organizations can help deepen financial markets; develop the financial sector through capacity building of banking and nonbanking institutions and human skills; and help create or improve the regulatory and supervisory infrastructure. Regional cooperation may be particularly useful in setting up stock markets on a regional rather than a national basis, since, for poorer countries, local equity markets tend to be very thin. There could be cost advantages (by economizing on administrative and supervisory overhead) and benefits for local and foreign portfolio investors in the form of greater choice and market liquidity. In addition, regional public bond markets, combined with integrated financial payments systems, might effectively reduce the risk of contagion of financial crises by facilitating a coordinated monetary policy response and reducing the possibility of temporary failure of trade finance. Some regional institutions are already engaged in such an agenda, as evidenced by the financial reforms of the

36. Independent Monitoring Group (2002).

WAEMU (Western) subregion of the CFA franc zone and the ECOWAS proposal for a second monetary zone. While the objective of mobilizing more resources from the savings of the poorest countries is ambitious—and some may even regard it as naïve or utopian—the fact remains that the "East Asian miracle" involved, to a large extent, poor countries with high savings rates (considerably in excess of those common in sub-Saharan Africa) *and* a reasonably efficient financial sector.[37]

However, an important caveat must be added. Regional rules and institutions should be designed, first and foremost, with regional needs in mind. To the extent that such rules and institutions reduce the scope for action on fiscal, monetary, financial sector, or exchange rate policies, as seems to be the case at least for some countries in the CFA franc zone and elsewhere in sub-Saharan Africa, they could hinder rather than help domestic investment and growth.[38]

In conclusion, meeting the needs of the poorest countries for resources—whether long-term or short—is the most demanding of all development challenges. It would be unrealistic to expect that regional cooperation, by itself, would help to bridge the enormous gap between availability and needs. Nonetheless, there may be ways in which regional cooperation can be a catalyst for greater or more effective aid and private flows or help to deepen local financial markets and increase the scope for domestic resource mobilization.

Bridging the Gap for Short-Term Financing

Most of the attention in the aftermath of the Asian financial crisis has dwelt on short-term measures to prevent or manage crises. While the 1998 proposal for an Asian Monetary Fund met with opposition from the IMF and some G-7 members, the 2000 Chiang Mai Initiative has been widely endorsed, despite lingering misgivings.

In the meantime, as a result of the 1997–98 crisis, Asian countries (including China, Hong Kong SAR, the Republic of Korea, India, Singapore, and Taiwan Province of China) have accumulated a large stock of foreign exchange reserves, estimated to be in excess of $2.5 trillion by June 2005. These resources give countries of the region a considerable war chest with which to fight speculative attacks. In that light, CMI bilateral swap and other arrangements

---

37. It is also true that economies such as the Republic of Korea and Taiwan Province of China benefited from large resource transfers from bilateral donors, particularly the United States.
38. Gottschalk (2003).

amounting to $36.5 billion in late 2004 scarcely tap this pool of reserves, although the CMI is viewed as a mechanism that will grow incrementally over time.[39]

The promise of the CMI as a regional mechanism for coping with financial instability (like the success of CAF in Latin America in attracting longer-term financing) illustrates an obvious fact about emerging market economies: their higher per capita incomes and their aggregate market size endow them with significant resources and access to capital. Given continued growth among such countries, it seems likely that such regional mechanisms, without industrial-country membership in some cases, will play an increasing role in meeting their short-term financing needs.

The much more difficult challenge is meeting the short-term financing needs of the poorer countries (including the LDCs and smaller lower-middle-income countries) in the face of natural disasters, declining and volatile commodity prices, and postconflict reconstruction.

For most of these needs, international mechanisms and the involvement of donors seem imperative. In the specific case of commodity-dependent countries, past approaches to stabilizing prices and protecting against shocks, including international commodity agreements, have experienced, at best, mixed success. There may be scope for subregional initiatives, however, in the areas of research and development, and quality control and assurance, to enhance supply capabilities, particularly to meet the increasingly stringent standards of consumers and buyers and to facilitate the production and export of higher-value-added products. Such activities could be financed through the Common Fund for Commodities (CFC).[40]

There may be scope for South-South cooperation as well in this area.[41] For example, developing countries with national stabilization funds for particular commodities (for example, Chile's Copper Stabilization Fund) could provide assistance (again funded through the CFC) to heavily commodity-dependent regions in creating similar funds on a regional basis, pooling revenues from the key commodities exported by member countries. Diversifying such funds to include revenues from more than one commodity would also serve as a stabiliz-

---

39. *The Economist*, September 15, 2005 (www.economist.com/displayStory.cfm?story_id= 4401162). For CMI bilateral swap arrangements as of November 2004, see www.aric.adb.org/ pdf/ProgressReportontheCMI10Nov04.pdf.

40. United Nations Conference on Trade and Development (2002).

41. Helleiner (1999).

ing force, assuming that different commodities are subject to somewhat different supply and demand cycles.

An Overall Balance

Finally, let us return to the questions posed at the outset of this paper with some tentative answers:

—What organizational and institutional characteristics contribute to regional financial organizations' playing an effective role?

It seems clear that regional groups comprising, or dominated by, emerging market countries are more effective because of their economic strength, deep financial markets, and readier access to markets. Put otherwise, they have significant domestic resources and some bargaining power in the global economy. Regional financial organizations in Asia and, to a lesser extent, in Latin America, enjoy these advantages. In addition, Asia is home to some donor countries able to provide concessional or grant financing to poorer countries in the region. Africa, comprising the poorest and lower-income countries, faces much graver difficulties in seeking a greater role for regional financial cooperation. To remedy these shortcomings, Africa must include nonregional donor or industrial countries in the membership of regional organizations, which can obviously raise other problems.

—What are the key financial constraints faced by different groups of developing countries with respect to short-term financing and longer-term financing?

The poorest and smaller countries face challenges across the entire spectrum—whether for short-term or longer-term purposes. All countries, including emerging market countries, face greater challenges in mobilizing short-term financing than longer-term financing, although in the case of the latter there seems greater likelihood that EMEs will be able to organize regionally along the lines of the Chiang Mai Initiative.

—To what extent can regional organizations play a key role in financial crisis prevention and management?

It is too soon to tell whether the Chiang Mai Initiative is up to the task of preventing or mitigating crises in East Asia. However, it could be argued that, as the CMI grows in scope, and the longer the region is spared further financial crises, the more effective CMI will be in making the region speculation-proof. As for poorer and smaller low-income countries, considerably more thought and discussion is needed to develop regional mechanisms to address their acute needs, whether for natural or manmade calamities, or for capital account, commodity, or aid shocks.

—How can regional financial organizations help bridge the large resource gap required for longer-term growth and development?

For the poorest and smaller countries, partnerships with donor countries seem inescapable for the foreseeable future. However, it seems important that the terms of the partnership be right for the developing countries. An excessively restrictive policy framework, ostensibly to appease donors, may constrain growth and development potential. For the emerging market countries, the experience of the CAF suggests that regional organizations can be very adept at mobilizing long-term development financing, provided the membership is appropriate (with prominent EME membership); portfolio composition and astute management are likely also key factors.

Clearly, more research is needed on the potential of regional financial organizations in order to reach a comprehensive assessment of their effectiveness, or prescriptions to improve their performance, including a better division of labor with the global organizations. However, it also seems clear that they can contribute significantly to the global financial architecture in meeting the particular needs of developing countries from very different parts of the world, facing considerably different opportunities and challenges.

References

Bhagwati, J. 1998. "Regionalism and Multilateralism: WTO, Mercosur et al." Paper presented to the Argentine Bankers' Convention, May. www.columbia.edu/~jb38/papers/Argen98.PDF.

Braga de Macedo, J., D. Cohen, and H. Reisen, eds. 2001. *Don't Fix, Don't Float.* Paris: OECD Development Centre Studies.

Chang, R. 2000. "Regional Monetary Arrangements for Developing Countries." Rutgers University. www.g24.org/chang.pdf.

Culpeper, R. 1997. *Titans or Behemoths? The Multilateral Development Banks.* Boulder: Colo.: Lynne Rienner.

Devlin, R., and L. Castro. 2002. "Regional Banks and Regionalism: A New Frontier for Development Financing." Buenos Aires: Inter-American Development Bank.

Economic Commission for Latin America and the Caribbean (ECLAC). 2002. *Growth with Stability: Financing for Development in the New International Context.* Santiago: ECLAC Books.

Emerging Markets Eminent Persons' Group. 2001. "Rebuilding the International Financial Architecture." Seoul: Institute for Global Economics (October).

English, P., and H. Mule. 1996. *The African Development Bank.* Boulder: Lynne Rienner.

Ethier, W. 1998. "The New Regionalism." *Economic Journal* 108 (July): 1149–61.

Gottschalk, R. 2003. "The Macroeconomic Policy Content of PRSPs: How Much Pro-Growth, How Much Pro-Poor?" Paper prepared for the North-South Institute Project on PRSPs and Poverty, Ottawa, October.

Hardy, C. 1995. *The Caribbean Development Bank.* Volume 3 of *The Multilateral Development Banks.* Boulder, Colo.: Lynne Rienner and the North-South Institute.

Helleiner, G. 1999. "Small Countries and the New World Financial Architecture." *Capítulos, Latin America in the International Financial Crisis* 56 (May/August).

International Monetary Fund (IMF). 2002. *Survey: Supplement.* September.

Independent Monitoring Group. 2002. *Enhancing Aid Relationships in Tanzania: Report of the Independent Monitoring Group.* Dar es Salaam: Economic and Social Research Foundation.

Kappagoda, N. 1996. *The Asian Development Bank.* Volume 2 of *The Multilateral Development Banks.* Boulder, Colo.: Lynne Rienner and the North-South Institute.

Kapur, D., and R. Webb. 1994. "The Evolution of the Multilateral Development Banks." In *International Monetary and Financial Issues for the 1990s.* Volume 4, Special issue. New York: United Nations Conference on Trade and Development (UNCTAD).

Manning, R. 2005. "Statement to the Seventy-Second Meeting of the World Bank-IMF Development Committee." Washington, September 25, Document DC/S/2005-0064.

Martin, M., with C. Rose-Innes. 2004. "Private Capital Flows to Low-Income Countries: Perception and Reality." In *Canadian Development Report 2004,* Chapter 2. Ottawa: North-South Institute.

Mistry, P. 1996. "Regional Dimensions of Structural Adjustment in Southern Africa." In *Regionalism and the Global Economy: The Case of Africa,* edited by J. J. Teunissen. The Hague: FONDAD.

Ocampo, J. A. 2002. "The Role of Regional Institutions." In *A Regional Approach to Financial Crisis Prevention: Lessons from Europe and Initiatives in Asia, Latin America and Africa,* edited by J. J. Teunissen. The Hague: Forum on Debt and Development (FONDAD).

———. 2003. "Capital-Account and Counter-Cyclical Prudential Regulations in Developing Countries." In *From Capital Surges to Drought: Seeking Stability for Emerging Economies,* edited by R. Ffrench-Davis and S. Griffith-Jones. London: Palgrave/Macmillan.

Park, Y. C. 2001. "Beyond the Chiang Mai Initiative: Rationale and Need for a Regional Monetary Arrangement in East Asia." Korea University. www.g24.org/ychp0904.pdf.

Quintela, C. 2000. "Corporación Andina de Fomento: Thirty Years Financing Sustainable Development." Presentation, Rio de Janeiro, September 25.

Rwegasira, D. 1996. "Economic Cooperation and Integration in Africa: Experiences, Challenges and Opportunities." In *Toward Autonomous Development in Africa,* edited by R. Culpeper and C. McAskie. Ottawa: North-South Institute.

Stiglitz, J. 2002. *Globalization and Its Discontents.* New York: W. W. Norton.

Strauss-Kahn, M. O. 2003. "Regional Currency Areas: A Few Lessons from the Eurosystem and the CFA Franc Zone." In *Regional Currency Areas and the Use of Foreign Currencies,* BIS Papers (Basel) 17 (May): 42–58.

Teunissen, J. J., ed. 2002. *A Regional Approach to Financial Crisis Prevention: Lessons from Europe and Initiatives in Asia, Latin America and Africa.* The Hague: FONDAD.

United Nations Conference on Trade and Development (UNCTAD). 2000. *The Least Developed Countries 2000 Report.* Geneva: United Nations.

———. 2002. *The Least Developed Countries 2002 Report: Escaping the Poverty Trap.* Geneva: United Nations.

3

Regional Development Banks:
A Comparative Perspective

FRANCISCO SAGASTI AND FERNANDO PRADA

This chapter compares the roles played by regional and subregional multilateral development banks (MDBs) in development financing and attempts to integrate fragmented data and information from a variety of sources.

Development financing institutions are situated at the intersection of the international development system and the international financial system. While there are several entities that straddle both systems, the MDBs occupy a unique place because of their specific characteristics and because they interact with most of the actors in both systems. Multilateral development banks are international financial intermediaries whose shareholders include both developing countries that borrow from them and developed countries that do not. They mobilize resources from private capital markets and from official sources to make loans on better-than-market terms, provide technical assistance and policy advice for economic and social development, and offer a range of complementary services to developing countries and to the international development community.

The MDB "model" is perhaps one of the most useful institutional innovations in development finance of the past six decades and, on the whole, these institutions have a reasonably positive track record. Neither private sources nor bilateral agencies could have leveraged financial resources so efficiently. Moreover, there are no other institutions capable of providing a comparable range of products and services to their member countries, including financial resource mobilization, capacity building, institutional development, knowledge brokering, and the provision of international public goods.[1]

MDBs must preserve a delicate balance among the three main functions they perform: *financial resource mobilization* with the aim of providing financial resources to developing countries through regular and concessional loans; *capacity building, institutional development, and knowledge brokering* through technical assistance, grants, policy dialogue, dissemination of best practice and research support; and *helping to provide regional and global public goods* that cannot be fully provided by national institutions. Not all MDBs are involved in these functions to the same extent, but collectively they cover all of them. There is an inherent tension between the financing and development functions of the MDBs, a tension that has been there since these institutions were created. They serve, on the one hand, as financial intermediaries, and on the other, as development agencies. Performing this delicate balancing act has become much more difficult in recent years, primarily because of the increasing number of issues that MDBs are required to address, the criticisms that have been leveled against them (especially the World Bank), and the debt service problems faced by many of their low-income borrowers. Moreover, in addition to their financing and development roles, these institutions are being asked to play a service role in the provision of regional and global public goods. Although regional and subregional institutions are not as important as the World Bank in the provision and financing of such goods, there is evidence that they are taking a more active role in the provision of regional public goods, and this applies in particular to the Inter-American Development Bank (IDB) and the Asian Development Bank (AsDB).[2]

Nevertheless, financial resource mobilization can be considered to be the primus inter pares of these three functions. Providing loans to borrowing member countries is an essential condition for the existence of an MDB, and neither of their other two functions could be performed without preserving their financial integrity and technical capacity to make loans.

---

1. See, in this regard, Bezanson and Sagasti (2000), Sagasti and Bezanson (2001), and Sagasti (2004).

2. Estevadeordal, Frantz, and Nguyen (2004). In late 2004, the IDB launched a new initiative to support the provision of regional public goods. It will allocate at least U.S.$10 million annually for this purpose during the next three years. Resources are being allocated through an open competition for proposals.

An Overview of the Regional and Subregional Development Banks

There are more than twenty institutions that qualify as MDBs according to the broad definition of multilateral development banks being used in this chapter. MDBs can be differentiated according to size, number, and characteristics of their shareholders, type of borrowers (public or private, income levels), geographic scope (global, regional, subregional), and by the sectors or activities they cover. Most studies of MDBs have focused on the World Bank, the oldest and largest of the MDBs, and on the regional development banks (Inter-American Development Bank, Asian Development Bank [AsDB], African Development Bank [AfDB], and European Bank for Reconstruction and Development [EBRD]), which come next in size and membership, and which were established during the 1950s and 1960s (with the exception of the EBRD, which was established in 1991). However, there are also many smaller MDBs ("subregionals") and international funds and institutions that can be considered multilateral development banks based on the characteristics of their operations (see table 3-1).[3]

The level of resources provided by MDBs to developing countries is lower than the direct foreign investment (U.S.$137 billion in 2003), remittances (U.S.$93 billion), and bilateral assistance (U.S.$49.5 billion) they receive. In addition, the share of MDBs in total net flows from multilateral sources varies across regions and levels of income. Net flows from regional development banks (RDBs) to developing countries were U.S.$66.7 billion during the period 1991–2002, nearly 30 percent of total net flows from multilateral sources (table 3-2). Excluding from this total the flows from the International Monetary Fund (IMF), which are mainly short term, RDBs provide more than 40 percent of total long- and medium-term net flows to developing countries from multilateral sources.

---

3. The European Investment Bank has been placed in the category of subregional development banks, even though it is very large and might belong in a category of its own. It operates in a wide variety of countries, including some relatively advanced European and transition countries, as well as in many developing countries. Other institutions, such as the Latin American Reserve Fund and the Arab Monetary Fund, provide short-term financial assistance to their member countries and therefore have not been considered here as MDBs; their functions are more like those of the International Monetary Fund (IMF). The Latin American Export Bank (BLADEX) is another special case. It focuses on trade transactions (export credit) and on capital market operations (guarantees). BLADEX has not been classified as an MDB because of its shareholding composition: of its 39.3 million shares, 16.1 percent are Class A (shares that can only be issued to Latin American Central Banks or banks in which the state or some government agency is the majority shareholder), 10.4 percent are Class B (issued to banks or financial institutions), and 73.5 percent are Class E (issued to any person whether a natural person or a legal entity).

There are important regional differences in the role that RDBs play in development financing. In Latin America, net flows from the IDB have steadily and significantly expanded, rising from U.S.$5.2 billion in 1991–94 to U.S.$15.9 billion in 1999–2002, and have surpassed by far those from the World Bank (U.S.$1.3 and U.S.$7.3 billion, respectively, in the same periods). RDB net flows are also higher than those of the World Bank in the region comprising the Middle East and North Africa (U.S.$3 billion from RDBs compared with U.S.$1 billion from the World Bank in the period 1991–2002), although financial flows from multilateral sources are not as large in that region as in Latin America.

The growth in financing from RDBs has occurred primarily in middle-income countries, where their net flows surpassed those of the World Bank: U.S.$42.5 billion compared with U.S.$40 billion for the period 1991–2002. If IMF flows to these countries are excluded, RDBs account for more than 50 percent of net multilateral flows. Lower-middle-income countries have received U.S.$7.2 billion from the World Bank and U.S.$12.3 billion from RDBs. Upper-middle-income countries received U.S.$30 billion from RDBs in the same period, although for this group of countries World Bank net flows were higher than those of RDBs (U.S.$33 billion). In contrast, low-income economies are heavily dependent on the World Bank, which accounted for 53 percent of total net multilateral flows (U.S.$41 billion in the period 1991–2002). The situation is similar for highly indebted poor countries (HIPC), where the World Bank contributed 64 percent of total net multilateral flows.

Evolution and Current Situation of the Regional and Subregional Development Banks

Financial Instruments and Services

The MDBs have product lines that include regular loans at below-market rates of interest;[4] concessional loans at very low rates of interest with long repayment periods; relatively small amounts of grant financing for technical assistance; train-

---

4. Some borrowing countries with very good credit ratings can obtain financing from international capital markets at lower rates than those offered by the MDBs, but these countries have also resorted to MDB financing in exceptional cases of distress. For example, the World Bank provided the Republic of Korea with a total of U.S.$8.6 billion in IBRD regular loans and U.S.$120 million in IDA soft credits through the years, with the last loan occurring in December 1994, before the Republic of Korea "graduated" and became ineligible for World Bank financing. Nevertheless, in the aftermath of the 1997 Asian crisis, the Republic of Korea returned to borrow from the World Bank and received a U.S.$3 billion loan as part of a U.S.$57 billion package provided by various international financial institutions and bilateral agencies.

Table 3-1. *The Family of Multilateral Development Banks*

Multilateral development banks	Year	Latin America and the Caribbean	Sub-Saharan Africa	Middle East and North Africa	South Asia	East Asia and Pacific	Europe and Central Asia
World Bank group							
International Bank for Reconstruction and Development (IBRD)	1944	Pr/Pu[a]	Pr/Pu	Pr/Pu	Pr/Pu	Pr/Pu	Pr/Pu
International Development Association (IDA)	1960	Pu	Pu	Pu	Pu	Pu	Pu
International Finance Corporation (IFC)	1956	Pr/Pu	Pr/Pu	Pr/Pu	Pr/Pu	Pr/Pu	Pr/Pu
Multilateral Investment Guarantee Agency (MIGA)	1988	Pr/Pu	Pr/Pu	Pr/Pu	Pr/Pu	Pr/Pu	Pr/Pu
Regional development banks (RDBs)							
Inter-American Development Bank (IDB)	1959	Pr/Pu					
Fund for Special Operations (FSO)	1959	Pu					
Inter-American Investment Corporation (IIC)	1989	Pr					
Multilateral Investment Fund (MIF)	1992	Pr					
African Development Bank (AfDB)	1964		Pr/Pu	Pr/Pu			
African Development Fund (AfDF)	1972		Pr/Pu	Pr/Pu			
Asian Development Bank (AsDB)	1966				Pr/Pu	Pr/Pu	Pr/Pu
Asian Development Fund (AsDF)	1973				Pu	Pu	Pu
European Bank for Reconstruction and Development (EBRD)	1991						Pr/Pu
Subregional development banks (SRDBs)							
European Investment Bank (EIB)	1958	Pr/Pu	Pr/Pu	Pr/Pu	Pr/Pu	Pr/Pu	Pr/Pu
Central American Bank for Economic Integration (CABEI)	1961	Pr/Pu					

Institution	Year						
Caribbean Development Bank (CDB)	1969	Pr/Pu					Pr/Pu
Andean Development Corporation (ADC)	1971	Pr/Pu					Pr/Pu
Nordic Investment Bank (NIB)	1976	Pr/Pu	Pr/Pu	Pr/Pu	Pr/Pu	Pr/Pu	Pr
Islamic Development Bank (IsDB)	1973		Pr/Pu	Pr/Pu	Pr/Pu	Pr/Pu	Pr/Pu
Islamic Corporation for Insurance of Investments and Export Credits (ICIEC)	1994		Pr	Pr	Pr	Pr	Pr
Islamic Corporation for the Development of the Private Sector (ICD)	1999		Pr	Pr	Pr	Pr	Pr
East African Development Bank (EADB)	1967		Pr/Pu	Pr/Pu	Pr/Pu		
Arab Bank for Economic Development in Africa (ABEDA)	1974		Pu	Pu	Pu	Pu	
West African Development Bank (BOAD)	1973		Pr/Pu	Pr/Pu	Pr/Pu		
North American Development Bank (NADB)	1994	Pr/Pu	Pr/Pu				
Other MDB-like funds							
Nordic Development Fund (NDF)	1989	Pr/Pu	Pr/Pu	Pr/Pu	Pr/Pu	Pr/Pu	Pr/Pu
International Fund for Agricultural Development (IFAD)	1977	Pr/Pu	Pr/Pu	Pr/Pu	Pr/Pu	Pr/Pu	Pr/Pu
Arab Fund for Economic and Social Development (AFESD)	1968	Pu	Pu	Pu	Pu		
Organization of Petroleum Exporting Countries (OPEC) Fund for International Development	1976	Pr/Pu	Pr/Pu	Pr/Pu	Pr/Pu	Pr/Pu	Pr/Pu
FONPLATA[b]	1976	Pu					

a. Pu = operations with the public sector. Pr = operations with the private sector.

b. Fondo Financiero para el Desarrollo de la Cuenca del Plata (Fund for Development of the Plata River Basin).

Table 3-2. *Regional Development Banks: Net Flows by Region, 1991–2002*
Billions of U.S. dollars

Multilateral financing sources[a]	1991–94	1995–98	1999–2002	Total 1991–2002	Relative share, 1991–2002 (percent)
All developing countries					
World Bank	25.42	31.51	23.95	80.87	35.7
IMF	7.48	35.36	20.62	63.46	28.0
Other	6.62	8.55	0.16	15.33	6.8
RDBs	20.53	24.65	21.55	66.73	29.5
Regions					
East Asia and Pacific					
World Bank	7.13	8.12	3.46	18.71	46.0
IMF	−0.61	12.65	−2.11	9.93	24.4
Other	0.13	0.30	0.08	0.51	1.3
RDBs	3.11	5.30	3.15	11.55	28.4
Europe and Central Asia					
World Bank	3.17	9.47	7.02	19.66	33.6
IMF	9.98	16.57	6.90	33.45	57.2
Other	3.50	−1.29	0.12	2.33	4.0
RDBs	0.35	1.94	0.71	2.99	5.1
Latin America and the Caribbean					
World Bank	−1.29	3.46	5.10	7.27	11.3
IMF	−4.79	9.54	15.83	20.58	32.0
Other	0.64	6.04	−1.64	5.04	7.8
RDBs	5.17	10.24	15.93	31.34	48.8
Middle East and North Africa					
World Bank	1.15	0.29	−0.37	1.07	10.7
IMF	0.09	1.10	−0.60	0.59	5.8
Other	1.41	2.94	1.03	5.38	53.5
RDBs	2.27	0.99	−0.26	3.01	29.9
South Asia					
World Bank	8.07	3.94	2.14	14.15	61.3
IMF	1.71	−4.33	0.02	−2.61	−11.3
Other	−0.01	0.24	0.28	0.51	2.2
RDBs	5.09	4.43	1.53	11.05	47.8
Sub-Saharan Africa					
World Bank	7.18	6.23	6.60	20.01	67.0
IMF	1.11	−0.17	0.59	1.53	5.1
Other	0.94	0.33	0.28	1.55	5.2
RDBs	4.55	1.74	0.49	6.79	22.7

Table 3-2. *(continued)*
Billions of U.S. dollars

Multilateral financing sources[a]	1991–94	1995–98	1999–2002	Total 1991–2002	Relative share, 1991–2002 (percent)
	Income level				
Low income					
World Bank	17.04	12.42	11.46	40.92	52.5
IMF	1.88	6.97	0.97	9.82	12.6
Other	1.30	1.11	0.62	3.02	3.9
RDBs	10.74	8.01	5.47	24.23	31.1
Middle income					
World Bank	8.38	19.08	12.49	39.95	26.9
IMF	5.60	28.39	19.65	53.64	36.1
Other	5.33	7.45	−0.47	12.31	8.3
RDBs	9.79	16.63	16.08	42.50	28.6
Heavily indebted poor countries					
World Bank	7.63	8.30	9.47	25.39	64.0
IMF	0.31	1.10	0.98	2.39	6.0
Other	0.99	0.95	0.88	2.82	7.1
RDBs	3.97	2.82	2.26	9.05	22.8

Source: World Bank (2004).

a. Other multilateral sources are export credit and rescheduling operations with the Paris Club.

ing and capacity-building activities; risk mitigation and management instruments (such as guarantees, equity participation and capital market operations to enhance private investment); debt management and debt reduction instruments; and additional mechanisms such as the convening of consultative groups to mobilize resources from other financial sources and the issuing of bonds in local currencies to strengthen the capital markets of developing countries. Table 3-3 presents a list of these financial mechanisms and their subtypes, including some innovative proposals that have not yet been fully implemented.[5]

5. The World Bank has been an important source of innovative financial instruments for developing countries, and these instruments have generally been rapidly emulated by RDBs and, to a lesser extent, by SRDBs. For example, regional development banks initially offered loans only through their regular windows, but established concessional windows during the 1970s after the International Development Association (IDA) was created. Similarly, the surge in private sector operations through the Multilateral Investment Guarantee Agency (MIGA) was promptly emulated by the RDBs during the 1990s.

Table 3-3. *MDB Financing Instruments and Their Degree of Use*

Financing instruments	Subtypes of financial instruments	Degree of use[a]
Regular loans	Project, program, and sector loans for the public and private sectors	++++
	Structural adjustment loans and balance-of-payments support	+++
	Emergency recovery loans (in case of disaster or unexpected events)	+++
	Loans to financial intermediaries (for example, development finance corporations)	+++
	Prearranged fast-disbursement loans conditional on previous performance	*
Soft (concessional) loans	Project, program, sector, and structural adjustment loans to the public sector	+++
	Temporary funds for countries with special needs (postconflict reconstruction, sudden deterioration of external conditions)	+
Grants (mostly to public institutions)	Assistance to public institutions for specific programs and projects	+++
	Technical cooperation, capacity-building, and institutional development grants	+++
	Emergency operations to deal with natural or manmade disasters	+++
Risk mitigation and management (mostly for the private sector)	Total, partial, and rolling guarantees (political, contractual, regulatory, credit, foreign exchange risks)	+++
	Financing for currency- and interest-hedging operations	++
	Equity participation and quasi-equity (common shares, preferred stock, C loans)	++
	Other instruments to promote private investment and trade: export credits, securitization, leasing, syndication, underwriting, trade insurance	++
Debt reduction and debt management	Funds for multilateral debt reduction (HIPC Initiative)	+++
	Debt reduction loans (for example, for buying back existing debt, debt service reduction)	++
	Funds for clearing arrears with multilateral development banks	++
	Soft loan buy-down mechanisms	*
Additional financial instruments	Mobilization of resources from bilateral and other multilateral sources (consultative groups)	+++
	Issuing bonds in developing countries to strengthen local capital markets	++

a. This column classifies the use of these instruments as follows:
* Proposed.
+ Being designed and tested.
++ In limited use (in some cases on a pilot scale).
+++ In moderate use (focus on certain countries and sectors).
++++ In extended and widespread use.

Regular loans are medium- or long-term loans, which constitute the main activity of the banks. They include: (1) project and program loans for the public and private sectors, the most frequent type of loans; (2) structural adjustment loans and balance-of-payments support, usually disbursed in tranches, subject to the implementation of agreed policy reforms and certain targets; (3) emergency recovery loans extended in cases of disaster or unexpected events; (4) loans to financial intermediaries, such as development finance corporations, and establishment of apex funds for microfinance; and (5) prearranged fast-disbursement loans conditional on previous performance, available to borrowers deemed creditworthy. Regional development banks and, to a lesser extent, subregional development banks (SRDBs) also have soft loan windows available to their poorest member countries. These include low-interest long-term concessional loans with an extended grace period for public sector investment projects and programs, for sectoral and structural policy reforms, for emergencies and postconflict reconstruction, and for budget support through a common pool of resources.

The World Bank disbursed an annual average of U.S.$17.7 billion during the period 2000–03, of which regular International Bank for Reconstruction and Development (IBRD) loans accounted for 66 percent and International Development Association (IDA) soft credits for 34 percent.[6] As shown in table 3-3, RDBs disbursed almost U.S.$19 billion and SRDBs more than U.S.$12 billion in the same period. Although the figures may vary because data from some SRDBs and MDB-like funds are reported in different currencies, it seems clear that regional and subregional institutions have been mobilizing large amounts of resources, surpassing those from the World Bank in several cases. The figures in table 3-3 corroborate this in the case of net flows, especially in the Latin American region.[7]

Table 3-4 indicates the relative importance of various types of financing instruments in each institution. The emphasis placed on certain types of operations by

6. During this time, the World Bank committed U.S.$17.3 billion. The level of financing grew in 2004 to U.S.$20.1 billion, mainly as a result of the increase of IDA commitments to nearly U.S.$10 billion, up from an annual average of U.S.$7.3 billion in the period 2000–03.

7. The data would need to be standardized in order also to compare net flows from SRDBs, which are poorly reflected in most statistical databases. For example, the World Bank's *Global Development Finance* does not include these flows. On the other hand, the OECD Creditor Reporting System includes some information about the CDB and IFAD and aggregate information on the Arab Funds (AFESD; the Kuwait, Saudi, and Abu Dhabi Funds, ABEDA; the OPEC Fund, and IsDB). It indicates that the CDB disbursed U.S.$0.55 billion in the period 2000–02 and had U.S.$0.42 billion in net flows; that IFAD disbursed U.S.$0.84 billion in the same period and had U.S.$0.46 billion in net flows; and that the Arab Funds disbursed U.S.$0.89 billion and had U.S.$0.32 billion in net flows. (For the full names of organizations abbreviated in this note, see table 3-1.)

Table 3-4. *Financial Resource Mobilization and Financing Instruments, Annual Average, 2000–03*

| | Estimated percentage of total portfolio | | | | | Other instruments (U.S.$ billions) | |
Multilateral development banks	Regular loans	Soft loans	Grants	Private sector operations and risk instruments[a]	Total amount (U.S.$ billions)	Debt instruments[b]	Additional instruments[c]
Regional development banks							
IDB group	83.3	5.0	0.4	11.3	6.71	1.29	1.87
AfDB, AfDF	40.4	36.9	20.2[d]	2.5	2.89	3.85	0.88
AsDB, AsDF	70.1	25.4	0.2	4.3	5.68	0.00	2.19
EBRD	25.9	0.0	0.1	74.0	3.26	...	5.82
Total[e]					18.54	5.14	
Subregional development banks							
EIB (2000–02)[f]	14.9	...	...	85.1	4.56	0.69	n.a.
CABEI	62.0	...	...	38.0	0.38	0.59	...
CDB	69.6	28.7	0.8	0.9	0.19	0.02	...
ADC (2000–02)	59.1	0.1	0.5	39.3	2.93	0.11	0.53
NIB (2003)[g]	93.4	...	...	6.4	0.79	0.01	...
IsDB group	46.2	9.1	4.3	40.4	2.92	0.14	0.05
EADB	69.5	...	...	30.5	0.04	0.01	...
ABEDA[h]	37.8	58.3	1.6	3.3	0.13	0.19	0.37
BOAD	46.0	...	n.a.	31.0	0.14	0.05	n.a.
NADB (1996–2002)	12.0	...	88.0[h]	...	0.06	...	...
Total[e]					12.14	1.81	

Other MDB-like funds

NDF (2003)	100.0	…	…		0.09	0.03
IFAD (2000–02)	7.5	86.7	5.8		0.28	0.28
AFESD (2003)	99.9	…	0.1		0.28	0.07
OPEC Fund (2003)	74.9	…	11.0	14.1	0.31	0.16
FONPLATA	97.9	…	2.1		0.03	0.03
Total[e]					1.10	0.57

n.a. Not available.

… Negligible.

a. Private sector activities (not included in the regular or soft windows), guarantees, and equity investment. It is assumed that all guarantees and equity instruments are designed for the private sector, although this is not entirely true in the case of guarantees and equity for public enterprises or guarantees for the public sector. When possible, private sector loans guaranteed by public institutions have also been included. In the case of the IsDB and CABEI, trade financing operations, which are assumed to be mainly a private sector activity, account for most of the resources.

b. Total commitments for debt reduction under the HIPC Initiative for thirty-seven countries. Twenty-three multilateral creditors have committed to provide HIPC relief amounting to U.S.$24.3 billion (2003 net present value terms)—over 99 percent of the total debt relief required. Global institutions, such as the IMF and the World Bank, could provide over U.S.$15.4 billion of this amount. Other multilateral institutions not included could provide U.S.$0.2 billion.

c. Cofinanced projects, included in total resources provided by banks, except in the case of EBRD and ABEDA, where the amounts shown constitute additional financing.

d. For AfDB, grants include resources committed for debt reduction.

e. The total amount is shown for each type of institution for comparative purposes only.

f. Includes only operations with developing countries (11 percent of total) and accession countries (8 percent of total), not European Union member countries (fifteen during the period under consideration).

g. Total amount includes European transition countries. Private sector operations and risk instruments include only guarantees; lending to the private sector is included in regular loans, most of them (82 percent) to Nordic companies.

h. Soft loans and grants are calculated taking into account the grant element of total loans. Only technical assistance grants are included. In the case of NADB, grants are preinvestment grants.

regional and subregional institutions reflects the diversity of financial needs. Institutions serving the African region are more focused on concessional loans and grants, for example. The AfDB and ABEDA have a higher proportion of these instruments than institutions operating in Central Asia and Europe, which are more focused on private sector activities. These differences between RDBs also apply at the subregional level. For example, the Caribbean Development Bank (CDB) operates in some of the poorest Caribbean countries and has a larger proportion of concessional lending than the Central American Bank for Economic Integration (CABEI), which has a clear mandate to improve intraregional trade (this is reflected in its higher proportion of trade finance and infrastructure operations). The ADC (Andean Development Corporation) and FONPLATA (Fondo Financiero para el Desarrollo de la Cuenca del Plata; in English, Financial Fund for Development of the Plata River Basin), operating mainly in middle-income countries, have specialized in other types of operations, such as infrastructure projects for regional integration and for improving competitiveness. These activities are in line with the general idea behind the creation of regional and subregional institutions: they play specific and localized roles, which are not always covered adequately by global or even by regional institutions.[8]

Some characteristics of the RDBs and SRDBs merit highlighting. First, the level of resource mobilization does not clearly differentiate RDBs from SRDBs. Some subregional institutions such as the Andean Development Corporation and the European Investment Bank (EIB) have disbursed more resources than regional institutions, and their close relations with international capital markets allow them to tap financial markets with relative ease. Although very few of its sovereign shareholders have an investment-grade rating for their debt, the ADC has been a preferred borrower in international markets, raising U.S.$1.3 billion in 2003 and U.S.$3.2 billion in 2002. It has an investment-grade rating of A/A2 by Standard & Poor's and Moody's, and the entrance of Spain as a shareholder, together with the fact that nonaccruing loans were less than 0.2 percent of its loan portfolio, have helped to secure this favorable rating. The EIB provides resources to developing, transition, and developed countries, although during the period 2000–02 its operations in developing countries accounted for only 19 percent of its total operations, which averaged U.S.$24.5 billion.

8. During the mid-1950s and the 1960s, the World Bank financed mainly infrastructure projects (75 percent of its total portfolio). The creation of the first RDB, the Inter-American Development Bank, in 1959, can be seen partly as a reaction by Latin American countries to World Bank lending policies that gave little attention to the social and agriculture sectors (which represented only 3 percent of the World Bank's portfolio). In the first ten years of IDB operations, these sectors received almost 50 percent of total IDB disbursements (Kapur, Lewis, and Webb, 1997).

Another special feature of some MDBs, closely related to their participation in private sector projects, is their capacity to cofinance projects by mobilizing funds from bilateral agencies, other multilateral institutions, or the private sector. Again, the heterogeneity of the available financial information is notable, although the figures provided by the RDBs are slightly more reliable. For example, the IDB and the AsDB committed U.S.$1.87 and U.S.$2.19 billion per year, respectively, to private sector projects during the period 2000–03, and they have leveraged about 35 percent and 48 percent, respectively, in additional resources. The EBRD, with private sector loans averaging U.S.$3.2 billion per year, mobilized U.S.$5.82 billion from various sources during the period 1999–2003. The instruments used to achieve this are quite diverse and include syndicated loans, grants, and concessional loans from other multilateral sources, guarantees, and private sector contributions. Guarantees appear to be the next step toward enhancing the capacity of regional institutions to leverage additional financing,[9] mainly from private sources and possibly focusing on infrastructure projects. The total number of guarantee operations during the period 2001–03 by the IBRD, the Multilateral Investment Guarantee Agency (MIGA), the Islamic Development Bank (IsDB), the IDB, and the AsDB was 124, of which fifty-two were infrastructure projects. The value of the guarantees was U.S.$4.9 billion, with infrastructure projects accounting for U.S.$2.8 billion.[10]

Participation in equity is another way to leverage resources and enhance the impact of regional institutions. In these operations, the MDBs risk a small amount of their own capital and buy shares in specific companies (equity investment) or in financial institutions. For example, the International Finance Corporation (IFC) generally subscribes to between 5 percent and 20 percent of a project's equity, but never more than 35 percent, and it is never the single largest shareholder in a project. The AsDB will only risk 25 percent of a project's cost or U.S.$50 million for each project, whichever is less (equivalent to less than 0.22 percent of AsDB paid-in capital and reserves in 2003); the EBRD only the lesser of 35 percent of the long-term capital of the obligor or 5 percent of EBRD paid-in capital and reserves (equivalent to about U.S.$225 million for each project); and the IDB only the lesser of 25 percent of project cost (or 40 percent for small countries) or U.S.$75 million (equivalent to 0.38 percent of IDB paid-in capital and reserves in 2003). When it comes time to withdraw from the project, these institutions divest their holdings by selling shares in the capital markets through a public offering.

---

9. These activities mainly involve RDBs, though it is worth noting that the Andean Development Corporation is one of the most active subregional users of guarantees.

10. Raymond (2004).

Portfolios and Specializations of the Regional Development Banks[11]

The sectoral composition of the MDBs' portfolio and its evolution over time is a good indicator of the degree of institutional specialization. As the MDBs have grown and matured, they have become involved in more complex development sectors and projects in which the participation of the private sector or other financial institutions is less probable. The MDBs have better mechanisms for managing risks, and they have accumulated experience in these relatively more difficult and uncertain operations. This evolution has coincided with a progressively higher involvement of the largest banks in the "soft" areas of development—education, health, institutional reform, technical cooperation, microfinance, and others—and with a reduction in the size of their investments in infrastructure and productive sector projects, which are less complex in terms of financial arrangements, risk, and estimation of returns.[12]

Figure 3-1 shows the evolution of the regional development banks in this regard. The RDBs have expanded their operations in all sectors over the past three decades—with the sole exception of the IDB Fund for Special Operations. The sector involvement of the RDBs has followed two main patterns. First, increasing importance has been accorded to the social sectors, mainly related to public financial support for social development and governance reforms during the 1990s and early 2000s. Second, there has been a progressive reduction of their involvement in the productive sectors and a corresponding increase in financing for other types of activities, including financing for the private sector, regional public goods, debt relief, support to nongovernmental organizations

11. The data in this section come from the OECD Creditor Reporting System, which has complete information from 1971 to 2002. Data for "the 2000s" therefore refer to the period from 2000 to 2002.

12. For example, the IBRD went from devoting 95 percent of its portfolio to infrastructure during the 1950s and 1960s to devoting 42 percent to the infrastructure and productive sectors and 10 percent to the social sectors during the 1970s. During the 1980s, social sector allocations rose to 18 percent, while the infrastructure and the productive sector remained at 35 percent, and structural adjustment (support for public finances and balance of payments) grew rapidly to 9 percent of the total portfolio. During the 1990s and in the period 2000–02, support for the productive sectors fell to only 5 percent, while funding for infrastructure, social sectors, and sector adjustment reached 35 percent, 30 percent, and 20 percent, respectively. The IDA, too, has moved from strong support for the productive sector (more than 45 percent) and infrastructure (25 percent) during the 1970s and 1980s to greater involvement in the social sectors during the 1990s and since the start of the new millennium (40 percent), allocating less than 10 percent to the productive sector, 20 percent to infrastructure, and 10 percent to structural adjustment operations.

Figure 3-1. *Evolution of the Sectoral Distribution of RDB Portfolios*[a]

Percent[b]

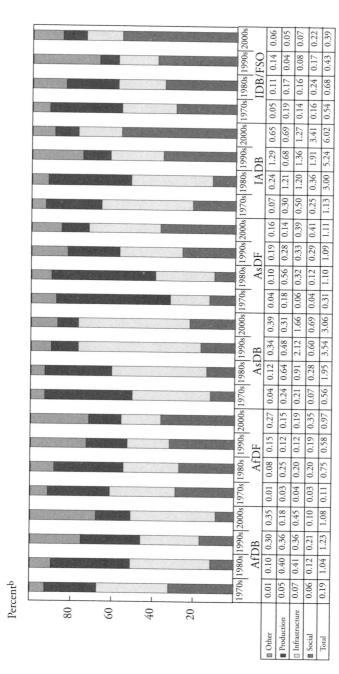

	AfDB				AfDF				AsDB				AsDF				IADB				IDB/FSO			
	1970s	1980s	1990s	2000s	1970s	1980s	1990s	2000s	1970s	1980s	1990s	2000s	1970s	1980s	1990s	2000s	1970s	1980s	1990s	2000s	1970s	1980s	1990s	2000s
Other	0.01	0.10	0.30	0.35	0.01	0.08	0.15	0.27	0.04	0.12	0.34	0.39	0.04	0.10	0.19	0.16	0.07	0.24	1.29	0.65	0.05	0.11	0.14	0.06
Production	0.05	0.40	0.36	0.18	0.03	0.25	0.12	0.15	0.24	0.64	0.48	0.31	0.18	0.56	0.28	0.14	0.30	1.21	0.68	0.69	0.19	0.17	0.04	0.05
Infrastructure	0.07	0.41	0.36	0.45	0.04	0.20	0.12	0.19	0.21	0.91	2.12	1.66	0.06	0.32	0.33	0.39	0.50	1.20	1.36	1.27	0.14	0.16	0.08	0.07
Social	0.06	0.12	0.21	0.10	0.03	0.22	0.19	0.35	0.07	0.28	0.60	0.69	0.04	0.12	0.29	0.41	0.25	0.36	1.91	3.41	0.16	0.24	0.17	0.22
Total	0.19	1.04	1.23	1.08	0.11	0.75	0.58	0.97	0.56	1.95	3.54	3.06	0.31	1.10	1.09	1.11	1.13	3.00	5.24	6.02	0.54	0.68	0.43	0.39

Source: Prepared by the authors using data from the OECD Creditor Reporting System.

a. The definition of sectors is taken from OECD data (Creditor Reporting System) for the period 1971 to 2002: *Production* means loans and projects for agriculture, forestry, fishing, industry, mining, trade and tourism; *Infrastructure* refers to transport and storage, communications, energy, banking and financial services, and business and other services; *Social* refers to education, health, population programs, water supply and sanitation, government and civil society, housing, and social services; *Other* covers multisectoral projects, structural adjustment, action related to debt, nonfood emergency and distress relief, support to NGOs, and all unallocated or unspecified projects or loans. The latter category has been aggregated for simplicity.

b. Annual average by decades, in billions of 2002 U.S. dollars and percentages.

(NGOs), and the development of capital markets. However, each bank has had a different pattern of expansion, for both the regular and concessional windows.

The share of social sector operations has expanded rapidly in most RDBs, with the sole exception of the African Development Bank.[13] Investment in social sector projects in areas such as health, education, and housing; social investment; and protection and rehabilitation after natural disasters has accounted for most of the social sector portfolio expansion of RDBs. These activities accounted for U.S.$1.1 billion per year on average during the 1970s and 1980s, but rose to U.S.$3.1 billion during the 1990s and 2000s. However, part of this growth is explained by the involvement of RDBs in state reform, social policies, and economic reforms, which also include large programs of public sector adjustment, budget support, and pension reforms.[14] These activities accounted for U.S.$1.5 billion per year on average during the 1990s and in the early years of the 2000s. In contrast, investment in this field was almost nil during the 1970s and the 1980s.[15]

RDB support for the productive sector as a percentage of the total RDB portfolio diminished during the 1990s and early 2000s from its 1970–80 levels. This took place as the public sector in many developing countries progressively reduced its direct participation in these activities through state-owned enterprises. Figure 3-1 shows that the sharpest reductions occurred at the AsDB (from 35 percent of the total portfolio on average during the 1970s and 1980s to 8 percent in the following decades) and at the IDB (from 32 percent to 9 percent in the same period).

However, this reduction of support for the productive sector through state-owned financial intermediaries has been compensated for to a certain extent by the introduction of new financial instruments that directly support private sector investments. These include operations with private banks and the development of domestic capital markets, which fall under the category of "financial infrastructure," according to the OECD classification scheme. This category comprises support for financial restructuring, financial intermediation, apex

13. This is explained mainly by the reduction of AfDB support for major water supply projects in Algeria, the Democratic Republic of the Congo, Morocco, and Nigeria, which started during the 1980s and mid-1990s with the construction of dams, canals, and water facilities. The projects in these four countries represented 52 percent of total investment in the social sectors (U.S.$1.3 billion) during this period.

14. According to OECD statistics, most of the financial support for institutional reform is classified as social sector investment; "government and civil society," one of the highest-growth areas during the 1990s and early 2000s, is included here.

15. The AfDF added U.S.$0.86 billion for these types of programs during the period 1990–2002, the AsDB and the AsDF U.S.$3.1 billion each, and the IDB group U.S.$12.1 billion.

funds for the formal and informal sectors, and capacity building for the management of new financial instruments, among other activities.[16]

Financial infrastructure operations have rapidly become a major component of RDB portfolios and are especially important at the AsDB (U.S.$7.2 billion, or 13.1 percent of the total portfolio during the period 1990–2002). However, these activities have been highly concentrated; for example, the U.S.$3.6 billion committed to the financial sector program in 1997 was largely directed to the Republic of Korea in the wake of the Asian crisis. In the case of the AfDB, financial market support represented 4.4 percent of the total portfolio during the period 1990–2002 (U.S.$1.4 billion), while at the IDB this figure was 3.3 percent (U.S.$2.3 billion). The AfDB concentrated its operations in Egypt, Morocco, South Africa, and Tunisia (U.S.$1.1 billion), while the IDB focused on Argentina and Mexico (U.S.$1.6 billion).

Along with financial sector and capital market support, the RDBs entered into new development financing fields during the 1990s. One of the most important has been the provision of regional public goods, especially those related to regional transport, energy and communication infrastructure, and environmental programs. Using a methodology devised by Te Velde, Morrissey, and Hewitt, and employing OECD data, Ferroni has estimated that RDB commitments to international public goods (IPGs) amounted to at least one-third of total multilateral IPG funding during the 1990s in all regions.[17] This would mean that the IDB invested almost U.S.$2.2 billion, or 3.9 percent of its total portfolio, during the 1990s; the AsDB about U.S.$3.8 billion, or 8.2 percent; and the AfDB group nearly U.S.$1.6 billion, or 8.8 percent of its loans in this period. Initiatives such as the New Partnership for Africa's Development (NEPAD), the Initiative for the Integration of Regional Infrastructure in South America, and the Plan Puebla-Panama will certainly increase this proportion, and this will probably be a field for RDB expansion in the future.

Regular and Concessional Windows: Graduation Policies

Because of the nature of the eligibility criteria applied by development banks, over time there has been a high level of correlation between the use of regular or

---

16. For example, the IsDB played a key role in supporting the banking industry and in developing capital markets in the Islamic countries during the 1990s. This was accomplished through entities such as the Accounting and Auditing Organization for Islamic Financial Institutions (AAOIFI), the International Islamic Rating Agency (IIRA), the Islamic Financial Services Board (IFSB), the International Islamic Financial Market (IIFM), the Liquidity Management Center (LMC), and the General Council of Islamic Banks and Financial Institutions (GCIBFI).

17. See Ferroni (2002); for the methodology, see Te Velde, Morrissey, and Hewitt (2002).

Table 3-5. *RDB Resource Allocation by Income Level*[a]

Annual average per country in each income category, in millions of U.S. dollars

Donor	Income group[b]	1970s	1980s	1990s	2000s
AfDB	Low	4.8	16.5	18.9	29.9
	Middle	2.5	50.2	75.4	105.5
AfDF	Low	3.5	17.8	14.5	30.3
	Middle	3.0	5.7	3.4	0
AsDB	Low	25.8	181.1	564.3	447.9
	Middle	24.8	136.9	89.7	46.0
AsDF	Low	28.9	76.8	48.0	69.3
	Middle	10.5	29.9	22.3	27.5
IDB	Low	19.8	13.1	30.1	40.5
	Middle	53.0	138.6	242.6	296.8
IDB Special Fund (FSO)	Low	29.7	14.7	48.6	130.6
	Middle	24.5	31.3	21.5	65.4

a. The amount indicated is the annual average received by countries in each income category. Being an average, the figure therefore also reflects the number of countries that received resources from each window.

b. The OECD income classification may differ from the classification criteria applied by each institution. The categories correspond to the OECD classification, where "Low" comprises LDCs (least-developed countries) and OLICs (other low-income countries); and "Medium" comprises LMICs (lower-middle-income countries) and UMICs (upper-middle-income countries).

concessional loans and the per capita income levels of RDB borrowers. As a country increases its income level, it eventually "graduates" from concessional to regular loans. Table 3-5 presents the annual average disbursed to countries according their income category.[18] It can be seen that the AfDB disbursed U.S.$105.5 million on average to each middle-income country borrower during the early 2000s, but only U.S.$29.9 million to low-income ones, while the African Development Fund (AfDF) disbursed U.S.$30.3 million to low-income countries and had no operations in middle-income countries. The IDB and its (concessional) Fund for Special Operations followed the same pattern. In the case of the AsDB group, both the regular and soft loan windows disbursed more resources to low-income countries. This pattern can be explained by the presence of large low-income bor-

18. The number of borrowing members has been variable owing to an increase in member countries and to their "graduation" or prioritization. For example, the AfDB lent to forty-five countries during the 1970s and 1980s, but to only thirteen countries during the 1990s and early 2000s, and the IDB Fund for Special Operations reduced the scale of its operations from twenty-one countries in the 1970s to only eight countries during the 1990s. The AsDB introduced new graduation policies during the 1990s.

rowers such as China, India, Indonesia, Pakistan, and Vietnam, which receive loans from both the regular and the concessional windows.

These findings are consistent with the graduation policies established by each institution. The AfDB group has a three-tier classification system to determine eligibility for each window, which is compatible with the World Bank's classification system (based on income category and debt sustainability). Under these criteria, thirteen African countries were eligible to borrow only from the regular (AfDB) window at the end of 2002, two members were eligible to borrow from both the regular and the concessional (AfDF) windows, and thirty-eight members were eligible to borrow only from the AfDF.

The AsDB changed its graduation policies in 1997 and now applies a two-stage process, classifying the countries first by income category and then assessing their debt repayment capacity. This is done using indicators such as debt sustainability, private capital inflows, gross domestic saving rate, country size, categorization as an HIPC, volatility of export growth, main external financing sources, access to IDA credits, and whether sovereign borrowing by the country is rated by Moody's and Standard & Poor's.[19]

The IDB has a four-tier country classification system (A, B, C, or D) to determine the eligibility of its members for assistance from its three windows: the Fund for Special Operations (FSO), which provides concessional loans; the Intermediate Financing Facility (IFF), whose lending terms are between those of the regular and concessional windows; and ordinary capital (OC), which provides regular loans.[20] The poorest borrowing countries (Group D) are the only ones with access to soft loans from the FSO, although they may also be eligible for loans from the ordinary capital or regular window. The IDB management decides whether to extend regular loans to FSO-eligible countries on a case-by-case basis, taking into account creditworthiness considerations. Countries in Groups C and D are eligible to

19. AsDB has a four-tier country classification: Group A receives concessional resources from the AsDF only; Group B1 from the AsDF, with limited amounts of ordinary capital resources (the regular or AsDB window); Group B2 from the AsDB, with limited amounts of AsDF resources; and Group C from the regular or ordinary capital resources of the AsDB. In 2003, cost-sharing limits for project loans were 80 percent for Group A, 75 percent for Group B1, 70 percent for Group B2, and 65 percent for Group C. Government contributions to technical assistance must be at least 15 percent of total costs for A countries, 20 percent for B1 and B2, and 30 percent for C countries.

20. The four-tier category is based on the size of a nation's economy. The IDB finances a percentage of the total costs of a project according to the following classification: For group A countries (Argentina, Brazil, Mexico, and the Bolivarian Republic of Venezuela), the IDB finances only 60 percent of the project; for group B (Chile, Colombia, and Peru), 70 percent; for group C (Bahamas, Barbados, Costa Rica, Jamaica, Panama, Suriname, Trinidad and Tobago, and Uruguay), 80 percent; and for group D (Belize, Bolivia, Dominican Republic, Ecuador, El Salvador, Guatemala, Guyana, Haiti, Honduras, Nicaragua, and Paraguay), 90 percent.

borrow from the IFF, with priority given to countries that are not eligible for FSO resources. Groups A and B can borrow only from ordinary capital or regular resources.[21]

The EBRD has different criteria for graduation and eligibility, since it does not have a concessional window. This policy derives from the EBRD's charter mandate of advancing transition toward market-oriented economies. The EBRD concept of graduation rests on three principles: (1) transition impact, defined as the effect of a project on the economy or society; (2) additionality, defined as the effect of the EBRD's catalyzing additional resources; and (3) sound banking—that is, assurance that the bank's investment is secure. These principles are used to define a phased graduation approach across market segments within a country. As a country advances, it will have fewer and fewer segments in which the principles of transition and additionality are met. Eventually, the country will graduate from EBRD operations entirely and secure access to international capital markets and other private sources of financing.

There are important differences between the RDBs in terms of sector allocations and income categories (see table 3-6). For example, while the regular window of the AfDB allocated 36 percent of its total portfolio to infrastructure in middle-income countries during the period 2000–02, the soft loan window allocated a similar amount to the social sectors in low-income countries. At the IDB, both the regular and soft loan windows allocated almost 57 percent of their total portfolios to the social sectors. The AsDB seems to be the most pro-poor of the regional development banks: on average, 87 percent of its total operations, including both regular and concessional windows, are oriented toward low-income countries (primarily China, India, Indonesia, Pakistan, and Vietnam). The AsDB allocates 52 percent of its total portfolio to infrastructure projects in low-income economies, while the AsDF utilizes 55 percent of its total portfolio for social sector and infrastructure projects in low-income countries.

Financial Standing of the Regional Development Banks

As indicated earlier, MDBs obtain funds for their regular loan windows from borrowings in the international capital markets and for their concessional loans from contributions by donors through periodic replenishments, which are complemented by resources from their net income. As a result of their preferred-creditor

---

21. In 1999 the IDB introduced a more rigorous method of determining eligibility. The grouping divides countries in Groups I and II, based on their GNP per capita in 1997. On the basis of their lower per capita income, the bank aims to channel 35 percent of its lending volume to Group II countries and the rest to Group I countries.

Table 3-6. *Country Categories and Sectoral Allocation of Portfolio, 2000–02*
Amount and percentage of total portfolio

Donor	Income group	Social Percent	Social U.S.$ billions	Infrastructure Percent	Infrastructure U.S.$ billions	Productive Percent	Productive U.S.$ billions	Other Percent	Other U.S.$ billions	Total Percent	Total U.S.$ billions
AfDB	Low	9.3		6.4		1.8		14.0		22.0	
	Middle		0.30	35.6	1.36	15.0	0.54	18.1	1.04	78.0	3.24
AfDF	Low	36.4	1.06	19.4	0.57	15.8	0.46	28.3	0.82	100.0	2.91
AsDB	Low	17.8		51.9		6.8		11.5		88.0	
	Middle	4.9	2.08	2.6	4.99	3.4	0.93	1.1	1.16	12.0	9.17
AsDF	Low	24.3		29.9		10.0		13.4		87.6	
	Middle	2.8	1.23	5.7	1.18	2.8	0.42	1.1	0.48	12.4	3.36
IDB	Low			1.3						1.3	
	Middle	56.6	10.22	19.8	3.81	11.5	2.08	10.8	1.93	98.7	18.05
IDB FSO	Low	40.0		9.9		7.9		8.8		66.6	
	Middle	16.6	0.67	7.5	0.21	3.6	0.13	5.6	0.17	33.4	1.18

status in relation to private lenders and their low gearing ratios in comparison with those of private financial institutions, the MDBs enjoy a high standing in the eyes of bond rating agencies, and this allows them to raise funds on favorable terms in international capital markets for their regular windows. Donor confidence in the effectiveness of MDB operations allows them periodically to raise nonreimbursable contributions from donor countries to continue operating their concessional loan windows, which constitute a large grant component.

Providing loans and a variety of financial and nonfinancial services to member countries requires a combination of market trust, strong donor commitment, and a high degree of institutional credibility. The evolution of MDB flows to developing countries, the introduction of more complex financial instruments, and the participation of these institutions in new development activities has only been possible because of their sound financial standing, and preserving the financial integrity of MDBs is an essential condition for their continued existence.

Table 3-7 presents a number of indicators that make it possible to compare the financial and administrative situations of the regional banks and the World Bank for 2002. Three issues are worth highlighting. First is the relationship between the size of the banks and their net income, administrative costs, staff, and the countries they serve. The AfDB is the smallest of the regional banks in terms of these indicators, even though it lends to fifty-three countries. In contrast, the IDB lends to twenty-six countries, but its total disbursements are about five times higher than those of the AfDB. The principal reason for this difference is that thirty-eight African countries, which are among the poorest and most severely indebted in the world, are eligible for concessional lending provided by the AfDF.

Second, in terms of average project size—calculated by dividing total commitments by the total number of projects approved—there is a significant divergence between the AfDB and the other banks. While the average project sizes for the AsDB, the World Bank, and the IDB are U.S.$79.94 million, U.S.$77.14 million, and U.S.$53 million, respectively, the AfDB average project size was only U.S.$23.5 million. This may be partly explained by the fact that the World Bank, the IDB, and the AsDB provide rather large loans to countries such as Argentina, Brazil, China, and India.

Third, there are different degrees of decentralization among the MDBs. The AsDB is the most centralized of the banks, with only fifty-six members of its staff (15 percent) in country or regional offices. In contrast, the World Bank, as part of its Strategic Compact, has undertaken a major expansion of field-based activities. As of June 2003, it had approximately 3,000 staff (34 percent of its total staff) working in over 100 country offices. The IDB had 543 (28 percent) in its country offices, out of a total staff of 1,912.

Table 3-7. *MDBs: Financial and Administrative Indicators, 2002*[a]

Billions of U.S. dollars unless otherwise indicated

	World Bank	AfDB	IDB	AsDB	EBRD
Financial indicators					
Authorized capital	189.57	29.24	100.95	47.29	22.49
Callable	178.09	26.34	96.61	43.90	16.58
Paid-in	11.48	2.90	4.34	3.25	5.91
Total commitments	18.51	2.77	4.55	5.68	4.43
Commitments from concessional window	7.28	1.31	0.41	1.63	. . .
Total disbursements	18.94	1.42	5.84	4.20	2.73
Disbursements from concessional window	2.80	0.74	0.31	1.14	. . .
Net income	5.34	0.31	0.71	0.98	0.54
Administrative indicators					
Administrative expenditure	1.04	0.15	0.33	0.14	0.18
Average size of projects	0.08	0.02	0.05	0.08	0.04
Total staff	8,800	1,259	1,912	2,220	907
Number of regional/ country offices	100	6	28	25	27
Number of staff in regional offices	3,000	56	543	321	237
Number of countries eligible for borrowing	142	53	26	35	27
Number of nonborrowing member countries	39	24	20	28	33

Source: Data for the World Bank were obtained from the *Annual Report 2003;* for the rest of the MDBs, data were obtained from 2002 annual reports.

a. Exchange rates for 2002: 1 unit of account = U.S.$1.35952; 1 U.S.$ = 0.88 euro.

A key aspect in the comparison of MDBs is the relationship between capital, equity, and level of disbursements, which is an important indicator of the financial strength of multilateral development banks. Discussions about MDB capital adequacy have emphasized the very conservative "one-to-one gearing ratio," according to which the outstanding loans of MDBs cannot exceed their total capital (which includes paid-in and callable capital, as well as reserves). They have also focused on the "risk-bearing capital ratio" (RBCR), which is considered a more adequate measure of financial strength. All MDBs have a ratio lower than 4, about half the average for the private sector (table 3-8), which indicates that the MDBs are managed quite prudently from a financial point of view. Another

Table 3-8. *Risk-Bearing Capital Ratio (RBCR) of the MDBs*[a]

Millions of U.S. dollars, except where noted

Multilateral development banks	Loans outstanding net of LLP	Paid-in	Retained earnings	RBCR 2003	RBCR 2000
World Bank group	111,762	11,748	27,031	2.88	3.82
Regional development banks					
Inter-American Development Bank Group	50,471	4,340	9,622	3.61	4.10
African Development Bank Group	7,642	3,239	2,271	1.39	2.01
Asian Development Bank Group	25,398	3,657	9,025	2.00	2.38
European Bank for Reconstruction and Development[b]	8,356	5,197	564	1.45	0.92
Subregional development banks					
European Investment Bank[b]	247,600	7,500	13,641	11.74	10.97
Central American Bank for Economic Integration	2,483	371	759	2.20	2.36
Caribbean Development Bank	512	155	257	1.24	1.09
Andean Development Corporation	6,387	1,319	887	2.90	2.91
Nordic Investment Bank[b]	10,552	404	1,235	6.44	n.a
Islamic Development Bank Group	990	3,942	1,685	0.18	n.a
East African Development Bank	103	37	10	2.20	n.a
Arab Bank for Economic Development in Africa	560	1,500	131	0.34	n.a
North American Development Bank	14	405	16	0.03	0.02
Other MDB-like funds					
Nordic Development Fund[b]	387	573	42	0.63	n.a
Arab Fund for Economic and Social Development	5,402	2,188	4,884	0.76	0.68
FONPLATA	221	46	325	0.60	0.59

Source: Financial statements of the institutions.

n.a. Not available.

a. Ratio between loans outstanding net of loan loss provisions (LLP) and the sum of paid-in plus retained earnings at the end of the fiscal year.

b. In millions of euros.

indicator used by rating agencies is the ratio of equity capital plus callable capital from AAA or AA shareholders divided by total risk assets (defined as loans to borrowing countries with ratings below investment grade).[22] As a consequence of their conservative financial practices, most MDBs, and particularly the World Bank, have consistently obtained the highest rating for their bond issues.[23]

A rather low risk-bearing capital ratio could indicate in some cases that the institution has not fully used its capacity to lend. Subregional banks such as the NADB (North American Development Bank), which have recently initiated their operations, have done so mainly with preinvestment grants and small pilot projects. FONPLATA has increased its level of lending for transport infrastructure during the 1990s, though its level of reserves could allow it to play a larger role in the Initiative for the Integration of Regional Infrastructure in South America (Iniciativa para la Integración de la Infraestructura Regional Suramericana, IIRSA) during the coming years. However, there are some banks operating in the Arab region and with Islamic countries that have had large levels of reserves and paid-in capital for some time, but have not significantly increased their lending levels. For example, the IsDB has levels of reserves and paid-in capital comparable to those of the AfDB, but its outstanding loans are only one-eighth of those of the latter. This could be a consequence of the limited absorptive capacity of its borrowing members, but also suggests that the IsDB has the potential to significantly expand operations in the future, possibly introducing new financial mechanisms or even initiating operations in other countries and regions. This could also be the situation of the EBRD, whose high level of paid-in capital allows it to have a highly favorable risk-bearing capital ratio and, from a purely financial perspective, would enable it to increase its lending operations significantly.[24]

22. This ratio should be maintained above 100 percent to be considered adequate. Current practice requires that reserves be increased when borrowing by a member might put the institution at risk of moving into nonaccrual status, which would imply increasing the share of net income allocated to reserves.

23. In contrast, the AfDB experienced severe financial difficulties and undertook a major reorganization during the second half of the 1990s. Total loan and grant approvals came to a peak in 1991, at U.S.$3.45 billion, and after that, the fund ran dry. In August 1995, Standard & Poor's lowered the bank's credit rating from AAA to AA+, because of the "increasing politicization" of the bank's corporate governance and management. The downgrade made it more expensive for the bank to borrow money on international markets. After a long period of institutional reforms, during which it was pledged U.S.$2.6 billion in a seventh replenishment and U.S.$3.4 billion in an eighth replenishment, the AfDB's credit rating was upgraded by S&P to AAA on July 25, 2003.

24. The EBRD's president, Jean Lemierre, indicated in its 2003 Annual Report that the bank is in a transition period. During the next few years, the EBRD will take more risks and will enter into new areas, such as helping to reduce intraregional disparities in borrowing countries, providing more support to small and medium-sized enterprises and making more aggressive use of risk mitigation instruments.

Other MDBs operate more like private sector institutions and are backed up by strong donors. This is the case of the EIB, which has allocated 85 percent of its portfolio to the private sector and directs a large proportion of its loans to developed countries. As a result of this special situation, it has the highest risk-bearing capital ratio of all the MDBs. Similarly, the NIB lends a significant part of its portfolio to private companies from Nordic countries (nearly 80 percent) to promote foreign direct investment, not only in developing countries, but also in Europe.

Loan Conditions and Costs

The World Bank regularly compares the average costs of RDB operations, using their spreads over LIBOR-based (London interbank offered rate) sovereign loans (see table 3-9). In general, the AsDB offers the most favorable terms for developing countries (around 35 basis points), which is consistent with the fact that it has the lowest institutional administrative costs and the highest average project size (see table 3-7). Nevertheless, all MDBs have rather low spreads, with the exception of the EBRD, which charges the highest rate and does not grant waivers or interest rate reductions as the other MDBs do. Although the AfDB has the least favorable financial indicators among the RDBs, its spread (56 basis points) is on the low side.

RDB concessional loans are provided on quite favorable terms. IDB/FSO loans have a twenty-five- to forty-year maturity and a five- to ten-year grace period, with an average annual rate of interest below 2 percent. AsDF loans have a thirty-two-year maturity (or twenty-four-year maturity in the case of fast-disbursing program loans) and an eight-year grace period, with 1 percent interest charge during the grace period and 1.5 percent during the amortization period. The AfDF lends at a zero interest rate, with a service charge of 0.75 percent per annum, a commitment fee of 0.50 percent, and a fifty-year repayment period, including a ten-year grace period.

The relatively better conditions granted by the AfDB are explained by changing conditions in the replenishment processes of the last decade, which have taken place on a three-year basis. Partly encouraged by the better financial results of the AfDB Group, donor countries are pledging more resources to the poorest countries in Africa through the bank's soft loan window. The last three replenishments—AfDF VII (1996–99), AfDF VIII (1999–2002), and AfDF IX (2002–05)—have spanned the crisis years of the bank and also its years of major reform and renewal. However, this reform did not quickly translate into larger replenishments of the AfDF. In fact, the fund experienced a dramatic decline of over 45 percent during the period 1996–98 and has not yet returned to the level achieved in 1991–93. The real value (in 2002 U.S. dollars)

Table 3-9. *Comparative Sovereign MDB Loan Charges*
LIBOR-based U.S. dollar loans as of June 30, 2004 (basis points)[a]

	IBRD					
	VSL[b]	FSLs[c]	IDB	AfDB	AsDB	EBRD
Interest spread						
Contractual spread	75	75	30[d]	50	60[d]	100
Risk premium	...	5	50[e]	...	...	...
Benefit of sub-LIBOR[f] funding cost	−31	−30	−34	−15	−35	...
Waivers	−25	−25	...	...	−20[g]	...
Net spread over LIBOR (I)	19	25	46	35	5	100
Charges						
Commitment charge	75	85[h]	25	75	75[i]	50
Waiver	−50	−50	...	−50	...	...
Net commitment fee	25	35	25	25	75	50
Spread equivalent of commitment fee[j] (II)	*17*	*22*	*17*	*17*	*30*	*34*
Front-end fee						
Contractual front-end fee	100	100	0	0[k]	100	100
Waiver	...	...	...	...	−100	...
Net front-end fee	100	100	0	0	0	100
Spread equivalent of front-end fee[j] (III)	*20*	*20*	*0*	*0*	*0*	*20*
Total spread equivalent over LIBOR (I + II + III)	56	67	63	52	35	154

Source: World Bank.

... Negligible.

a. Numbers may not add to totals because of rounding.

b. Variable spread loan.

c. Fixed spread loan.

d. This is a variable spread.

e. Represents premium for interest rate cap.

f. The IBRD average cost margin (sub-LIBOR spread) shown is for VSL rate settings from January 15, 2004, through July 14, 2004. Sub-LIBOR spreads for IDB and AfDB shown are the current sub-LIBOR spreads for the U.S. dollar. The sub-LIBOR spread for ADB represents rebate for the first six months of 2004.

g. ADB will waive 20 basic points on its public sector loans outstanding from July 1, 2004 through June 30, 2005.

h. For the first four years, an additional commitment charge risk premium of 10 basis points is charged on the undisbursed amount over and above the contractual commitment charge.

i. The commitment charge is applicable to the following proportion of the loan amount, less the cumulative disbursements: 15 percent in the first year, 45 percent in the second year, 85 percent in the third year, and 100 percent in the fourth year and beyond.

j. Spread equivalent computations for commitment charge and front-end fee use an evenly distributed disbursement profile of eight years. Repayment terms used are as follows: final maturity: seventeen years; grace period: five years; level repayment of principal. Disbursement profiles and payment terms vary across MDBs and hence spread equivalent charges would vary based on the disbursement profile and payment terms used.

k. In February 2001, the AfDB Board passed a resolution authorizing the bank's management to impose a front-end fee of up to 50 basis points if the financial condition of the bank warrants it.

of AfDF VI (1991–93) is estimated at U.S.$1.95 billion and that of AfDF IX at U.S.$1.91 billion. The AsDF IX replenishment will cover the period 2005 to 2008; the twenty-eight members of the AsDB have pledged their contributions and reached agreement on a U.S.$7 billion replenishment.

Following guidelines established in 1995 at the time of the negotiations for the eighth general capital increase of the IDB, the last replenishment of its concessional window, the Fund for Special Operations, was agreed in December 1998. Board members managed to strike an elaborate set of compromises that were closely related to the negotiations on how to fund IDB participation in the HIPC Initiative. These agreements stipulated, among other things, that nonborrowing countries would make additional contributions to cover the cost of IDB participation and to fund the U.S.$136 million for the FSO agreed at the time of the eighth general capital increase. It was also agreed that resources from the bank's net income would not be used to pay for its participation in HIPC and that any shortfall in nonborrowing country contributions to the FSO would be covered by periodic transfers from IDB net income up to the end of 2004. There are no plans for future replenishments of the FSO, since only five countries qualify for operations from this window.

The Political Economy of Multilateral Development Banks

In general, RDBs and SRDBs are very heterogeneous, not only in the countries and regions they serve, but in allocations and financial instruments, size and financial strength, specialization, selectivity, costs charged to their borrowers, and strategies for leveraging resources, among other characteristics. The complexity and heterogeneity of these institutions is related to the interaction between their stakeholders and constituencies and their relative power—what may be called the "political economy" of the RDBs. The arena where, in the final analysis, key political economy issues are settled is the management of net income, in which the banks determine how their net income (what would be called profits in private financial institutions) will be allocated among competing uses: bolstering reserves, providing grants, and reducing the cost of borrowing, according to the outcomes of the interaction processes between their diverse stakeholders and constituencies, especially their sovereign shareholders.

Changing Constituencies and Multiplicity of MDB Stakeholders

At any given time, MDBs are subject to a multiplicity of competing pressures that shape their behavior and performance. These institutions are a natural point of convergence for demands from many different actors whose preferences and interactions help define the characteristics, orientation, and personality of each MDB. Moreover, these actors and their power relations change over time as some old ones fade out and new ones emerge and as their agendas and demands shift and evolve.

MDBs are owned by their government shareholders and have to respond to their political agendas and expressed preferences. Shareholder perceptions are influenced by a variety of domestic constituencies, particularly in the developed member countries, where many groups have the capacity to exert pressure on their government representatives to the MDB boards and, in some cases, directly influence senior management at these institutions. In regional and subregional MDBs, relations between shareholders and their constituencies are less complex than in the World Bank, which must contend with the greater heterogeneity of the international community at the global level. Regional and subregional organizations should be able, at least in principle, to do a better job of accommodating the interests of smaller countries, give them more participation in decisionmaking, and allow them to enjoy a greater sense of ownership.

Other development financing institutions, including the World Bank, other MDBs, and bilateral agencies, heavily influence the operations of RDBs. This takes place in the field and in specific sectors, where these institutions often have different approaches to development issues and where pressures to improve development effectiveness and coordination are increasing. Joint projects, cofinancing, technical cooperation between MDBs, and cross financing are other expressions of the complex relations between these institutions.[25]

Financial market investors seek an appropriate balance between risk and return. Those that purchase MDB bonds accept relatively lower returns because of the very low risk of default on these bonds. The financial strength of MDBs, their preferred-creditor status, and the support of nonborrowing shareholders allow them to enjoy a most favorable treatment from bond rating agencies. They compete with private corporations, sovereign borrowers, and other financial institutions to attract capital, but in general have a privileged position as bond issuers in international capital markets. At the same time, joint operations with private firms and corporations are a growing segment of many MDB portfolios, which allows them to cofinance projects and to leverage and channel additional resources to their member countries. These complex competition-collaboration interactions impose new demands on the MDBs and require efforts to harmonize the diverse interests of capital market investors and other stakeholders.

---

25. For example, the IDB often has provided funds to subregional institutions. CABEI, ADC, and FONPLATA are among the institutions eligible for IDB loans.

Other constituencies whose influence over the MDBs has been growing include academic institutions, which continuously generate new approaches to development issues and have placed many issues on the agenda of the MDBs, including the provision of global public goods, gender considerations, environmental concerns, and human rights, among others; socially and environmentally concerned private sector firms, many of which are interested in forging partnerships with MDBs; and private foundations, trade associations, and professional bodies that focus on issues such as social capital formation, environmental stewardship, community development, and corporate social responsibility.

In a growing number of situations, MDBs are being challenged to accommodate an increasingly wide variety of diverging and often conflicting interests, particularly those of NGOs and other advocacy groups. MDBs have opened numerous avenues of consultation with these organizations and have attempted to respond to their views and concerns. However, several single-issue NGOs remain implacably confrontational, escalating demands at the slightest signal that their initial concerns may be addressed. The absence of clear rules and procedures to ensure the public accountability of NGOs makes it especially difficult to find common ground between such groups and other MDB stakeholders. Nevertheless, a number of MDB-NGO committees set up during the 1990s have collaborated to address some of the shortcomings of the banks' operations, particularly in areas that have an impact on human rights and environmental issues. The challenge for the senior management and executive boards of these institutions, which are also important MDB constituencies, is to distinguish legitimate concerns amidst a cacophony of discordant voices and vociferous demands.

However, in spite of this growing diversification of constituencies, the "owners" and most powerful constituencies of the MDBs are their shareholders. They ultimately decide what MDBs do, define the maneuvering room for their management, and determine how they will evolve. Table 3-10 lists the main shareholders in twelve of these institutions, differentiating between borrowing and nonborrowing members. In general, borrowing members in subregional development banks have greater voting power than those in regional development banks. The relatively better position of borrowing countries in the AfDB can be explained by the fact that nonregional members were not admitted until 1982, which means that the bank was entirely owned by its developing country members during its first eighteen years. The United States is the largest shareholder in all of the MDBs in which it participates, with the exception of the African Development Bank, where Nigeria has a larger share. For example, the United

Table 3-10. *Voting Power in Selected MDBs, 2003 or Last Year for Which Information Is Available*[a]

Percent

Multilateral development banks	Voting power		Main shareholders	
	Nonborrowers	Borrowers	Nonborrowers	Borrowers
RDBs				
IDB group	49.98	50.02	USA (30), Canada (4)	Brazil, Argentina (10.8 each), Mexico (5.8)
AfDB	39.99	60.00	USA (6.6), Japan (5.4), Germany (4.0)	Nigeria (9.0), Egypt (5.1), Libya (3.7)
AsDB	57.14	42.86	Japan (12.9), USA (12.9), Australia (4.51)	China (5.53), India (5.44), Indonesia (4.72), Republic of Korea (4.39)
EBRD	87.95	12.05	USA (10.15), France, Italy, Germany, UK, Japan (8.64)	Russia (4.06)
SRDBs				
EIB		100.00		Germany, France, Italy, UK (16.28 each)
CABEI (2001)	37.10	62.90	Taiwan Province of China (8.3), Mexico (6.8)	Costa Rica, El Salvador, Honduras, Guatemala, Nicaragua (10.20 each)
CDB (2001)	39.98	60.02	Canada, UK (9.05 each), Germany, Taiwan Province of China, Italy (5.47 each)	Jamaica, Trinidad and Tobago (17.45 each)
ADC		100.00		Peru, Colombia, Bolivarian Republic of Venezuela (26 each)
IsDB		100.00		Kuwait (6.86), United Arab Emirates (7.76), Turkey (8.65), Egypt (9.48), Iran (9.59), Libya (10.96), Saudi Arabia (27.33)

(continued)

Table 3-10. *(continued)*
Percent

Multilateral development banks	Voting power		Main shareholders	
	Nonborrowers	Borrowers	Nonborrowers	Borrowers
ABEDA		100.00		Saudi Arabia (20.8), Libya (14.23), Kuwait (13.13), Iraq (12.58), United Arab Emirates (10.94)
NADB		100.00		USA and Mexico (50 each)
Other MDB-like funds				
FONPLATA (1999)		100.00		Argentina, Brazil (33.3), Bolivia, Paraguay, Uruguay (11.1 each)

Source: Financial statements of the various institutions compiled and elaborated by the authors.

a. When information about voting power was not available, it was calculated as a percentage of the share subscriptions of the main shareholders.

States has a dominant position in the IDB, where it holds 31 percent of the shares, but in fact has much greater decisionmaking power than this percentage suggests.[26]

Net Income Management

The growing and conflicting pressures faced by MDBs find clear expression in the management of their net income. Achieving an appropriate balance among the three main functions of MDBs involves difficult decisions on the size and the allocation of net income. First, there is the need to use net income to increase reserves and strengthen their financial position and risk-bearing capacity. Second, a shift to more complex operations and engagements with stakeholders requires more and better-trained staff, as well as a larger presence in the field, both of which increase administrative expenses and reduce the margin left after subtracting these from operating income (less interest paid and related charges) in order to determine net income. Third, a portion of net income is used to

---

26. Strand (2003) argues that even though the United States has 31 percent of the shares and of voting power in the IDB, in effect it has 76 percent of the "effective voting power," which is calculated using "power indices" that consider a variety of voting scenarios by possible voting coalitions and other ways of influencing the final outcomes of voting processes. This would mean that the United States exerts de facto control over this institution.

Table 3-11. *MDB Gross Income from Loans and from Investments*
Billions of U.S. dollars

	2002		2003	
Institution	Loans	Investment	Loans	Investment
World Bank	6.89	0.73	5.72	0.41
IDB (OC)	2.63	0.32	2.71	0.30
IDB (FSO)	0.12	0.02	0.15	0.02
AsDB	1.70	0.33	1.38	0.30
AsDF	0.16	0.13	0.18	0.15
AfDB	0.39	0.07	0.32	0.10
AfDF	0.09	0.02	0.07	0.03

Source: Financial statements of the various institutions, compiled and elaborated by the authors.

fund the banks' soft loan windows and for grants to cover the cost of providing public goods and to finance special operations (such as emergency relief), both of which increase administrative expenditures. Finally, some MDBs use part of their net income to cover the costs of their participation in debt cancellation under the HIPC Initiative.

The two main sources of income for MDBs are loan portfolios and the management of liquid assets, although some MDBs have also generated small amounts of income from charges for nonlending services to their members and other clients (see table 3-11). Income from loans can be raised in only two ways. First, the volume of lending may be increased, but this may lead to pressures to lend more than would be strictly appropriate. Second, loan charges may be increased, but this may make the MDBs noncompetitive with capital markets for countries with access to them—especially when transaction costs to borrowers (delays, conditionality) are factored in. Without adequate safeguards, any of these options may lead to a deterioration of the loan portfolio, primarily because loans to less creditworthy borrowers may represent a higher proportion of loan assets and because countries that would be better credit risks may elect not to borrow from MDBs.

Investment income from the management of liquid assets can be raised by increasing the resources at the disposal of the MDBs for short-term investment in capital markets, and by assuming higher market risks in the expectation of obtaining higher returns. However, this source of income is rather volatile and subject to capital market swings, which makes it unreliable. It cannot be counted upon at times of international financial crisis, which is presumably when it would be most needed. The option of increasing loan charges to augment operating and net income has been adopted by some MDBs.[27] This is closely related to the question of "graduation" of borrowing countries and has problematic aspects, not least of which is that there is a limit to such increases if the MDBs wish to remain relevant to all their shareholders. For example, governments in high- and middle-income developing countries with access to private sources of finance may prefer to borrow in capital markets, thus reducing the demand for MDB loans, which in turn would have a negative impact on the quality of MDB portfolios.

Each MDB has taken a different approach to the management of net income (see table 3-12). These approaches are influenced by differences in power relations and interests among major shareholders, which have pressed for different allocations of net income to reserves, transfers to concessional lending windows, the provision of grants, and reductions in loan charges. The World Bank is facing pressures to allocate more resources to the International Development Association, its soft loan window, and to increase the proportion of grants provided through IDA to its poorest member countries. In addition, in 2004 it also allocated U.S.$80 million to the Trust Fund for Gaza and the West Bank and U.S.$25 million for the recently created Low-Income Countries Under Stress (LICUS) Implementation Trust Fund.[28]

The RDBs have used net income primarily to bolster reserves in order to strengthen their financial position. The IDB and the EBRD use more than 90 percent of their net income for this purpose, although the former has also used net income to cover the cost of its participation in the HIPC Initiative and to make up for any shortfall in member country contributions to the FSO, its concessional window (U.S.$27.2 million in 2003). The AfDB and the AsDB have a more complex pattern of net income allocation. The former has used, on average, more than U.S.$70 million in the past three years (25 percent of net income) to finance a variety of regional initiatives and to contribute to its soft loan window (the AfDF). The AsDB has allocated almost 30 percent of its net income to its soft window (the AsDF) and to technical assistance programs for member countries.

27. In the case of the IDB, in the first half of 2003 it set its lending spread at 0.5 percent. The inspection and supervision fee and credit commission were each set at 0.5 percent, reflecting partial waivers of 0.5 percent and 0.25 percent, respectively. For the second half of 2003 the bank applied the new standard ordinary capital loan charges established by the new capital adequacy policy—that is, a lending spread of 0.3 percent, a credit commission of 0.25 percent, and no charge for inspection and supervision. For 2003 the Board of Directors of the AsDB approved a waiver of 50 percent of the front-end fee for loans approved in 2003 to public sector borrowers. The effect of this waiver was to reduce net income by U.S.$3 million.

28. The World Bank's net income increased from U.S.$1.2 billion in 1998 to U.S.$3.4 billion in 2003 owing to increases in investment income, and fell to U.S.$1.2 in 2004 because of a reduction in loan income and because of loss provisions.

The SRDBs have also emphasized the use of net income to strengthen their financial position. The charters of some organizations, for example CABEI and FONPLATA, specify that net income must be allocated only to the general reserve. Others, such as the IsDB and ADC, must allocate part or all of their net income to the general reserve until the amount in that reserve reaches a certain threshold expressed as a percentage of subscribed capital—25 percent in the case of the IsDB and 50 percent in the case of the ADC.

Concluding Remarks

This chapter describes the main characteristics of the family of multilateral development banks, focusing on the regional development banks and, to a lesser extent, on the subregional development banks. It shows that these institutions play a key role in development finance and that they fill a niche that has not been adequately covered by global institutions such as the World Bank and the International Monetary Fund, and certainly not by private sector financing entities. They provide a unique combination of financial resource mobilization, capacity building and institutional development, and provision of regional and subregional public goods. No other international institution performs these three sets of functions as they do.

Because of the relative maturity of the World Bank's portfolio, at the beginning of the twenty-first century RDBs and SRDBs are providing higher net financial flows to their borrowers, and subregional institutions are in a better position to do so than regional development banks. At the same time, a sort of de facto division of labor has evolved among these institutions in the financial instruments they use, the services they provide, the countries they serve, and the sectors and activities they focus on. Yet in spite of their heterogeneity, all MDBs share a key concern: preserving their financial strength and high standing in international capital markets, where they place bonds to fund regular lending operations, and in the main donor countries that fund their soft loan windows.

The growing interactions between the various MDBs, and between these institutions and other entities involved in development finance (bilateral agencies, international institutions, foreign investors, private banks, investment funds, foundations, and individuals sending remittances, among others), are creating in some regions (especially Latin America and, to a lesser extent, Africa and the Middle East) multiple networks of financial institutions that are involved in increasingly complex operations to support the development efforts of member countries. This has led to the emergence of a large variety of stakeholders and constituencies, a change that is making the governance of multilateral development

Table 3-12. *Uses of Net Income in the MDBs*

	Net income (millions of U.S. dollars)		Uses (percent of 2003 net income)				Notes
MDBs	2002	2003	Reserves	Soft loan window and grants	Other		
World Bank	2,778	5,344	36.9	10.1*	33.0**		*IDA (U.S.$300 million) and HIPC Trust Fund (U.S.$240 million). **Compliance with Financial Accounting Standard 133 (U.S.$854 million), Pension Reserve (U.S.$953 million).
RDBs							
IDB	728	2,433	98.1	1.1*	...		*Allocation to the Fund for Special Operations to cover unpaid contributions (U.S.$27.2 million).
FSO	81	114	...	100.0**	...		**U.S.$75.2 million to the Intermediate Financing Facility and U.S.$37.5 million for the HIPC Initiative.
AfDB	308	160	74.9	25.1	...		The percentages relate to 2002 net income. In 2003 the Board of Governors approved allocations of U.S.$77.3 million out of 2002 net income, 15.8 percent to the HIPC Initiative, 43.8 percent to the AfDF, 17.5 percent to the Special Relief Fund for African Countries Affected by Drought, and 22.5 percent to the special fund for postconflict assistance to the Democratic Republic of Congo.
AsDB	979	458	48.3	28.8*	22.9**		The percentages relate to 2002 net income. *U.S.$200 million to the AsDF, and U.S.$80 million to the Technical Assistance Special Fund (TASF). **U.S.$224.8 million to the cumulative revaluation adjustments account.
EBRD	108	378	9.5		91.5		The amount is in euros. €30.2 million was transferred to the general reserve and the remaining €360 was posted as retained earnings.

Source: Financial statements of the various institutions, compiled and elaborated by the authors.
n.a. Not available.
. . . Negligible.

SRDBs

CABEI	49	53	100.0	...	...	According to its charter, the net income of the bank must be transferred to the general reserve.
CDB	18	21	100.0	...	...	The Board of Governors decides every year how to allocate net income, but it has usually been allocated to the general reserve.
ADC	127	136	75.4	14.6*	10.0**	The percentages relate to 2002 net income. *U.S.$18.5 million was allocated to a special fund for technical cooperation grants. **10 percent of net income is allocated to a special reserve until it equals 50 percent of subscribed capital.
IsDB	92	101	100.0	...	...	The annual net income of the bank must be transferred to the general reserve until it equals 25 percent of the bank's subscribed capital. Any excess of net income over the above limit is available for distribution to the member countries. In 2003 U.S.$2.8 million was allocated to technical assistance grants.

Other MDB-like funds

AFESD	259	404	94.8	5.2	...	0.2 percent of net income has been allocated to Arab scholars, 5.0 percent to technical assistance, 10.0 percent to the general reserve, and the remaining 84.8 percent to the additional reserve.
FONPLATA	n.a.	6	100.0	...	...	The annual net income of the bank must be transferred to the general reserve.

banks a rather difficult proposition, although in the case of SRDBs, the smaller number of member countries simplifies these problems to a significant extent.

Multilateral development banks in general, and regional and subregional development banks in particular, have proved to be a most useful institutional innovation for supporting the development efforts of their member countries. If they did not exist, it would be necessary to invent them. Yet much remains to be done before their emerging complementarity-cooperation-rivalry interactions evolve toward the creation of a veritable "system" of MDBs at the global level and in some specific regions.

References

Bezanson, K., and F. Sagasti. 2000. *A Foresight and Policy Study of Multilateral Development Banks.* Institute of Development Studies, Sussex University, for the Ministry of Foreign Affairs, Sweden.

Estevadeordal, A., B. Frantz, and T. R. Nguyen, eds. 2004. *Regional Public Goods: From Theory to Practice.* Washington: Inter-American Development Bank.

Ferroni, M. 2002. *Regional Public Goods: The Comparative Edge of Regional Development Banks.* Prepared for the conference "Financing for Development: Regional Challenges and the Regional Development Banks" at the Institute for International Economics, Washington, February 19.

Kapur, D., J. Lewis, and R. Webb. 1997. *The World Bank: Its First Half Century.* Vol. 1: *History.* Brookings.

Raymond, P. 2004. "Comparative Review of IFI Risk Mitigation Instruments." Presentation at Water Week: Diving into Implementation, Washington, World Bank, February 25, 2004.

Sagasti, F. 2004. "La banca multilateral de desarrollo en América Latina." In *Gobernabilidad e Integración Financiera: Ámbito Global y Regional,* edited by J. A. Ocampo and A. Uthoff. Santiago: Libros de la CEPAL.

Sagasti, F., and K. Bezanson. 2001. *Financing and Providing Global Public Goods Expectations and Prospects.* Development Financing 2000, Study 2001: 2. Institute of Development Studies, University of Sussex, for the Ministry of Foreign Affairs, Sweden.

Strand, J. 2003. "Measuring Voting Power in an International Institution: The United States and the Inter-American Development Bank." *Economic Governance* (Springer Verlag) 4: 19–36.

Te Velde, D. W., O. Morrissey, and A. Hewitt. 2002. "Allocating Aid to International Public Goods." In *International Public Goods: Incentives, Measurement, and Financing,* M. Ferroni and A. Mody, eds. Amsterdam: Kluwer Academic.

World Bank. 2004. *Global Development Finance 2004: Harnessing Cyclical Gains for Development.* Washington.

4

Regional Exchange Rate Arrangements: The European Experience

CHARLES WYPLOSZ

Regional arrangements generally remain controversial. They are sometimes seen as a threat to multilateralism, and multilateralism is, in principle, first best. The argument for multilateralism and against regionalism is best developed for trade arrangements: regional agreements have a trade-creating effect within the region but also a trade-diverting effect in the rest of the world, and for that reason could quite possibly reduce overall welfare. Yet the threat is not substantiated by historical developments over the past decades. Baldwin develops a convincing domino theory according to which regional trade arrangements prompt multilateral arrangements as those left out face additional incentives to reach multilateral agreements that they were resisting beforehand.[1] The domino theory is dynamic; trade diversion is static.

Applying the general presumption against regionalism in the matter of exchange rate arrangements is even more misleading. The International Monetary Fund (IMF) was created to promote multilateralism in exchange rate arrangements largely in reaction to the self-destructive wave of beggar-thy-neighbor devaluations during the interwar period. This is why the IMF and many countries are unhappy with regional arrangements. Yet a number of factors ought to be taken into account.

---

1. Baldwin (1997).

First, there is no international monetary system, not since the end of the Bretton Woods system. Every country is free to choose the arrangement that it deems most desirable, without having to make sure that it fits other countries. True, the Articles of Agreement of the IMF ban exchange market manipulations of the beggar-thy-neighbor type, but there is no rule that prevents regional agreements. Regional arrangements do not impair a nonexisting system.

Second, existing regional arrangements do not encourage collectively negative behavior toward nonmembers. The euro floats freely, as does the East Caribbean dollar. The CFA franc is tied to the euro. It is very unclear how third parties can be hurt by such arrangements. Trade blocs have not been found to create adverse trade diversion, and currency blocs are even less likely to do so.

Third, a direct impact of regional arrangements is to reduce the risk of currency crises, which often have unpredictable contagious effects. For instance, European currencies used to be regularly buffeted by speculative attacks; this is now history with the advent of the monetary union, which, so far at least, has not led to exchange rate instability elsewhere. Preventing contagious crises is one of the most urgent tasks of the international monetary "system" and regional arrangements are arguably the most efficient response.

The recent interest in regional exchange rate arrangements has been stimulated by the "hollowing-out view," sometimes also called the "two-corner solution." This view holds that there is no workable middle ground between floating and hard pegs (currency boards or the adoption of a foreign currency). It predicts that traditional fixed exchange rate regimes are doomed in a world of unfettered capital flows. According to this view, countries that wish to limit exchange rate flexibility have to go all the way to hard pegs. The regional counterpart to a hard peg is a monetary union.

The creation of the euro has also contributed to the rising popularity of regional arrangements. Up until its birth in 1999, the euro project was often greeted with suspicion and warnings of impending disaster.[2] At the time of this writing, six years later, predictions that the arrangement is doomed can still be heard, but they sound increasingly hollow. The truth is that the euro has been a stunning success. Gone are the days of speculative attacks and wide inflation differentials in Europe. The debate on whether the European Central Bank (ECB) is performing well is vigorous, as it should be. To be sure, it is imperfect, as has historically been the case with almost all new federal institutions. Some populist European politicians blame the euro for every difficulty, and their criticisms often fall on sympathetic ears, but their arguments are weak and unfounded.

2. See Feldstein (1997).

Regional monetary unions can work, as do other regional arrangements, such as Europe's previous exchange rate mechanism.

Yet it would be equally misleading to believe that the European example can be easily transferred elsewhere. Over the past fifty years, Europe has achieved a remarkable degree of economic and financial integration. Twenty-five countries now share a single market for goods and services, and twelve countries have adopted a common currency, the euro. Over the next decade, a few more countries will join the single market and ten more countries could adopt the euro. This process is also being matched, to some degree, by political integration, with efforts under way to align foreign policies and internal security. Not all is perfect, though, and formidable challenges remain on the agenda, if only to improve the existing governance structure initially designed for the first six countries that formed the European Community in 1958.[3] Yet, the depth and breadth of the arrangement is unprecedented, and it brings together countries that were often at war with each other over the past thousand years. War is unthinkable today, and it is precisely the desire to avoid it that has underpinned the effort and the readiness to give up significant elements of national sovereignty.

The thesis of this chapter is that Europe's story carries a number of important lessons but also several warnings. For instance, it argues that the commitment to fixed exchange rates has always taken precedence over capital mobility. Exchange rate stability has been seen as a precondition for trade integration, the only way of establishing a level playing field for international competition. The decision to adopt a common currency came very late, much as capital mobility was restrained for decades, and it was reached only after a high degree of trade integration had been achieved, accompanied by the establishment of powerful supporting institutions. Put differently, regional trade integration, exchange rate stability, and institution building came first, capital mobility and monetary union came later. A key question is whether this sequencing can be modified and whether the pace can be accelerated. The answer is that both are quite unlikely.

The following section examines the reasons why small open or would-be open economies care about exchange rate stability and how stability can be achieved. It reviews how Europe has dealt with this issue. It emphasizes that choosing an exchange regime must go hand in hand with the choice of a capital mobility regime. The following sections then describe in detail the gradual hardening of exchange rate arrangements in Europe and examine the lessons of that experience.

---

3. These countries are Belgium, France, Germany, Italy, Luxembourg, and the Netherlands.

Figure 4-1. *Official IMF and de Facto Exchange Rate Regimes*

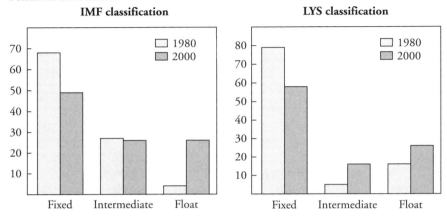

Percent of all countries

Source: Levy-Yeyati and Sturzenegger (2002).

The Logic of Soft Pegs

Regime Choice

Despite its appeal, the hollowing-out hypothesis is not proving valid in practice, at least not yet. A few well-known cases of adoption of hard pegs in the 1990s (currency boards in Argentina, Bulgaria, Estonia, and Lithuania; dollarization in Ecuador and El Salvador) do not signal mass migration to hard pegs. Many countries have announced that they will let their currency float freely, but these announcements have not always been followed by concrete action. Figure 4-1 shows the official exchange rate regime reported to the IMF and the actual regime found to exist by Levy-Yeyati and Sturzenegger.[4] The figure reveals that the proportion of pegged exchange rate regimes has declined between 1980 and 2000, with an equal increase in freely floating regimes. Levy-Yeyati and Sturzenegger confirm the decreasing popularity of pegged regimes but find that migration has taken place toward intermediate regimes (crawls, managed floats). Much the same picture emerges from the classification by Reinhart and Rogoff, who use a very different procedure to identify exchange regimes.[5]

---

4. See Levy-Yeyati and Sturzenegger (2002).
5. Reinhart and Rogoff (2004).

The evidence against the hollowing-out hypothesis is of considerable importance. This hypothesis is based on the entirely correct view that when capital is freely mobile pegged regimes are unstable, unless the use of monetary policy is purely and simply abandoned and all efforts are directed toward upholding the peg. But in this case, the peg becomes a hard one; there is no sustainable midway. In fact, the evidence seems to suggest that many countries do not wish to move to the extremes. They exhibit both "fear of floating"[6] and "fear of pegging." Resistance to adopting formal pegs is explained by the loss of monetary independence and by the risk of inviting speculative attacks. Resistance to freely floating is explained by the high degree of volatility that exchange rates then display.

Central to the hollowing-out hypothesis, therefore, is the view that full capital mobility is the natural evolution. What the evidence shows, however, is that most developing countries are reluctant to remove all restrictions on capital mobility, following the approach of most developed countries. It was not until the late 1980s that full capital mobility became the norm among developed countries. As is argued below, this is what led to the adoption of the euro.

Put differently, the choice of an exchange rate regime cannot be dissociated from the capital mobility regime. The hollowing-out hypothesis, a reincarnation of what used to be called the "impossible trinity," can be restated as follows: if a country opts for a regime of full capital mobility, the only sustainable exchange rate regimes are the extreme ones—hard pegs or free floating. If a country opts for a high degree of exchange stability, it must restrict capital mobility.

Forms of Exchange Rate Stability

Exchange rate stability does not necessarily mean a peg. Bretton Woods–style fixed-but-adjustable pegs with fluctuation bands represent one way of achieving a degree of stability, but they are not the only way. In the presence of high but moderate inflation, pegs require recurrent depreciations, which can take the form of crawling pegs with various adjustment frequencies. A close substitute is a managed float, whereby the authorities allow the exchange rate to depreciate over time if need be, but limit the range of fluctuation around the trend.

This view of exchange rate stability focuses on the behavior of the exchange rate—an important policy consideration, but not the only one that matters. Equally important is the commitment aspect. A peg announcement, whether it concerns a fixed-but-adjustable rate or a crawling band, commits the authorities in two ways. First, monetary policy must be constrained. This constraint can be relaxed somewhat by delinking domestic financial markets from international

6. See Calvo and Reinhart (2000).

conditions through limits on capital mobility, but the effectiveness of such capital controls is limited. Second, announcing a band of fluctuation, no matter how wide it is, means that its hedges are open to speculative pressure. When the exchange rate comes close to any hedge, the situation usually becomes untenable. Thus a peg announcement carries with it an implicit invitation to speculation. Capital controls offer some protection; indeed, this is where they are effective, for they provide some breathing room in the midst of a currency crisis.[7]

The managed float is the increasingly popular regime. It seems to offer the best of all worlds, allowing the authorities to limit short-run fluctuations while accommodating long-run trends and removing the commitment that invites speculative attacks. This view is misleading, however. Markets are good at spotting the implicit strategy and they will test the implicit limits of fluctuations. If there are no such limits, or if they are fuzzy, the stabilization effect is lost. If the authorities do enforce limits, the difference with explicit bands is cosmetic. Much the same applies to the width of the fluctuation bands. Narrow bands impose a tight constraint on monetary policy; wide bands produce an effect that differs little from that of a free float, except that they will occasionally be subject to speculative pressure.

In the end, there is no free lunch: restricting the volatility of the exchange rate can only be achieved by subjecting monetary policy to fairly strict constraints. There are various ways of achieving this aim; they all require discipline. This is why a peg, of one form or another, is sometimes referred to as an anchor. As such, it is a desirable tool, comparable to other monetary policy rules, such as inflation targeting or money growth rules. For small open economies, this may be the best rule, as the next section argues.

Why Exchange Rate Stability Matters: The Case of Europe

There are several reasons for wanting to limit exchange rate variability. The most commonly cited reasons are a quest for stability for trade purposes, a strategy of importing monetary discipline, and a lack of sufficiently deep financial and exchange markets. This section argues that, in Europe, the key motivation was trade.

Financial and exchange markets were shallow in Europe in the 1950s. After the move to current account convertibility in 1958, capital account restrictions remained widespread, partly motivated by the belief that this would help make

---

7. This statement relates only to the usefulness of controls during speculative attacks. There is a huge body of literature on the usefulness of capital controls and on their distortionary impact. Most of it is extremely critical of capital controls because they entail high costs and few benefits. Rogoff (2002) offers one such sober assessment.

Table 4-1. *Year of Liberalization in Postwar Europe*

Country	Internal	External
Austria	1981	n.a.
Belgium	1978	1990
Denmark	1980	1988
Finland	1970	. . .
France	1985	1989
Germany	None	1981
Ireland	1969	1992
Italy	1983	1990
Netherlands	1981	1986
Norway	1984	. . .
Portugal	n.a.	1992
Spain	1966	1992
Sweden	1983	. . .
Switzerland	1975	1980
United Kingdom	1971	1979

Sources: Exchange controls from Bakker (1996), p. 220; credit ceilings from Cottarelli and others (1986), unpublished appendix.

n.a. Not available.

. . . Not applicable.

the fixed exchange rate system work. By the late 1970s, Europe had deep enough markets to operate reasonably efficient exchange markets, yet capital restrictions remained widespread. The United Kingdom liberalized in 1979, but it did not join the exchange rate mechanism (ERM) of the European Monetary System, instituted that same year. Within the system, Germany was the first country to make the move, in 1981, and for a long while it remained the only country to have done so (see table 4-1). In these preliberalization years, there were many bad reasons to maintain capital controls and one good one: the fear that unlimited capital mobility could endanger exchange rate stability.

It is often claimed that most countries wanted to use the nominal exchange rate as an anchor to import the Bundesbank's discipline. This is a revisionist view of the situation, at least until the 1980s. To start with, the assumption underlying the discipline argument was that Europe's inflation rate would remain close to that of the United States during the Bretton Woods period and then stay close to the German rate. It also assumed that Europe's inflation would be lower than in the other industrialized countries, which have been floating for most of the post–Bretton Woods era (Canada, Japan, Switzerland, the United Kingdom, and more recently, Australia and New Zealand). Figure 4-2 does not

Figure 4-2. *Inflation in the OECD Area*

Percent

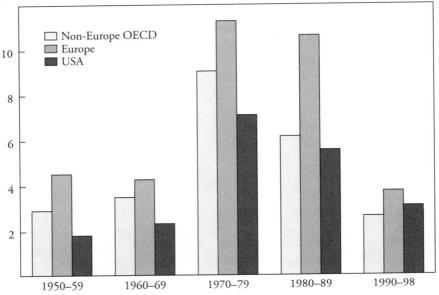

Source: IMF.
a. "Non-Europe" is Australia, Canada, Japan, New Zealand, Switzerland, and the United Kingdom.

bear out these assumptions. On average, Europe (excluding the floaters, Switzerland and the United Kingdom) exhibits the worst inflation performance in the Organization for Economic Cooperation and Development (OECD) area. If discipline was the motivation, it did not work. Most likely, it was not.

The view that exchange rates can be used as an anchor is fairly recent, at least in European official thinking. The argument that the inflation anchor served as the motivation for setting up the European Monetary System (EMS) mixes up the timing. It was only after the wave of currency crises of 1983, after France had adopted the "franc fort" strategy, that the EMS started to function asymmetrically, with the German mark as its recognized anchor. When the EMS was created, reference was explicitly made to nominal exchange rate stability, not to the desire to anchor inflation to best practice in Germany. Realignments were not only possible but actively practiced and always justified as a "correction" of accumulated inflation differentials. In fact, the EMS was explicitly set up as a symmetric system, with no central currency. Its rules carefully avoided adopting the Bretton Woods presumption that countries with high inflation and weak currency would bear the burden of adjustment in case of misalignment and market pressure. Responsibility for exchange market interventions was strictly bilateral, with unlimited support from the strong to the weak currency country. Much to the discomfort of the Bundesbank,[8] the EMS was officially aiming at a "regression toward the mean," not at imposing the Bundesbank's rigorous best practice.

The view that exchange rate stability promotes trade has no theoretical support (uncertainty can either encourage or discourage international trade, depending on assumptions) and limited empirical support. See, for example, works by Kenen and Rodrik regarding the effects of short-term volatility in real exchange rates in a sample of industrialized countries and by de Grauwe on the impact of exchange rate volatility in the European Union; stronger evidence has been adduced by Rose and by Helliwell and Parsley and Wei on the border effect. At any rate, the quest for exchange rate stability has been crucial. Policymakers happened to believe that nominal exchange rate stability matters for trade, possibly for good reasons.[9]

Evidence on the stability of intra-European exchange rates is presented in figure 4-3a for the key French franc/German mark exchange rate. The top chart of figure 4-3a displays the real exchange rate between these two currencies over the period 1971–98, at the end of which both currencies ceased to exist. The top chart in figure 4-3b shows the real exchange rate between the franc and the United States dollar. The contrast is sharp and is confirmed by the two middle charts in both figures, which depict the behavior of the pound sterling, a non-EMS currency (except for a very short period in 1992). Much the same pattern applies to the other EMS currencies. For comparison purposes, the bottom chart in figure 4-3a shows the real exchange rate between the Argentina peso and Brazil real over the period 1980–2003. Much as is the case for Britain and its European partners, the bilateral volatility between these two currencies (peso and real) is of the same order of magnitude as their volatility against the dollar, exemplified in the exchange rate between the Argentine peso and the U.S. dollar in the bottom chart of figure 4-3b. Clearly, the European countries that wanted to stabilize their bilateral exchange rates succeeded.

---

8. As documented in Eichengreen and Wyplosz (1993), the Bundesbank had arranged for a private agreement with the German Treasury that would suspend the intervention clause if it determined that it was threatening price stability. This clause was invoked during the lira crisis in September 1992.

9. Kenen and Rodrik (1986); de Grauwe (1988); Rose (2000); Helliwell (1998); Parsley and Wei (2001).

Figure 4-3a. *Real Exchange Rates*[a]

Sample average = 100

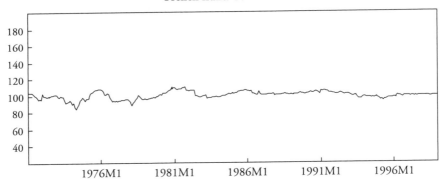

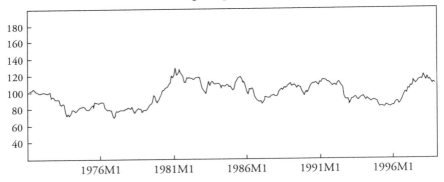

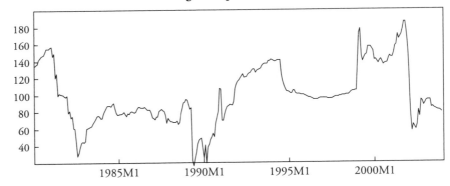

Figure 4-3b.

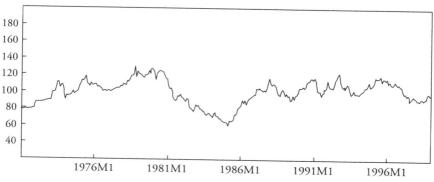

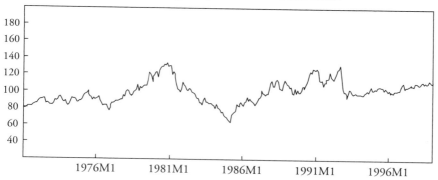

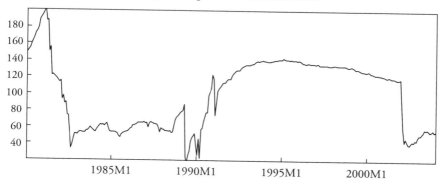

Source: IMF.
a. The index uses the consumer price index.

It is important to note that it is not the *nominal* exchange rate that was stabilized, but the *real* rate. This remark is important for two reasons. First, while the target was the real exchange rate, the instrument was the nominal exchange rate. The procedure was to make frequent use of the ERM provisions for realignment and to base these realignments explicitly on purchasing power parity (PPP). Second, the above observation confirms that the goal was not to use the exchange rate as a nominal anchor to achieve uniformly low inflation. Germany was attached to price stability and achieved it throughout the period. Other countries, notably France and Italy, had more tolerance for inflation, and periodically realigned their exchange rates to reestablish competitiveness.[10] But the inflation performance of the United Kingdom was similar to that of France and Italy. If the United Kingdom did not join the ERM it was not because of inflation, but because it accorded less importance to exchange rate stability than its partners. Clearly, inflation differentials were considerably more modest than those observed in Latin America, for example. It is likely that the arrangement would not have been possible in the face of large inflation differentials. In that sense, exchange stability promoted discipline.

Summarizing, this section argues that the European countries have identified real exchange rate stability as a key policy target. The discipline argument for exchange rate stability focuses on the nominal, not the real, exchange rate: nominal rates were anything but stable, and the inflation performance of the European countries has been worse than that of most other developed countries. The view that exchange rates were kept pegged because the markets were too shallow to be efficient is not convincing, either. That may have been true in the 1950s and the 1960s, when the currencies were simply not convertible, but it was not true in the 1970s and beyond.

Exchange Rate Arrangements in Europe

This section briefly describes the different arrangements adopted in Europe since the end of World War II. It illustrates two key aspects of Europe's monetary integration: a constant quest for internal exchange rate stability and a succession of daring advances and temporary setbacks. Europe's approach to exchange rate coordination has been gradual and pragmatic. It has mainly reacted to events, both external (such as the end of the Bretton Woods system) and internal (such as the removal of capital controls), shunning any grand design. The 1971 Werner Plan to launch a common currency within two years never took off. The project

10. The Netherlands is one country that actively used the exchange rate as an anchor and undertook never to devalue it against the German mark.

was adopted twenty years later, but only when it had become obvious that the ERM could not cope with full capital mobility, even though policymakers might not have realized this necessity.

Brief Historical Overview

Bretton Woods. The Bretton Woods agreements provided indirectly for fixed exchange rates within Europe, but they were not a joint undertaking, nor were they intended to further any specific European goals. The agreements matched European interests, but they also matched those of the United States, which was equally preoccupied with the restoration of trade links. Faced with an acute shortage of dollar balances, European countries did not move to establish currency convertibility from the outset. As they concentrated on developing bilateral payment agreements, both among themselves and with non-European countries, they started to work out their own arrangements.

The European Payments Union. The European Payments Union (EPU) was set up in 1950 to simplify the cumbersome web of some two hundred bilateral payment agreements. It worked as a multilateral clearing system, focusing on the overall balances of payments of its member countries within the union. Generally considered a success, the EPU is credited with helping to bring about the resumption of intra-European trade. The EPU had some drawbacks, however, notably its tendency to encourage trade among its members to the detriment of nonmembers.

Convertibility. The next major move, the restoration of currency convertibility in 1958, was decided collectively, concurrent with the adoption of the Treaty of Rome, which created the European Common Market. Convertibility initially only concerned the current account. For many more years the financial account remained subject to fairly draconian restrictions in most countries. The arrangement provided for a high degree of exchange rate stability, with few realignments. The first major depreciation, by the United Kingdom, did not occur until 1967. It was followed by a depreciation of the French franc and a revaluation of the German mark, both in 1969.

The snake. By the time the Bretton Woods system collapsed during the period 1971–73, further imbalances had accumulated inside Europe. After a series of realignments, most European countries undertook to maintain limited margins of fluctuation for their bilateral exchange rates, while the other developed countries let their currencies float. The resulting arrangement, known as the European "currency snake," was a mixed success. Most countries were able to keep up with the arrangement, but speculative pressure forced others—especially France, Italy, and Sweden—to withdraw from the snake. Outside Britain, there was no serious questioning of the wisdom of keeping exchange rates pegged.

The Werner Plan. The main setback for monetary integration during this period was the abandonment of the Werner Plan. Completed in 1970 and endorsed by the Council of Ministers in 1971, the Werner Report had recommended the rapid adoption of a common currency. It mapped out three stages, including the pooling of foreign exchange reserves for joint interventions. The turmoil surrounding the breakup of the Bretton Woods system led the larger countries to aim at more modest steps, partly out of pragmatism, partly as a pretext to escape a move that was clearly ahead of policymakers' thinking. The smaller countries, which were seeing their own policy autonomy decline, were frustrated by the failure but unable to shake the domination of the larger countries.

The European Monetary System. Monetary integration soon took another direction, however. The EMS was agreed upon in 1978 and began operating in 1979. Eight of the then nine members of the European Community became active members of the exchange rate mechanism. When the euro was launched in January 1999, all members of the European Union were part of the ERM, with the exception of Greece, Sweden, and the United Kingdom. Greece joined the ERM later that year.[11]

The European Monetary Union. During its first ten years of existence, the ERM underwent frequent crises. By the early 1980s its survival was very much in doubt, especially as a series of attacks affected the French franc in the wake of the election of President François Mitterrand. The political reaction turned out to be another show of support for fixed exchange rates. The authorities rededicated themselves to a new ERM, one in which the German mark would play the role of central currency. This "greater Deutschmark area" gradually asserted its credibility and came to be seen as such a success that policymakers grew emboldened and resolved to move to the next logical step, monetary union.[12] But the success of the ERM was concealing a buildup of tensions. The combination of accumulated imbalances and a major policy mistake—denial of the fact that German unification would require a revaluation of the mark—triggered a round of violent speculative attacks. Two countries (Italy and the United Kingdom) left the ERM, and many were forced to devalue, some of them several times. The ERM was radically changed when its margins of fluctuation were widened to the

---

11. Among European nonmembers of the European Union, Switzerland has traditionally steered its own currency alongside the German mark, even though it has always been very careful not to declare an official linkup, and has occasionally used the exchange rate as a tool of monetary policy.
12. A detailed review of this evolution is provided by Kenen (1995).

point of irrelevance. Yet, while the ERM currencies were officially quasi-floating, unofficially the monetary authorities endeavored to keep them within narrow margins, in fact quietly mimicking the defunct ERM.

The Exchange Rate Mechanism: A Sophisticated Arrangement

The ERM, which lasted in its first incarnation for twenty years, is of more than historical interest. To start with, it still plays an important role, as the new European Union members are expected to participate in the mechanism as a preliminary step toward joining the monetary union.[13] More important, perhaps, is the fact that it was the success of the ERM that convinced policymakers to go to the next step, monetary union. This is why it is of general interest to critically review its main features.

When the ERM was launched, two main requirements shaped its design. The first one was to provide a tool for stabilizing the intra-European exchange rates that had been buffeted in the years following the demise of the Bretton Woods system. It had to be sturdier than the currency snake. The second requirement was of a political nature. The other countries were unwilling simply to tie their currencies to the German mark, even though it was already the most stable European currency.

The solution to the second issue was to make the ERM fully symmetric. In contrast with the hub-and-spoke arrangement of Bretton Woods, exchange rates were fixed bilaterally, producing a matrix of bilateral parities that became known as "the grid." Each bilateral rate could fluctuate by +/−2.25 percent around its declared parity.[14] In addition, the responsibility of maintaining the exchange rate within the agreed upon margin of fluctuation was shared by each pair of countries, with no presumption that more had to be done by the weaker currency. Symmetry was the response to political sensitivities.

The solution to the first question was an unprecedented commitment that, if need be, the parities would be defended by unlimited interventions, conducted by both countries whose bilateral rate was pushed to its declared margin of fluctuation. In addition, other ERM member countries could be asked to provide support, either through interventions or through short-term loans. Cohesion and mutual support was the answer to economic fragility.

13. The new exchange rate mechanism (ERM II) was established when the euro was launched. Initially, its only member was Denmark. Seven of the ten new European Union members have now joined Denmark, and the three remaining ones have the obligation to join the mechanism "soon."

14. The Italian lira was given a temporarily larger margin of +/−6 percent.

Table 4-2. *Exchange Rate Mechanism (ERM) Realignments*

Date	Sept. 24, 1979	Nov. 30, 1979	Mar. 22, 1981	Oct. 5, 1981	Feb. 22, 1982	June 14, 1982
Number of currencies involved	2	1	1	2	2	4
Date	Mar. 21, 1983	May 18, 1983	July 22, 1985	Apr. 7, 1986	Aug. 4, 1986	Jan. 12, 1987
Number of currencies involved	7[a]	7[a]	7[a]	5	1	3
Date	Jan. 8, 1990	Sept. 14, 1992	Nov. 23, 1992	Feb. 1, 1993	May 14, 1993	Mar. 6, 1995
Number of currencies involved	1	3[b]	2	1	2	2

a. All ERM currencies realigned.
b. In addition, two currencies (pound sterling and lira) left the ERM.

Furthermore, both upon entry and subsequently, the choice of every bilateral parity had to be agreed collectively and by consensus of all member countries. This was designed to prevent any beggar-thy-neighbor manipulation by a group of member countries. It was also seen as a justification for the collective defense of existing parities.

Thus the ERM was much more than a "European Bretton Woods." It was an ambitious undertaking that removed decisions on exchange rate parity from national hands. It sent the signal that any attack on a particular currency would be met by a collective defense. It also envisioned an active management of parities, so that realignments would not come to be seen as a system failure, but rather as an indication of flexibility.

Indeed, the ERM went through a large number of realignments, as shown in table 4-2. From its inception in March 1979 until January 1987, no fewer than twelve adjustments were deemed necessary, on average one every eight months. Interestingly, these realignments were usually anticipated by the markets and thus preceded by speculative attacks. These attacks, however, were not lethal because capital controls limited the volume of required interventions and also because corrective realignments were promptly enacted.

Interventions by both of the central banks concerned were compulsory when any bilateral margin was reached, but it soon became apparent that waiting for that to happen was risky. When pressed against its limit, an exchange rate offers

Table 4-3. *Foreign Exchange Market Interventions*[a]
Billions of U.S. dollars

	1979–82	1983–85	1987–87	1988–89
All currencies				
Inside ERM				
At margin	20.5	15.4	22.3	0.9
Intramarginal	29.2	48.6	113.7	32.4
In U.S. dollars	139.4	78.4	53.7	29.5
Bundesbank				
Inside ERM				
At margin	3.1	1.7	3.3	0
Intramarginal	0	0	0	0
In U.S. dollars	25.4	18.9	5.4	12.4

Source: Gros and Thygesen (1998).
a. Algebraic sum of purchases.

speculators one-way bets—either a realignment occurs and large gains are reaped, or there is no realignment and the cost of speculating is virtually nil—that make attacks irresistible. This is why, gradually, most interventions became increasingly intramarginal—that is, aimed at keeping the bilateral rates well within the margins of fluctuation, as table 4-3 shows. The table also indicates that dollar interventions, aimed at stabilizing bilateral parities within the ERM via the stabilization of U.S. dollar parities, became less important, but never negligible, as interventions in ERM currencies assumed greater importance.

Table 4-3 also reveals an important asymmetry between the Bundesbank and the other central banks. While most other central banks increasingly relied on noncompulsory intramarginal interventions, the Bundesbank limited its own interventions to fulfilling its obligation of providing bilateral support at the margin. This is one aspect of the process that led to the progressive emergence of the German mark as the de facto center of the system. Simplifying somewhat, initially the ERM worked in a symmetric way; all central banks stabilized their bilateral parities mainly by managing their currencies against the dollar, as in the Bretton Woods system. Eventually, all countries dropped the dollar in favor of the mark, while the Bundesbank steered the evolution of the European currencies against the dollar.

There is another reason for this evolution. All the countries that were running higher inflation than Germany and that had been forced to devalue repeatedly under speculative pressure gradually accepted the view that they ought to aim at a lower inflation rate. From 1987 onward, they effectively adopted the

German mark as the anchor and committed to holding their exchange rate parities unchanged. In fact, they proceeded to closely follow the Bundesbank's policy. This approach worked in the sense that inflation gradually declined everywhere toward the German level. With nominal exchange rates stable for several years, the ERM was seen as a major success. The idea of irrevocably fixing exchange rates by adopting a common currency followed almost naturally, leading to the Maastricht Treaty.

Meanwhile, however, the inflation differentials that had accumulated in the effort to achieve inflation convergence had resulted in the overvaluation of some currencies. The collective removal of capital controls in 1990 meant that the unavoidable realignments would be a dangerous affair. Indeed, when speculation started, triggered by difficulties in ratifying the Maastricht Treaty, two currencies were forced to leave (the Italian lira and the pound sterling, which had joined a few months before at an overvalued rate) and the margins of fluctuation had to be widened to a huge +/−15 percent. The ERM was in shambles, but the decision to launch the euro had been firmly taken, which provided for continuing currency stability.

The late difficulties of the ERM illustrate three general points. First, any system of pegged rates has to be flexible. Using the exchange rate as an anchor is a possibility for one country, not for a system. Such a strategy has to shape monetary policy in the country that adopts it; it is a disciplinary device. Within the ERM, with its symmetric nature and promise of mutual support, the discipline aspect is weakened and any slippage affects all members. Second, it is impossible to maintain pegs when capital is fully mobile. Strict monetary policy discipline is a necessary but not sufficient condition in a world where self-fulfilling crises are conspicuous. Third, it is quite striking that the system worked well when it was symmetric but failed when Germany had become the de facto center. This does not mean that a hub-and-spoke system cannot work, but it does suggest that a regional system can work without a center if all the rest is well thought through.

The Monetary Union

The European Economic and Monetary Union (EMU) is less original than the ERM. In a number of respects it mimics arrangements that can be found in many federal countries. This section therefore does not attempt to provide a detailed description of the EMU; rather, it deals with the originality of the undertaking and points out a few key distinguishing features.

The main challenge is to build adequate institutions. At the technical level, the situation is fairly straightforward: a single currency requires a single monetary authority, and there are not many possible monetary strategies. To be sure, debates rage on the strategy of the ECB, but these are details. More complex is the governance issue of turning over the important power of carrying out monetary policy to a multinational authority. While the broad design will inevitably be inspired by arrangements in federal states, the fact that Europe remains a union of independent nation-states greatly complicates matters.

The solution adopted offers a mix of federal and international arrangements. The decisionmaking power is given to the European System of Central Banks, the Eurosystem. Its decisionmaking body is the Governing Council, composed of the six members of the ECB Executive Board and the governors of the national central banks (NCBs) of the participating countries. The Executive Board is of a federal type, as its members serve in a personal capacity. Yet, they are appointed by the member states, which inevitably means that nationality matters a great deal. As could be expected, the emerging pattern is that the large member countries (France, Germany, Italy, and Spain) have managed to appoint one of their nationals and intend to keep it that way, and the two remaining positions are filled by nationals of the smaller countries. Of course this runs completely counter to the spirit of the principle that board members are appointed solely on the basis of their competence and in no way serve as representatives of their countries. Similarly, the fact that the NCB governors serve on the Governing Council ex officio is another contradiction to the nonrepresentativeness principle.

More worrisome is that the size of the Governing Council is due to expand as new countries join the EMU. With eighteen voting members, the decision-making process is already highly unlikely to permit deep exchanges of views. The council could grow to thirty-one members if all current European Union members adopt the euro, and with more countries slated to enter the European Union, the Governing Council could become even larger. This difficulty is well recognized but politically delicate. The Eurosystem has proposed capping the number of voting members at twenty-five, resorting to a complex rotation system that would take account of the size of countries.

Even more worrisome is the widely discussed "democratic deficit." The Eurosystem is completely independent: the members of its Governing Board are all appointed to long terms and cannot be removed from office. Yet independence brings with it the question of accountability. The chosen solution has been to make the ECB accountable to the European Parliament. However, the European Parliament has no formal power over the ECB, except for confirming the appointments of Executive Board members. It cannot make suggestions on future policies; it can only comment on past policies. The result is a weak ex post process, with no serious consequences if the Parliament disagrees with the actions of the Eurosystem.

These issues reflect the political and institutional difficulties of a monetary union. Although Europe is unique in having a structured governance system (the European Council, which brings together the heads of state and government, and the Council of Ministers) and an elected Parliament, the current organization is not fully satisfactory. It is true that the EMU has functioned quite well so far, and it is hard to foresee major difficulties, which suggests that the arrangements are not fundamentally flawed, yet criticism is endemic and might weaken governance if serious difficulties were to arise.

Fiscal Policy: Coordination and Discipline

The final issue of interest concerns the treatment of fiscal policy. If capital is freely mobile, the more exchange rates are fixed, the less monetary policy can be used for macroeconomic stabilization purposes. As a result, fiscal policy becomes the main, if not the only, macroeconomic stabilization tool. Yet in the absence of fiscal policy discipline, any monetary policy commitment, including exchange rate stability, is bound to be undermined. In addition, it is often asserted that, because they affect exchange rates, fiscal policies must be coordinated. Thus the tighter the degree of cooperation on the exchange rate, the more limits have to be put on the implementation of national fiscal policies, in effect reducing the scope for national macroeconomic stabilization policies. An alternative is to restrict capital mobility, preferably using a version of the Chilean *encaje*.[15] Such restrictions do not provide full freedom to carry out long-lasting divergent policies, especially policies that result in lasting inflation differentials, but they make exchange rate realignments manageable.

On the other hand, the closer the exchange rate linkage within the region, the more each country depends on the behavior of the others. It is often claimed that the overall policy mix matters for regional interest and exchange rates, especially in a monetary union. This is misleading. If the region is closely integrated in international financial markets, each country is too small to have an impact on the regional interest rates. This is true even for the European monetary union. The collective stance matters if the region is large, as Europe is, but this means that fully coordinated policies might have an impact. Given that, in each country, fiscal policy is highly political and hard to design, full coordination is extremely unlikely.

What remains true is that one country's default, especially if that country is large relative to the others in the region, could have a serious effect on the whole region. This is why fiscal discipline becomes a regional concern, in particular

---

15. The *encaje* is a system of capital controls that works by imposing costs on inflows. These costs decline with maturity, mimicking the desirable properties of the Tobin tax.

within a monetary union. Europe has adopted the Stability and Growth Pact, an agreement to limit budget deficits to 3 percent of GDP. This pact is ill-conceived for two reasons. First, what is required is long-run debt sustainability, not limits on annual deficits. Annual deficits are far too constraining, and a rigid ceiling is far too demanding. Second, the Stability and Growth Pact includes a procedure whereby the Council of Ministers can tell individual countries what they should do with their budget deficits and fine them if they fail to heed the recommendations. This is an extremely intrusive approach that threatens sovereignty in a sensitive domain. These two flaws have become increasingly visible and have led to a complete breakdown of the pact, which was "suspended" in November 2003 when the council should have initiated the fine procedure against the two largest countries, France and Germany.

The European experience illustrates both the need for some commitment to fiscal discipline and the need for a sensible procedure to ensure compliance. Suggestions for improvement have been advanced by Sapir, Wyplosz, and others.[16] They suggest shifting the target away from annual deficits and toward the debt level and include various proposals for involving the member states more directly.

What Does the European Experience Tell Us?

This section draws on the European experience to explore possible options for other regions that also feel the need to stabilize their exchange rates.

Sequencing: Where to Go and How to Get There

As noted earlier, there are many ways of stabilizing exchange rates within a region, ranging from soft managed floats to hard monetary unions. Europe has climbed the ladder from soft to hard pegs, using each step to develop institutions that were then used to prepare for the next step, but without ever committing to taking the next step.

Europe's sequencing has very much followed the traditional sequencing approach initially proposed by McKinnon.[17] It first liberalized intraregional trade with the creation of the Common Market in 1958, and then gradually integrated itself into world trade through a succession of accords under the General Agreement on Tariffs and Trade (GATT). It also instituted current account convertibility upon launching the Common Market and then very gradually adopted financial account convertibility, achieving full capital liberalization in

---

16. See, for example, Sapir (2003) and Wyplosz (2002a).
17. See McKinnon (1979).

1990 as part of the Single European Act. Retaining capital controls made it possible to operate the ERM for a decade. Exchange rate agreements started with fixed-but-adjustable exchange rates until capital liberalization forced a choice between the two extreme corners, and most countries opted for the monetary union corner. Thus Europe followed all the textbook prescriptions, and it worked. The exception is the gap of the 1990s, when full capital mobility was in place but the monetary union had not yet come to be. This forced the de facto suspension of the ERM through the adoption of very large margins of fluctuation, which was a way of upholding the mechanism, at least notionally. Yet this period was accompanied by continuing exchange rate stability (see figure 4-3) for one notable reason: by then the decision to launch the euro had been taken and a firm date had been set. While this latter sequencing was entirely fortuitous, it is rich with lessons. It establishes the crucial role of expectations in underpinning exchange rate stability. It also demonstrates the importance of institutions; the 1990s were dedicated to fulfilling the EMU entry conditions, and these visible efforts at convergence provided an anchor, underpinned by the gradual buildup of the Eurosystem.

The European process thus provides a roadmap that is feasible, not only because it has already been followed, but also because it accords well with basic principles. Does this mean that monetary union is the only destination and gradualism the only way to get there? Probably not. Southeast Asia is one example of a region where some degree of exchange rate stability has been achieved since the 1997–99 crisis through unofficial managed floats. The Chiang Mai Initiative offers some support, but it remains a partial and bilateral effort.

At the other end of the spectrum, can regions immediately jump to a monetary union without the intermediate step of a system of fixed and adjustable exchange rates, such as the ERM? In theory, such a leapfrogging strategy is possible. The European approach of gradualism is not based on economic principles. As a regime change, it can be achieved virtually instantaneously—in fact, it must be achieved instantaneously—and this is how it happened in Europe on January 1, 1999. True, that moment was preceded by a long period of mandatory convergence, but that was a protection requested by Germany to ensure that the "culture of price stability" would become sufficiently ingrained that the euro could be as good as the German mark. This does not have to be the case in other instances, provided that inflation differentials are limited, an issue taken up below.

On the other side, the European principle of gradualism is based on political and institutional principles. The process has been one of continuous erosion of national sovereignty, brought about through confidence-building steps. A monetary union also requires institutions, not just a common central bank—which can be put in place reasonably quickly—but also all the accompanying appointment and control mechanisms discussed earlier. In addition, it may take years to design and print banknotes.

Thus while there is no fundamental economic reason to prevent the adoption of a common currency without transiting through an ERM-type agreement, the lead time needed to get a monetary union up and running spans years. This constraint raises the question of what happens along the way, bearing in mind that excessive turmoil may jeopardize the whole project. One solution is to quietly build up the required institutions while allowing all future member currencies to float freely. If this period is characterized by wide fluctuations, it may be difficult to pinpoint the rate at which the disappearing currencies will be converted into the new collective currency. The risk is that some conversion rates may result in overvaluation. This would seriously threaten the eventual monetary union, for years of painful deflation might be needed to eliminate the overvaluation. Another solution is a managed float designed to erase wide fluctuations, which would make it possible to test possible conversion rates. However, managed floats are never a panacea, for markets are likely to test the intentions of monetary authorities, which may necessitate heavy interventions. The best that can be done under such circumstances is to conduct tightly coordinated interventions, assuming that large reserve stocks have previously been accumulated. While such interventions are unlikely to succeed, they can do so if they are supported by an agreement to adopt a common currency by a clearly established date. A necessary condition for this option to work, however, is that national monetary and fiscal policies be conducted with sufficient prudence so as not to undermine the project itself.

In the end, we come back full circle. ERM-type arrangements and Maastricht-style convergence programs are not strictly required to move toward a monetary union. Yet, given the unavoidable lead time, the transition period is fraught with potentially lethal dangers. A key concern is that the choice of conversion rates can only be based on past behavior, which in turn requires sufficient exchange rate stability during the transition period. In addition, once the monetary union starts, inflation rates will have to be broadly similar.[18] Given that inflation rates tend to be sticky, inflation convergence needs to be fairly complete before the monetary union is launched in order to avoid overvaluation. Hence a high degree of coordination is required during the transition period.

---

18. National inflation rates in a monetary union do not have to be equal. There may be temporary fluctuations related to varying macroeconomic conditions. There may also be trends reflecting different productivity gains (the Balassa-Samuelson phenomenon).

Institutions

Exchange rate arrangements cannot operate in a void. "Light" arrangements, such as loosely coordinated managed floats, can be accommodated without dedicated institutions, as has been the practice in Southeast Asia. More ambitious agreements do require institutions. Even light arrangements must be supported by domestic institutions, a view now well recognized in the literature.[19]

An obvious characteristic of institutions is that they take time to build and to establish themselves. In a way, therefore, they are needed before they exist. The early buildup of institutions may well be a key factor in the success of Europe's integration. The European Commission was set up by the Treaty of Rome in 1958, when the Common Market was launched. Its powers and ambitions were initially quite limited. Over the years, it has become the advocate for integration, binding together two opposing forces. On the one hand, it embodies the collective interest and the gains from cooperation. On the other hand, it derives its powers from governments, which represent national interests. This explains its often arcane decisionmaking process and many of its shortcomings. The commission's inherent internal contradiction is not often appreciated: its role is to manage those elements of national sovereignty that have been given up by its member states, but it needs approval from those same member states, which are instinctively loath to relinquish politically sensitive decisionmaking powers. The fact that the commission exists, and that it has seen the range of its responsibilities grow considerably since it was created, cannot be overestimated. Not only does the commission act as the lobby for integration, it also undertakes the background work needed to prepare for further steps. When the time is politically ripe—which can never be anticipated—everything needed to take the project forward is readily available in the commission's drawers. Besides the commission, Europe has built up a vast array of institutions as it has gradually expanded the scope for cooperation beyond economics. Each step is usually characterized by the same uneasy compromise between integrationist and nationalistic forces. A good example is the European Parliament, which became the handy, if weak, body to which the ECB is accountable.

Because exchange rate arrangements must involve some reduction in national sovereignty, entering into them is never an easy decision, and it is likely to need prodding and technical support. Countries contemplating such arrangements should have a budding institution that can study the concepts and propose various solutions. It should not have any power, but it should be clearly regional in ori-

---

19. See, for example, Persson and Tabellini (2000) and Drazen (2000).

Figure 4-4. *Treasury Bill Rates in Europe, 1992–2000*

Percent

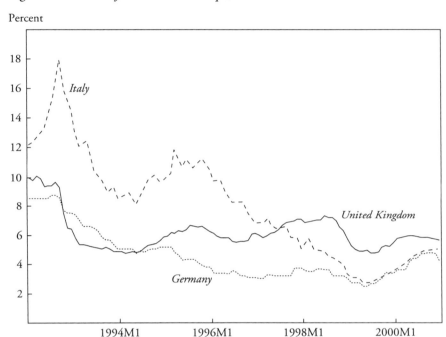

Source: IMF.

entation from the outset. An advantage is that it would need to report regularly to the ministers of finance, thus encouraging and framing their deliberations.

The Role of Financial Markets

In the matter of exchange rate arrangements, financial markets are both foes and friends. They are foes because they are prone to challenge policies whenever they detect vulnerability. Some vulnerabilities are the consequence of bad policies, in which case an early warning is not unproductive, even if it is painful. But in a world where self-fulfilling crises feed on intrinsic vulnerabilities, markets can impose excessively high standards of good behavior. When policies are well designed, however, markets can produce powerful support. A good example is the run-up to the monetary union in Europe. When it became clear that Italy would join the EMU, its interest rates quickly converged with those of Germany and stayed there (see figure 4-4). Not only did this convergence represent a vote of confidence in the undertaking, but it solidified the link between the lira and the mark until the euro was launched. In contrast, the British rate has retained a life of its own, reflected in euro-pound exchange rate fluctuations. A further lesson is that the European bond markets have become integrated, thus holding up the promise of a deep and efficient market. This has been a bonus to the smaller countries and has provided ex post justification of capital liberalization.

The implication is that markets ought to be called upon when they can provide support and kept at bay when they can be disruptive. If exchange rate arrangements are of the soft peg variety, they are highly vulnerable to speculative pressure. This observation provides a solid case for restraining capital flows. If the decision is to go all the way to a monetary union, the markets can support the process, but only if it is well crafted and politically guaranteed. Until this happens, the markets are likely to spot cracks in design and political will and tear up the project, another argument for imposing restraints.

Finally, is regional financial market integration a substitute for an exchange arrangement? To start with, if some of the national markets are already integrated with world markets, regional integration means de facto global integration. As argued earlier, financial market integration sharpens the choice of an exchange rate regime—the hollowing-out hypothesis. Consequently, such a move can either provide impetus for a hard exchange arrangement (monetary union) or force free floating. Regions that include countries that are conducting a substantial amount of trade among themselves are unlikely to find a high level of exchange rate volatility.

Conclusions

Europe has provided the two most accomplished examples of regional exchange rate arrangements: first the ERM and now a monetary union. Are these arrangements that should and can be emulated elsewhere? This chapter argues that small open economies that have intensive trade links, or that wish to intensify trade links, are naturally interested in stabilizing their internal exchange rates. It also argues that the European approach has followed sound, well-recognized principles. For these reasons, it offers a blueprint that could be adopted in other regions.

Yet it is not an example that will be easy to follow. The strategy of achieving a deep level of economic integration was built upon much wider objectives than just a common market. At the heart of the process has been the desire to put to rest centuries of war. Fresh memories of mutual destruction have made it easier for Europeans to agree to ever wider transfers of sovereignty, in spite of determined opposition and profound national divergences. Indeed, it is not by chance that the decision to share a common currency closely followed an exceptional event, the collapse of the Berlin Wall.

Another important feature of the European process is that there was never any master plan. Integration has always been characterized by a process of muddling through, taking two steps forward and one step back, with deep and lingering divergences as to what the end objective should be. But each integration step has made the next one more likely. Success in one area emboldened political leaders to contemplate another even bolder project in another area. More crucially perhaps, each important step has been matched by some additional institutional buildup, which has provided the backbone for further moves. It is difficult to overstate the importance of the early creation of institutions to support the integration process, no matter how imperfect those institutions are.

Another important consideration is that for a significant period many European countries have kept capital controls in place in a world where full capital mobility was the exception, not the rule. When the worldwide process of liberalization picked up speed, Europe had already moved a long way down the road of regional exchange rate stability. Given its attachment to and success with exchange rate stability, when forced to choose between a free float and a monetary union as the result of its own financial liberalization, the choice was relatively straightforward.

The European solution of operating soft pegs for an extended period, while keeping the ultimate aim of a monetary union unspecified, requires that capital controls be retained or, in some instances, reestablished. This worked in Europe, and it can work elsewhere as well. But if capital controls are ruled out, the menu of available choices shrinks and becomes polarized. Soft pegs are unlikely to last very long, leaving two alternatives: regional floating or a reasonably speedy move to a monetary union. A monetary union requires strong political will, especially in regions that have been hesitant to consider transfers of sovereignty and have not yet put in place the institutions that will be required to prepare and implement the necessary steps. These include establishing a regional central bank, providing for some form of democratic accountability, and adopting measures that will guarantee fiscal discipline. But it seems that it will take exceptional circumstances to effectively move in that direction.

This is why, after all, a slow process may be more realistic, even if its evolution must be measured in generations, not years. The first step in such a process is joint management of exchange rates—either fixed and adjustable pegs backed by capital controls as in the ERM, or joint management of floats. This is why the capital mobility regime is a key preliminary decision. The role of capital controls remains an open and controversial issue. It is sometimes claimed that capital controls are no longer feasible in today's globalized world. This claim is unsubstantiated. Nevertheless, countries that have already liberalized their capital movements, and often paid a high price for it,[20] are unlikely to reverse course. At any rate, if capital flow liberalization is considered desirable, such a step must be accompanied by substantial exchange rate flexibility. In either case, regions that wish to limit bilateral exchange volatility cannot escape setting up a dedicated institution and establishing ERM-type multilateral agreements of mutual support.

References

Bakker, Age F. P. 1996. *The Liberalization of Capital Movements in Europe.* Amsterdam: Kluwer Academic.

Baldwin, R. 1997. "The Causes of Regionalism." *World Economy* 20, no. 7: 865–88.

Calvo, G., and C. Reinhart. 2000. "Fear of Floating." *Quarterly Journal of Economics* 117, no. 2: 379–408.

Cottarelli, C., G. Galli, P. Marullo Reedtz, and G. Pittaluga. 1986. "Monetary Policy through Ceilings on Bank Lending." *Economic Policy* 3: 673–710.

de Grauwe, P. 1988. "Exchange Rate Volatility and the Slowdown in Growth in International Trade." *IMF Staff Papers* 35: 63–84.

Drazen, A. 2000. *Political Economy in Macroeconomics.* Princeton University Press.

Eichengreen, B., and C. Wyplosz. 1993. "The Unstable EMS." *Brookings Papers on Economic Activity* 1: 51–124.

Feldstein, M. 1997. "The Political Economy of European Monetary Union: Political Reasons for an Economic Liability." *Journal of Economic Perspectives* 11, no. 4: 23–42.

Gros, D., and N. Thygesen. 1998. *European Monetary Integration.* 2nd ed. Harlow, United Kingdom: Longman.

Helliwell, J. F. 1998. *How Much Do National Borders Matter?* Brookings.

Kaminsky, G., and C. Reinhart. 1999. "The Twin Crises: The Causes of Banking and Balance-of-Payments Problems." *American Economic Review* 89, no. 3: 473–500.

Kenen, P. B. 1995. *Economic and Monetary Union in Europe: Moving beyond Maastricht.* Cambridge University Press.

Kenen, P. B., and D. Rodrik. 1986. "Measuring and Analyzing the Effects of Short-Term Volatility in Real Exchange Rates." *Review of Economics and Statistics* 68: 311–19.

Levy-Yeyati, E., and F. Sturzenegger. 2002. "Classifying Exchange Rate Regimes: Deeds versus Words." Universidad Torcuato di Tello.

McKinnon, R. 1979. *Money in International Exchange: The Convertible Currency System.* Oxford University Press.

---

20. There is substantial evidence that financial opening is followed by currency crises. See, for example, Kaminsky and Reinhart (1999) and Wyplosz (2002b).

Parsley, D., and S.-J. Wei. 2001. "Limiting Currency Volatility to Stimulate Goods Market Integration: A Price-Based Approach." Working Paper 8468. Cambridge, Mass.: National Bureau of Economic Research.

Persson, T., and G. Tabellini. 2000. *Political Economics: Explaining Economic Policy*. MIT Press.

Reinhart, C., and K. Rogoff. 2004. "The Modern History of Exchange Rate Arrangements: A Reinterpretation." *Quarterly Journal of Economics* 119, no. 1: 1–48.

Rogoff, K. 2002. "Rethinking Capital Controls: When Should We Keep an Open Mind?" *Finance and Development* 39, no. 4: 55–56.

Rose, A. 2000. "One Money, One Market: Estimating the Effect of Common Currencies on Trade." *Economic Policy* 30: 7–46.

Sapir, A., P. Aghion, G. Bertola, M. Hellwig, J. Pisani-Ferry, D. Rosati, J. Viñals, and H. Wallace. 2003. *An Agenda for a Growing Europe*. European Commission.

Wyplosz, C. 2002a. "Fiscal Discipline in EMU: Rules or Institutions?" Paper prepared for the Group for Economic Analysis of the European Commission.

———. 2002b. "How Risky Is Financial Liberalization in the Developing Countries?" *Comparative Economic Studies* 44, nos. 2–3: 1–26.

5

European Financial Institutions: A Useful Inspiration for Developing Countries?

STEPHANY GRIFFITH-JONES, ALFRED STEINHERR,
AND ANA TERESA FUZZO DE LIMA

Since its beginning, European integration has been accompanied by the creation of major financial mechanisms. Such mechanisms and the resulting financial transfers have been seen as both an economic and a political condition for making economic integration effective and equitable. These mechanisms have included grants (through the Structural Funds), loans (mainly through the European Investment Bank), and most recently, guarantees (European Investment Fund).

These financial mechanisms have had two major aims: (1) reducing income differentials between countries and regions within the European Community (and later the European Union), particularly those resulting from trade liberalization, and (2) allocating major financial resources to facilitate the functioning of an increasingly integrated market, for example by financing interconnection of national networks in transport and telecommunications. While other aims have later been added, these two remain central.

It is important to stress that very large—and growing—resources have been allocated in Europe consistently for these aims. To an important extent this

The authors would like to thank José Antonio Ocampo for very valuable suggestions for this paper. We are very grateful to Peter Holmes for his insights on the role of structural funds in European convergence.

dynamic has been driven by the relatively poorer countries, which during the negotiations over their joining the European Community have put as a precondition the creation, or sharp increase, of grants and loans. The first such case was when Italy—before joining the European Economic Community in the mid-1950s—pressed for the creation of the European Investment Bank, largely to help fund infrastructure in the poorer southern part of Italy. Similarly, when other countries joined, the Structural Funds and the Cohesion Fund were created to address their needs. More recently, pre-accession funds have been put in place to prepare transition economies for joining.

This chapter focuses mainly on the experience of the European Investment Bank (EIB), a bank that lends far more than the World Bank. However, we first analyze the broader context of fiscal (grants) mechanisms linked to European integration. We outline their historical evolution, describe their rationale and main features, and highlight their scale. As we discuss, fiscal transfers via the structural funds have represented very high proportions of the GDP of poorer countries (between 3 and 4 percent of GDP for Portugal and Greece during the 1990s). In the 1990s an interesting innovation was introduced: significant fiscal transfers were made to Eastern European countries before they joined the European Union (EU), via special mechanisms. Thus significant resources (both loans and grants) have been transferred recently even during pre-accession periods.

The next section is dedicated to the EIB, which was created to help achieve the goal of economic convergence. In the bank's early stages, capital markets were incomplete and underdeveloped, so there was a strong case, both theoretically and politically, for dealing with such market imperfections through the creation of a public bank. Another interesting feature of the evolution of the EIB is its relatively low level of lending in the initial phase (first decade), with very large increases afterward. This section concludes by outlining key policy issues at the EIB today.

In developing countries, particularly the relatively poorer ones, where market imperfections still prevail, especially in capital and credit markets for long-term finance, the role of regional public banks in integration processes is probably more similar to that of the EIB in its early stages—that is, explicitly supporting, via loans, a regionally integrated infrastructure and providing assistance to poorer regions. Nonetheless, the issue of greater focus on mechanisms such as guarantees and other risk-bearing instruments, rather than on pure loans, also has increasing relevance for integration among developing countries. In the final analysis, the central lesson from the EIB experience is the importance of a large and dynamic public bank to support integration and convergence processes.

Fiscal Transfers within the European Union

The original broad European aim was to reduce disparities between regions by providing large-scale funding. In the late 1980s, a narrower rationale was adopted.[1] The European Community would not take responsibility for addressing those disparities that predated its existence, but it was necessary to find a means by which additional disparities that might be created in poorer regions by trade liberalization would be compensated financially. The political goal was to maintain support for the integration process in poorer countries.

European regional policy has developed gradually, influenced by successive periods of deepening and widening of the European Union. The major stages and the financing mechanisms created are outlined in table 5-1.

Funds for Equitable Development

In the preamble to the Treaty of Rome, which created the European Economic Community (EEC) in 1957, the member countries explicitly called for ensuring "harmonious development by reducing the differences existing between the various regions and the backwardness of the less favored regions." In keeping with this clear objective and with the underlying vision that financial transfers are both a political and an economic condition for making economic integration effective and equitable, from its inception the European Community created major financial mechanisms, including both loans and grants.

These major institutional mechanisms created in the EEC responded to widely accepted studies in economics that have shown that trade liberalization contributes, via economies of scale and other mechanisms, to more rapid growth overall, but owing to inherent asymmetries also leads to relatively less rapid growth (or even decline) in relatively poorer areas.[2] Besides creating mechanisms to reduce potentially growing inequalities between regions and countries as a result of trade liberalization, from the start the EEC allocated major financial resources to interconnect national networks (in transport and telecommunications, in particular) and to facilitate the functioning of an increasingly integrated market. Broader aims, such as educational and cultural exchanges and improvements in the environment, have also been funded.

The European Investment Bank was created at the same time as the EEC to further the objectives of harmonious development and compensation of less favored regions. It committed a high proportion of its loans to finance infra-

1. See Griffith-Jones, Kimmis, and Fuzzo de Lima (2003).
2. See Griffith-Jones, Stevens, and Georgiadis (1992) and Griffith-Jones, Kimmis, and Fuzzo de Lima (2003).

Table 5-1. *Development of European Union Regional Policy and Main Financing Mechanisms*

Year	Context	Main events
1957–75	The preamble to the Treaty of Rome refers to the need "to strengthen the unity of their [the countries of the European Community] economies and to ensure their harmonious development by reducing the differences existing between the various regions and the backwardness of the less favored regions."	1958: The *European Investment Bank* is set up under the Treaty of Rome to provide long-term loans in support of European integration. A key objective of the EIB is to strengthen the economically weaker regions. 1958: The two sector-based Structural Funds, the *European Social Fund* (ESF) and the *European Agricultural Guidance and Guarantee Fund* (EAGGF), are established.
1975–85	The northern enlargement of the European Union increases regional imbalances. The United Kingdom lobbies for an EU regional policy in its accession negotiations.	1975: The *European Regional Development Fund* (ERDF) is created to redistribute part of the member states' budget contributions to the poorest regions.
1985–93	The introduction of the Single European Act, together with further enlargement involving three less-developed countries—Greece in 1981, and Spain and Portugal in 1986—provides further impetus for EU regional policy.	1986: The *Single European Act* lays the basis for a genuine cohesion policy designed to offset the burden of the single market for southern countries and other less favored regions. 1989–93: The *European Council* in Brussels in February 1988 overhauls the operation of the Structural Funds and doubles the resources allocated to them.
1993–2000	The Treaty on European Union, which comes into force in 1993, designates cohesion as one of the main objectives of the union, alongside economic and monetary union and the single market.	1993: The *Cohesion Fund* is created to support projects in the fields of the environment and transport in the least prosperous member states. Alongside the Structural Funds, a new *Financial Instrument for Fisheries Guidance* (FIFG) is created. In 1994, the *European Investment Fund* is created to provide guarantees for infrastructure and investment in small and medium-sized enterprises (SMEs).

(continued)

Table 5-1. *(continued)*

Year	Context	Main events
	In 1993, the Copenhagen European Council invites the central European countries to apply for membership in the European Union. The present enlargement process is launched in 1997.	The *PHARE Program,* set up in 1989 to provide support to the countries of central Europe during transition, is reoriented in 1993. From 1997, PHARE becomes totally focused on pre-accession assistance, becoming the first of three pre-accession instruments.
2000–06	The future enlargement of the European Union, with the addition of ten central European countries, will increase the demands on the EU budget for cohesion.	1999: The Structural Funds and the Cohesion Fund are reformed. The *Instrument for Structural Policies for Pre-accession* (ISPA) and the *Special Accession Program for Agriculture and Rural Development* (SAPARD) complement the PHARE Program to promote the economic and social development of applicant countries in central Europe. In 2000, the European Investment Fund becomes part of the EIB, focusing on venture capital and guarantees for institutions financing SMEs.

Source: Information compiled by the authors.

structure in poorer regions and countries. Italy, where there was much poverty in the south, played a key role in pressing for the bank's creation.

Several Structural Funds were created to provide grants for poorer regions and specific sectors (especially agriculture). The three funds created initially were the European Social Fund, the European Agriculture Guidance and Guarantee Fund (the basis for the Common Agricultural Policy), and the European Regional Development Fund. An additional large fund, the Cohesion Fund, was created when Portugal and Spain joined, as a result of pressure from the new members, particularly Spain.

In 1989, when the Berlin Wall fell and the transition to the market and democracy began in Central and Eastern Europe (CEE), the then European Community quickly created fairly generous mechanisms to support the CEE countries' transition to the market. The transfer of know-how was considered just as important as the financial assistance provided, if not more so. The previously existing European Investment Bank lent on an important scale to these countries, and a new development bank, the European Bank for Reconstruction and Development (EBRD), was established in support of the transition. In spite of its name, the EBRD does not respond solely to European interests; its board of directors comprises both European and other members—Japan, the United States, and others—and in the years after its creation it lent not only to the European region but also to the former Soviet Union. The EBRD is thus different from the EIB, which was established as, and remains, a European bank.

In 1997 the Council of the European Union officially launched the current round of European Union enlargement, with ten countries from Central and Eastern Europe negotiating accession. To assist the accession process, the financial instruments and mechanisms previously used to support transition to the market in those countries were transformed fairly easily and seamlessly into mechanisms for preparing them for integration into the European Single Market, which is a significantly more advanced stage of trade integration than a free-trade area. Moreover, during the 1990s, pre-accession funding became far larger than in the past, and its aims became more ambitious, focusing particularly on countries preparing to integrate effectively into the single market while also providing resources for poorer regions and people, as well as supporting cross-border communications. Post-accession funding will become slightly less generous than in the past (especially for agriculture), but will still be large.

Since their creation, the Structural Funds and the Cohesion Fund have been the main instruments of social and economic cohesion policy in the European Union. Through the four Structural Funds, the European Union grants financial assistance to resolve structural, economic, and social problems.[3] The Structural Funds underwent major reform in 1988 and again in 1993 when the Cohesion Fund was introduced.

Since the 1988 reforms, European Union structural policy has become even more significant in financial terms. By 1999 the Structural Funds and the Cohesion Fund together accounted for around one-third of the budget for EU policies and amounted to some 0.5 percent of the EU's GDP. Such funding represented very high proportions of the GDP of the poorer countries: almost 4 percent for Portugal and Greece (see table 5-2).

To put this in perspective, the Marshall Plan for the reconstruction of postwar Europe was equivalent to around 1 percent of the annual GDP of the United States and contributed an average of 2 percent of the European annual GDP over the period 1948–51. EU structural intervention is lower per year, at

---

3. The four Structural Funds are the European Regional Development Fund (ERDF), the European Social Fund (ESF), the European Agriculture Guidance and Guarantee Fund (EAGGF), and the Financial Instrument for Fisheries Guidance (FIFG).

Table 5-2. *European Union Structural Funds, 1989–1993, and Structural Funds and Cohesion Fund, 1994–1999*
Millions of ECUs[a]

Country or region	1989–93 (millions of ECUs and percent of EU-12)	1989–93 (percent of GDP)[b]	1994–99 (millions of ECUs and percent of EU-15)	1994–99 (percent of GDP)[c]
Belgium	740 (1.2)	0.11	1,808 (1.3)	0.18
Denmark	402 (0.6)	0.08	741 (0.5)	0.11
Germany	6,015 (9.5)	0.13	19,519 (14.1)	0.21
Greece	7,528 (11.9)	2.65	13,980 (10.1)	3.67
Spain	13,100 (20.8)	0.75	31,668 (22.9)	1.74
France	5,907 (9.4)	0.14	13,334 (9.6)	0.22
Ireland	4,460 (7.1)	2.66	5,620 (4.1)	2.82
Italy	10,753 (17.1)	0.27	19,752 (14.3)	0.42
Luxembourg	55 (0.1)	0.17	83 (0.1)	0.15
Netherlands	725 (1.1)	0.07	2,194 (1.6)	0.15
Portugal	8,450 (13.4)	3.07	13,980 (10.1)	3.98
United Kingdom	4,816 (7.6)	0.13	11,409 (8.2)	0.25
EU-12	62,951 (100)	0.29		
Austria			1,432 (1.0)	0.19
Finland			1,503 (1.1)	0.40
Sweden			1,178 (0.8)	0.37
EU-15			138,201 (100)	0.51

Source: European Commission.
a. ECU: European currency unit.
b. Based on annual average Structural Fund totals, and on average GDP in the period 1989–93.
c. Based on annual average Structural Fund totals, and on GDP in 1994.

around 0.5 percent of GDP, but is far higher in cumulative terms, since it has represented a long-term commitment for a large number of years.

There has been a dramatic increase in the level of funding available through the Structural Funds over the past forty years. In 1961, about €8.6 million was allocated through these funds. This figure had risen to €11.8 million by 1971. Total EU expenditure on the Structural Funds had reached nearly €14 billion by 1991 and some €32 billion by 2001.[4]

In terms of the distribution of funds, table 5-2 shows that between 1989 and 1993 the five recipients of the largest share of Structural Fund financing were Spain (21 percent), Italy (17 percent), Portugal (13 percent), Greece (12 percent),

4. European Commission, *Annual Report on the Structural Funds* (2000).

and Germany (9 percent). In the later 1994–99 period, for which the figures include financing from the Cohesion Fund, the major recipients were again Spain (23 percent), Italy (14 percent), Germany (14 percent), Portugal (10 percent), and Greece (10 percent). Table 5-2 also indicates the importance of these funds to the economies of the recipient countries by showing the annualized funding received as a proportion of their GDP. In both periods, EU structural funding represented a significant proportion of GDP for Portugal, Greece, Ireland, and Spain. In 1994–99 Structural Funds accounted for 4.0 percent of GDP for Portugal, 3.7 percent for Greece, 2.8 percent for Ireland, and 1.7 percent for Spain.

In the case of poorer countries such as Portugal and Spain, where time allows for more precise measurement of outcomes, the impact of post-accession EU funds has been broadly positive, especially in contributing to convergence with average European income per capita; it can also be seen in physical developments, such as the increase in new road and rail links, particularly those connecting with other European states. These advances have greatly facilitated both the integration of trade and integration in the broader sense.

There does remain some debate about the exact contribution made by the Structural Funds as opposed to that of the overall process of integration. Recent studies have shown a positive trend toward convergence between richer and poorer states of the European Union (unlike in other regions of the world),[5] and there can be little doubt that the integration process has played a significant part.[6] First Italy, then the poorest states in the EU-15 (Spain, Greece, Portugal, and Ireland) all saw a process of catching up. Ireland came from behind to an above-average position in income per head.

There is a little more debate about the specific contribution made by the Structural Funds themselves. Work by the European Commission and by several academics on country convergence has supported the view that the Structural Funds have played an important role.[7] It is certainly the case that for smaller poorer countries the receipt of up to 4 percent of GNP in financial transfers can make a substantial difference. In the Irish case, it is widely believed that these funds were well used and that they contributed to the emergence of Ireland as a high-tech economy. The convergence that has occurred within the EU has been a convergence of national levels of income per head, while within countries there has been something of a divergence between richer and poorer regions in relative terms. In Greece, Portugal, and Spain, it is the richer regions that have caught up the fastest with the rest of the European Union.

5. See Milanovic (2002).
6. Ben-David (1996); Ben-David and Kimhi (2000).
7. See EU (2004) and, for example, Solanes (2001).

The broad conclusion of analysts is that while EU funds seem to have had a positive effect at the country level, the results at the regional level have been more nuanced.[8] The evidence is consistent with the view that EU funds have made a positive impact on growth where the policy environment is favorable. The extreme example of this, of course, has been Ireland. The Greek experience, in contrast, to some extent indicates the limitations of transfers when absorptive capacity is insufficient.[9]

The European Commission, meanwhile, in its latest (2004) *Cohesion Report,* finds evidence that since 1988 the "Objective 1 regions"—those entitled to maximum EU regional support—have been growing faster. A simple regression of growth by region against receipt of EU funds does indeed show a positive correlation, but the association is weak, implying that other factors need to interact with the funds themselves. It can be concluded that there is evidence that structural funds have had a positive impact on the growth of poorer countries. However, the nature of the link is complex.

Unfortunately, neither the European Commission nor the authorities that have received such assistance have formally evaluated the effectiveness of different pre-accession instruments. Our analysis, interviews, and experience suggest that a structural program such as the pre-accession financing program offered to the Central and Eastern European countries is far superior to the more ad hoc, substantially lower pre-accession financing provided to Portugal. (Spain had no pre-accession grants, though it had pre-accession EIB loans.) However, the effort needed to achieve successful integration into Europe was also smaller for Spain and Portugal than it was for the CEE countries. This was because European integration had progressed significantly further when the CEE countries joined than when Spain and Portugal joined, owing especially to the creation in 1992 of the Single European Market. The accession funding for countries such as Portugal and Spain was focused mainly on the original aims of EU funding: redistribute to facilitate convergence and support investment, especially in infrastructure, to help European integration. However, a fairly dominant additional aim of pre-accession funding to the CEE countries was linked to the vast effort of harmonization of regulations and standards to meet EU norms (broadly called the Acquis Communtaire) so as to join a well-advanced single market.

Given their larger scale and their greater flexibility, EIB loans are an extremely valuable part of the pre-accession package in areas such as infrastructure, small and medium-sized enterprises (SMEs), and others. In both Spain and Portugal, as

8. See Funck and Pizzati (2003).
9. See EIB (2000).

well as in the Central and Eastern European countries, EIB loans were disbursed more easily and in a more streamlined way than grants.

Lessons Learned for Other Regional Integration Experiences

Financial mechanisms for accession can contribute to convergence between rich and poor countries and regions if they are both adequately funded and effective. The scale and coverage of the financing mechanisms used by the European Union to aid countries before and after accession has been extensive. European Union grant financing and EIB loans have together represented a meaningful proportion of each country's GDP and total investment. Added to this, the budget figures for EU Structural Funds do not immediately convey their significance for the economically weaker areas of the EU. As resource transfers are very heavily concentrated in the poorer areas, where economic activity is relatively low, they are of considerable size. Also, as Structural Fund allocations are based on the principle of cofinancing, with individual member states contributing resources to supplement the EU funding, they can act as a catalyst for higher levels of resource transfers to poorer regions. Naturally, the scale of resources made available through grants in the European case has been linked to the ability and willingness of the richer countries in the EU—particularly Germany in the initial phases—to make such resources available.

Policies designed to improve economic and social cohesion among member states are also very important in political terms. First, they help to unite member countries around a common goal. In the European context, for example, there has always been a strong sense of a European model of society, comprising elements such as a social market economy, free trade, democratic systems, and social cohesion. The financial mechanisms to support regional integration in the European Union are very much rooted in a desire to uphold this model of society. Second, cohesion policies are important in order to maintain the support of poorer and weaker states and regions for trade integration. Indeed, Portugal and Spain have been among the most steadfast supporters of the European integration process. Though the level of enthusiasm for integration may be somewhat lower at present in regional groupings in developing countries, or in the proposed Free Trade Area of the Americas, even free-trade areas require sustained political support.

A general lesson from early and later entrants seems to be that financial assistance works better the more decentralized the decisions are. Decentralized decisions (both in countries and in regions) not only are more efficient and make the best use of local knowledge and experience; they can also play an important role in fostering institutional development. Greater effectiveness and agility are also supported by the EIB, which has opened offices in member countries, and by the European Commission country offices, which have been given greater autonomy to approve programs without involving Brussels.

Though the European experience shows that it is valuable to provide support in a number of dimensions, the experience in different countries, from Portugal to the Czech Republic, suggests that effectiveness improves with a focus on a fairly limited number of programs linked to the priorities defined in the trade integration program. As Devlin and colleagues point out, a limited number of programs—together with other factors such as clear objectives and work programs—helps make cooperation successful.[10] Problems of absorptive capacity, especially in smaller countries, can more easily be overcome if assistance is narrowly focused and specific, because this facilitates provision of sufficient finance and technical assistance that can help overcome problems of implementation.

The EU Structural Funds were initially universal, although they were heavily concentrated on poorer nations and regions (including poorer regions in richer countries). Later, a targeted fund—the Cohesion Fund—was created to provide financing for environment and infrastructure projects in the poorer countries only.

Infrastructure integration has received a great deal of priority and funding. However, other areas (such as educational and cultural exchanges, research, integration, and environmental improvements) have also been funded, as European integration is seen as being broader than purely trade or even economic integration.

The European Investment Bank

The 1957 Treaty of Rome, which created the European Economic Community, contained several provisions for the creation of instruments that could contribute to "harmonious development" and the reduction of regional disparities. The European Investment Bank, one of the most powerful of those instruments, was established by the treaty "to contribute to the balanced and smooth development of the Common Market in the interest of the Community." The EIB was intended as a source of relatively low interest loans and guarantees that would facilitate the financing of: "(a) projects for developing less developed regions; (b) projects for modernizing or converting undertakings or for developing fresh activities called for by the progressive establishment of the common market; (c) projects of common interest to several Member States, which are of such size or nature that they cannot be entirely financed by the various means available in the individual Member States."[11]

10. Devlin, Estevadeordal, and Krivonos (2002).
11. Treaty of Rome, Article 130.

The EIB was created, therefore, as *a bank to support the European integration process.* Its three objectives reflected three major concerns expressed during the negotiation of the Treaty of Rome. The first was to help reduce the gulf between relatively prosperous and relatively poorer regions. This concern also reflected the fear that, if not compensated for, European integration could increase imbalances. In the treaty negotiations, the Italian government pressed strongly for the creation of the EIB, precisely for this purpose; according to some sources, the creation of the EIB and its concentration on lending to southern Italy were a precondition for Italy to join the EEC. The second major concern was to help "senile industries," or areas where such industries were dominant, that were not able to compete on their own and required support to modernize, convert, or develop new activities. The third concern was the need to finance investment that would help to integrate the European economies and that would apply to several member states or to the EEC as a whole, particularly in the area of cross-frontier communications (especially transport). This concern was related to the fact that much of the existing infrastructure at the time was geared toward meeting domestic needs; the creation of the EEC led to new cross-border needs. It is noteworthy that these three aspects (possibly in somewhat different proportions) could also be central supportive measures in other integration processes.

Because currencies in the mid-1950s were still not fully convertible and capital markets were underdeveloped, there was a strong case, both theoretically and politically, for dealing with these market imperfections through the creation of a public bank. The main mission of this bank would be to assist in channeling savings from the more developed parts of the EEC to the less developed parts (regional development). At the same time it was recognized that a customs union was needed to complete and transform an essentially juxtaposed national infrastructure into an integrated European infrastructure (European integration).

The European Commission was given responsibility for making funds available on a grant basis to assist lagging regions. As there was a limited supply of grant money, and as it was felt that for many projects the problem was not lack of returns but financial constraints, it made sense to complement grant facilities with loans. This was the job given to the EIB.

The Institutional Setup

The EIB is an international nonprofit organization with headquarters in Luxembourg. Its shareholders are the member countries of the European Union. The bank is designed as the *Hausbank* of the European Union. As such, it receives its strategic lending mission (what type of lending, in which parts of the outside world) from its Board of Governors after discussion in the Ecofin Council. It follows the policies set by the European Commission and ensures that the projects it finances respect European guidelines (European environmental guidelines, for example). The EIB follows a division of labor with the commission (for example on economic forecasts) and with other international organizations such as the World Bank and the International Monetary Fund (IMF). Its own policy analysis is therefore very limited. The EIB does not systematically make sectoral policy analyses (a World Bank or European Commission job) or macro policy analyses (an IMF or European Commission job), and therefore abstains from making policy recommendations.

As a result, the EIB has a very lean staff (some 1,200 in 2004) and low expenses in relation to loan volume. Its activity is focused on the European Union (close to 90 percent of outstanding loans), although over time it has increasingly been asked also to operate outside the EU.

The EIB was set up in 1957 with subscribed capital of €1 billion. After its last capital increase and before enlargement on May 1, 2004, its *subscribed capital* stood at €150 billion and its paid-in capital at €7.5 billion. Reserves stood at €18.5 billion, bringing its funds up to €25.9 billion. After enlargement on May 1, 2004, subscriptions of new members increased the total to €163.6 billion. Each member state's share in the bank's capital is calculated in accordance with its economic weight within the EU (expressed in GDP) at the time of accession.

Lending and Pricing Policies

The EIB's lending has been limited to financing projects. Recent developments create more flexibility. The focus on project lending excludes trade financing or program financing, such as balance-of-payments support, poverty reduction, sector reforms, and the like.[12] In general, the bank lends up to 50 percent of the project cost, and often provides as little as one-third of the total funding required. This implies that the multiplier effect on recipient economies is increased. Sometimes, at the request of political authorities in the country concerned, this limit is increased to 75 percent to speed up financial support during downturns of the business cycle or to respond to other priorities. This introduces an interesting explicit element of countercyclicality in the lending operations of the EIB that should help support economic activity—especially investment—in periods of economic downturn.

12. Member states have national vehicles to provide and commercial banks to carry out trade financing. In less developed areas this may not be the case. For this reason, the main financial mission of the Black Sea Trade and Development Bank (BSTDB), for example, is trade financing.

For a project to receive EIB financial support it must first be eligible. This means it must fall into one of the categories of projects to which the bank lends. Then it must satisfy the bank's exacting borrower quality standards. If the borrower is not a government, it must provide adequate guarantees. In addition to the quality conditions to be satisfied by the borrower, the project must be financially and economically sound. Since the main objective of the bank is to contribute to the European Community's economic performance (regional development, European infrastructure, high environmental standards, European competitiveness, and energy security), the project must be financially sound and must have a high social return. This social return (the internal rate of return augmented by externalities such as employment creation) is always difficult to assess, leaving scope for political desiderata. The bank's Board of Directors is the arbitration court for such matters.

To assess a project's social return and conformity to EU policies (such as international competitive bidding and environmental standards), it is evaluated by a team of lending officers, economists, and engineers. For less sophisticated borrowers, this evaluation can lead to project modification and improvement. The scope for such enhancements is obviously limited for projects put forward by sophisticated corporations. The technical and economic evaluation of projects of reputed corporations in the European Union is therefore much more limited.

In its lending activity the bank needs to observe *subsidiarity*. This means, in principle, that the bank lends to projects only when there are no other means available. This is a sound theoretical principle but a difficult one to make operational. At some price other funds tend to become available to solid borrowers, who are the borrowers to whom the bank currently tends to lend. But if subsidiarity has to be assessed on the basis of the alternative financing cost, what is the cutoff spread? In current practice, borrowers make the decision. If the bank's offer is more favorable in terms of cost than the alternatives, borrowers request a bank loan, and the bank's more favorable offer contributes to the success of the project. It might be more efficient if the EIB were to define a benchmark (which would naturally be adjusted over time) that would indicate the minimum cutoff spread over alternative funding for which the EIB would lend. While subsidiarity is a difficult issue to deal with, the EIB attaches great value to cooperating closely with banks and other financial institutions.

The EIB is a not-for-profit institution and therefore prices its loans with the aim only of covering costs. Given its very high degree of financial solidity, it enjoys a triple-A rating. It therefore borrows at the best terms, with only a slight spread over triple-A-rated government debt. A markup is added to this cost of funding to cover administrative costs. Given the high lending volume per employee (personnel costs account for 80 percent of total administrative costs), these costs are small. In line with the increase in outstanding loans per employee, the cost-covering markup declined to 15 basis points in the early 1990s.

The markup calculation was then changed to reflect more directly costs incurred per project. A major problem is that the administrative cost is concentrated on origination and therefore not related to loan maturity. Hence it would be best to compute a single up-front fee. For a variety of reasons, however, a markup embodied in the interest rate is preferred, and a modulation of the markup for very long maturities has therefore been introduced. The administrative cost of a €1 billion loan is not a hundred times the administrative cost of a €10 million loan. Repeat loans also generate lower costs. Modulation now generates markups in the range of 5 to 15 basis points. The combination of a low financial cost with a very low administrative markup means that the bank's lending conditions are extremely attractive for borrowers, even when compared with those of other international financial institutions such as the World Bank or the EBRD.

As this description of EIB pricing makes clear, there is no explicit subsidy in EIB lending. Rather, the strong financial backing of the bank minimizes the cost of resources to the bank, an advantage passed on to customers. There is, however, an implicit subsidy. All members of the European Union are treated as equal. Therefore, lending to governments is priced equally, without a risk premium and independent of country ratings. These ratings vary in the European Union from triple-B to triple-A. Borrowers outside the European Union benefit from an EU guarantee, since the EIB is carrying out lending outside the EU on the basis of an EU mandate. Accordingly, the EIB does not charge a risk premium, and borrowers receive a de facto subsidy provided by the European Union.

The Rationale

Market imperfections. A public sector bank finds the justification for its existence in market imperfections.[13] When the bank was created, the major market imperfections were capital controls, a little-developed and segmented capital market, and uneven development of the banking sector across the European Community. Indeed, it could be argued that markets were incomplete or even missing for longer-term funding in the relatively poorer countries of the EC— first the south of Italy; then new entrants such as Greece, Ireland, and Portugal; and more recently, the new accession countries in Central and Eastern Europe. What are the justifications today?

---

13. For more discussion, see Stiglitz (1998).

Except for rated borrowers, the market is still characterized by pronounced market imperfections arising from information asymmetries. Asymmetric information arises because one party to the contract (the borrower) has more and better information than the other party (the lender or investor). Asymmetric information leads to two problems in the financial system: adverse selection and moral hazard.

The asymmetric information problem illustrates that the provision of reliable information is crucial to the ability of financial markets to perform their function efficiently and to distinguish good from bad credit risks. One solution to the asymmetric information problem is for a lender to collect the necessary information to screen and monitor investments. This is what banks usually do when they establish a long-lasting and, ideally, exclusive (from the banks' point of view) relationship with a close customer. But in general, there are two barriers to information collection. The first is its cost, particularly when more than one lender is potentially or actively involved. The second problem is the free rider problem— that is, the fact that investors who do not spend resources on collecting information can still take advantage of information that other institutions have collected. If bank A lends to a firm, it gives a signal to other potential lenders that it has collected information that it finds satisfactory. The value of this signal that disseminates information to the market is positively correlated with the reputation of bank A and becomes a "public good." This provides incentives to free riding.

One solution to the problem of asymmetric information is for a public bank to incur the cost of information collection. The EIB does this and acts as a "delegated monitor."[14] It carries out a very detailed evaluation of projects, going beyond the typical analysis of a commercial bank, and then monitors the loan carefully. Because the bank has established a high reputation as a careful evaluator and as a conservative bank with an excellent track record (very few EIB loans have experienced difficulties), the value of the signal sent when it approves a loan is high. The bank finances only part of a project, but its participation is a signal to free riding banks that they may confidently finance the remainder of the capital needs.

The project focus of EIB lending diminishes the moral hazard somewhat. Monitoring in such cases is easier than with a general loan to a company, since diversion of funds to other uses with higher risk is more limited. Moreover, a large part of bank lending is carried out with repeat borrowers that value access to EIB funding.

It could be argued that the role of the EIB could be further strengthened if it lent more to riskier borrowers. In the future, the EIB might be induced by

14. Leland and Pyle (1977).

market forces to shift a larger part of its operations from providing funds without assuming risks (it currently requires guarantees, which means that the guarantors bear the risks) to operations in which the EIB would assume more of the risks (for example, via guarantees) and private lenders would provide the loans.

In fact, the EIB has already started making this shift through the creation of the European Investment Fund (EIF), of which the EIB is the largest shareholder. The EIF provides guarantees, takes equity participation, and supports venture capital funds, thus taking on this new role of assuming risk. Interesting lessons may exist here for regional banks' lending to developing economies.

Completing the market: long-term funding and support for national market development. The EIB lends to the *public* and *private* sectors. During the first decades of its operations, its lending was heavily concentrated in the public sector, which at that time was almost exclusively responsible for infrastructure projects in many countries. Such projects are highly capital-intensive and require long periods of financing. The bank was designed as a long-term lending institution because market imperfections have been most pronounced in that segment. Since its creation, the bank has made loans with maturities of up to thirty years, depending on project needs. Over time, as capital markets have developed and the expertise needed to finance infrastructure has evolved and spread, the private sector has gained importance.

The bank lends in any convertible currency requested by customers. It lends at fixed rates for the life of a loan, at variable rates, or with options for resetting or conversion of lending conditions. EIB loans also benefit from a grace period for gradual repayment, which is normally three years, but may be more if the project profile makes a longer grace period desirable.

Because few banks lend for long maturities at fixed rates, the bank has acquired a unique reputation for fixed-rate long-term lending.[15] The social value of fixed-nominal-rate lending is, however, debatable. Simulations carried out by bank staff suggest that it would have been cheaper in the long run for borrowers to have borrowed from the EIB at variable interest rates than at fixed rates. Fixed interest rates do have the advantage of providing stable payments. However, this is valid only for nominal interest payments; in contrast, since variable interest rates tend to be more closely correlated with inflation, variable interest rates might actually generate more stable real interest payments.

An interesting and positive side-product of the EIB has been its contribution to the development of bond markets in local currencies of member states. Such

---

15. Before the introduction of the euro, long-term loans, even at variable interest rates, were not generally available in many countries of today's "Euroland."

borrowings by a well-recognized regional bank with a triple-A rating may make significant contributions to the development of local bond markets. The EIB played a significant role in this respect in the capital markets of Greece, Portugal, and Spain during the 1990s and since then has done so in the emerging markets of Central Europe.

Financial Strength of the Bank

The authors of the bank's establishing agreement had a clear vision of its mission and of how to accomplish that mission. However, these views obviously reflected the financial knowledge and market conditions of the 1950s, and increasingly they need to be interpreted flexibly in the current context.

One compelling argument for the bank's founders was that it should be made as financially strong as possible. This was rightly seen as having two advantages: first, a low likelihood of recourse to shareholder money, and second, a low cost of funding from capital markets for the projects funded by the bank. As less-than-triple-A-rated banks realize benefits from creating triple-A-rated special vehicles, less-than-triple-A-rated governments can do the same. In the terminology of economics, this is a *coordination gain*.

The first step toward financial solidity is a generous endowment of equity capital. The bank has a gearing ratio between outstanding loans and *subscribed* capital of 250 percent. The ratio of the World Bank, in comparison, is 100 percent. However, the conservative nature of the EIB's gearing ratio becomes apparent from the second quality feature: 5 percent of the subscribed capital has to be paid in, and the unpaid 95 percent is a *contingent* capital guarantee of shareholders. Moreover, should a shareholder be unable to pay up, then all others are collectively liable. This provides very strong capital backing.

The third qualitative feature is on the assets side. All loans must be adequately guaranteed by a first-class third party. For a long time, guarantees were provided mainly by governments. This was the case when EIB lending was mostly concentrated in the public sector. Over time, the share of lending to the private sector has increased steadily. Third-party guarantees have mainly been provided by first-class banks (meaning banks with at least a single-A rating).

A test of the contribution of asset quality to the bank's solidity is provided by a computation of the Basel I capital adequacy ratio. Although the bank is not subject to the Basel framework, such a computation is instructive. Until the early 1990s, more than half of the outstanding loans enjoyed a government guarantee and hence a zero risk weighting. The remainder of the loan book was supported by bank guarantees with a 20 percent risk weighting. It comes, therefore, as no surprise that the bank's capital adequacy ratio exceeded 100 percent, far in excess of the minimum requirement of international commercial banks of 8 percent. Over time, with a rising share of lending to the private sector, the capital adequacy ratio has declined gradually, but it was still very comfortable at over 30 percent in 2003.

As a result of the bank's very prudent and conservative approach to lending, it has not lent to weaker economic actors without strong securities or third-party guarantees. Loan performance therefore has been exceptionally good, and provisions are large relative to modest past loan losses. Since only a few loans have been nonperforming over its forty-six-year existence, the bank's recourse to guarantors has also been modest. The reverse side of this coin is that potential borrowers with excellent credit standing and high-quality guarantees could also find money elsewhere.

The need for third-party guarantees became increasingly recognized as problematic and overly conservative—problematic because the bank sought increasingly to lend to the private sector but also to maintain very high quality. Focusing on top borrowers and insisting on third-party guarantees turned out to be both contradictory and not market conforming. The commercial cost of a third-party guarantee, added to the bank's lending rate, made the package unattractive for borrowers with a top standing and hence access to the capital market.

To make its loans more attractive to prime lenders, the bank introduced "single signature" loans, which are loans without a third-party guarantee. They are unlike loans with a third-party guarantee, which are priced on the basis of the bank's "opportunity" refinancing cost (that is, what the bank would pay if it had to refinance on capital markets on the day of fixing the lending rate for a loan).[16] With the hedging techniques available, this "opportunity" rate corresponds, on average, to the bank's actual cost of refinancing, plus a markup to cover administrative costs. In addition, a risk premium is added to single-signature loans. This risk premium is computed by the bank using advanced financial models, with external ratings as input. Additional securities such as mortgages or revenue pledges are accepted by the bank and reflected in the size of the risk premium.

Returns from lending and other investments generate a surplus, because all projects funded with borrowed resources must be cost-covering. This surplus (technically not a profit because it remunerates only the factor of production) is added to the bank's reserves and makes it possible to augment capital by converting reserves into paid-in capital without cash payments by existing shareholders. Of course, the gearing ratio of the EIB is defined in terms of subscribed

16. Until the late 1980s lending rates were set on the basis of actual borrowing costs. The change to "opportunity" cost was a response to market developments.

capital. But as 5 percent of subscribed capital must be paid-in, there is an implicit relationship with paid-in capital. The bank can satisfy this constraint by transferring funds from reserves to paid-in capital.

Since 1991 all capital increases of the EIB have been self-financed in this way. This obviously makes it easier to increase capital. Had the EIB been obliged to pay out dividends and then call on shareholders for fresh capital, it might have been more difficult to sustain lending growth with capital increases.

The return to convertibility of member countries in preparation for the Economic and Monetary Union (EMU) facilitated the bank's access to national capital markets.[17] A big jump was achieved with the EMU, representing for the bank a significant improvement in funding through large issues in just one currency, the euro. Moreover, increasing financial sophistication made the management of the bank's asset liability position and its currency risk easier. Today it has become standard to borrow in currencies for which the bank has no direct use but for which funding costs are interesting and to swap the proceeds into euros. At present, the bank has virtually no compelling immediate financial need for expansion.

The bank's choice to minimize the risk on its balance sheet and to transfer lending risk to other parties results in very limited risk diversification in its lending portfolio. This, in combination with the setting of lending rates to ensure that costs are covered, makes it impossible to securitize some parts of the loan portfolio without loss: any investor in an EIB unsecuritized bond would have more security and the same interest rate. For that reason, in an environment of growing lending volumes, the EIB carries a large historic loan book that needs to be supported by ever more subscribed capital.

Historical Evolution of Lending

Exponential lending growth. The activity of the EIB was fairly slow to develop (see figure 5-1). During its first ten years of operation, total loans amounted to only €7.983 billion, in comparison with €42.332 billion in 2003 alone, both expressed in 2003 euros (see table 5-3).

In terms of growth of lending adjusted for price increases, the highest growth rates were achieved during the period 1965–73, when the average annual real growth rate was 20 percent (excluding the setup period, during which growth rates are meaningless). During the period 1974–85 the average annual real growth rate declined to 15 percent, and since 1985 it has been around 8 percent. Even in recent years, between 1995 and 2003, the average annual real

---

17. It needs to be recognized, however, that the EIB had always received preferential treatment from national authorities, which provided considerable advantages for reducing funding costs.

Figure 5-1. *EIB Lending Growth, 1959–2003*

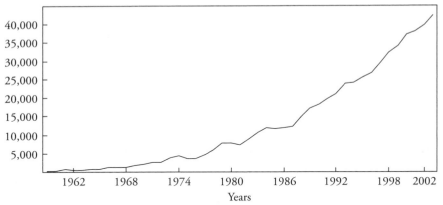

Millions of 2003 euros

Source: Prepared by the authors using EIB data.

growth rate was 7 percent, which was still much higher than real GDP growth in the European Union.

During the second decade, from 1969 to 1978, the total lending volume increased to €35.019 billion (in 2003 euros), which was four times greater than the lending volume during the first decade. This increase was due to more lending within the six-member European Community and to an expansion of the community. Italy was the largest borrower, followed by the United Kingdom. Lending outside of Europe amounted to less than 10 percent of the total, but as a result of the first oil shock, lending to the energy sector came close to 30 percent of total lending. And global loans became modestly significant, reaching 8 percent of total lending.

During the period 1979–88 the EIB became a bank with a recognized role in Europe. Total lending for the decade increased to €105.151 billion, in 2003 euros (three times as much as the previous decade). Global loans continued their march to greater significance, reaching over 20 percent of total lending. Lending to countries outside of Europe declined to 7 percent of the total.

The total for the next decade, 1989–98, was €238,349 million, in 2003 euros. Unified Germany and the former socialist countries became major borrowers. Two sectors dominated: infrastructure accounted for nearly 50 percent of total lending and global loans for 25 percent. Remarkably, global loans accounted for nearly 50 percent of lending to France and Germany, two coun-

Table 5-3. *Total EIB Lending*
Millions of 2003 euros

Decade	Amount
1959–68	7,983
1969–78	35,019
1979–88	105,151
1989–98	238,349
1999–2003	191,396
Total	577,899

Source: Prepared by the authors using EIB data.

tries that are not generally considered underrepresented in retail banking and that have numerous savings banks whose primary function is to lend to SMEs.

During the five years between 1999 and 2004, the lending volume reached €191.396 billion (in 2003 euros), and the bank became a global name. For the first time since 1958, Italy was replaced by Germany as the bank's top borrower, with Spain not far behind. Because accession countries were treated as if they had already joined the EC, lending outside the community exceeded 19 percent of the total. As to the sectoral distribution, energy declined strongly, global loans exceeded 30 percent, and health and education took off.

Among the sectors supported by the EIB, agriculture has never received much attention, and global loans (given to financial intermediaries to support SMEs) were modest during the first two decades (see table 5-4).[18] The public sector was the predominant borrower of financing for infrastructure, energy, and capital-intensive state industries (airlines, electricity generation and distribution, telephone systems, etc.).

As already pointed out, one of the key aims of the EIB was and is to contribute to convergence of poorer regions and countries by focusing lending on them. Griffith-Jones and colleagues deflated total allocations of EIB lending by country, by years of membership, and by population for the period 1959–90 (see table 5-5) and found that the countries obtaining the largest loans from the EIB during that period (per capita and per year of membership) included Ireland, Portugal, Greece, and Spain.[19] These were then the poorest countries in the European

18. Global loans are credit lines that the EIB grants to a financial intermediary, which deploys the proceeds to support SMEs. Although the effectiveness of this instrument is debatable, in the absence of a retail network, cooperation with retail banks is the only way the EIB can channel resources to SMEs.

19. See Griffith-Jones, Stevens, and Georgiadis (1992).

Table 5-4. Total EIB Lending by Sector
Millions of euros, values adjusted for each range of years[a]

Years	Agriculture, fisheries, forestry	Energy	Global loans, grouped loans	Health, education	Industry	Infrastructure	Services	Total
1959–68	1	177	10	0	440	509	0	1,137
1969–78	14	2,914	760	2	2,163	3,689	26	9,568
1979–88	375	17,173	14,493	102	6,206	21,441	258	60,048
1989–98	458	30,486	48,921	1,346	20,178	94,210	1,916	197,515
1999–2003	235	16,394	59,193	9,540	14,395	82,168	3,978	185,904
Total	1,083	67,144	123,377	10,990	43,382	202,017	6,178	454,172

Source: Prepared by the authors using EIB data.
a. All the data are in nominal terms.

Table 5-5. *EIB Lending, Deflated by Time of Membership and Population, 1959–90*

Member country	Indicator
Belgium	0.4
Denmark	4.2
Germany	0.2
Greece	2.9
Spain	2.9
France	0.7
Ireland	5.5
Italy	1.9
Luxembourg	0.5
Netherlands	0.2
Portugal	5.5
United Kingdom	1.4

Source: Griffith-Jones, Stevens, and Georgiadis (2002).

Community (with the exception of Denmark, which was not so poor, but also obtained high levels per capita and per year of membership). This provides strong indicative evidence that the EIB performed an important redistributive role.

Reasons for sustained growth. This very slow evolution of the bank's lending during the first twenty years, and the continued rather rapid expansion of activity over the past twenty years, are all the more remarkable because the very reason for the creation of the EIB—namely, capital controls and an underdeveloped capital market—disappeared with the reforms undertaken in the late 1980s and early 1990s in preparation for the EMU. To put it more provocatively, the EIB only started to flourish when its original raison d'être vanished. Why?

There are no convincing reasons for the slow start. Surely, it was wise to build up operations slowly, to gain experience in the field and to focus on economically promising projects within a narrow range. As a new bank, the EIB first had to establish a solid reputation. In addition, the underdeveloped, split-up European capital market put constraints on the refinancing capability of the bank, a constraint that has disappeared with the development of the European capital market. Most of the lending took place in European currencies, since borrowers preferred not to take an exchange risk. Financial markets in Europe were still national markets and were not yet sufficiently developed to allow the bank to borrow in the more mature U.S. market and then swap the proceeds into European currencies.

The successive enlargements of the European Union automatically expanded the lending volume. The following example will help to quantify the impact of EC expansion. Out of the total lending of €198.325 billion in the period

1999–2003, €86.530 billion went to the six original members of the community (EU-6). If Germany had maintained its borrowing at the same level as France (before unification Germany always borrowed less than France), then lending to these six countries would have totaled €74.363 billion. It can thus be concluded that EU expansion accounted for over 60 percent of activity.

Among the most significant recent decisions by the EIB is the decision to increase lending in the health and education sectors in recognition of the importance of such investments for economic growth. During the period 1999–2003, health and education accounted for 5.14 percent of total lending. Meanwhile, global loans accounted for 31.85 percent, but the share of industry was only 7.75 percent. If global loans, services, health, and education were subtracted from the adjusted EU-6 lending of €74.363 billion mentioned above, lending in the six countries would have dropped to some €45 billion, or only 23 percent of the total. Hence lending outside the initial EU-6 and to sectors that initially played little or no role accounted for 78 percent of the expansion in EIB lending.

In addition to these factors, a growing mandate to support the political objectives of the European Union beyond its borders sustained the growth of EU lending. The first lending mission outside the European Community concerned projects in African, Caribbean, and Pacific countries. In the early 1990s Latin America and the poorer countries in Asia became eligible. Of course, the biggest impact on EIB lending outside the EU came from the opening up of the former socialist countries of Central and Eastern Europe, where the EIB is by far the largest lender. In 2003 the EIB lent more than €4 billion to CEE countries, or about the amount of its total lending in 1985. Also, for geopolitical symmetry, lending to Mediterranean countries picked up.

Until the turn of the century, the bank limited its lending outside the European Union to 10 percent of its overall lending. In 2003, lending outside the EU represented 19.26 percent, of which 10.85 percent went to acceding and accession countries and 8.41 percent to countries in the rest of the world. Since the expansion of the EU on May 1, 2004, a large part of the bank's lending has once again become internal, and lending outside the EU has gone back down to close to 10 percent of the total.

Given that the capital adequacy ratio of the EIB is so large, and its expertise so valuable, it may be worthwhile to consider whether it should increase its lending to the developing world.

Lessons for New Regional Development Banks

Analysis of the EIB experience suggests a number of structural and operational features of interest for other regional development banks (RDBs).

—A regional development bank should be endowed with a small, first-class professional staff in order to establish a reputation beyond reproach. Management should execute its mission as set by the bank's establishing agreement and by its board of governors (the finance ministers of member states). To minimize political horse trading, maximize social acceptance, and optimize the economic effects of the bank's interventions, an advisory board composed of nongovernment experts should provide an opinion on all lending projects for which the social rate of return is below a set benchmark. Otherwise, all loans should be required to yield a social rate of return at or above the benchmark.

—The activity of a regional development bank should be focused. For project lending, a list of eligible projects might prove useful. This list should recognize the importance of education and health for human capital formation. As the development of regional trade is a key objective, trade financing should be among the top priorities. Also, transnational investment projects (pipelines, train and road connections, airports, and seaports, for example) should receive priority status.

—There should be no a priori restrictions on either private or public sector counterparts. Particular priority could be attached to private-public partnerships. Financial support for any lending project should be limited to the amount needed to stimulate cofinancing and increase the multiplying effect.

—Borrowing and lending in local currencies of the regional development bank should receive priority, with the double aim of avoiding foreign exchange risk for the borrower and assisting in the development of regional capital markets. However, this will absorb regional savings. Therefore, borrowing in foreign currencies should not be excluded. Loans should be made available for long maturities on a variable-rate basis. This will facilitate shorter-term borrowing by the RDB for longer-term loans, minimize the risk for the borrower in real terms, and, experience suggests, reduce the long-term cost of borrowing.

—Subsidiarity (that is, the risk that RDB loans will take business away from private banks or capital markets) will most likely not be an issue in emerging markets. To gain professional independence in carrying out its tasks as defined by its board of governors, and to ensure maximum economic impact from its financial interventions, the bank could set a minimum social rate of return (that is, the financial rate of return, plus the positive or negative value of externalities) as an absolute condition for loan acceptance.

—Asymmetric information is a problem everywhere, but even more so in markets with less developed financial markets. An important role of the RDB is therefore investment in project information and signaling to potential cofinanciers. To perform this role effectively, the RDB first needs to establish an impeccable reputation. It must also assume some of the risks. Risk is the greatest stumbling block in credit markets. It would be difficult to sell off the risk, and the signaling power would be diminished.

—The regional development bank should be endowed with a comfortable capital base. Because public coffers are not plentiful in emerging countries, it might be useful to complement the paid-in capital with subscribed, but not paid-in, capital for possible contingencies. The RDB should be allowed to retain any surpluses to build up reserves. With strong risk management and a high-quality loan portfolio, the RDB can obtain an international credit rating above those of member countries. The goal should be triple-A. This is achievable with strong management, a good loan portfolio, cost- and risk-covering prices, and a solid capital base. Weak ratings of member countries are a disadvantage, but not a decisive one (with respect to paid-in capital, *pecunia non olet,* so that only contingent capital would be affected by a discount factor). This will allow the economies in the region to have access to better borrowing conditions.

—Over time, as the regional development bank's growing balance sheet requires additional capital to maintain the bank's gearing ratio, certain loans might be securitized. This would avoid capital increases and focus the role of the RDB on loan originating.

—Pricing of loans should cover the financial cost, the risks taken, and the administrative costs. A small profit could be added to strengthen the capital base. With a triple-A rating and a lean staff, lending rates can be hundreds of basis points lower than the rates of private banks or the financing costs of local governments.

References

Ben-David, D. 1996. "Technological Convergence and International Trade." Discussion Paper 1359. London: Centre for Economic Policy Research.

Ben-David, D., and A. Kimhi. 2000. "Trade and the Rate of Income Convergence." Discussion Paper 2390. London: Centre for Economic Policy Research.

Commission of the European Communities. 1996. *The First Cohesion Report.* Brussels.

———. 2001. *Regular Report on the Czech Republic's Progress towards Accession.* Brussels.

———. 2002. *The Second Report on Economic and Social Cohesion.* Brussels.

Devlin, R., A. Estevadeordal, and E. Krivonos. 2002. "The Trade and Cooperation Nexus: How Does the Mercosur-EU Process Measure Up?" In *An Integrated Approach to the European Union-Mercosur Association,* edited by P. Giordano. Paris: Institut d'Etudes Politiques de Paris.

European Commission. 1997. "The Single Market Review." Subseries VI: Aggregate and Regional Impact. Vol. 2: *The Cases of Greece, Spain, Ireland and Portugal.* Brussels.

————. 2004. *A New Partnership for Cohesion—Convergence, Competitiveness, Cooperation. Third Report on Economic and Social Cohesion.* Luxembourg.

————. Various years. *Annual Report on the Structural Funds.*

European Investment Bank. 1985, 1987, 1988, 1989. *EIB Annual Reports.* Luxembourg.

————. 1997. *40 Years' Activity.* Luxembourg.

————. 2000. "Regional Convergence in Europe: Theory and Empirical Evidence." *Economic and Financial Studies* 5, no. 2. Luxembourg.

————. 2001. *The Bank's Operations in the Accession Countries of Central and Eastern Europe: Review of Current and Future Lending Policy.* Luxembourg.

————. 2001. *EIB Contribution to Regional Development: A Synthesis Report on the Regional Development Impact of EIB Funding on 17 Projects in Portugal and Italy.* Luxembourg.

————. 2003. *Statute of the European Investment Bank.* Luxembourg.

————. 2004. *The EIB Group Activity Report 2003.* Luxembourg.

European Investment Bank Group. 2001. *The EIB Group Activity Report 2001.* Luxembourg.

European Union. 2004. *Cohesion Report.* Brussels.

Funck, B., and L. Pizzati, eds. 2003. *European Integration Regional Policy and Growth.* Washington: World Bank.

Griffith-Jones, S., J. Kimmis, and A. Fuzzo de Lima. 2003. "Financial Mechanisms for Accession: Lessons from the European Union to a Free Trade Agreement of the Americas." IDS Research Paper. Brighton: Institute of Development Studies.

Griffith-Jones, S., C. Stevens, and N. Georgiadis. 1992. *Regional Trade Liberalisation Schemes: The Experience of the EC.* Brighton: Institute of Development Studies.

Leland, H. E., and D. H. Pyle. 1977. "Information Asymmetries, Financial Structure, and Financial Intermediation." *Journal of Finance* 32 (May): 371–87

Milanovic, B. 2002. "Worlds Apart: International and World Inequality 1950–2000." Washington: World Bank.

Solanes, J. G. 2001. *The Impact of European Structural Funds on Economic Convergence in European Countries and Regions.* Universidad de Murcia, Spain.

Stiglitz, J. 1998. "IFIs and the Provision of International Public Goods." *EIB Papers* 3, no. 2: 116–33.

6

Macroeconomic Coordination in Latin America: Does It Have a Future?

JOSÉ LUIS MACHINEA AND GUILLERMO ROZENWURCEL

For most developing countries, open regionalism has emerged as a sensible response to the ongoing turbulent and asymmetric process of economic globalization: it avoids the huge costs associated with both isolationism and outright liberalization. Moreover, the successful experience of the countries that now form the European Union has made regional integration an increasingly attractive option for the developing world.

Whenever regional integration is intended to go beyond just a free-trade agreement, macroeconomic coordination becomes a key issue. From a theoretical standpoint, the underlying idea is simple: when economies are interdependent, the events that take place and the policies implemented in each of them will, through various transmission channels, affect the performance of all the rest. Under these conditions, macro policy coordination appears to be a means of internalizing the effects of reciprocal interrelationships on decisionmaking in each economy while improving the results for all concerned.

This idea has spread beyond the borders of the Old World, but for a variety of reasons, repeated attempts to implement macroeconomic coordination mechanisms outside Europe, and in Latin America in particular, have run into numerous difficulties. Be that as it may, regional integration agreements are now a well-established reality on the world scene, and Latin America is no exception. In many cases, moreover, the participants in these agreements are seeking to go beyond improving trade relations and to set for themselves decidedly more ambitious integration goals. The reasons are not solely economic, but involve wider political and cultural motivations as well.

If the movement in this direction grows stronger, then it is natural to expect that coordination efforts will not be abandoned. Exploring the obstacles that will have to be overcome and the circumstances under which these initiatives can be profitable therefore becomes a necessary task. It is clear that this task can be completed satisfactorily only if the specific nature of the economic interdependence and political conditions and factors existing in each case are taken into account. Contributing to the efforts to achieve this objective in Latin America is the primary motivation for this analysis.

In the following sections we look at the particular characteristics of the economic interdependence entailed in the integration agreements existing in Latin America, with emphasis on how they differ from those in Europe. We assess the experience with macroeconomic coordination in the Southern Common Market (Mercosur), the region's largest trading bloc. An effort is made here to draw some lessons applicable to the other integration schemes in the region. Finally, we raise the question of how the demand for coordination can be increased in Latin America and seek to identify the main obstacles, opportunities, and incentives in this regard.

Reasons for Macroeconomic Coordination: How Much Economic Interdependence Is There in Latin America?

A high level of interdependence among countries is one of the main reasons for increasing the coordination of macroeconomic policies, since interdependence implies that each member of the group is affected by what happens in the other countries. The degree of interdependence among a group of countries is usually measured on the basis of the trade and financial links existing among them.

Trade Interdependence

Intraregional trade has followed quite different trends in the various subregional integration schemes in Latin America throughout the 1990s and thus far in the present decade. As figure 6-1 shows, Mercosur and the Andean Community (AC) grew steadily up to 1997–98, both in dollar value and in the share of total trade activity accounted for by intraregional trade. This trend changed abruptly when the international crisis erupted, however, and intraregional trade's share of the total dropped significantly, although the Andean Community managed to

Figure 6-1. *Share of Intraregional Exports in Total Regional Exports, 1985–2003*

Percent of total exports

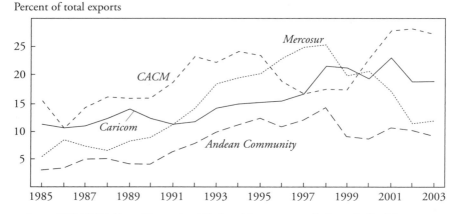

Source: ECLAC, Division of International Trade and Integration, on the basis of official data.

maintain the dollar value of such trade near the highs recorded in 1997–98, while in Mercosur it fell steeply. In the Central American Common Market (CACM), on the other hand, the dollar value of intraregional trade (without including *maquila* activities) has risen steadily throughout this period, and intraregional trade's share of the total, although it has fluctuated sharply, has also exhibited an overall increase. Within the Caribbean Community (Caricom), intraregional trade expanded considerably, both in dollar value and when measured as a percentage of total trade until 1998, and it has remained fairly steady since then.

Figures 6-2 and 6-3, in turn, assess the trade interdependence existing in the different Latin American economic blocs and other regional agreements. This comparison is based on two indicators: (a) intraregional trade with respect to total trade, and (b) intraregional trade in terms of GDP. For Latin America and the Caribbean, the indicators show that interdependence in subregional integration agreements, although it increased over the past decade, is still substantially less tight than in other regions. These findings become particularly evident when intraregional trade is analyzed in terms of GDP. The differences between the two indicators are primarily attributable to the openness of the individual countries.

In any event, the expansion of intraregional trade is limited by the size of the blocs. There are enormous differences in this respect: whereas the European Union (EU) accounts for 37.2 percent of world trade, no subregional agreement in Latin America accounts for more than 1 percent, with the sole exception of Mercosur, which, though it is the largest bloc in the region, accounts for only 1.4 percent of world trade.

Figure 6-2. *Share of Intraregional Exports in Total Regional Exports, 1990–91 and 2000–03*[a]

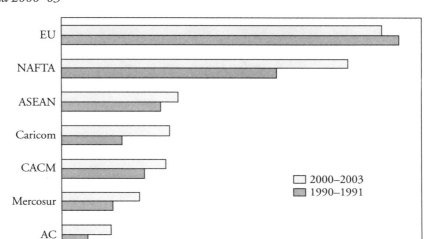

Percent

Source: ECLAC, Division of International Trade and Integration, on the basis of official data.

a. The figures given are annual averages. EU: European Union; NAFTA: North American Free Trade Agreement; ASEAN: Association of Southeast Asian Nations; Caricom: Caribbean Community; CACM: Central American Common Market; Mercosur: Southern Common Market; AC: Andean Community.

Financial Integration

The reciprocal externalities operating among the countries of Latin American subregional blocs have not been transmitted solely via trade channels, however. Macroeconomic spillovers from financial markets have also been extremely significant, even though the integration of financial transactions or related activities within domestic financial markets is virtually nil.[1] Financial conditions in the countries of subregional blocs are connected in two ways. On the one hand, since external vulnerability is a trait shared by all the member countries, changes in international financing conditions tend to have a more or less similar impact on all their economies. On the other hand, the contagion effects deriving from the imperfect information prevailing in international financial markets tend to magnify their financial interdependence. The strong correlation between the

1. Machinea and Rappoport (2004).

Figure 6-3. *Intraregional Exports as a Percentage of Regional GDP, 1990–91 and 2000–03*[a]

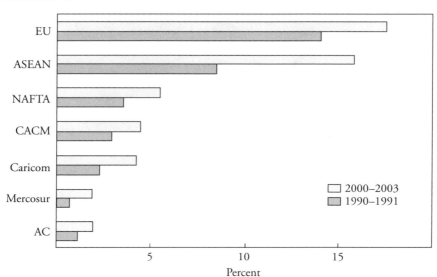

Percent

Source: ECLAC, Division of International Trade and Integration, on the basis of official data.
a. The figures given are annual averages.

country risk ratings in Mercosur—in particular those of the largest economies of the bloc—until shortly before Argentina's default is a good illustration of this point (see figure 6-4).[2]

In fact, empirical studies have shown the existence of strong interconnections among financial markets in emerging countries that are clearly influenced by geographic proximity, trade links, and economic policy similarities.[3] Moreover, there is evidence that a country's currency crises are more closely associated with exchange rate misalignments with a partner in a trade agreement than with the rest of the world.[4] However, when contagion is measured through the impact of

2. One exception is the absence of contagion in the final phases of the Argentine crisis. This could be attributed to the "absence of surprise" as events unfolded, which enabled investors to pre-pare themselves by reallocating their assets gradually. During the preceding months, however, there was an impact on other countries in the region, and during 2002 the crisis severely affected Uruguay. Although there are different definitions of contagion, references here are to a situation in which a crisis in another country increases the probability of crisis in the home country, after con-trolling for the economic fundamentals (Eichengreen, Rose, and Wyplosz, 1996).
3. Inter-American Development Bank (2002, chap. 7).
4. Fernández-Arias, Panizza, and Stein (2002).

Figure 6-4. *Country Risk: December 1993–September 2004*

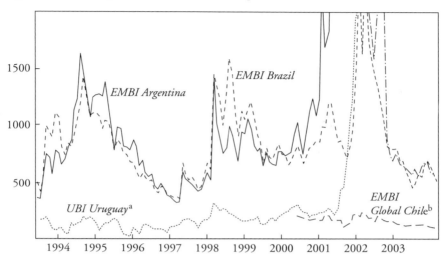

Source: ECLAC, on the basis of data from JP Morgan Securities and the Uruguay Republic Pension Fund (AFAP).
a. Uruguay Bond Index (UBI). Since May 2003, Uruguay has changed the reference bond basket.
b. Global Bond 2009 Sovereign Spread over United States Treasury (UST) bond yields.
EMBI = Emerging Markets Bond Index.

a change in one country's capital flows on the other partners' flows, the evidence is more ambiguous.[5]

These trade-related and financial externalities notwithstanding, their presence has not generated a reciprocal demand for permanent macroeconomic cooperation. The reason is simple: although the expansion of intraregional trade was regarded as a long-lasting phenomenon, every time one of the two largest partners was overtaken by a crisis, the most prevalent reaction was a fear of financial spillovers. In such situations, the usual response of policymakers in the other countries has been to send out signals that differentiate them from their distressed neighbor in an effort to influence the mainstream perception on financial markets.[6] Their reason for doing so is that the adverse effects to be expected in the short run have been of such a magnitude, and the decisionmaking horizon

---

5. This issue is described in more detail in Inter-American Development Bank (2002, chap. 7).
6. The extreme case was the Argentine government's behavior in 1999 after Brazil's devaluation.

for governmental and private sector actors has shortened to such a point, that the ratio between the perceived costs and benefits of integration has grown drastically worse.

Dependence or Interdependence?

Statistics on interdependence for the bloc as a whole often conceal considerable differences between countries, which are often due to differences in their size. Figures 6-5 and 6-6 indicate the level of dependence or interdependence in different regional agreements based on two indicators: (1) distribution of regional GDP, and (2) intensity of reciprocal trade between the largest partner in each agreement and the rest of the bloc. The figures show that there are considerable differences in country size within the North American Free Trade Agreement (NAFTA) and Mercosur. In such cases, there are fewer coordination incentives for the largest country. In NAFTA, in particular, it is unthinkable that the United States would be prepared to coordinate its fiscal and monetary policies with Canada and Mexico. Although concern for its neighbors may lead the United States to help them in critical situations such as Mexico's "tequila crisis" in 1994, it is extremely unlikely that it would ever agree to have Mexican or Canadian representatives sitting on the U.S. Federal Reserve Board.

Other Reasons for Coordination

Incentives for cooperation are not only related to size and economic interdependence. Beyond trade and financial interdependence, there may be other economic or political reasons for coordination among members of an agreement. European integration is a clear example of this. But without doubt, large size differences among the partners reduce the incentives for coordination. Additional motives for coordination may include cyclical synchronism, its importance in introducing discipline in the face of domestic pressures, and its use as a mechanism to reduce macroeconomic volatility and to build up government credibility within a country.

Cyclical synchronism. Benefits from macroeconomic coordination increase (or the costs decrease) to the extent that the countries belonging to the regional agreement face similar situations. If cycles are synchronous, economic policy decisions will be similar, and therefore the cost of forgoing autonomous policies will be lower.

Countries in subregional blocs in Latin America have historically registered low synchronism in economic cycles, at least when they are compared against countries of the European Union and the Association of Southeast Asian Nations

Figure 6-5. *Regional GDP Distribution, 1990–2003*[a]

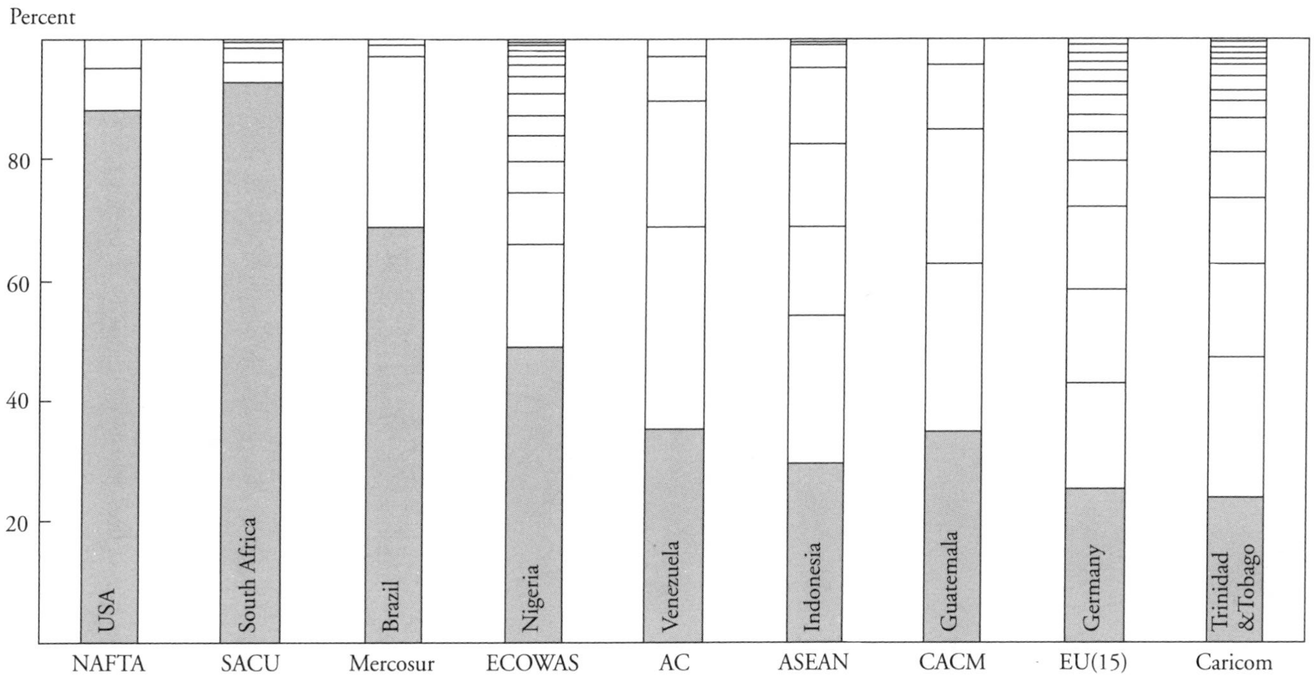

Percent

Source: ECLAC, Division of International Trade and Integration, on the basis of official data for Mercosur, AC, CACM and Caricom; and World Development Indicators 2004 for NAFTA (North American Free Trade Agreement); SACU (Southern African Customs Union), EU (European Union), and ECOWAS (Economic Community of West African States).

a. Annual average.

Figure 6-6. *Degree of Interdependence of Core Countries in Some Integration Schemes, 1989 and 2002*[a]

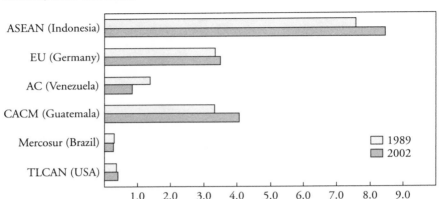

Source: ECLAC, Division of International Trade and Integration, based on IDB (2002) *Integration 2002 Report*, chap. 7 (box 7.1), p. 48.

a.The indicator was estimated with the following formula:

$$\varphi_{int} = \left\{ \left(\frac{X_{jb}}{X_{jTOT}} \right) \middle/ \left[\frac{\sum_{\substack{n=i \\ j \neq i}} X_{ij}}{\sum_{\substack{n=i \\ j \neq i}} X_{iTOT}} \right] \right\}.$$

The formula shows the ratio between the exports of the larger country *j* to the regional integration agreement *B*, and the sum of the exports of the rest of the member countries *i* to the larger country *j*. In both cases, exports are normalized by the respective total exports. In parentheses, the left axis shows the larger country in terms of its share of regional GDP, considering figure 6-7.

(ASEAN) (see figure 6-7). Within this context, the CACM countries are found to have a relatively high level of correlation, while Mercosur and the Andean Community evidence the lowest level of synchronism in the region.[7] Nevertheless, some studies suggest that, at least in the case of Mercosur, during the 1990s the cycles of the member countries, and particularly those of the two largest partners, were somewhat more closely synchronized than in the past.[8] This has occurred mainly as the result of external financial disturbances that have affected all the countries of the bloc.

Domestic resistance. Similarly, a macroeconomic coordination agreement can serve to implement measures that have met with domestic resistance. However,

7. De la Cuba and Winkelried (2004).
8. Lacunza and others (2003); Fanelli and González Rozada (2003); Machinea (2003a).

Figure 6-7. *Cyclical Synchronism: Weighted Average of Correlation Coefficient, 1962–2002*

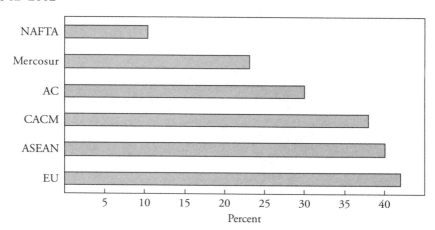

Source: Machinea (2003c).

the importance of the role of regional agreements in imposing some degree of internal discipline depends on whether the agreement is perceived by the actors involved as being advantageous for the country. While this has been the case for Europe, it has not necessarily been so for Latin America and the Caribbean.

"Borrowing credibility." It is not clear whether macroeconomic policy coordination is an effective means of building domestic credibility in the region. Unlike in Europe, it is difficult to find in the region countries that have strong enough reputations to generate credibility for other nations by partnering with them in the area of macroeconomic policy. Even more important, countries in Latin America do not have strong enough reputations to emerge unharmed from an association with a country that has a history of severe instability.

Finally, while a country's volatility affects its partners in different ways, exchange rate volatility typically attracts the most attention because of its effects on trade and on the political economy of the integration process. As can be seen in figure 6-8, although exchange rate volatility is not so intense in Central America, it is particularly severe in Mercosur and is also quite significant in the Andean Community, the two largest economic blocs in Latin America.

There are several reasons for these large exchange rate volatilities, notable among them the different domestic macroeconomic policies and the coexistence of different exchange rate regimes. In particular, the coexistence of dollarization in

Figure 6-8. *Volatility of Bilateral Real Exchange Rates*

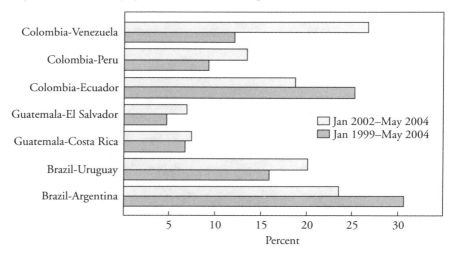

Percent

Source: ECLAC, on the basis of official data.

Ecuador and convertibility in Argentina with more flexible exchange regimes in the rest of Latin America explains part of the volatility from 1998 on, the period in which the countries of the region experienced similar large financial shocks.[9]

The potential advantages of macroeconomic coordination as a means of reducing economic volatility, in particular exchange rate volatility, and improving economic performance in the members of a regional agreement are discussed in the following sections.

Macroeconomic Coordination: The Experience of Mercosur from a Latin American Perspective

Regarding the size of the economies involved, Mercosur is Latin America's largest integration initiative to date. When it was created, the member countries committed themselves to structuring a customs union, which, over time, was to develop into a common market.

The difficulties that Mercosur is currently experiencing, however, raise serious doubts about the possibility of achieving significant progress on integration in

---

9. See Machinea (2003a) and Fanelli and González-Rosada (2003) for a detailed discussion of the Mercosur case.

the near future. Questions about its functioning, and even its usefulness for the economic development of its members, have been raised with particular force in recent years. To differing degrees and intensities, many of the obstacles facing Mercosur are similar to those being encountered in other integration agreements in the region.

From that vantage point, this section first analyzes how the Mercosur integration process has evolved. It then looks at recent changes in the nature and intensity of the interdependence among the countries of this bloc. Finally, the main lessons to be learned from the failed attempt at macroeconomic coordination made in 2000 are discussed.

Evolution of the Integration Process: From Hope to Disenchantment

Mercosur was established in 1991, and by the middle of that decade the integration process was already having difficulty meeting the commitments it had made to eliminate nontariff barriers, adopt a common external tariff, establish special import regimes and a common customs code, and harmonize procedures to deal with unfair trade practices. The virtual absence of any supranational institutional structure was a significant factor in these difficulties.

The difficulties went largely unnoticed while the two largest countries of the bloc were experiencing rapid growth. In 1997, however, there was a significant break in the trend toward the elimination of trade restrictions, which occurred when Brazil, in order to curb the growth of its current account deficit caused by a sharp appreciation of the exchange rate, decided to impose general import restrictions, which also applied to its partners under the agreement.[10]

The negative macroeconomic performance of the past few years has been transmitted to the countries' intraregional trade. As a result, intraregional trade as a share of total trade fell from 25.3 percent in 1998 (before the international financial crisis began to affect the region) to 12 percent in 2003.

As a result of the deterioration in the macroeconomic situation triggered by events in the international arena from 1998 on, the weaknesses of the integration process became more apparent as the recession increased the countries' sensitivity to trade problems and caused relations between the member countries to worsen even further, undermining their countries' already debatable willingness to create even a minimal institutional framework and significantly weakening not only the integration process but also trade relations within the bloc.

---

10. As a matter of fact, in 1992, again in a context of significant exchange rate appreciation, Argentina had already resorted to the temporary establishment of a 10 percent statistical duty on imports of any origin.

As was discussed in the previous section, the conditions for extending integration and establishing macroeconomic cooperation mechanisms within Mercosur, and in Latin America in general, are comparatively less favorable than those that prevailed in the process that led to the establishment of the European Union. First, the degree of trade integration that can be attained by Mercosur, and for that matter the other integration schemes in Latin America, is unlikely to approach the levels seen in the European Union or NAFTA for a number of reasons, including one quite simple factor: the enormous differences in the size of their respective markets. Second, cyclical synchronism is still quite low, and even though the cycles have become more synchronized in the 1990s, this has mainly been the result of spillovers arising from external financial disturbances. Third, the extreme volatility of exchange rates, added to the deep economic crises of recent years and the fact that the region has grown more slowly than the rest of the world, have led to a proliferation of intraregional trade restrictions, significantly weakening not only the integration process but also trade and political relations within the bloc.

Fourth, in times of crisis, the political horizon is shortened to a minimum and the authorities' discount rate soars. It is therefore not surprising that the benefits of integration, which tend to make themselves felt over the long term, appear to be outweighed by its costs, which are evident in the short term. There are two clear manifestations of this effect. On the one hand, whenever sharp macroeconomic fluctuations in either of the two largest members of the bloc have significantly altered intraregional trade flows in ways that have adversely affected their neighbors, sectoral pressures and the public's reaction have inevitably given rise to policy responses oriented toward counteracting those effects. These policy measures have generally been aimed at restraining imports from the country that, either because of the presence of recessionary conditions or because of a devaluation of its currency, was in a better competitive position in the regional market. On the other hand, every time a country is in deep trouble, the partners' foreseeable reaction is to try to distance themselves from the neighbor that is experiencing difficulties. As a result, instead of creating demand for coordination, financial interdependence has repeatedly generated political conflicts within the bloc.

It may be argued that if progress were made in macroeconomic coordination, intraregional trade would be strengthened, the correlation of the countries' cycles would be increased, and favorable conditions would be created for deepening their integration.[11] It is clear, however, that such cooperation requires a minimum set of political and economic conditions that have thus far not been seen in Mercosur. Moreover, in view of the scale of economic problems, the

11. Frankel and Rose (1996).

political will of the relevant parties becomes a critical factor. In addition to facing unfavorable economic conditions, Mercosur has also exhibited weaknesses on the political front.[12]

At this writing in 2006, Mercosur is in trouble. The remaining exceptions to the common external tariff have prevented consolidation of the customs union and, what is more, new nontariff barriers have appeared. Although a technical secretariat was created in 2002 and, more recently, a Commission of Permanent Representatives was established, given these bodies' small budgets and diffuse functions, the bloc still has virtually no institutional structure.

The Attempt at Macroeconomic Coordination in 2000: Lessons from a Failed Experiment

Although the need to coordinate macroeconomic policies is explicitly stated in the first article of the Treaty of Asunción, which sanctioned the creation of Mercosur, given the relative weakness of the macroeconomic spillovers among the countries of the bloc, in the beginning the demand for coordination was not significant.

However, in 2000 an attempt to advance in this direction was made that, although overtaken by later events, set a precedent that may be useful to analyze. The ministers of finance and the presidents of the countries' central banks agreed in their first meeting of that year: (1) to establish common targets on macroeconomic matters and in financial services; (2) to develop performance indicators based on a common methodology; (3) to begin regular publication of a series of harmonized fiscal indicators starting in September 2000; (4) to set jointly agreed goals in relation to the fiscal deficit, the public debt, and inflation in March 2001; (5) to complete and update a survey and comparative analysis of current regulations relating to financial and capital markets, including payment systems, with a view to moving toward the integration of these markets; and (6) to establish a macroeconomic monitoring group made up of high-level officials whose first task would be to evaluate the consistency of the joint methodology to be used to prepare the indicators.

It proved possible to harmonize the statistics on the fiscal deficit, public debt, and prices in a relatively short span of time. Then, in December 2000, the ministers of finance and the presidents of the countries' central banks met in Florianopolis, Brazil, to set targets for the fiscal deficit, public debt, and inflation that would enter into force beginning in 2002. The target set for prices was a ceiling rate for the annual increase in the consumer price index (CPI) of 5 percent

---

12. The difficulties of deepening integration in the economic sphere have been an obstacle for strengthening the political relationships within the bloc.

until 2005 and 4 percent beginning in 2006 (in this case on the basis of the core inflation rate of the CPI, to be estimated using a harmonized methodology). As for fiscal matters, a maximum value of 3 percent was set for the consolidated deficit, and a downward trend was projected for the debt/GDP ratio starting in 2005, with a maximum limit of 40 percent to be reached by 2010 at the latest. The discussion of goals related to the external sector, including targets for the current account and the short-term external debt, was left for the future.

At the meeting in Florianopolis it was not possible, however, to make significant progress in developing incentives for compliance with these goals. What the authorities did succeed in agreeing upon was that any country that deviated from these goals should inform the macroeconomic monitoring group of the corrective measures it would take to return to the established limits, and that it would have to apply those measures within one year from the date of presentation to the group. It was also agreed that the ministers of finance and the presidents of the countries' central banks could make public comments on such measures as they deemed appropriate.

Two lessons can be learned from this experience. First, it was demonstrated that it is possible to achieve results fairly quickly if people at the highest political decisionmaking levels are involved and if capable technical bodies exist. A second lesson is of a more negative nature and concerns the rewards and penalties required to ensure compliance with the goals. In this connection, the results were not very significant. This issue may not be a serious drawback in the initial phases of an experiment of this nature, but it brought to light the absence of effective mechanisms for securing compliance with the commitments assumed.

The deterioration of the Argentine economy that culminated in its collapse in late 2001 and 2002, coupled with the worsening situation in the other countries of the bloc, led to the introduction of new trade restrictions, exceptions to the common external tariff, and heated disputes among member countries. As a result, this first attempt at coordination came to an abrupt end. The conclusion is clear: when there is excessive instability and high exchange rate volatility in one of the countries concerned, especially one of the larger ones, macroeconomic cooperation becomes unworkable.

The Future of Macroeconomic Coordination in Latin America and the Caribbean:

Is it possible to increase the demand for coordination? Above all else, individual countries need to have responsible macroeconomic policies that guarantee a minimum level of stability. It is impossible to coordinate policies without reasonably stable economies. Viewed from this standpoint, stability can be considered, to a certain extent, an initial basic condition for the emergence of a demand for policy coordination between neighboring countries.

In principle, the strengthening of trade integration tends to generate greater incentives for coordination. However, regional experience shows that reinforcing such integration alone is not sufficient to increase the demand for coordination. It is therefore essential to find other incentives for this coordination, and especially for ensuring compliance with the agreements reached by the parties.

Bearing this need in mind, this section presents an analysis of the main obstacles and opportunities for macroeconomic cooperation and coordination in Latin America. The discussion first looks briefly at the question of where to start and how to gradually shift from "softer" to "harder" forms of coordination. It then moves on to the issue of rules and incentives for coordination. The difficulties raised by exchange rate volatility as well as the type of macroeconomic policy mix called for under exchange rate floats, the currently prevailing regime in the region, are then examined. Finally, the feasibility and implications of the integration of domestic financial markets, as well as the role that subregional stabilization funds or other financial instruments might play, are explored.

Where to Begin

Given the complexity of the factors involved, macroeconomic coordination processes can only progress gradually. There is consensus about this issue in the literature, which is also supported by the European experience. Periodic meetings, exchange of information, standardization of statistics, and the creation of supranational forums for policy debate are necessary procedures for gradually building the mutual trust and knowledge that are critical to avoiding the "prisoner's dilemma" and the creation of incentives for opportunistic behavior.[13]

Seen from this vantage point, the exchange of information can be considered an initial way of implementing cooperation policies. Although information exchange is a "soft" form of coordination that has no direct effect on macroeconomic performance, it does enable countries to become better acquainted, improve their understanding of each other's specificities and circumstances, and achieve a common vision, which is far from happening in Latin American integration processes.

13. Ghymers (2001). The Macroeconomic Dialogue Network (REDIMA), an ECLAC initiative launched in 2000, has played an important role in promoting this approach, albeit with mixed results, in Mercosur, the Andean Community, and CACM, the three Latin American subregional integration agreements.

The integration process will be strengthened if countries set up and maintain a supranational technical forum in which they can meet regularly and systematically take on certain tasks (such as the standardization of statistics and harmonization of indicators), assess other experiences, analyze various aspects of the integration process, and, when the time comes, formulate criteria and options for convergence. This forum could function informally, but its institutionalization would send a strong signal of the importance attached to the goal of coordination.

Nevertheless, if there is political will to make progress toward integration, a long-term approach should be adopted. The establishment of mutual confidence should not be taken for granted but should be seen as the first objective to be achieved through an "institutional investment" that requires the allocation of resources, concrete action, and continuity over time.

During this initial phase of "soft" coordination, it is crucial to achieve a minimum level of national macroeconomic stability (exchange rate stability in particular), especially for the larger members of the bloc, which because of their size bear the responsibility of its leadership. Only if this minimum objective is achieved will more concrete coordination mechanisms appear to be an attractive way of reinforcing the credibility of the larger countries and of enabling the smaller countries to "buy credibility" for their own macroeconomic policies.

Toward a "Harder" Form of Coordination

The main objective of the second stage of macroeconomic coordination is to sustain stability in the long term. This requires the adoption of more explicit coordination mechanisms. As suggested by the European experience, this implies establishing goals for the convergence of a set of macroeconomic variables.

The convergence of certain variables at predetermined values established by common agreement does not guarantee that these values will be maintained in the future. Furthermore, a commitment to hold the fiscal deficit below a certain level may limit a country's capacity to implement countercyclical policies. Sustaining macroeconomic stability over the long run requires institutions that encourage fiscal and monetary responsibility, nominal price flexibility, and factor mobility. Some scholars therefore believe that carrying out the institutional reforms needed to ensure lasting stability in each country is more important than setting convergence objectives.[14]

However, as the experiences of some countries in the region show, institutional reforms are not irreversible either. Thus, although such reforms are surely

14. See, for example, Eichengreen (1998).

vital, mutual commitment to the convergence of certain key variables at credible levels may enhance the policy consistency and stability of the economies involved. In addition to exchange rate issues, which are discussed later, the question of macroeconomic convergence raises other matters, such as the fiscal situation, inflation, and, given the region's external vulnerability, its exposure to changes in international market conditions.

Fiscal convergence is necessary to prevent any one country's lack of discipline from damaging its own financial market, increasing its country risk, and, via contagion effects, impairing the flow of capital to the region as a whole. Given its intertemporal dimension, the effort to achieve convergence should include the fiscal deficit and the public debt, measured as proportions of GDP. To avoid curtailing the possibility of implementing countercyclical policies, the deficit that should be taken into account for these purposes is the structural deficit (adjusted for cyclical variations). In light of the region's track record in such matters and its governments' lesser borrowing capacity, the limit for the structural deficit should be lower than the level set in Europe. For countries that are initially above the limit, the adjustment period allowed to align themselves with the target should be reasonably brief. A low deficit does not, however, guarantee a government's solvency if its debt is too high—hence the need to place a ceiling on the public debt. Since satisfying this condition may not be feasible immediately, the adjustment period allowed will have to be longer than the period set for convergence on the deficit target.

Because high inflation also tends to contribute to volatility, the first objective of setting an inflation target is to reduce uncertainty. In floating exchange rate regimes, inflation targets also help to curb volatility in the nominal exchange rate.

The external vulnerability of the region is precisely what makes it necessary for macroeconomic coordination to include targets for the external sector.[15] These targets would be the current account deficit and short-term external debt. Fiscal policy may not be sufficient to achieve these objectives in the face of large capital flows. In the event of massive capital inflows, for instance, it might be necessary to impose restrictions on short-term capital movements.

Rules and Incentives for Coordination

Establishing explicit macroeconomic coordination mechanisms—through, for example, the adoption of convergence targets—will be useful only if those targets are feasible and if compliance with the relevant agreements can be enforced to a reasonable extent. The need to ensure that targets are feasible raises the

15. This is suggested by Lavagna and Giambiagi (2000), Zahler (2001), and others.

question of just how strict the rules should be, while the need to enforce compliance is linked to the issue of incentives.

Adopting rules that are too strict could make compliance excessively costly or simply impossible under certain circumstances; knowledge is never complete, and there is no way of predicting all eventualities. Thus a certain degree of policy flexibility has to be maintained in order to deal with unexpected critical situations. Excessive flexibility, however, could undermine the credibility of the commitments undertaken.

Striking the right balance is not simple in any case, but especially not for the countries of the region. On the one hand, adopting policies based on strict rules seems to be the only option for governments whose good reputations are often in doubt. On the other hand, many such policies in the region have failed to take account of the intrinsic vulnerability of the economies involved and have therefore been unsuccessful because policymakers lack enough maneuvering room to respond to unexpected shocks. The collapse of the convertibility regime in Argentina is the most recent example of this type of situation.

In any event, integration agreements aimed at furthering macroeconomic coordination in the region can clearly afford to grant little leeway in the establishment of common targets. It therefore becomes vital to determine which alternatives could be used to stimulate cooperation.

The high costs of irresponsible policies in the current context of economic globalization already constitute an incentive for macroeconomic discipline, which is also encouraged by the conditionality of agreements with the IMF and other multilateral credit agencies.[16] To a certain extent, these factors act implicitly as exogenous coordination variables.

More explicit use could be made of incentives at the international level in promoting macroeconomic coordination. For instance, multilateral financial institutions could play an important role if program design took into account the regional agreements already in place.[17] What is more, convergence targets would be much more influential if the criteria used for setting them were agreed with those same institutions. Similarly, the rules established by the Bank for International Settlements for the prudent regulation of national financial systems could be adapted and used as a basis for regional financial

---

16. In Mercosur, for instance, all countries have concluded agreements with the IMF in recent years.

17. The Brazilian devaluation of 1999, which was supported by the IMF, and its impact on neighboring countries provides a good example of the negative externalities that the IMF could help to mitigate if its recommendations took account of regional interdependence.

integration agreements. It would be a mistake to ignore external incentives because of potential political susceptibilities, especially when internal incentives are weak.

Indeed, the European experience shows that the most powerful coordination incentive, especially for smaller countries, is the enhanced reputation associated with achieving convergence targets. Unfortunately, this incentive may not apply in the Latin America and Caribbean region for some time. For economic agents, the main sign that a government is implementing its macroeconomic policy responsibly is compliance with agreements concluded with the IMF and other multilateral financial institutions, and this does not seem about to change anytime soon.

The gains afforded by reducing exchange rate volatility with major trading partners are another incentive for coordination. Of course, the importance of this factor will increase in proportion to the volume of intraregional trade. Although this factor is present in the integration agreements in Latin America and the Caribbean, it clearly cannot come to be as important as it has been in the European experience.[18]

Another incentive that has also been considered in Europe is the threat of direct sanctions (either financial or of other sorts). For this kind of incentive to be effective, noncompliance must entail possible exclusion from the agreement. When the number of countries involved is too small or their economic size is too different, it is extremely unlikely that direct sanctions can be enforced. In Latin America this is clearly the case with Mercosur: the exclusion of Uruguay or Paraguay would have enormous costs for the integration project, while the departure of Brazil or Argentina would signify the end of the agreement altogether. Direct sanctions do not seem easy to impose in the other Latin American subregional agreements either.

Although moral sanctions are "softer" than financial penalties, they are also an incentive worth considering. In principle, the fact that their cost is tolerable but not negligible makes moral sanctions viable and capable of making some contribution to the objective of coordination. One possibility is to set up an independent assessment committee, made up of regional and international experts, tasked with periodically checking compliance with agreements and

18. See Ghymers (2002). In retrospect, however, it can be seen that direct sanctions have not played such an important role in the European Union. In fact, in recent years, instances of noncompliance by some countries of the bloc have gone unpunished. It is quite clear that the reason for this is that the countries concerned, Germany and France in particular, are among the most important ones in the union.

making recommendations where appropriate. Logic would dictate that the assessments should be public in order to have some effect.

It does not seem too bold to conclude that the incentives mentioned here are not enough to make macroeconomic cooperation an attractive option for existing subregional integration agreements in Latin America and the Caribbean. This issue is discussed again later, after a review of the available alternatives for limiting exchange rate volatility and an analysis of the viability of subregional funds in that context.

Options for Limiting Exchange Rate Volatility

It is impossible to deepen an integration process without curtailing variations in the exchange rates of the countries involved, given their direct influence on trade and the political economy of integration.[19] In a significant sample of developed and developing countries, Fernández-Arias, Panizza, and Stein observed that the negative effects of exchange rate mismatches tend to be greater in relation to other countries within the region than with the rest of the world;[20] this is probably attributable to the part played by "regional goods"— that is, goods that, for different reasons, are mainly traded within the region where they are produced.

In principle, it is to be expected that, as a result of increased uncertainty, both the level of the exchange rate and exchange rate fluctuations would have adverse effects on foreign trade. This is especially true if there is high volatility and if there are no adequate hedging instruments to cover risk, as is common in less-developed countries.[21] In the specific case of Mercosur, many applied studies have found that variations in the exchange rate do have some effect on intra-regional trade.[22]

Significant variations in exchange rates also affect the political economy of the process. When the exchange rate is devalued in a given country (especially a large country within the region), the appreciation of the other countries' exchange rates shifts the internal balance of forces in favor of anti-integration sectors, generates more protectionist pressures, and reduces governments' capacity for cooperation. The negative reactions are much more dramatic during a regional recession than during a period of growth.

---

19. For a detailed discussion, see Machinea (2003b).
20. See Fernández-Arias, Panizza, and Stein (2002).
21. This hypothesis is supported by several empirical studies (Devlin and others, 2001; Estevadeordal, Frantz, and Saez, 2001; Giordano and Monteagudo, 2002).
22. Heymann and Navajas (1991, 1998).

There are various causes of fluctuations in the exchange rate. At the national level, monetary and fiscal excesses are obviously a major determining factor. In a context of high capital mobility, the effects manifest themselves primarily in public and external debt (especially short-term debt). External structural disturbances affect the real equilibrium exchange rate as well. When such disturbances are asymmetrical—that is, when they affect the various countries involved in the integration process in differing ways—then there is a change in the real equilibrium exchange rates between those countries.

Domestic fundamentals and external disturbances are not the only causes of exchange rate variability in the short and long terms, however. Under conditions of high capital mobility, the exchange market behaves much like any other financial assets market. As pointed out by Frankel and Rose, asymmetrical access to relevant information, imperfect transmission of information between market participants, and their heterogeneous nature may give rise to herd behavior or bandwagon effects that could trigger sharp appreciations or devaluations in nominal and real exchange rates.[23]

Last, the implications of having coexisting different exchange rate regimes must also be considered. It is not particularly controversial to state that nominal wages and prices are not completely flexible, that purchasing power parities cannot be accurately determined, and that nominal devaluations account, in large part, for the performance of the real exchange rate.[24] The exchange rate regime is therefore a relevant factor in accounting for the real exchange rate, and the coexistence of different systems affects real exchange rate variations across countries. This manifests itself when countries from a given region experience a symmetrical external disturbance that changes the equilibrium exchange rate of all the countries in relation to the rest of the world without altering the equilibrium parity among them.

Regardless of its causes, exchange rate volatility is a formidable barrier to moving forward with integration. The question is how to control it. Monetary union is the most expedient means since, by definition, it eliminates exchange rate variations between the countries involved. For economic and political reasons, however, this option is not feasible within the subregional integration groupings in Latin America and the Caribbean.

With monetary union ruled out, at least for the foreseeable future, it is vital to consider alternative options. As previously stated, the coexistence of different exchange rate systems contributes to large exchange rate variations resulting

23. Frankel and Rose (1995).
24. See Froot and Rogoff (1995); and Obstfeld (2000).

from common external disturbances. In fact, floating regimes are prevalent in most Latin American countries at present.

Given the fact that international financial and commodities markets continue to be highly unstable, the currency float prevailing in the region seems to be the most advisable option. In this respect, Eichengreen and Taylor showed that the variability of exchange rates is lessened when countries adopt floating exchange rate systems and steer monetary policy toward a particular inflation rate (inflation targeting).[25] The explanation behind this phenomenon is that, in most cases, countries with fixed exchange rates face rather abrupt exchange rate adjustments when they abandon exchange rate parity.

However, as noted by Calvo and Reinhart, the difficulties associated with flexible exchange rates should not be underestimated.[26] On the one hand, it is true that a float facilitates adjustments in the equilibrium rate when circumstances call for it. On the other hand, it is equally true that the fluctuations permitted by this regime, particularly in the context of heightened capital mobility, are not always due to "fundamental" reasons, at least in the short and medium terms. In principle, the advantage of adjusting the real equilibrium exchange rate more quickly comes at the cost of greater uncertainty.

Besides, in countries where dollar-denominated debt is widespread, whether in the public or private sector, the problems that arise with abrupt fluctuations in the exchange rate are significant, owing to their effects on financial assets. If dollarization is so widespread that it encompasses bank claims and, above all, if deposits are dollarized as well, then the situation becomes even more complicated: the likelihood that an unforeseen devaluation would trigger a currency and financial crisis and prompt a drastic slowdown in production levels increases dramatically.[27]

In addition to the challenges posed by a floating regime in reducing the variability of the exchange rate in each country, its implications for the rest of the region must also be considered. A floating exchange rate system tends to facilitate exchange rate stability among the countries of a given region when all of the countries are affected similarly by external shocks. However, exchange rate flexibility increases variability when disturbances, whether external or internal, are asymmetrical.

An analysis by Fanelli and González Rozada of the cyclical co-movements of Argentina, Brazil, and Uruguay offers two important findings in this connec-

25. Eichengreen and Taylor (2002).
26. Calvo and Reinhart (2002).
27. See Rozenwurcel (2003).

tion.[28] Although the authors focus on Mercosur, its applicability in the rest of the region is more than plausible. They find that common external shocks arising from volatility in international financial markets are an important factor in explaining the common component shared by the economic cycles of the three countries and that the spillovers among them are considerable. They also find, however, that the idiosyncratic component accounts for most of the cycle of each country (approximately 85 percent), leaving only 15 percent to be explained by the common component.[29]

The large size of the idiosyncratic component present in the cycles of the members of the bloc reveals significant differences in their respective production structures, in addition to the existence of marked asymmetries in the shocks they are exposed to, as well as a lack of policy coordination. An immediate consequence of this is that, although they have similar exchange rate regimes, significant sources of exchange rate volatility persist among Mercosur partners.

A second conclusion to be drawn is that if countries belonging to a trading bloc decide to coordinate their macroeconomic policies and adopt common macroeconomic targets, this could certainly help reduce exchange rate fluctuations, even though the exchange rate itself may not be a target. In fact, policy differences among the various countries are responsible for much of the lack of synchronization in their economic cycles. Therefore, coordinating macroeconomic policy would not only deactivate an important source of instability in each country, but would also eliminate one of the mechanisms that amplifies external shocks.

Coordination under Floating Exchange Rate Regimes

Given that floating regimes are inherently unstable, if exchange rate volatility is to be reduced a managed float is preferable to a free float. Nevertheless, in order to manage the float, the authorities must intervene in the foreign exchange market, and in order for them to do this, sufficient reserves must be available and monetary effects must not put pressure on prices.

In truth, central bank interventions can have different objectives. At present, China and other Asian countries, for example, have aimed their exchange rate policies at maintaining a devalued real exchange rate as part of their development strategy.[30] The pros and cons of this approach fall outside the scope of this chapter. Nonetheless, according to Rodrik, one of the few stylized facts that can

---

28. Fanelli and González Rozada (2003).

29. A common external shock could have a different impact on the partners as a result of idiosyncratic reasons related to the economic and financial structure.

30. See Dooley, Fokerts-Landau, and Garber (2003, 2004).

be deduced from a careful analysis of concrete experiences of economic development is that policy prescriptions "travel" poorly from one country to the next.[31]
In particular, considering the economic conditions needed to make a policy of
this nature viable, in terms of both reserve accumulation and inflation, such an
alternative in most Latin American countries is unlikely to materialize.

Therefore, the main aim of exchange rate policies in the region should be to
smooth out short-term swings, which generate "noise" that engenders uncertainty and has a negative effect on expectations and economic performance. Any
intervention on the part of monetary authorities, though, must not hinder
adjustments in the real exchange rate to accommodate disturbances that undermine its long-term equilibrium.

At any rate, a managed float entails a trade-off in terms of the objectives of
monetary policy, since the monetary effects of exchange rate interventions can
lead to inflation. This issue cannot be taken lightly in Latin America, where
many countries have a long history of inflation.

In particular, as long as financial deepening continues to be very limited and
dollarization rather widespread, as is the case in many Latin American countries,
managed floats may cease to be feasible when strong external shocks occur.
What should be done in such extreme cases? One possibility is to let the
exchange rate float freely. If the real parity is at a reasonable level and if fiscal
and monetary policies are managed responsibly, regulating short-term capital
movements seems to be a better option.

Although restrictions on capital flows continue to be a subject of heated
debate, considering the high volatility exhibited by globalized financial markets,
there are good theoretical reasons for using them.[32] Moreover, empirical evidence
suggests that, although they have costs and do not work perfectly, when implemented sensibly such restrictions can be efficient in moderating flows, modify-
ing their composition, and smoothing out swings in the exchange rate.[33]

Until now, the motivation behind regional integration has not explicitly fig-
ured in this discussion on monetary and exchange rate policy under a floating
regime. However, it is evident that even if all members of a regional agreement
adopt a floating exchange rate, the differences in their monetary and exchange
rate policies may seriously hinder any reduction in the volatility of exchange
rates in the region.

31. Rodrik (2003).
32. See Rodrik (2003); Rogoff (2002); Ffrench-Davis and Larraín (2003); Ocampo and Chiappe (2003); and DeLong (2004).
33. Ffrench-Davis and Villar (2005).

Therefore, if the objective of furthering integration is to be maintained, it is very important—in addition to setting common macroeconomic targets, particularly inflation targets—for the countries to gradually make progress on the coordination of their exchange rate policies, starting with the definition of common criteria for intervention, then moving on to the harmonization of regulations pertaining to capital movements and, possibly, the adoption of a system of currency bands. Of course, in an area as sensitive as this, major advances cannot be expected to occur quickly. However, in principle the countries could agree on a mechanism for consulting with one another concerning possible courses of action to follow in extreme situations. This exercise would not imply any concrete commitments for action, but it would be the starting point for the joint learning process that is needed in order to propose more ambitious objectives later on.

Integration of Regional Financial Systems and Macroeconomic Stability

The existing subregional agreements in Latin America do not, at present, provide any major incentives for financial integration.[34] On the contrary, thus far contagion effects have been the only source of externalities operating between financial systems in the region. Under certain conditions, however, the regional integration of domestic financial systems can generate positive synergies among member countries and can help to reduce macroeconomic volatility.

In fact, the vulnerability of the countries' financial systems is a main source of macroeconomic instability in the region. Raising and harmonizing the regulatory standards of the members' financial markets in accordance with international best practices can therefore be seen as a means of complementing macroeconomic coordination in relation to monetary, fiscal, and exchange rate matters as part of a concerted effort to reduce volatility and deepen regional integration.[35]

The harmonization of financial regulations is a good starting point for the financial integration process because it does not involve any weakening of the independence of national policymakers and institutions. Thus it will not be perceived as a vehicle for contagion among the financial systems of each country.

The contribution that financial harmonization can make to macroeconomic stability is not, however, the only reason for promoting the integration of financial systems at the regional level. In time, this form of integration can also help

---

34. This subject is discussed in depth in Machinea and Rappoport (2004).

35. The fragility of domestic financial systems in the region and the magnitude of the shocks to which they are exposed would seem to indicate that the regulations to be adopted should be stricter than those required to meet the Basel standards. Factors that are not addressed by those standards, such as currency mismatches or public debt risk, should also be taken into account, however. The regulations to be established should therefore be based on modified "Basel plus" standards.

to reduce transaction costs and further the development of a regional capital market. In order for this to occur, however, the harmonization of prudential regulations would have to be extended, during a second stage, to include convergence among other financial institutions. In particular, consideration should be given to the adoption of similar mechanisms for deposit insurance and the creation of a regionwide payments system.

This step, unlike the harmonization of regulations, can indeed affect the countries' risk of contagion, since it would increase the interdependence of their financial systems. The timing of the announcement of such measures is therefore just as important as their proper implementation.

Stabilization Funds and Other Subregional Financial Agreements

There are very good reasons why the majority of the countries in the region have recently adopted floating exchange rate regimes. But the inherent volatility of the exchange rate does not disappear even when the fundamentals are kept in order and monetary policy is managed responsibly. The difficulties that this poses on the domestic level and for regional integration processes are even greater because the countries have a very limited capacity to intervene in order to curb the instability of foreign exchange markets. Macro-level coordination may contribute to achieving this objective, but it is not sufficient in itself.

The European experience of the past few decades shows that various mechanisms for regional cooperation in the exchange rate and financial sphere have played a very important role in stabilizing parities within the region.[36] Of course, in the European case there was another fundamental element that is lacking in the region: in Europe some of the countries had convertible currencies and could thus intervene in exchange markets with their own currencies.[37]

The idea of creating supranational funds to contribute to regional stability has begun to gather momentum in Latin America as a result of the severe crises that erupted on international financial markets in the 1990s.[38] These crises revealed shortcomings and delays in the provision of assistance by the International Monetary Fund to emerging economies, which are attributable only in part to the fact that resources and capacities were overwhelmed by the scale of the events in question. Other reasons include the extensive discussions related to conditionality clauses and, in some cases, to the "wait and see" attitude toward the results of policies. If this diagnosis is correct, regional and subregional funds

36. See Giovannini and Mayer (1991) and Eichengreen and Ghironi (1996).
37. The best-known case is Germany's intervention to defend the value of the franc in 1992.
38. Ocampo (1999); Mistry (1999); Agosin (2001); Machinea (2003a).

that would act as lenders "of first resort" could be an effective complement to the role of the IMF as a lender of last resort.[39]

In fact, a subregional stabilization fund has already been operating in Latin America for quite some time. The Latin American Reserve Fund (Fondo Latino-americano de Reservas, FLAR) was created in 1978 by the countries of the Andean Community. More recently, in 1991, Costa Rica also joined the fund. The main purpose of FLAR is to provide short-term financing aimed at crisis prevention and management. Only shareholders are eligible for loans. FLAR's financing played an important countercyclical role in the recent period of high volatility in the international environment: its loans peaked in 1996 and 1999, helping GDP growth in the Andean countries to recover quite rapidly from two severe external shocks.

From the point of view of subregional integration processes, having a mechanism that could help countries to cushion the effects of external shocks and change investors' perceptions before contagion spreads to their neighbors would be very helpful. In addition to facilitating the adjustment of the country or countries concerned, it would minimize the defensive reactions of partner countries in their attempts to distance themselves from a troubled neighbor. Moreover, subregional funds could serve as an incentive for macroeconomic coordination. This would be the case if compliance with the agreed goals for convergence were required in order for requesting countries to receive assistance from the fund.

The effectiveness of these subregional funds will of course depend on the volume of resources available. Thus, unless developed countries provided support, it seems improbable that funds of this type could soften the impact of simultaneous abrupt reversals in capital flows, particularly when their scale is significant and they trigger contagion effects in neighboring countries of the region (see figure 6-9).

On the other hand, because variations in the terms of trade do not show any significant correlation and the magnitude of their impact is much less than that of financial disturbances, these funds could be quite useful in responding to this type of shock even if resources come only from the countries of the region (see figure 6-10).

With regard to Mercosur, during the 1990s the maximum impact of fluctuations in the terms of trade was on the order of U.S.$6.3 billion in 1999 and for the rest of the decade never reached even one-third of that figure.[40] In contrast, capital outflows amounted to almost U.S.$16 billion in 1999 and exceeded

39. Mistry (1999).
40. These figures are from Machinea (2003a).

Figure 6-9. *Volatility of Private Capital Flows, 1971–2000*[a]

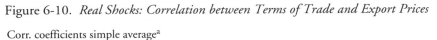

Source: Machinea (2003c).
a. Annual changes > 20 percent of total exports.

Figure 6-10. *Real Shocks: Correlation between Terms of Trade and Export Prices*

Corr. coefficients simple average[a]

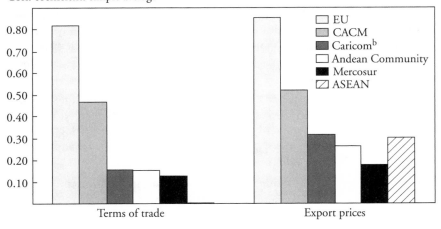

Source: Machinea (2003c).
a. Correlation coefficients are expressed as the simple average of the correlation coefficients among the rates of growth of each country member.
b. Because not all data were available, only four countries were included for Caricom: Guyana, Haiti, Jamaica, and Trinidad and Tobago, which represent 63 percent of regional GDP.

U.S.$10 billion two years previously. Accordingly, a regional fund on the order of U.S.$5 billion (which in 2000 was just over 10 percent of the total reserves of the countries in the region) would be able to offset almost 80 percent of annual losses resulting from variations in the terms of trade on the scale of the worst fluctuations experienced in the 1990s, but its coverage would be scarcely more than 30 percent of annual capital outflows, similar to the highest levels recorded in that decade.[41]

In addition to the level of resources, the creation of subregional funds poses a second problem: the differences in size of the countries that might be involved. In fact, the creation of a fund exclusively for Mercosur, for example, would seem very difficult to implement. Taking into account the fact that Brazil generates approximately 65 percent of the region's GDP and 60 percent of its foreign trade, it would be almost impossible for a fund established solely by the current members to help that country to cushion adverse shocks.

The problem of size asymmetries becomes less severe as the number of countries participating in such a fund rises.[42] The drawback is that a fund formed by member countries of different subregional blocs would make its potential role as an incentive for macroeconomic coordination within each bloc much more difficult to implement.

Conclusions

The progress made in the area of macroeconomic cooperation and coordination in Latin America has so far been rather poor. From an economic viewpoint, the lack of synchronization among cycles weakens demand for coordination. One of the main causes of this is the low level of trade interdependence. In fact, the relative scale of intraregional trade in the existing integration schemes is substantially lower than in other economic blocs, and there is little reason to expect that it will increase very much in the future.

Moreover, since financial integration is virtually nil, the reciprocal externalities existing on this front are due exclusively to contagion effects generated by the frequent shocks brought about by the highly volatile nature of globalized financial markets. Adverse macroeconomic spillovers caused by contagion tend to lead

41. Regional funds could therefore contribute to stabilization but would not eliminate the need to review the role of multilateral financial agencies. In particular, the possibility of offsetting at least part of the effects of capital flow volatility would require, as a minimum, the reformulation by the IMF of its Compensatory Financing Facility to transform it into an automatic disbursement line.

42. Agosin (2001), for example, proposes that all the countries of South America establish a joint fund.

countries to try to differentiate themselves from their neighbors in times of crisis. This in turn exacerbates political tensions and weakens integration processes.

The perception that coordination with regional partners can engender more negative than positive externalities tends to create a vicious cycle. As in the prisoner's dilemma, each country expects that the other will behave in a non-cooperative way and acts accordingly, thereby further undermining incentives for coordination.[43]

Under these conditions, it is justifiable to wonder whether it is reasonable for subregional blocs to continue trying to coordinate their macroeconomic policies. The response depends on the objective being pursued. In other words, it depends on whether or not the aim is to deepen cooperation and further the integration process.

If the decision is not to advance beyond trade linkages, then a free-trade area will be sufficient, and macroeconomic coordination will be mostly unnecessary. This choice implies accepting the idea that the importance of subregional blocs will fade as the conclusion of bilateral free-trade agreements with other countries and regions becomes more frequent.

The other option is to deepen the integration process. This implies that countries are willing to move forward toward the creation of a common market, which in turn would involve agreeing on common protection levels and hence a similar development agenda. For example, relatively high levels of protection for certain production sectors make sense only if the aim is to develop those sectors within the agreement. However, if the production strategies of the various countries differ, it will be difficult for them to form a customs union.

It is clear, therefore, that this option entails accepting some loss of sovereignty and calls for a strong political will to back it up. This is true for any country, but in particular for the larger partners in the agreement, for which the loss of autonomy is more costly. In other words, when economic interdependence among the members of an integration agreement is highly asymmetrical, the larger partners have the responsibility to provide leadership in order to move the integration process forward.

Only under these conditions does it make sense to pursue macroeconomic coordination. However, in this case, the following dilemma arises: in order to deepen integration, macroeconomic policies must be coordinated, but in order for demand for coordination to emerge, a significant degree of economic interdependence is required. While the example of Europe is usually cited to demonstrate that the demand for coordination increases with the level of interdependence, it

43. Ghymers (2002).

is also true that, from an evolutionary perspective, the same example reveals that coordination and interdependence can become complementary factors and can be developed together as part of a recursive process.

Nevertheless, macroeconomic coordination in Latin America entails greater difficulties than those that confronted Europe in the early stages of its integration process. In Latin America there is no exogenous exchange rate coordination mechanism such as prevailed under the Bretton Woods agreements in the initial phase of the European integration process. Moreover, the situation is compounded by the governments' lack of sufficiently strong reputations, the fragility of the countries' domestic financial systems, and the scale of the external shocks now affecting the region. In any case, although concrete forms of coordination will vary according to the specific characteristics of the different integration agreements, there are certain lessons to be drawn from international experience and certain common features of Latin American economic conditions that should be taken into account in all cases.

Macroeconomic coordination can only move forward gradually. The complexity of the factors involved and the need to generate the necessary confidence and mutual understanding make this inevitable. In addition, a basic minimum degree of domestic macroeconomic stability, and above all, exchange rate stability, must be achieved initially, especially among the principal partners in the bloc. Only if this minimum objective is achieved will the perceived benefits of coordination outweigh its costs and the use of more concrete mechanisms have greater appeal.

These more concrete mechanisms, therefore, must wait for a more advanced stage in which it will be possible to set convergence goals so as to consolidate macroeconomic stability and its long-term sustainability. Given the region's external vulnerability, in addition to the usual targets (fiscal deficit, public debt, and inflation), coordination in Latin America must include goals for the external sector relating to such variables as the current account deficit and the short-term external debt. In addition, measures designed to harmonize prudent regulations in financial markets can also contribute to macroeconomic stability.

Obviously, the adoption of convergence goals will contribute to regional stability only if countries strive to fulfill them. Incentives, therefore, are a crucial issue. Apart from the "exogenous" incentives for macroeconomic discipline deriving from agreements with multilateral financial institutions, endogenous incentives must also be present. In the European experience, the chance to build stronger reputations proved to be a powerful incentive for the fulfillment of such goals. But, for the time being at least, this is clearly not true in Latin America. Supervision of compliance with convergence goals by a committee of experts, and dissemination of the corrective measures that it recommends in the event of noncompliance, may gradually lend greater importance to this incentive, but only in the long run. The adoption of effective sanctions does not appear to be a very credible alternative either, especially when the countries do not perceive the costs of being excluded from an integration agreement as being very high.

In sum, for one reason or another, the incentives that were present in the European experience are not strong enough to bring about macroeconomic coordination in Latin America. That being the case, the creation of stabilization funds and other subregional financial mechanisms can become significant additional incentives for macroeconomic coordination. Stabilization funds capable of providing fast-disbursing resources to facilitate the adjustment of member countries to external shocks could prove to be an efficient complement to the role of the IMF. If, in addition, the fulfillment of commitments with regard to convergence targets were one of the requirements for receiving disbursements, these funds could also encourage macroeconomic coordination. Subregional development banks, besides being an effective complement to multilateral lending institutions in certain areas, can play an important role in easing countries' access to the international financial markets. Moreover, they can be an effective tool for promoting intraregional trade and furthering financial integration.

Nevertheless, the establishment of such institutions entails several difficulties. In the case of stabilization funds, in particular, sharp asymmetries can render the fund useless for the larger countries, such as Brazil in Mercosur. The participation of a larger number of countries in the fund would make this problem less severe, but to maintain its role as an incentive for coordination, it would be necessary to increase the number of partners in the bloc. Irrespective of the asymmetries that exist, given the positive correlation of capital flows to countries of the region, the amount of resources needed to cushion the impact of common financial shocks could be very high. However, these funds could be useful for terms-of-trade shocks and, in small and even medium-sized countries, financial shocks as well. Large-scale funds would require support from developed countries, as is the case with the Chiang Mai Initiative in Asia.

Finally, there is the problem of exchange rate volatility. Addressing this phenomenon is crucial in order to achieve deeper integration: the volatility of bilateral exchange rates not only undermines intraregional trade, but also exacerbates political tensions within the integration scheme. The adoption of similar exchange rate regimes helps to alleviate the problem. But the exchange rate floats that have tended to prevail in the region—which have been adopted in order to cope with the persistent instability of international financial markets—exhibit difficulties that should not be underestimated. From the standpoint of regional integration, in particular, the existence of major asymmetries in the shocks to which countries of the region are exposed means that important sources of exchange rate volatility continue to exist. The coordination of macroeconomic policies can help to reduce this volatility but will not eliminate the problem.

For this reason, in addition to ensuring that monetary policy is consistent with the objective of smoothing out exchange rate fluctuations and refraining from ruling out the introduction of restrictions on capital flows, it is very important for the countries to move toward some degree of coordination of their exchange rate regimes. Clearly, in an area as sensitive as this, major advances cannot be expected overnight. Nevertheless, countries could, as a first step, agree on a mechanism for consulting with one another concerning possible courses of action, without committing themselves to specific measures but with a view to setting more ambitious objectives later on.

In any event, the volatility inherent in flotation regimes will not disappear even if the fundamentals are kept in line and appropriate mechanisms for macro-economic policy coordination are in place. These difficulties are compounded by the magnitude of the external shocks to which the countries of the region are exposed. Thus the creation and strengthening of the subregional stabilization funds might serve as a tool for cushioning the impact of these shocks, facilitating macroeconomic cooperation, and advancing toward deeper integration.

References

Agosin, M. 2001. "Fortalecimiento de la cooperación financiera internacional." *Revista de la CEPAL* (ECLAC) no. 57 (April).

Calvo, G., and C. Reinhart. 2002. "Fear of Floating." *Quarterly Journal of Economics,* 117, 2.

De la Cuba, M., and D. Winkelried. 2004. "Una moneda común? Nuevas evidencias para América Latina." Documento de Trabajo 17. Washington: Institute for the Integration of Latin America and the Caribbean (INTAL)–ITD (April).

DeLong, J. B. 2004. "Should We Still Support Untrammeled International Capital Mobility? Or Are Capital Controls Less Evil than We Once Believed?" *The Economists' Voice* 1, no. 1. Berkeley Electronic Press.

Devlin, R., A. Estevadeordal, P. Giordano, J. Monteagudo, and R. Saez. 2001. "Estabilidad macroeconómica, comercio e integración." *Integración & Comercio* no. 13. Buenos Aires: IDB–INTAL.

Dooley, M., D. Fokerts-Landau, and P. Garber. 2003. "An Essay on the Revived Bretton Woods System." Working Paper 9971. Cambridge, Mass.: National Bureau of Economic Research.

———. 2004. "The Revived Bretton Woods System: The Effects of Periphery Intervention and Reserve Management on Interest Rates and Exchange Rates in Center Countries." Working Paper 10332. Cambridge, Mass.: National Bureau of Economic Research.

Eichengreen, B. 1998. "Does Mercosur Need a Single Currency?" Research Paper C98-103. University of California, Berkeley: Center for International and Development Economics.

Eichengreen, B., and F. Ghironi. 1996. "EMU and Enlargement." Prepared for the Conference on Economic and Monetary Union organized by D. G. EcFin of the European Commission, Brussels, March 21–22, 2001. Revised version appears in *EMU and Economic Policy in Europe,* edited by Marco Buti and Andre Sapir. Edward Elgar, 2003.

Eichengreen, B., and A. Taylor. 2002. "The Monetary Consequences of a Free Trade Area of the Americas." Paper prepared for the conference "FTAA and Beyond: Prospects for Integration in the Americas." BID–INTAL/Harvard University, Uruguay.

Eichengreen, B., A. Rose, and C. Wyplosz. 1996. "Contagion Crises." Working Paper 6370. Cambridge, Mass.: National Bureau of Economic Research.

Estevadeordal, A., B. Frantz, and R. Saez. 2001. "Exchange Rate Volatility and International Trade in Developing Countries." Washington: Inter-American Development Bank.

Fanelli, J., and M. González Rozada. 2003. "Business Cycles and Macroeconomic Policy: Coordination in Mercosur." Documento de Trabajo 16/2003. Buenos Aires: Universidad Torcuatro Di Tella, Centro de Investigación en finanzas, Escuela de Economía Empressarial.

Fernández-Arias, E., U. Panizza, and E. Stein. 2002. "Trade Agreements, Exchange Rate Disagreements." Washington: Inter-American Development Bank.

Ffrench-Davis, R., and G. Larraín. 2003. "How Optimal Are the Extremes? Latin American Exchange Rate Policies during the Asian Crises." In *From Capital Surges to Drought: Seeking Stability for Emerging Economies,* edited by R. Ffrench-Davis and S. Griffith-Jones, pp. 245–68. London: Palgrave/Macmillan.

Ffrench-Davis, R., and L. Villar. 2006. "The Capital Account and Real Macroeconomic Stabilization: Chile and Colombia." In *Seeking Growth under Financial Volatility,* edited by R. Ffrench-Davis. New York: Palgrave/Macmillan.

Frankel, J., and A. Rose. 1995. "Empirical Research on Nominal Exchange Rates." In *Handbook of International Economics,* Vol. 3, edited by G. Grossman and K. Rogoff. Amsterdam: Elsevier.

———. 1996. "The Endogeneity of the Optimum Currency Area Criteria." Working Paper 4805. Cambridge, Mass.: National Bureau of Economic Research.

Froot, K., and K. Rogoff. 1995. "Perspectives on PPP and Long-Run Real Exchange Rates." In *Handbook of International Economics,* Vol. 3, edited by G. Grossman and K. Rogoff. Amsterdam: Elsevier.

Ghymers, C. 2000. "La coordinación de las políticas macroeconómicas en la zona euro: orígenes, desarrollo y retos actuales, con algunas posibles conclusiones para América Latina." En *La política fiscal en América Latina: Una selección de temas y experiencias de fines y comienzos de siglo.* Serie Seminarios y Conferencias, no. 3. Santiago: Economic Commission for Latin America and the Caribbean (ECLAC).

———. 2001. "Economic Policy Coordination: Main Issues and the Redima Approach for Latin America Countries." Santiago: ECLAC.

———. 2002. "América Latina y la coordinación de políticas económicas." *Estudios Internacionales* 35, no. 138: 71–87.

Giordano, P., and J. Monteagudo. 2002. "Exchange Rate Instability, Trade and Regional Integration." Washington: Inter-American Development Bank.

Giovannini, A., and C. Mayer, eds. 1991. *European Financial Integration.* Cambridge University Press.

Heymann, D., and F. Navajas. 1991. "Coordinación de políticas macroeconómicas: Aspectos conceptuales vinculados con el MERCOSUR." Working Paper 45. Buenos Aires: Comisión Económica para América Latina y el Caribe (CEPAL).

————. 1998. "Coordinación de políticas macroeconómicas en MERCOSUR: Algunas reflexiones." In *Ensayos sobre la Inserción Internacional de la Economía Argentina*. Working Paper 81. Buenos Aires: CEPAL.

Inter-American Development Bank. 2002. *Beyond Borders: The New Regionalism in Latin America. Economic and Social Progress in Latin America*. Washington.

Lacunza H., J. Carrera, M. Cicowiez, and M. Saavedra. 2003. "Cooperación macroeconómica en Mercosur: Un análisis de la interdependencia y una propuesta de coordinación." Presented in *Jornadas de Economía Monetaria e Internacional*. Universidad Nacional de la Plata.

Lavagna, R., and F. Giambiagi. 2000. "Hacia la creación de una moneda común: Una propuesta de convergencia coordinada de políticas macroeconómica en el MERCOSUR." In *Coordinación de Políticas Macroeconómicas en el MERCOSUR*, edited by J. Carrera and F. Sturzenegger: Mexico City: Fondo de Cultura Económica.

Machinea, J. 2003a. "La inestabilidad cambiaria en el Mercosur: causas, problemas y posibles soluciones." INTAL–ITD Working Paper IECI-06d. Buenos Aires: INTAL.

————. 2003b. "Currency Crises: A Practitioner's View." In *Brookings Trade Forum 2002*, edited by Susan M. Collins and Dani Rodrik. Brookings.

————. Machinea, José Luis. 2003c. *Mercosur: en busca de una nueva agenda. La inestabilidad cambiaria en el Mercosur: Causas, problemas y posibles soluciones*. Buenos Aires: Banco Interamericano de Desarrollo (BID).

Machinea, J., and V. Rappoport. 2004. "Financial Safety Nets and Regional Integration." *Integration and Trade* 8, no. 20: 7–44.

Mistry, P. 1999. "Coping with Financial Crisis: Are Regional Arrangements the Missing Link?" In *International Monetary and Financial Issues for the 1990s*, Vol. 10. Geneva: United Nations Conference on Trade and Development (UNCTAD).

Obstfeld, M. 2000. "International Macroeconomics: Beyond the Mundell-Fleming Model." University of California, Berkeley, Institute of Business and Economic Research.

Ocampo, J. A. 1999. "Reforming the International Financial Architecture: Consensus and Divergences." *Temas de Coyuntura* (CEPAL), no. 1.

Ocampo, J. A., and M. L. Chiappe. 2003. *Counter-Cyclical Prudential and Capital Account Regulations in Developing Countries*. Expert Group on Development Issues (EGDI). Stockholm: Swedish Ministry for Foreign Affairs, Almqvist & Wiksell International.

Rodrik, D. 2003. "Growth Strategies." Working Paper 10050. Cambridge, Mass.: National Bureau of Economic Research.

Rogoff, K. 2002. "Rethinking Capital Controls: When Should We Keep an Open Mind?" *Finance and Development* 39, no. 4: 55–56.

Rozenwurcel, G. 2003. "The Collapse of the Currency Board and the Hard Way Back to Normality in Argentina." www.networkideas.org/featart/featart_Argentina.htm (May).

Zahler, R. 2001. "Estrategias para una cooperación monetaria." *Integración & Comercio* (Buenos Aires, BID–INTAL) 5, no. 13 (January–April).

7

Subregional Financial Cooperation: The Experiences of Latin America and the Caribbean

DANIEL TITELMAN

The countries of Latin America and the Caribbean have made significant progress in building a system of institutions for financial cooperation and integration. In addition to promoting productive and social investment financing via development banks, another aim of financial integration has been to facilitate intraregional trade and help finance the countries' short-term liquidity needs.

The foreign debt crisis of the 1980s undermined regional financial cooperation and integration, except among the institutions covering the countries of the Andean Community, which were more dynamic during the 1980s crisis. Starting in the 1990s, there was a revival in financial integration schemes. Indeed, in the subset of member countries of the Andean Community, the Central American Common Market, and the Caribbean Community, the subregional banks now contribute approximately 46 percent of the funding from development banks.

To deepen regional and subregional financial integration and cooperation, these institutions must be able to respond to the new challenges and demands arising from changes in national and international financial systems. However, support for balance-of-payments financing requirements continues to be one of

The author wishes to thank Andras Uthoff and José Antonio Ocampo for their comments. He is also grateful to Gabriela Clivio and Cecilia Vera for their efficient work on statistics and constructing indicators.

the weakest areas of financial cooperation in the region. In addition to being an important source of funding, the development banks should facilitate the countries' access to international financial markets by taking greater advantage of their credit risk rating and of instruments that help the countries to access financial resources in international capital markets.

This chapter examines the financial cooperation dynamic in the countries of the Andean Community, the Central American Common Market, and the Caribbean Community. In particular, it discusses the development of the Andean Development Corporation, the Central American Bank for Economic Integration, the Caribbean Development Bank, and the Latin American Reserve Fund.

Old and New Challenges of Regional Financial Cooperation

Latin America and the Caribbean is one of the regions in the developing world that has made the most progress on economic integration. The process of financial and monetary cooperation in the region has been closely linked with the countries' commercial integration. Growth in intraregional trade led to the creation of institutions for facilitating payments derived from commercial transactions among the countries. Clearing systems and agreements were established. In 1960 the Clearing System for the Central American Common Market was created; in 1965 the Agreement on Reciprocal Payments and Credits was set up in the framework of the Latin American Free Trade Association (LAFTA), now the Latin American Integration Association (LAIA); and in 1977 the Multi-lateral Clearing System for the Caricom member countries was set up.

At the same time that these payment agreements were implemented, financial institutions were created to address collectively the problems of low savings and undeveloped financial systems. The Andean Development Corporation (Corporación Andina de Fomento, CAF) was created in 1968 to serve the Andean Community; the Central American Common Market (CACM) created the Central American Bank for Economic Integration (CABEI) in 1961; and the Caribbean countries (Caricom) created the Caribbean Development Bank (CDB) in 1969.

A factor common to all these subregional institutions was their development bank status. In general, they were created to support the economic and social development of their member countries. Therefore their functions focused mainly on mobilizing medium- and long-term resources for financing productive investment, preferably in areas that would foster economic complementation among the member countries.

The foreign debt crisis that struck the region in 1982 undermined the operation of the financial integration schemes, hitting clearing systems hardest and development banks to a lesser extent. Of course, the crisis did not have the same impact on all of the subregional schemes. While systems of multilateral trade clearing and balance-of-payments support virtually stopped operating in Central America and the Caribbean, this did not happen with the LAIA Reciprocal Payments and Credit Agreement or with the Andean group's financial institutions.

In fact, CAF operations increased significantly beginning in 1983. Between 1983 and 1990, CAF approved loans worth U.S.$2.727 billion, corresponding to around 85 percent of total loans approved between 1971 and 1990. CABEI approved loans worth an average of U.S.$91 million per year, whereas for the period 1984–89, CDB approved average annual loans of U.S.$51 million, a figure rather higher than the U.S.$30 million per year approved in the period 1971–80 (see table 7-1).

In spite of the difficulties financing external accounts, one of the weakest links in the region's financial integration has been the inability to get collectively organized to provide support for balance-of-payments financing needs. In the Central American sphere, the Central American Monetary Stabilization Fund (Fondo Centroamericano de Estabilización Monetaria, FOCEM) was created to provide financial support for the member countries' balance of payments. Its resources came from contributions from the countries, plus any extraregional resources that FOCEM was able to capture. In practice, FOCEM operations have been suspended since 1983.

A different fate awaited the Andean Reserve Fund (Fondo Andinas de Reservas, FAR), created in 1978, which became the Latin American Reserve Fund (Fondo Latinoamericano de Reservas, FLAR) when Costa Rica joined in 1989. Originally, this institution was created to provide short-term liquidity for financing balance-of-payments imbalances of members of the Andean Group (now the Andean Community: Bolivia, Colombia, Ecuador, Peru, and the Bolivarian Republic of Venezuela). FLAR now focuses on providing support to the member countries' balance of payments, granting credit and securing third-party loans; improving the liquidity of international reserve investments; and helping to harmonize the member countries' monetary, exchange rate, and financial policies. FAR/FLAR played an important role in supporting the short-term liquidity needs of the Andean countries during the 1980s and 1990s. One of the principal benefits it confers on its member countries is timely and rapid access to resources in excess of the countries' individual contributions.

Challenges of Financial Integration

Attempts to improve and deepen the processes of financial integration in the region must recognize previous efforts to build regional and subregional financial

Table 7-1. *Latin America and the Caribbean: Loans Approved by Development Banks, 1971–90*
Millions of current U.S. dollars

Bank	Annual average, 1971–80	1981	1982	1983	1984	1985	1986	1987	1988	1989	1990
IDB	1,294	2,493	2,744	3,045	3,567	3,061	3,037	2,361	1,682	2,618	3,881
World Bank	1,462	3,153	2,988	3,460	3,028	3,698	4.771	5,152	5,264	5,842	5,965
Subregional banks	169	200	238	160	180	224	353	475	664	637	1,112
CAF	56	21	58	83	101	160	264	309	524	474	812
CABEI[a]	83	141	132	45	25	26	33	126	77	110	199
CDB	30	39	49	32	54	38	56	40	63	53	101
Total	2,925	5,846	5,970	6,665	6,775	6,983	8,161	7,988	7,610	9,097	10,958

Source: Prepared by the author, using official data from the Inter-American Development Bank (IDB), World Bank, Andean Development Corporation (CAF), Central American Bank for Economic Integration (CABEI), and Caribbean Development Bank (CDB).

a. For CABEI, the annual average is for the period 1961–80.

institutions and adapt these institutions to meet the demands that arise from changes in national and international financial systems. In the financial sphere, closer integration and increasingly volatile capital flows have heightened the financial vulnerability of the region's economies, which has led to recurrent financial and economic crises that have undermined their capacity for economic growth.

In this context, numerous authors have argued that strengthening regional and subregional financial institutions is important in order, first, to complement global institutions, and second, to provide instruments and public goods that are provided neither by the international financial system nor by global financial institutions.[1] (For the purposes of this essay, we shall concentrate on the functions appropriate to subregional development banks and to mechanisms for financial balance-of-payments support.

Since the 1990s, the dynamic of the business cycle in the countries of the region has been closely correlated with inflows and outflows of financial capital.[2] This preponderance of financial variables in determining the cycle is not exclusive to the region, but is a phenomenon that has accompanied this phase in the globalization process, stemming from closer financial integration worldwide. This means that the countries of the region are facing international financial problems that are common to all developing and emerging economies. Economic crises have been marked by problems of financial and commercial contagion typical of what may be called "latest-generation" crises. The 1990s have witnessed a number of crises that reflect components of regional and extraregional contagion. The tequila crisis in 1995 was an example of regional contagion, whereas the Asian crisis of 1997 and the Russian crisis of 1998 were examples of extraregional contagion.

Since, in addition to terms-of-trade shocks, there have been external shocks of a financial, exchange rate, or monetary nature affecting the countries' capacity to finance their balance of payments, it is more important than in the past to have regional institutions to facilitate the capture of resources to cover temporary liquidity requirements. Recent experience shows that, individually, the economies of the region have not been successful in mitigating financial shocks and have had to make costly economic adjustments to tackle their liquidity problems. The economies are unable to generate adequate levels of international reserves to cope with sudden changes in capital flows; the international financial system has not been capable of providing short-term financing during crisis

---

1. See Culpeper (this volume); Ocampo (2002a and 2002b); Mistry (1999); Economic Commission for Latin America and the Caribbean (2002a); and Agosin (2001).
2. Economic Commission for Latin America and the Caribbean (2002b).

periods; and last, even though the IMF did step in with exceptional financing, it imposed very onerous economic conditionalities and was not fast or flexible enough. Furthermore, added to the difficulties specific to each country, there is a component of regional crisis contagion, which makes it more difficult for the countries to access financial resources in international markets. For this reason, promoting and expanding institutions such as FLAR is seen to be a key element of regional financial integration.

In addition to helping to cope with balance-of-payments crises, a regional fund such as FLAR should promote greater coordination of macroeconomic policies, which would lessen vulnerability to regional and extraregional shocks. Lack of harmonization in macroeconomic policies and sharp fluctuations in bilateral exchange rates have conspired against more decisive progress toward commercial and financial integration among the countries of the region.

In spite of closer financial integration with the rest of the world, the countries of the region still have severely limited domestic and foreign savings to finance productive and social investment. In this respect, development banks, as well as catalyst institutions for medium- and long-term financial resources, continue to be important for promoting and boosting economic growth. Multilateral development banks, both regional and subregional, have played an important role in providing external financing to the region. During the 1990s, multilateral development banks provided three-quarters of the net capital inflows to countries in the region with a per capita income of less than U.S.$2,000. These resources helped in part to offset the adverse effects of external shocks. In countries with a per capita income of between U.S.$2,000 and U.S.$4,000, resources from multilateral banks represented around 14 percent of net capital inflows. However, in the wealthier countries—that is to say, countries with a per capita income of more than U.S.$4,000—resources from multilateral development banks accounted for around 11 percent of total net inflows. Also, multilateral development banks granted more favorable financial conditions for credits than did private sources of financing, with lower interest rates and a longer term.[3]

Since the ability to access foreign capital flows continues to be a key factor in the economic growth dynamic, development banks must support and facilitate access to private external financing in order to improve the term and costs. Since lending by these institutions is generally countercyclical, they also play a role in stabilizing financial flows. An issue of vital importance for the region is financial risk management. The weak structure of most national financial systems has hampered financing of productive activity and innovation. Regional

3. Titelman (2002).

and subregional development banks must therefore support the emergence of new national, subregional, and regional financial instruments.

Over and above providing financial resources, regional and subregional development banks must take a more prominent role in the financial development of the countries in the region, which evidence varying levels of financial deepening. Legal problems, the supervision and regulation of national financial systems, and the capacity to manage financial risk would all be alleviated by the presence of subregional financial institutions acting in a complementary capacity with more global financial institutions.

Subregional or regional financial institutions can enhance the work of global institutions by playing a complementary role. The ability to incorporate specific regional or subregional requirements into the structure and operation of development finance institutions enables them to provide development banking, emergency financing, and technical support services. Last, recent experience shows that the countries' sense of ownership is crucial to institution building and increases their willingness to accept the imposition of conditionalities by financial institutions, which leads to greater flexibility for lending resources.[4]

Subregional Development Banks

Regional and subregional development banks have been major sources of funding for all the economies of the region, in particular for relatively less developed countries. During the period 1990–2003, these institutions approved credits to the region worth an average of U.S.$15 billion per year. This figure is almost three times the average annual U.S.$5 billion approved in the period 1971–89. During the 1990s, subregional development banks contributed around 20 percent of total resources, in contrast to only around 5 percent in the period 1971–90 (see table 7-2).

Development banks have been actively involved in the subregional sphere. The Andean Development Corporation (CAF) was created to support the sustainable development and integration of the countries of the Andean Community, and the countries eligible to receive financial resources therefore include all the Andean countries (Bolivia, Colombia, Ecuador, Peru, and the Bolivarian Republic of Venezuela). However, CAF membership has grown over time to include a very large group of Latin American and Caribbean countries, together with Spain. At present, CAF grants loans and extends lines of credit to corporations, lending institutions, and public and private banks financing foreign trade

4. Ocampo (2002a); Agosin (2001).

Table 7-2. *Latin America and the Caribbean: Loans Approved by Development Banks, 1971–2003*
Millions of current U.S. dollars, unless otherwise noted

Bank	Annual average, 1971–89	1990	1991	1992	1993	1994	1995	1996	1997	1998	1999	2000	2001	2002	2003
Loans approved															
IDB	1,976	3,881	5,419	6,023	5,963	5,255	7,304	6,766	6,017	10,063	9,486	5,267	7,854	4,549	6,810
World Bank	2,735	5,965	5,237	5,662	6,169	4,747	6,061	4,438	4,563	6,040	7,737	4,064	5,300	4,366	5,821
Subregional banks	254	1,112	1,578	2,115	2,569	2,768	2,708	2,955	3,482	3,721	2,655	2,832	3,855	4,079	4,170
CAF	134	812	1,300	1,773	2,096	2,160	2,258	2,314	2,900	2,672	2,182	2,323	3,198	3,291	3,304
CABEI[a]	82	199	171	272	402	566	358	569	532	932	336	330	572	680	681
CDB	38	101	108	70	70	43	92	73	51	117	137	179	85	108	185
Total	4,965	10,958	12,234	13,800	14,701	12,770	16,073	14,159	14,062	19,824	19,878	12,163	17,009	12,994	16,801
As a percentage of the total approved															
IDB	40	35	44	44	41	41	45	48	43	51	48	43	46	35	41
World Bank	55	54	43	41	42	37	38	31	32	30	39	33	31	34	35
Subregional banks	5	10	13	15	17	22	17	21	25	19	13	23	23	31	25
Total	100	100	100	100	100	100	100	100	100	100	100	100	100	100	100

Source: Prepared by the author using official data from Inter-American Development Bank (IDB), World Bank, Andean Development Corporation (CAF), Central American Bank for Economic Integration (CABEI), and Caribbean Development Bank (CDB).
a. For CABEI, the annual average is for the period 1961–89.

and working capital operations. In addition, it provides the financial sector with global credits and lines of credit for channeling resources to a variety of projects in the productive sector. It also offers governments and government bodies development bank services for special financing of physical infrastructure and integration projects. Added to this, it provides investment bank services, such as shareholding, acquisition, and guarantee for the issue of securities, and structuring and financing projects with limited guarantees (limited-recourse financing, cofinancing, syndicated loans, financial guarantees, and others). Furthermore, it offers financing for projects to promote human development and integrate marginalized groups (such as indigenous peoples).

In the Caribbean subregion, the Caribbean Development Bank was created in 1969 to contribute to the growth and economic development of the Caribbean member countries (Caricom) and to promote cooperation and economic integration among them, paying special attention to the needs of the region's less-developed countries. To this end, the bank has applied the Caricom definition of less-developed country to the following countries: Anguilla, Antigua and Barbuda, Belize, Dominica, Grenada, Montserrat, Saint Kitts and Nevis, Saint Lucia, and Saint Vincent and the Grenadines. Added to these are the British overseas territories of the British Virgin Islands, the Cayman Islands, and the Turks and Caicos Islands. In addition, there are the borrower member countries: Bahamas, Barbados, Guyana, Jamaica, and Trinidad and Tobago. The CDB provides financing to the governments of its borrower member countries and to public and private sector entities from those countries. Furthermore, it grants loans to private sector entities without a government guarantee and invests in shares in those enterprises.

On the Central American isthmus, the Central American Bank for Economic Integration (CABEI) gears its activities toward investment financing, giving precedence to the export, basic services (infrastructure, electricity, communications), and agricultural sectors, and in general to projects in the productive sector that foster economic complementation among the member countries. It operates several funds, the most prominent of which are the Central American Economic Integration Fund (Fondo Centroamericano de Integración Económica), the Housing Finance Fund (Fondo Financiero de la Vivienda), the Export Promotion Fund (Fondo para la Promoción de Exportaciones), the Fund for Promoting Central American Exports (Fondo de Fortalecimiento de Exportaciones Centroamericanas), the Technical Cooperation Fund (Fondo de Cooperación Técnica), and the Regional Debt Conversion Fund (Fondo Regional para la Conversión de Deuda). The member countries eligible for financing are Costa Rica, El Salvador, Guatemala, Honduras, and Nicaragua.

A fourth and smaller institution, FONPLATA (Fondo Financiero para el Desarrollo de la Cuenca del Plata; in English, Financial Fund for the Development of the Plata River Basin), was created in 1971 to act as the financial body of the Cuenca del Plata treaty.[5] Its main objective is to finance studies, projects, programs, and works intended to promote the economic development and the physical integration of the Plata River basin. The fund began operating in 1977 with initial capital of U.S.$160 million contributed by its member states (33 percent by Argentina and Brazil and 11.11 percent by Bolivia, Paraguay, and Uruguay). As of December 2003, the total authorized capital of the fund was U.S.$390 million. From the beginning of its activities up to December 2003, FONPLATA had approved sixty-two financing operations for a total of approximately U.S.$593.5 million. The total financing of projects carried out by the fund, together with local contributions and resources from other multilateral as well as national sources, amounts to U.S.$2,482 million. The fund has mainly financed preinvestment and investment projects in the transport sector (70 percent of the total).[6]

Regional and subregional development banks are able to offer a wide range of instruments and services (see table 7-3). These are linked largely with the provision of financing, access to financial markets, financial development, technical training, and disaster financing. The only development bank authorized to provide funds for balance-of-payments support is CABEI, via the Central American Monetary Stabilization Fund. However, as mentioned earlier, this fund ceased to operate in the early 1980s. As illustrated below, the importance and use of the instruments also differ significantly from one subregional bank to another.

Relative Importance of Subregional Banks

Beginning in the 1990s, the relative importance of financing from subregional development banks increased (see tables 7-4 and 7-5). In the Andean countries, CAF contributed around 56 percent of the total resources approved by the development banks for the Andean Community countries. From 1995 on, except in 1998–99, CAF has been the main source of multilateral financing for the Andean countries, attaining 68 percent of the total approved during 2002.

On the Central American isthmus, CABEI has also increased its loans, albeit to a lesser extent and with more ups and downs. CABEI had significant growth between 1995 and 1998 (from U.S.$358 million approved in 1995 to

5. Signatories to that 1969 treaty were Argentina, Bolivia, Brazil, Paraguay, and Uruguay. The objective of the treaty is to join efforts to promote economic development and the physical integration of the member countries.

6. See www.fonplata.org.

Table 7-3. *Products and Services of Multilateral Financial Institutions*

	Worldwide	Regional	Subregional		
Product or service	World Bank	IDB	CABEI	CAF	CDB
Investment	x	x	x	x	x
Preinvestment		x	x	x	x
Cofinancing	x	x	x	x	x
Trust funds	x	x	x	x	x
Guarantees	x	x		x	
Access to the capital market	x	x		x	x
Technical cooperation and counseling	x	x	x	x	x
Training	x	x	x	x	x
Capacity building	x	x		x	
Second-tier banking	x	x	x	x	
Development of the capital market	x	x			x
Sectoral restructuring	x	x	x	x	x
Venture capital for SMEs and rural enterprises		x	x	x	
Balance-of-payments support			x		
Disasters	x	x	x	x	x

Source: Maldonado (2003).

Table 7-4. *Loans Approved by Development Banks, 1995–2004*
Millions of current U.S. dollars

	1995	1996	1997	1998	1999	2000	2001	2002	2003	2004
Andean Community countries										
IDB and World Bank	2,133	1,924	1,392	2,996	2,558	2,152	1,917	1,559	4,124	2,329
CAF	2,258	2,314	2,900	2,673	2,182	2,323	3,198	3,290	3,304	3,503
Central American Common Market countries										
IDB and World Bank	876	626	593	1,233	1,027	513	1,079	1,043	513	760
CABEI	358	569	532	932	336	330	572	680	681	800
Caricom countries										
IDB and World Bank	345	506	176	189	334	270	310	326	242	221
CDB	92	73	51	117	137	179	85	108	185	94

Source: Prepared by the author using the annual reports of the Inter-American Development Bank (IDB), World Bank, Andean Development Corporation (CAF), Central American Bank for Economic Integration (CABEI), and Caribbean Development Bank (CDB).

Table 7-5. *Loans Approved by Development Banks, 1995–2004*
Percent of GDP

Bank	1995	1996	1997	1998	1999	2000	2001	2002	2003	2004
Andean Community countries										
IDB and World Bank	0.9	0.8	0.5	1.1	1.0	0.8	0.7	0.6	1.6	0.7
CAF	0.9	0.9	1.0	1.0	0.8	0.8	1.1	1.2	1.3	1.1
Central American Common Market countries										
IDB and World Bank	2.0	1.4	1.2	2.3	1.8	0.9	1.8	1.6	0.8	1.0
CABEI	0.8	1.3	1.1	1.7	0.6	0.6	0.9	1.0	1.0	1.1
Caricom countries										
IDB and World Bank	2.0	2.7	0.9	0.9	1.5	1.1	1.3	1.3	0.9	0.8
CDB	0.5	0.4	0.3	0.6	0.6	0.8	0.3	0.4	0.7	0.3

Source: Prepared by the author using annual reports of the Inter-American Development Bank (IDB), World Bank, Andean Development Corporation (CAF), Central American Bank for Economic Integration (CABEI) and Caribbean Development Bank (CDB).

U.S.$932 million in 1998), before shrinking significantly in 1999 and 2000 and recovering in 2001. In comparison with other multilateral sources (the World Bank and Inter-American Development Bank [IDB]), CABEI has contributed an average of around 40 percent of the total financing approved by these institutions for the Central American countries, reaching a maximum of 57 percent in 2003. Disbursements increased from U.S.$310 million in 1995 to U.S.$864 million in 2002, when they were equivalent to 51 percent of total disbursements by the multilateral institutions.

In the Caribbean region, the CDB also increased its loan portfolio, from U.S.$108 million approved in 1991 to U.S.$179 million approved in 2000, only to fall again and recover in 2003, when it approved loans worth U.S.$185 million. As a source of multilateral financing for the Caribbean subregion, it accounted for around 30 percent of total loan approvals between 1992 and 2002. Disbursements grew from U.S.$59 million in 1995 to U.S.$119 million in 2002, and in the period 1995–2002 they were equivalent to 23 percent of the total disbursed by multilateral development banks.

Measured in terms of the gross domestic product (GDP), subregional banks' financing flows are equally significant. For the period 1995–2004, CAF approved loans equivalent to 1.0 percent of the GDP of the Andean Community countries. During the period 1995–2004, CABEI approved average resources equivalent

Table 7-6. *CAF Loans by Economic Sector, 1971–2003*
Millions of current U.S. dollars

	Cumulative 1971–90	Cumulative 1991–2000	2001	2002	2003
Productive sectors	1,379	4,209	985	122	362
Infrastructure	628	5,383	1,290	1,872	1,667
Social sectors	0	922	353	536	311
Economic reforms	0	528	195	0	172
Long-term	2,007	11,042	2,823	2,530	2,512
Short-term	953	10,934	375	760	792
Total approved	2,960	21,976	3,198	3,290	3,304
As a percentage of the total approved					
Productive sectors	47	19	31	4	11
Infrastructure	21	24	40	57	50
Social sectors	0	4	11	16	9
Economic reforms	0	2	6	0	5
Long-term	68	50	88	77	76
Short-term	32	50	12	23	24
Total	100	100	100	100	100

Source: Prepared by the author using Andean Development Corporation annual reports.

to 1.0 percent of the GDP of the Central American countries. The resources approved by the CDB were on average around 0.5 percent of the Caricom countries' GDP (see table 7-5).

Term and Sectoral Allocation

Over the past decade, CAF has progressed significantly in its capacity to provide medium- and long-term resources. The proportion of long-term resources has increased considerably more than short-term resources. While for the period 1991–2000 long-term loans represented around 50 percent of the total approved, between 2001 and 2003 they rose to 80 percent. A significant part of this financing was directed toward infrastructure investment, accounting for 24 percent in 1991–2000 and rising to 50 percent in 2001–03. The productive sector also receives major loan allocations, absorbing 15 percent of the total approved in 2001–03, followed by the social sector (see table 7-6). This contrasts with the IDB and the World Bank, which in recent years have directed a major part of their financing to the social sector.

Between 1970 and 2003, the CDB approved financing for a total of some U.S.$2.7 billion, which went mainly to infrastructure (30 percent), financial

Table 7-7. *CDB Total Financing by Economic Sector, 1970–2003*[a]
Millions of U.S. dollars, unless otherwise noted

	Cumulative 1970–89	Cumulative 1990–2000	2001	2002	2003
Productive sector	344	120	0	13	32
Infrastructure	604	136	10	24	33
Social sector	228	31	29	10	11
Natural disasters	81	0	5	41	0
Other financing	668	147	75	26	28
Total approved	1,925	434	119	114	189
As a percentage of the total approved					
Productive sector	18	28	0	12	17
Infrastructure	31	31	8	21	17
Social sector	12	7	24	9	6
Natural disasters	4	0	4	36	0
Other financing	35	34	63	23	15
Total	100	100	100	100	100

Source: Prepared by the author using data from the Caribbean Development Bank.
a. Total financing includes loans, grants, and equity.

markets, and financing activities (34 percent), and to a lesser extent to the productive sector (18 percent), the social sector (11 percent), and natural disasters (4 percent). In recent years the CDB has mobilized more resources for financing social sector projects and tackling the aftereffects of natural disasters, which accounted for 36 percent of the resources approved in 2002 (see table 7-7).

CABEI has traditionally channeled an important part of its resources to financing infrastructure, which accounted for 45 percent of approved resources between 2001 and 2003. Financing for the productive sector increased in relative importance from 14 percent of loans approved in the period 1961–90 to 42 percent in the period 1991–2003 (see table 7-8).

Credit Risk Rating, Access to Financial Markets, and Countercyclical Financing

One of the main characteristics of the Latin American and Caribbean economies in recent years has been their irregular access to international capital flows. This reflects flaws in the market at the level of both the countries and the international financial system. In this context, subregional development banks can

Table 7-8. *CABEI Loans by Economic Sector, 1961–2003*[a]

Millions of U.S. dollars, unless otherwise noted

	Cumulative 1961–90	Cumulative 1991–2000	2001	2002	2003
Productive sector	318	1,299	156	203	315
Infrastructure	1,382	1,149	180	269	321
Social sector	311	448	54	96	93
Other	228	152	10	1	0
Total approved	2,239	3,048	400	569	729
As a percentage of the total approved					
Productive sector	14	42	39	36	43
Infrastructure	62	38	45	47	44
Social sector	14	15	14	17	13
Other	10	5	2	0	0
Total	100	100	100	100	100

Source: Prepared by the author using data from the Central American Bank for Economic Integration (CABEI).

a. Amounts are as of June of every year.

play a significant role in intermediating financing funds from international markets to the countries of the region.

As can be seen in table 7-9, CAF, CDB, and CABEI have a much higher investment rating than their member countries (A, AAA, and Baa1, respectively), based, among other things, on the fact that they have exceeded the Basel reserve requirements, to the tune of 30 percent, 43 percent, and 47 percent respectively in 2002. These institutions therefore find themselves in a position that allows them to intermediate private financing funds at a lesser cost than their member countries. This can facilitate access to financing for a number of relatively less developed countries, while reducing the cost of these resources.

While the main function of subregional development banks is to generate medium- and long-term financial resources, they must also play a role in stabilizing financial flows and providing countercyclical financing. Experience shows that these institutions did indeed contribute in this way during the 1980s and 1990s. In general, although they have differing dynamics, development banks have increased their loan approvals during crisis periods and, in addition, they have had a countercyclical component (see figure 7-1). The decline in private financial flows toward the Andean Community countries, beginning in 1999, was partially offset by an increase in flows from CAF, which reduced the negative effect of diminished private flows.

Table 7-9. *Long-Term Debt Rating in Foreign Currency, according to Moody's*

Regional group	Rating	Loan
CACM		
Costa Rica	Ba1	
El Salvador	Baa3	CABEI
Guatemala	Ba2	Baa1
Honduras	B2	
Nicaragua	B2	
Caricom		
Barbados	Baa2	
Belize	Ba3	
Guyana		
Jamaica	B1	
Surinam	B1	
Trinidad and Tobago	Baa3	CDB
Antigua and Barbuda		AAA (S&P)
Dominica		
Grenada		
Montserrat		
Saint Kitts and Nevis		
Saint Lucia		
Saint Vincent and the Grenadines		
Andean Community		
Bolivia	B3	
Colombia	Ba2	
Ecuador	Caa1	CAF
Peru	Ba3	A
Venezuela (Bolivarian Rep. of)	B	

Source: Prepared by the author using data from the Andean Community, the Central American Bank for Economic Integration, the Caribbean Development Bank, and Bloomberg.

Share Capital and Sense of Ownership

One argument in favor of regional and subregional financial institutions is that countries eligible to receive resources have more say and decisionmaking power to influence the policies and instruments of such institutions than of global institutions. As a result, regional and subregional financial institutions have more flexibility to disburse resources in a timely manner, with conditionalities that, in many instances, are more in line with the countries' needs and realities. As the countries feel better represented, it makes them more likely to comply with the financial commitments they acquire with such institutions.

Figure 7-1. *GDP Growth, Loan Approvals, and Inflow of Private Capital,*
1991–2003[a]

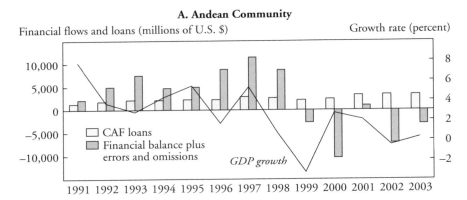

A. Andean Community

Financial flows and loans (millions of U.S. $)   Growth rate (percent)

CAF loans

Financial balance plus errors and omissions

GDP growth

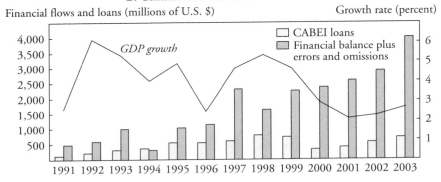

B. Central American Common Market

Financial flows and loans (millions of U.S. $)   Growth rate (percent)

GDP growth

CABEI loans

Financial balance plus errors and omissions

C. Caricom

Financial flows and loans (millions of U.S. $)   Growth rate (percent)

CDB loans

Financial balance plus errors and omissions

GDP growth

Source: Prepared by the author on the basis of data from the countries and from the Andean Community, Central American Bank for Economic Integration, and Caribbean Development Bank.

a. Private capital has been estimated from the financial balance (FB) and the errors and omissions (E&O) of the balance of payments.

Table 7-10. *CAF Loan Portfolio Delinquency, 1999–2003*

Loan type	1999	2000	2001	2002	2003
Portfolio of outstanding loans (millions of U.S. dollars)	4,188	4,478	5,455	6,062	6,597
Recovered/mature loans (percent)	100	100	100	100	100
Delinquency as a percentage of the loan portfolio	0.07	0.12	0.00	0.00	0.00

Source: Prepared by the author, using data from the countries, the Andean Development Corporation (CAF), and the Inter-American Development Bank (IDB).

The main shareholders of CAF are the Andean countries, which own around 96 percent of its share capital and are the chief recipients of funds, with the remaining 4 percent of shares distributed among Brazil, Chile, the Dominican Republic, Jamaica, Mexico, Panama, Paraguay, Spain, Trinidad and Tobago, and Uruguay. The CAF shareholder structure means that the Andean countries take an active part in defining the corporation's objectives, ensuring greater harmonization between the institution's activities and the countries' requirements. Unlike in CAF, CDB shareholders include countries from other regions of the world, such as Germany, Italy, the United Kingdom, Canada, and Taiwan Province of China, together with Colombia, Mexico, and the Bolivarian Republic of Venezuela from the region. Member countries eligible for financing represent 57 percent of the share capital. The CACM member countries own 72 percent of the share capital of CABEI. The remainder is distributed among Taiwan Province of China (11 percent), Mexico (9 percent), and Argentina and Colombia (4 percent each).

In comparative terms, CAF has a very good recovery rate for its loan portfolio. Between 1999 and 2003, which were economically difficult years for the region, CAF had almost no delinquency in its loan portfolio (see table 7-10).

Development banks have centered their financial management on granting credits, as well as providing supplementary nonfinancial services. Only recently have they started using new instruments for facilitating access to capital markets. The standardization of products and processes has been shown to have a significant impact on reducing intermediation costs and on facilitating access to new forms of asset financing, which is a positive area for development banks to break into. Trust management, the provision of guarantee funds and insurance, and asset securitization are all promising activities. For instance, acting in a second-tier capacity, development banks can perform credit securitization. This is where subregional development banks buy portfolios of callable loans from first-tier commercial banks or from national development banks, package them, and place them on the securities market. This allows them to transfer the credit risk to the securities market, giving national banks new lending capacity.

Though not new, loan guarantee and insurance schemes have attracted growing interest in recent years as instruments for facilitating access to financing. This type of instrument reduces the financial risk and credit transaction costs, which should result in better terms and conditions. Since subregional development banks have a greater capacity to distribute risk than national banks, they can play an important role in this type of instrument. Guarantee funds can be used to support other instruments that improve and facilitate financial intermediation for productive development, such as the venture capital industry. In Latin America and the Caribbean, little use is made of venture capital funds for financing investment.

To promote their role in this type of activity, subregional development banks should forge closer links with national development banks to create synergies between national financial instruments and subregional instruments. Subregional banks could also provide technical assistance to harmonize the various instruments and ensure that they have legitimacy in the various national markets, to train investors in using these instruments, and to finance the cost of initiating and implementing the new instruments.

Balance-of-Payments Support and Regional Reserve Funds

One of the weakest links in regional financial integration is support for balance-of-payments financing. The only institution in the region active in this field is the Latin American Reserve Fund (FLAR), which currently covers Bolivia, Colombia, Costa Rica, Ecuador, Peru, and the Bolivarian Republic of Venezuela. FLAR activities have three objectives: to provide financial support for its member countries' balance of payments; to improve the terms for its member countries' reserves investments; and to help to harmonize its member countries' monetary and financial policies.

In order to provide balance-of-payments financing, FAR/FLAR operates as a credit cooperative in which the member countries' central banks are able to take loans in proportion to their capital contributions. There are different credit facilities:

—Credits for balance-of-payments support are issued for a three-year term, with a one-year grace period, capped at 2.5 times the paid-up capital (except for Ecuador and Bolivia, where it is 3.5 times the paid-up capital), and their approval requires the consent of the board of directors.

—Credits for restructuring the external national debt are issued for a three-year term, with a one-year grace period, capped at 1.5 times the paid-up capital, and their approval requires the consent of the board of directors.

—Liquidity credits are issued for a term of up to one year, capped at 1.0 times the paid-up capital, and their approval requires the authorization of the chief executive officer.

—Standby credits are issued for a term of up to six months, capped at 2.0 times the paid-up capital, and their approval requires the authorization of the chief executive officer.

—Treasury credits (repos) are issued for a term of one to thirty days, capped at 2.0 times the paid-up capital and 50 percent collateralized, and their approval requires the authorization of the chief executive officer.

—The Andean peso is an accounting unit created to facilitate payment between the central banks and other authorized holders. However, this currency has been little used.

Relative Importance

Between its creation and the end of 2003, FAR/FLAR disbursed credits worth a total of U.S.$4.9 billion, consisting chiefly of credits for balance-of-payments support and liquidity credits. During the worst years of the debt crisis, 1982–84, FAR/FLAR increased its resource contribution significantly. The same happened in the 1995 and 1998–99 crises (see table 7-11).

During the period 1978–2003, FAR/FLAR contributed average resources equivalent to 60 percent of IMF exceptional financing to the Andean Community countries. In the 1978–89 period, FAR/FLAR channeled resources of around U.S.$3 billion, of which Ecuador received 25 percent; Bolivia and Colombia around 23 percent each; Peru, 20 percent; and the Bolivarian Republic of Venezuela, 9 percent. Of the U.S.$1.9 billion disbursed during the period 1990–2004, Ecuador received 46 percent; Peru, 26 percent; Bolivia, 10 percent; Costa Rica, 8 percent; Colombia, 6.5 percent; and the Bolivarian Republic of Venezuela, 1 percent. For the beneficiary countries, these funds have helped significantly to relieve liquidity restrictions. Measured in export terms, these flows have reached major proportions in the different countries. In Bolivia, for example, flows were equivalent to 30 percent of exports in 1985–86; in Peru they were 11 percent in 1991; in Ecuador, 11 percent in 1998; and in Colombia, 12 percent in 1984. From the international reserves perspective, the figures are even higher, with Bolivia showing flows equivalent to 35 percent of its international reserves in 1985–86; Peru, 13 percent in 1991; Ecuador, 28 percent in 1998; and Colombia, 30 percent in 1984.

Table 7-11. *FAR/FLAR Disbursements and IMF Exceptional Financing, 1978–99*[a]
Millions of U.S. dollars

	1978	1979	1980	1981	1982	1983	1984	1985	1986	1987	1988	1989
FAR/FLAR disbursements[b]												
Bolivia			39	53	53	53	30	165	190		28	96
Colombia						50	529	85				
Ecuador					105	67	127	34	250		93	54
Costa Rica												
Peru	15	18				195				20	130	240
Venezuela (Bolivarian Rep. of)										271		
Total	15	18	39	53	158	364	686	284	440	291	251	390
IMF exceptional financing[c]												
Bolivia	38	11	96		27	19			135		91	58
Ecuador						218	40	86	89	49	78	20
Costa Rica		27	20	62		119		35				
Peru	107	229	145		331	176	107					
Venezuela (Bolivarian Rep. of)												974
Total	145	267	261	62	358	532	147	121	224	49	169	1,052

An important aspect of FAR/FLAR funding is its timeliness and speed, and it has always contributed crisis funding to its member countries with a clear anticyclical impact (see figure 7-2). In some cases, FAR/FLAR was the only institution to contribute resources for crisis situations, as was the case for Peru in 1988, when its GDP fell by 8.4 percent and FAR/FLAR disbursed resources worth U.S.$130 million, whereas the IMF contributed no emergency financing.

Bolivia and Ecuador are the two countries to have received the most FAR/FLAR disbursements. These countries are granted privileged access to this fund: they can use 3.5 times their capital for balance-of-payments support credits, whereas other countries can use only 2.5 times their capital. As table 7-12 shows, when the debt capacity with FAR/FLAR is added to the member countries' international reserves, the ratio of short-term debt to international reserves

1990	1991	1992	1993	1994	1995	1996	1997	1998	1999	2000	2001	2002	2003
121	48	20											
117					234	34		494	125				
													156
129	403												
23													
390	451	20			234	34		494	125				156
31	31	51		44	26	49	23	46	23	15	24		
32	25			142						150	48	98	
	76	6											
			897				221						
1,843	317					508							
1,906	449	57	897	186	26	557	244	46	23	165	72	98	

Source: Prepared by the author using data from the countries, the Latin American Reserve Fund, and the International Monetary Fund.

a. The FAR/FLAR accounting year is from July to June; for the IMF it is a calendar year.

b. FAR/FLAR contingency financing is not detailed by country because it is zero for every year. The same applies to disbursements, because of debt restructuring, except for 1995 and 2003, when funds worth U.S.$200 million and U.S.$156 million were disbursed to Ecuador and Costa Rica, respectively. Also, not included in FAR/FLAR disbursements by country are countries that always had zero disbursements for any reason during the period 1978–2004.

c. IMF disbursements do not include the reserve tranche.

drops significantly in Bolivia, Ecuador, and Costa Rica, countries that contribute a smaller quota to the IMF.

Financing and Sense of Ownership

FAR/FLAR resources come mainly from paid-up capital from the member countries, which defines their debt capacity with the fund. In December 2003, of its equity of U.S.$1,554 million, 90 percent came from paid-up capital (U.S.$1,386), 9 percent from reserves, and 1 percent from net profits. The member countries have always paid off their loans with FAR/FLAR, even in situations of moratorium on external national debt. For example, during the 1980s and 1990s, Peru and Ecuador restructured their international obligations, defaulting in international financial markets. However, these countries continued to comply

Figure 7-2. *FLAR Member Countries: GDP Growth and FLAR Disbursements, 1978–2003*

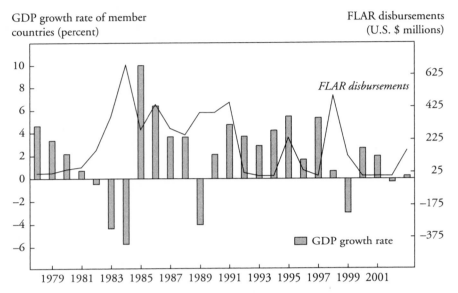

Source: Prepared by the author, using data from the countries and figures from the Latin American Reserve Fund.

with their obligations to FAR/FLAR, an indication that the member countries have endowed it with preferred-creditor status.

Preferred-creditor status reflects a number of factors. One is a sense of ownership, which has been reflected in speedy and timely financing, owing to the fact that loan approvals require the authorization of either the board of directors, which is made up of the member countries' central banks, or the chief executive officer, depending on the type of credit. This has given it an operational advantage over the IMF, which is not necessarily reflected in the amounts, but is reflected in the timeliness and relevance of the credits. Another is that the sense of ownership has been reflected in rules stipulated in the central banks' articles of agreement and accounting rules. Under these rules, the central banks must register any loans granted by FAR/FLAR as liabilities in the international reserves account, thereby providing an additional guarantee of repayment. At present, FAR/FLAR has a Moody's rating of Aa2 and a Standard & Poor's rating of A+. These ratings reflect the preferred-creditor status of FAR/FLAR. FLAR member countries have consistently honored their obligations, even

Table 7-12. *Impact of FAR/FLAR on Financial Vulnerability: Short-Term Debt and International Reserves, March 2003*
Millions of dollars, except where indicated

	Bolivia	Colombia	Costa Rica	Ecuador	Peru	Venezuela (Bolivarian Rep. of)
Subscribed capital	234	469	234	234	469	469
Paid-up capital	157	313	133	157	313	313
IMF quotas	233	1,053	222	414	878	3,721
Short-term debt	370	3,800	1,499	2,316	2,335	3,720
International reserves	893	10,844	1,497	1,004	9,721	12,107
Short-term debt/ international reserves (percent)	41	35	100	231	24	31
Short-term debt/increased international reserves (percent)[a]	26	33	82	149	22	29

Source: Prepared by the author using data from the countries, the Latin American Reserve Fund, and the International Monetary Fund.

a. The quotient of short-term debt over increased international reserves is calculated by adding to international reserves the debt capacity in FAR/FLAR, which is equal to 2.5 times the paid-up capital, except for Bolivia and Ecuador, where it is 3.5 times.

while encountering severe economic stress and being in default to their commercial creditors, giving it repayment priority over other creditors in the event of a moratorium, with the result that FLAR has a zero default record in its basic loan operations.[7]

Feasibility of Expanding FLAR Regional Coverage

In spite of prudent and relatively stable macroeconomic management by many of the countries of the region, they have proven to be highly sensitive to volatility in international capital movements. This vulnerability reflects flaws in international financial markets, insufficiently developed domestic financial markets, and the countries' low level of international reserves, which has made them unable to cope with problems of contagion and speculative attacks on their currencies. Therefore it is of paramount importance to boost regional financial cooperation by strengthening a regional reserve fund.

7. Moody's (www.moodys.com); Standard & Poor's (www.standardandpoors.com).

In an examination of the viability of expanding the FLAR area of coverage, Agosin argued that, despite the significant covariance between the capital flows to the different countries of the region, it is not so great as to make a regional reserve fund financially unviable.[8] Insofar as crises in the region have a clear sequential component, a regional fund is feasible and, furthermore, could help to curb mechanisms of crisis transmission between countries. If this fund were endowed with 15 percent of the reserves of the eleven countries of the region (including all the large countries, except Mexico), it could provide financing to cope with capital outflows equivalent to the entire short-term foreign debt of all the countries in question.[9] Thus by contributing around 15 percent of their international reserves, the countries could help to resolve short-term financial problems.

FLAR should not focus solely on providing support for balance-of-payments financing and short-term liquidity; it should also support coordination of the macroeconomic and monetary policies of the countries in the region. The fact that the countries feel a greater sense of ownership of this institution facilitates use of the fund to promote the coordination of monetary, exchange rate, and fiscal policies. FLAR, together with the member countries' central banks, could promote periodic assessments of the progress of the economies, as well as help to establish common standards for regulation and financial supervision. Stepping up the regional effort to monitor the countries' economic performance and helping to establish early warning systems for crisis risk could alleviate contagion problems and reduce financial vulnerability.

Summary and Conclusions

The countries of Latin America and the Caribbean have succeeded in building a major system of regional and subregional financial institutions, which was undermined by the foreign debt crisis of the 1980s. The effects of this crisis were not uniform throughout the various subregions and institutions. In general, clearing agreements, and to a lesser extent development banks, were the hardest hit. However, FAR/FLAR discharged its duty of providing balance-of-payments support. Within the subregional sphere, the financial institutions of the Andean Community were the least affected, and during the 1980s they maintained a better performance than those of the Central American Common Market or the Caribbean Community.

8. See Agosin (2001).
9. Agosin (2001).

The participation of subregional development banks has increased significantly since the 1990s, growing at an annual rate of around 10 percent, to the
point where they now channel roughly 46 percent of this type of financing to
the Andean Community, CACM, and Caricom countries. CAF is the most
dynamic and has mobilized the largest volume of resources. Loans have tended
to favor countries with a lower relative income and have focused mainly on
financing infrastructure investment. The subregional development banks have
disbursed a significant volume of resources, accounting for an average of around
1 percent of GDP of the Andean and Central American subregions and 0.5 percent of the Caribbean GDP.

Given the current characteristics of the process of financial integration by the
countries of the region with the world economy, subregional development banks
should not limit their role to acting as a complementary source of funding for
their member countries. In addition to providing countercyclical financing, they
should expand their functions to include supporting and facilitating the countries' access to international financial markets by taking greater advantage of their
better credit risk rating; and they should promote the emergence of instruments
to help these countries capture resources in international markets.

Subregional development banks must also actively support national and
regional financial development. Proper management of economic and financial
risk is key to stimulating and facilitating economic growth. Since subregional
development banks are more able to distribute risk than national banks, they
have an important role in promoting new financial instruments that reduce the
risks and costs of accessing financial flows. A promising area in this respect is
the deepening of domestic and subregional capital markets by means of asset
securitization, guarantee funds, and insurance mechanisms. This calls for stronger
ties with development and commercial banks and the countries' capital markets.

With respect to support for short-term liquidity needs and balance-of-payments
financing, FAR/FLAR has played a major role in providing timely emergency
financing to its member countries, in particular relatively less developed countries. In the case of Bolivia and Ecuador, it has loaned resources equivalent to
35 percent of Bolivia's international reserves and 28 percent of Ecuador's. Furthermore, when debt capacity with FAR/FLAR is added to the international reserves
of FAR/FLAR member countries, the short-term debt/international reserves ratio
drops significantly in Bolivia, Ecuador, and Costa Rica, which reduces these
countries' financial vulnerability. In addition, FAR/FLAR has played a clear
countercyclical role, complementing exceptional financing from the IMF.

However, because FAR/FLAR has such limited geographic coverage, balance-
of-payments support via emergency financing continues to be one of the weakest

links in regional financial integration. Given the characteristics and dynamics of the latest generation of balance-of-payments crises, an essential task in the process of intra- and extraregional financial integration is to strengthen and expand FAR/FLAR. Since the covariance between capital flows to the different countries is significant but not excessively high—reflecting a major sequential component of crises in the region—it is feasible to expand the geographic coverage of FAR/FLAR. This would help to reduce contagion of crises between countries.

References

Agosin, M. 2001. "Strengthening Regional Financial Cooperation." *CEPAL Review* (ECLAC, Santiago, Chile), no. 73 (April): 31–50.

Banco Centroamericano de Integración Económica (BCIE). Various years. *Annual Report.*

Corporación Andina de Fomento (CAF). Various years. *Annual Report.*

Banco de Desarrollo del Caribe (Caribbean Development Bank, CDB). Various years. *Annual Report.*

Economic Commission for Latin America and the Caribbean (ECLAC). 1990. "La cooperación regional en los campos financiero y monetario." LC/L.603. Santiago.

———. 2002a. "Introductory Note on Regional Schemes." Prepared for the Interregional Conference on Financing Development, Mexico, January.

———. 2002b. *Latin America and the Caribbean in the World Economy, 2000–2001.* Santiago.

Emerging Markets Eminent Persons' Group Seoul Report. 2001. *Rebuilding the International Financial Architecture.* Seoul, October.

Ffrench-Davis, R., and A. Di Filippo 2003. "El rol de las instituciones regionales en la globalización." *Estudios Internacionales* (IEI, University of Chile) 36, no. 141: April–June.

Fondo Latinoamericano de Reservas (FLAR). Various years. *Annual Report.*

Inter-American Development Bank (IDB). Various years. *Annual Report.*

Maldonado, R. 2003. "La cooperación financiera en América Latina y el Caribe: las instituciones financieras subregionales en el fomento de las inversiones y del comercio exterior." *Serie de Comercio Exterior.* CEPAL.

Mistry, P. S. 1999. "Coping with the Financial Crisis: Are Regional Arrangements the Missing Link?" *International and Monetary Financial Issues for the 1990's.* Vol. 10. UNCTAD.

Ocampo, J. A. 2002a. "Recasting the International Financial Agenda." In *International Capital Markets: Systems in Transition,* edited by John Eatwell and Lance Taylor. Oxford University Press.

———. 2002b. "Reforming the International Financial Architecture: Consensus and Divergence." In *Governing Globalization: Issues and Institutions,* edited by Deepak Nayyar. Oxford University Press.

Titelman, D. 2002. "Development Financing in the Context of Financial Volatility." *Serie Financiamiento del Desarrollo* 121. CEPAL.

———. 2003. "Banca de desarrollo y financiamiento productivo." *Serie Financiamiento del Desarrollo* 137. CEPAL.

World Bank. Various years. *Annual Report.*

8

Regional Financial Integration in East Asia: Challenges and Prospects

YUNG CHUL PARK

The large currency crises of the past decade have been regional in nature.[1] This feature of financial crises suggests that neighboring countries have a strong incentive to engage in mutual surveillance and to extend financial assistance to one another in the face of potentially contagious threats to stability. Regardless of whether the sudden shifts in market expectations and confidence were the primary source of the Asian financial crisis, foreign lenders were so alarmed by the Thai crisis that they abruptly pulled their investments out of the other countries in the region, making the crisis contagious. The geographic proximity and economic similarities (or similar structural problems) of these Asian countries prompted a blanket withdrawal of foreign lending and portfolio investment, with differences in economic fundamentals often being overlooked. If the channels of contagion cannot be blocked off through multilateral cooperation at an early stage in a crisis, countries without their own extensive foreign reserves will not be able to survive independently. Hence, neighbors have an interest in helping put out a fire (a financial crisis) before it spreads to them.[2]

The author wishes to acknowledge helpful comments from José Antonio Ocampo on an earlier draft.
1. See Glick and Rose (1999).
2. Ito, Ogawa, and Sasaki (1999).

But as long as a crisis remains confined to a specific country or region, there is no urgent political need for unaffected countries to pay the significant costs associated with playing the role of firefighter.

The formation of a regional financial arrangement in East Asia reflects in part frustration with the slow reform of the international financial system.[3] The sense of urgency concerning reform of the international financial architecture has receded considerably in the G-7 countries. The slow progress has been further complicated by the perception that the current international architecture is defective. The lack of global governance, including a global lender of last resort and international financial regulation, is not likely to be remedied anytime soon.[4] As long as there continue to be structural problems on the supply side of international capital—such as volatile capital movements and exchange rate gyrations of the U.S. dollar, the euro, and the yen—the East Asian countries will remain as vulnerable as ever to future crises. It is thus in the interest of East Asians to work together to create their own self-help arrangements. The Chiang Mai Initiative (CMI) of the Association of Southeast Asian Nations plus Japan, China, and the Republic of Korea (ASEAN+3) is one such available option. However, it is equally important that individual East Asian countries continue to undertake financial sector restructuring and development. Without sound financial institutions and adequate regulatory regimes, Asian financial markets will remain vulnerable to external shocks. Regional policy dialogue should also contribute to strengthening the efforts to restructure and advance the development of financial markets in East Asia. The CMI has emerged as a regional forum for policy dialogue and also for concerted regional efforts at financial reform in the region.

Three pillars—liquidity assistance, monitoring and surveillance, and exchange rate coordination—are essential for regional financial and monetary cooperation. However, the development of this cooperation and its related institutions will follow an evolutionary path, as was the case with European monetary integration. A shallow form of financial cooperation may comprise no more than a common foreign reserve pooling or mutual credit arrangements such as bilateral swaps. In other words, some kinds of shallow financial cooperation are conceivable without any commitment to exchange rate coordination, under which the exchange rates of participating countries would be pegged to each other or would vanish through the adoption of a common currency. The East Asian countries presently appear to be pursuing this form of financial cooperation.[5]

3. See Park and Wang (2002).
4. See Sakakibara (2003).
5. See Henning (2002).

Although a full-fledged form of monetary integration is not viable at this stage, East Asia may begin to examine the feasibility and desirability of cooperation and coordination in exchange rate policies.[6]

Evidently, there is a rising sense of East Asian identity today. After the proposal to create an Asian monetary fund was aborted, the leaders of ASEAN responded by inviting China, Japan, and the Republic of Korea to join in an effort to build a regional mechanism for economic cooperation in East Asia. The ASEAN+3 summit in November 1999 released a Joint Statement on East Asian Cooperation that covers a wide range of possible areas for regional cooperation. Recognizing the need to establish regional financial arrangements to supplement the existing international facilities, the finance ministers of ASEAN+3 at their meeting in Chiang Mai, Thailand, in May 2000 then agreed to strengthen the existing cooperative frameworks in the region through the Chiang Mai Initiative.

The purpose of this chapter is to examine the current process and future prospects for regional financial and monetary cooperation in East Asia. More specifically, it sketches an institutional design for a regional financial architecture encompassing the three major pillars (liquidity assistance arrangements, policy dialogue and surveillance, and exchange rate coordination). Through an evolutionary process of enlargement and consolidation of the CMI, this study envisions the creation of an Asian monetary fund that is fully equipped with liquidity support facilities and a monitoring and surveillance mechanism. The chapter does not, however, contemplate any manifest collective exchange rate coordination under the ASEAN+3 framework.

The chapter is organized as follows: The following sections successively discuss the economic rationale for a regional financial arrangement in East Asia; developments in the Chiang Mai Initiative; and major barriers to financial cooperation and integration in East Asia.

Economic Rationale for a Regional Financial Arrangement in East Asia

The 1997–98 Asian financial crisis brought home the need to create a regional mechanism of defense against future crises in East Asia. However, other events have also encouraged the regional integration movement. This section discusses some of these developments as background for an examination of whether they

6. East Asian currency union remains a very remote possibility, but this does not necessarily mean that a currency union could not be envisaged as a long-term objective.

can maintain the momentum for enhanced regional cooperation and lead to financial market integration and monetary unification in the long run.

Trade Integration and Stability of Bilateral Exchange Rates

Since the early 1990s, many of the East Asian countries have made sustained efforts to deregulate and open domestic markets, including financial markets, to foreign competition. As a result of market orientation and trade liberalization, East Asia has seen a large increase in intraregional trade and investment. In terms of imports, intraregional trade in East Asia (among the ASEAN+3 countries and Taiwan Province of China) accounted for 46 percent of the region's total trade in 2001, when the entire region was still recovering from the crisis (see table 8-1). There is every indication that this trend will continue.

Financial liberalization and market opening has also contributed to both regional and global integration of financial markets in the East Asian countries. And there is growing awareness that further integration of intraregional trade in goods, services, and financial assets will call for stabilization of the bilateral exchange rates for East Asian currencies. With deepening in regional trade integration, East Asia is bound to lose disproportionately more than other regions from trade disruptions caused by currency crises. Stability of bilateral exchange rates would also facilitate and increase the benefits of capital mobility in the region.

In the aftermath of the East Asian crisis, the flexible exchange system became the accepted norm in the new international financial architecture. The new consensus, however, did not last very long. Williamson and Frankel argue that intermediate regimes such as the "basket, band, and crawl" system are more likely to be appropriate than "two-corner solutions" for many emerging market economies (EMEs). In particular, Williamson advocates several intermediate regimes with soft margins. Fischer suggests that developing countries that are not exposed to capital flows could choose from a wide variety of intermediate regimes and that flexible exchange rate systems suitable for EMEs could include crawling bands with wide ranges.[7]

If East Asian countries find it desirable to follow some type of intermediate regime, a case can be made for creating regional financial cooperative arrangements that could help stabilize bilateral exchange rates in the region. Although the ASEAN+3 authorities have no plans for transforming the CMI into a monetary union, the East Asian countries could use the CMI as a framework for developing an East Asian common currency area in the long run, after a transition

---

7. See Williamson (2000); Frankel (1999); and Fischer (2001).

period during which a mechanism for the coordination of exchange rate policies would be established.

The IMF and Capital Account Crisis Management

A 2003 International Monetary Fund (IMF) report makes it clear that East Asia suffered a capital account crisis in 1997 and 1998, which required a management and resolution strategy different from the traditional IMF recipe for crises originating from current account deficits. A large increase in capital flows into some of the East Asian countries set off an asset market boom and a precipitous increase in the current account deficit, thereby making these countries vulnerable to speculative attacks. The perception of vulnerability of these countries triggered a sharp and large capital outflow, which was further aggravated by the panic and herding behavior of foreign investors. Once the dollar peg became indefensible, the value of the currencies plummeted. Many banks and corporations with balance sheet mismatches could not service their foreign-currency-denominated debts and eventually became insolvent. A sharp contraction in the level of output then followed.

The crisis resolution strategy of the IMF was twofold. First, it imposed tight monetary and fiscal policies with the aim of stabilizing the exchange rate and generating current account surpluses by contracting domestic demand. These policies, together with weak currencies, were expected to help lure back foreign investors. Second, the IMF required the crisis countries to undertake a wide range of reforms in the corporate, financial, and public sectors to strengthen the structural foundation of their economies. These reforms were intended to help the affected countries return to the pre-crisis path of robust growth; they were also viewed as critical to restoring international lenders' confidence in their economies.

Once the crisis broke out, output contraction and the turbulence of foreign exchange and other financial markets in one country were rapidly transmitted to other economies in the region through trade and financial market linkages. Pronouncements by international financial institutions, including the IMF and policymakers from the G-7 countries, that the crisis countries had serious structural problems in their financial, corporate, and public sectors did little to inspire confidence in these economies.[8] Indeed, to some extent the IMF crisis management program actually helped fuel contagion of the crisis.

At this writing nine years after the crisis, assessments of the success of the structural reforms are mixed. A 2001 World Bank report continued to argue that

8. Furman and Stiglitz (1998).

Table 8-1. *Trade Shares in East Asian Countries*
Percent

	Exports from																	
	East Asia			China			Japan			Republic of Korea			Other NIEs			ASEAN 4		
Exports to	1980	1990	2001	1980	1990	2001	1980	1990	2001	1980	1990	2001	1980	1990	2001	1980	1990	2001
							A. Export data											
East Asia	32.0	36.2	42.2	52.9	66.9	44.9	21.8	24.2	32.6	28.5	33.0	38.9	31.3	39.9	49.5	54.2	50.6	47.4
China	2.8	4.6	9.8	0.0	0.0	0.0	3.9	2.1	7.7	0.0	0.0	12.1	4.0	15.7	24.2	0.8	2.1	4.4
Japan	10.2	8.2	8.9	22.3	14.8	16.9	0.0	0.0	0.0	17.4	19.4	11.0	6.3	6.9	6.6	34.6	24.4	16.1
Republic of Korea	2.7	3.8	4.0	0.0	0.7	4.7	4.1	6.1	6.3	0.0	0.0	0.0	1.3	2.3	2.6	1.7	3.9	3.7
Other NIEs[a]	9.3	12.3	11.5	26.4	47.0	19.6	6.7	8.3	9.4	6.2	8.6	9.0	6.0	4.5	4.7	13.8	16.0	15.9
ASEAN 4[b]	7.0	7.1	8.1	4.3	2.9	3.8	7.0	7.7	9.3	5.0	5.0	6.8	13.7	10.6	11.5	3.2	4.2	7.2
South Asia[c]	1.7	1.4	1.5	1.1	1.5	1.5	1.6	1.2	0.8	2.0	1.7	1.8	2.8	1.9	2.1	1.1	1.3	1.8
Central Asia[d]	0.0	0.0	0.1	0.0	0.0	0.4	0.0	0.0	0.0	0.0	0.0	0.3	0.0	0.0	0.0	0.0	0.0	0.0
CER[e]	2.8	2.2	2.0	1.4	0.8	1.5	3.1	2.8	2.2	1.5	1.7	1.6	4.3	2.2	2.0	1.8	1.8	2.5
USA	21.4	25.7	21.0	5.4	8.6	20.4	24.5	31.7	30.4	26.4	29.9	20.8	19.4	23.0	10.3	18.8	19.4	20.0
EU	14.6	17.7	14.9	13.1	10.1	15.4	14.0	20.4	16.0	15.5	15.4	13.1	17.9	17.2	14.0	13.6	16.7	15.0
Others	27.5	16.8	18.2	26.1	13.6	15.9	35.1	19.6	18.0	26.0	18.3	23.4	24.3	15.9	22.1	10.4	10.2	13.2
World	100	100	100	100	100	100	100	100	100	100	100	100	100	100	100	100	100	100

B. Import data[f]

East Asia	30.4	38.7	45.8	33.3	49	32.3	20.7	23.4	36.2	33.4	34.4	39.9	47.9	57.1	62.8	41.1	46.2	50.8
China	3.9	7.8	15	0	0	0	3.1	5.1	16.6	0.1	0	9.4	10.8	22.6	29.9	2.8	2.6	5.6
Japan	11.2	12.8	9	27	14.7	0.3	0	0	0	26.3	26.6	18.9	20.4	17.8	12.2	24.3	25.6	19.8
Republic of Korea	1.8	3.4	5.4	0	0.5	13.7	2.2	5	4.9	0	0	0	2.3	3.8	4.1	2	3.4	5.1
Other NIEs[a]	3.1	6.4	5.1	4	29.6	8.5	1.5	2.4	2	1.2	2.2	3	4.3	3.6	3.8	8.3	10.6	10.9
ASEAN 4[b]	10.4	8.2	11.2	2.4	4.2	9.8	14	10.9	12.7	5.9	5.6	8.6	10.2	9.2	12.8	3.8	4.1	9.4
South Asia[c]	0.9	1.1	1.4	1	1.7	2.4	0.9	1	0.8	0.3	0.7	1.1	1.2	1	1.5	0.7	1.5	1.6
Central Asia[d]	0	0	0.1	0	0	0.6	0	0	0	0	0	0.1	0	0	0	0	0	0
CER[e]	4.7	4.1	3.4	6.4	2.9	3.6	5.6	6	4.7	3.4	4.4	4.4	2.3	1.6	1.4	4.3	3.8	3.1
USA	17	17.8	14.5	20	12.7	15.4	17.4	22.5	18.3	21.9	24.3	15.9	13	11.5	10.3	16.1	13.9	12.9
EU	8.8	14.9	12.9	14.7	17.6	20.9	5.9	16.1	12.8	7.2	13	10.6	11.7	11.8	10.5	13.5	16.4	11.7
Others	38.3	23.4	22	24.6	16.2	24.8	49.5	31	27.3	33.6	23.4	28	23.9	17.1	13.5	24.2	18.3	19.9
World	100	100	100	100	100	100	100	100	100	100	100	100	100	100	100	100	100	100

Source: International Monetary Fund, *Direction of Trade Statistics Yearbook*, various years.

a. Singapore, Hong Kong SAR.

b. Indonesia, Malaysia, Philippines, Thailand.

c. India, Sri Lanka, Bangladesh, Pakistan.

d. Kazakhstan, Uzbekistan.

e. Closer Economic Relations (CER) Trade Agreement between Australia and New Zealand.

f. Country A's exports to Country B are estimated by country B's imports from country A.

progress on structural and institutional reforms remained key to retaining confidence and resilience to shocks in East Asia.[9] One lesson of the Asian situation is that when a crisis in a country originates in the capital account, policy coordination or at least policy dialogue and review among neighboring countries is essential to prevent contagion of the crisis. Another lesson is that an appropriate response to a capital account crisis is to serve notice to international financial markets that the country in crisis is prepared to supply—either by itself or in cooperation with regional or global financial institutions, including the IMF—as much liquidity as it takes to thwart an impending speculative attack.

These lessons clearly suggest that regional financial cooperative arrangements such as the CMI could complement the role of the IMF in managing a capital account crisis. In the absence of policy dialogues and exchanges of information among neighbors, individual countries may not be able to find the causes of large changes in capital flows and exchange rates, or more important, respond to the crisis if it spreads. An efficient regional policy coordination mechanism will help monitor and make necessary policy adjustments in response to changes in market expectations. Even smoothing out high-frequency movements in the nominal exchange rate in individual countries may have to be coordinated at a regional level in order not to send wrong signals to foreign exchange markets. Unless the countries in the region maintain close working relationships in coordinating policies and exchanging information, they will not be able to make a prompt assessment of the nature of the crisis and mount a quick response.

The IMF could monitor capital flows within and between regions and also the behavior of market participants. But given its narrow mandate and its small staff, the IMF may not have either the institutional or the professional capacity to keep track of developments in the financial markets of all of its member countries. Since the Fund obtains most of its macroeconomic and market information from the authorities of member countries, its ability to prescribe preventive measures to countries vulnerable to the crisis may be limited. At best it can serve as a lender and as a crisis manager. However, the Asian experience demonstrates that the crisis management ability of the IMF is severely constrained.

At the time of the crisis, the CMI countries as a whole held about U.S.$700 billion in foreign reserves. The total financing required from the IMF, other international financial institutions, and a number of donor countries to restore financial stability in Indonesia, the Republic of Korea, and Thailand amounted to U.S.$111.7 billion. If the IMF had been ready to supply a large amount of

9. World Bank (2001).

liquidity to the crisis countries, or if the thirteen countries had established a cooperative mechanism through which they could pool their reserves to assist other countries in need of financial support, they could have nipped the Thai crisis in the bud and minimized its contagion by supplying only a small fraction of their total reserves. In view of the large loss of output and the fall in employment in the region, such a cooperative response would indeed have been desirable.

Inasmuch as East Asia suffered a liquidity crisis, compounded by the panic and herding behavior of foreign investors, a more effective IMF crisis management strategy—instead of tightening monetary and fiscal policy—would have been to supply a large amount of short-term financing to replenish foreign exchange reserves at the first sign of a speculative attack. Such a strategy could have stopped the spread of the crisis and the ensuing slump throughout the region.[10] At the time of the crisis, there were neither regional nor global lenders of last resort to deal with the bank-run problems that East Asian countries were facing. With its limited financial resources, the IMF could not manage the East Asian crisis by itself; it had to enlist the financial support of the G-7 and other countries. This situation is testimony that, as a global institution, the IMF would be more effective in resolving crises if it established cooperative relations with its regional counterparts and hence encouraged the development of regional financial mechanisms.

Once established, an East Asian monetary fund could serve as an institution complementary to the IMF by providing additional resources and by working with the Fund to prevent and manage financial crises. It could also support the work of the IMF by monitoring economic developments in the region and taking part in IMF global surveillance activities. As Henning notes, it is difficult to assess ex ante whether resources supplied through regional financial arrangements are really additional to those supplied by the international community.[11] The "additionality" problem arises in principle whenever there are multiple sources of

---

10. Contagion is geographically concentrated, making a regional grouping for support logical. In addition to providing financial assistance in tandem with international support, a regional financial cooperation mechanism may conduct policy reviews and initiate a dialogue process. Policy dialogue, including monitoring and surveillance, is the bedrock on which coherent policy formation under regional financial arrangements rests. A monitoring and surveillance process would provide prompt and relevant information for assessing the situation of countries in trouble and the potential contagious effects of a crisis to neighboring countries. Furthermore, a joint exercise based on a regionwide early warning system would facilitate closer examination of financial vulnerabilities in the region. In addition, the regional policy dialogue process would contribute to ensuring effective implementation of high-quality banking and financial standards and promoting financial market development in East Asia.

11. Henning (2002).

finance and conditionality, yet it appears to have been managed successfully in numerous historical cases. Potential conflicts can be avoided through consultation and coordination, which may be provided in part by the United States and the East Asian governments.

Limited and Slow Progress in International Financial Reform

One of several developments that have reinforced regionalism in East Asia has been slow progress in the reform of the international financial system. The need for reform is no longer so urgently felt in the G-7 countries, despite the economic collapse of 2001–02 in Argentina and the growing trade imbalance between the United States and East Asia. The slow progress has been further compounded by the perception that none of the many proposals for a new architecture may be effective in sustaining global financial stability. In particular, as long as the structural problems on the supply side of international capital markets are not addressed, the East Asian countries fear that they will remain as vulnerable to future crises as they are now.[12]

Griffith-Jones and Ocampo show that there has been no international reform agenda acceptable to both developing and developed countries.[13] The 2002 Monterrey Consensus produced a new international agenda, but it is not altogether clear whether the new agenda will be put into action. Some of the progress that has been made is asymmetrical in the sense that the reform has focused on strengthening the financial and corporate sectors of developing and emerging market economies instead of rectifying imperfections in international capital markets. Some of the advances in the new architecture have also been jeopardized by the growing reluctance of developing countries to support large IMF financing. Finally, it should be noted that developing countries have been largely excluded from the key institutions and forums involved in international financial reform.

It is natural that many emerging market economies, faced with the uneven and slow process of the reform, would consider developing their own mechanisms of defense against future financial crises. One such defensive measure is the CMI in East Asia. Instead of waiting until the G-7 creates a new architecture—whose effectiveness would be questionable, at best—the East Asian countries have taken the initiative of working together to create their own system of defense, and have fortified themselves by accumulating large amounts of reserves to deal with sudden and unexpected capital outflows.

12. Park and Wang (2002).
13. Griffith-Jones and Ocampo (2001).

Accumulating Reserves: A War Chest or Insurance?

Many developing and emerging market economies, in particular those in countries that have fallen victim to financial crises, have taken recourse to amassing foreign reserves as a defense against future crises. Before the onset of capital account liberalization in the early 1990s, foreign currency reserves were held mainly for transactions purposes. The rule of thumb was to hold reserves in an amount equivalent to imports for three to four months. This implicit rule appears to be no longer acceptable. In order to meet the increased volume of their capital account transactions, but above all in order to build a war chest large enough to stave off future speculative attacks, many East Asian emerging market economies have accumulated large amounts of reserves.

For example, at the end of 2005, the volume of reserves as a share of GDP in the Republic of Korea was almost 27 percent, which was more than four times the level in 1996. Similar developments have taken place in other crisis-hit parts of East Asia (see table 8-2). In Taiwan Province of China, the ratio of reserves to GDP almost doubled between 1996 and 2005. The ratio climbed to 54 percent at the end of 2005 from about 20 percent in 1997 in Malaysia. Although reserve accumulation has been relatively modest in both Thailand and the Philippines, these countries have added almost 10 percentage points to their ratios since the end of 1997. The thirteen East Asian countries that constitute ASEAN+3 held collective foreign currency reserves estimated at more than U.S.$2.5 trillion at the end of 2005. By any measure, this level is excessive and costly, and it represents a clear case of misallocation of resources.[14] If these reserves are pooled, a mere 10 percent of the total would be sufficient to provide a formidable line of defense against any future crises.

In theory, floating rates and capital account liberalization are supposed to reduce the amounts of reserves to be held for the prevention of crises. Except for China, Hong Kong SAR, and Malaysia, all the crisis countries have been on a flexible exchange rate system and have deregulated their capital account transactions to a considerable degree since the 1997 crisis. However, the shift to floating rates and participation in international financial markets over the past five years has not reduced their reserve holdings relative to their output, largely because capital flows have been unstable and capital account liberalization has not improved their access to international capital markets.

14. In a speech at a Tokyo conference, Stiglitz argued that the existing dollar-based reserve system benefits the United States, whereas developing countries bear a disproportionate burden of holding large amounts of reserves to counter volatility in the currency market. He went on to say that an Asian monetary fund, which would have given a quicker remedy to the Asian financial crisis, could be an alternative model, providing a good basis for a new global regime (see Stiglitz 2002).

Table 8-2. *Foreign Exchange Reserves and Current Account Balances, 1996–2005*

Country	1996	1997	1998	1999	2000	2001	2002	2003	2004	2005
Foreign exchange reserves (billions of U.S. dollars)										
Republic of Korea	34.0	20.4	52.0	74.0	96.1	102.8	121.3	155.3	199.1	210.4
China[a]	107.0	142.8	149.2	157.7	168.3	215.6	291.1	408.2	618.6	769.0
Hong Kong SAR	63.8	92.8	89.6	96.3	107.6	111.2	111.9	118.4	123.5	122.3
Taiwan Province of China	88.0	83.5	90.3	106.2	106.7	122.2	161.7	206.6	242.0	253.8
Thailand	37.7	26.2	28.8	34.1	31.9	32.4	38.0	41.1	49.8	52.1
Indonesia	24.0	20.6	22.7	23.5	28.5	27.2	31.0	35.0	36.3	34.7
Malaysia	27.0	20.8	25.6	30.6	29.1	30.5	34.2	44.5	66.7	70.5
Philippines	10.0	7.3	9.2	13.2	13.0	13.4	13.1	13.5	16.2	18.5
Singapore	77.0	71.4	75.0	77.2	80.4	75.4	82.0	95.7	112.8	116.6
Current account balance (billions of U.S. dollars)										
Republic of Korea	−23.0	−8.2	40.4	24.5	11.0	8.2	6.1	12.3	28.9	15.5
China[a]	7.2	37.0	31.5	15.7	20.5	17.4	35.4	45.9	68.7	100.3
Hong Kong SAR	−3.5	−6.2	3.9	10.5	8.8	9.9	12.6	16.2	16.4	24.7
Taiwan Province of China	10.9	7.1	3.4	8.4	9.3	17.9	25.6	29.2	18.6	10.9
Thailand	−14.7	−3.0	14.2	12.4	9.2	6.2	7.0	8.0	7.3	. . .
Indonesia	−8.5	−5.8	4.1	5.8	8.0	6.9	8.1	7.5	3.1	. . .
Malaysia	−4.5	−5.9	9.5	12.6	8.9	7.3	7.2	13.4	14.9	. . .
Philippines	−3.9	−4.4	1.5	7.9	9.3	1.3	4.2	3.3	2.0	. . .
Singapore	13.9	16.9	21.0	21.3	21.7	16.1	18.7	28.2	27.9	31.5
Foreign exchange reserves (percent of GDP)										
Republic of Korea	6.5	4.2	16.2	17.8	21.0	21.3	22.2	25.7	29.3	26.6
China[a]	13.1	15.8	15.8	15.9	15.5	18.3	22.9	28.9	38.7	42.4
Hong Kong SAR	41.4	54.3	55.0	60.5	65.8	68.3	69.3	75.0	74.5	69.1
Taiwan Province of China	31.5	32.7	32.6	35.9	36.4	43.5	57.3	72.2	75.0	73.8
Thailand	20.7	17.3	25.7	27.5	26.0	28.0	29.9	28.7	30.5	29.2
Indonesia	10.6	9.6	23.0	16.2	18.9	19.3	17.9	16.8	14.1	12.4
Malaysia	26.7	20.8	35.0	37.7	32.6	34.6	36.0	43.2	56.6	53.7
Philippines	12.1	8.8	14.9	17.3	27.4	18.6	16.8	16.7	18.8	19.8
Singapore	83.7	85.2	99.9	89.3	82.2	88.8	94.3	104.8	105.6	101.0
Current account balance (percent of GDP)										
Republic of Korea	−4.4	−1.7	12.6	5.9	2.4	1.7	1.0	2.0	4.2	2.0
China[a]	0.9	4.1	3.3	1.6	1.9	1.5	2.8	3.3	4.3	5.5
Hong Kong SAR	−2.3	−3.6	2.4	6.6	5.4	6.1	7.8	10.2	9.9	14.0
Taiwan Province of China	3.9	2.8	1.2	2.8	3.2	6.5	9.1	10.2	5.8	3.2

Table 8-2. *(continued)*

Country	1996	1997	1998	1999	2000	2001	2002	2003	2004	2005
Thailand	−8.1	−2.0	12.7	10.0	7.5	5.4	5.5	5.6	4.5	...
Indonesia	−3.8	−2.7	4.2	4.1	5.3	4.9	4.7	3.6	1.2	...
Malaysia	−4.4	−5.6	13.1	15.9	9.9	8.3	7.6	12.9	12.6	...
Philippines	−4.8	−5.3	2.4	10.3	19.7	1.8	5.3	4.2	2.3	...
Singapore	15.1	20.2	23.3	24.0	22.2	19.1	21.5	30.9	26.1	27.2

Sources: International Financial Statistics (IFS) database, the International Monetary Fund, and the Asia Regional Information Center (ARIC).

a. Estimates by the International Institute of Finance.

With growing financial integration, the adequacy of reserve holdings in emerging market economies is often gauged by the amount of short-term foreign borrowings, and a good benchmark is that the ratio of reserves to short-term foreign debts should be equal to or higher than 1.[15] Even when this benchmark is applied, the reserve holdings of the crisis-hit countries in East Asia are excessive. In the Republic of Korea and Indonesia, the ratio has been higher than 2. China and Thailand hold reserves six and four times, respectively, as large as their short-term external liabilities (see table 8-3). If emerging market economies in East Asia and elsewhere have to hold more reserves than their short-term foreign indebtedness, then questions arise as to whether these countries should borrow at all from the short end of international capital markets and whether they should open their financial markets.

Commercial banks hold reserves equal to only a small fraction of their short-term deposit liabilities; they can do so because, among other things, they have access to the domestic lender of last resort. In the absence of a global and regional lender of last resort, financial institutions in EMEs cannot engage in term transformation involving foreign currency loans. Could EMEs instead make arrangements with international banking institutions to establish private contingent lines of credit from which they could draw in case they come under speculative attack? The Mexican experience is instructive in this regard: the availability of contingent credit lines does not increase liquidity once a financial crisis breaks out, because the banks that provide contingent credit lines to the central bank withdraw other credits extended to firms and financial institutions to reduce their country exposure.[16]

---

15. The short-term foreign debt benchmark therefore suggests that reserve holdings for other uses must be secured by long-term foreign borrowing or the accumulation of current account surpluses.

16. Carstens (2001).

Table 8-3. *Ratio of Foreign Reserves to Short-Term Debt, 1998–2004*

Year	Indonesia	Republic of Korea	Thailand	China
1998	0.90	1.33	1.01	8.60
1999	1.49	1.74	1.74	10.39
2000	1.46	1.95	2.18	12.87
2001	1.08	2.45	2.42	4.26
2002	2.37	2.42	3.19	5.50
2003	2.72	2.81	3.77	5.30
2004	2.25	3.30	4.10	5.90

Source: Asia Regional Information Center (www.aric.adb.org).

Owing to the limited availability of private contingent lines of credit, together with the absence of a global or regional lender of last resort, EMEs may have to hold a larger amount of reserves, and to do so they may have to run a sizable surplus on the current account, as the East Asian crisis countries have done since the crisis in 1997. However, this reserve accumulation in EMEs has undesirable implications for future trade relations between developing and developed countries and for the growth of the world economy.

As a growing number of EMEs increase their holdings of reserves by running current account surpluses, trade relations between developing and developed countries are likely to suffer from tension and unnecessary conflicts. The large accumulation of reserves in EMEs may also sap global growth as it reduces global aggregate demand. Therefore, both developing and developed countries will find it in their interest to search for other schemes that can reduce EMEs' holdings of foreign exchange reserves. For example, a group of countries, not necessarily from the same region, may decide to pool a certain percentage of their reserves to create new credit facilities for short-term liquidity support. Individual countries belonging to the arrangement could then reduce their holdings by borrowing from these new credit facilities.

Regional Financial Arrangements: Building Blocks?

Any argument supporting regional trade and financial arrangements must address the fundamental question of whether they, whatever form they may take, are conducive to an orderly global integration of trade and financial markets. Although many misgivings have been expressed about the role of the growing number of recent regional economic arrangements, the experience of the past decade—in particular that of the European Union—suggests that such arrangements have not interfered with multilateral trade and financial liberalization.

In other words, they have been building blocks rather than stumbling blocks for a more integrated world economy. There is no evidence to suggest that an East Asian financial arrangement would be oriented toward a withdrawal from the global economy and that, hence, it would erect barriers to global financial integration.

Lawrence points out that the forces that were driving the wave of regionalism in the early 1990s differed fundamentally from those driving earlier moves toward regionalization and that the regional initiatives represented efforts to facilitate their members' participation in the world economy rather than their withdrawal from it.[17] Trade and financial developments since then have not been at odds with this observation. Many developing countries are motivated to join regional groupings as a means of facilitating implementation of a strategy to liberalize and open their economies. Since most of the East Asian EMEs are pursuing outward-looking development strategies geared to promoting exports and attracting foreign investment, they would have very little to gain by forming a regional arrangement designed to thwart globalization.

Ever since the proposal for creating an Asian monetary fund was first made, the opponents of a regional financial arrangement in East Asia have raised two issues. First, they argue that the ASEAN+3 countries have yet to develop the economic, social, and political conditions needed to support such an arrangement. When these conditions are not met, there is a danger that a regional arrangement for financial cooperation such as the CMI could undermine the role of the IMF and other global financial institutions. Specifically, regional financial arrangements may aggravate the moral hazard problems associated with excessive borrowing and the application of loose macroeconomic policies by participating economies. The opponents also contend that there is no need for regional financial arrangements, because the new information and communication technology, together with capital account liberalization, is driving financial globalization at an unprecedented speed.

Many of the countries participating in the CMI have been embroiled in territorial, political, and economic disputes with one another. Scholars have argued that East Asia lacks the tradition of integrationist thinking and the web of interlocking diplomatic agreements that would encourage European-style monetary and financial cooperation.[18] Therefore, "any monetary arrangement that seeks to stabilize exchange rates in the absence of the necessary political preconditions

---

17. Lawrence (1996).
18. See, for example, Eichengreen (2000); Eichengreen and Bayoumi (1999); and Bayoumi, Eichengreen, and Mauro (1999).

will be fragile and crisis-prone."[19] They are also concerned that regional mechanisms for financial cooperation would not be endowed with the necessary lending discipline and proper surveillance of the sovereign states participating in the arrangements.

In response to these views, it can be argued that the ASEAN+3 countries have participated in various regional groupings and in the process have accumulated a great deal of experience in managing cooperative arrangements with other countries. The ASEAN states have more than thirty years' experience with regional cooperation. Since its inception in 1967, ASEAN has helped to consolidate unity, promote free trade, and provide mutual financial assistance among member states. The ASEAN+3 countries have also been active members of the Asia-Pacific Economic Cooperation (APEC) group. Some of these countries also participate in the Manila framework and in other regional cooperative arrangements, such as the Executives' Meeting of East Asia–Pacific Central Banks (EMEAP) and the South East Asian and South East Asia, New Zealand, and Australia associations of central banks (SEACEN and SEANZA), which have served as informal forums for policy dialogue.

Nevertheless, it may be true that East Asians are not prepared to negotiate an international treaty that includes provisions for sanctions and fines for countries that do not adjust their domestic policies accordingly. This unwillingness would make it difficult for the regional fund to impose politically unpopular policies on member countries and hence could pose a serious problem concerning policy discipline.[20] However, moral hazard is not a problem that besets only regional arrangements. The IMF is not immune to this problem. The moral hazard concern is so serious that some people even question whether the IMF should continue to play the role of quasi-lender of last resort, and to them creation of regional monetary funds must be anathema.[21]

---

19. Bayoumi, Eichengreen, and Mauro (1999, p. 2).

20. Eichengreen finds it useful to distinguish between technical assistance and financial assistance (Eichengreen 2000). It is true that there is no reason to discourage competition in the market for technical assistance. Governments should be free to choose the source of technical assistance with the best track record. However, his concern is that if multiple monetary funds were available, East Asian governments would have an incentive to shop around for the most generous assistance and the least onerous terms. He seems to believe that Asian monetary fund conditionalities would be much softer than IMF conditionalities. His point should be taken when Asians consider further development beyond the CMI that assumes IMF conditionality as a given.

21. See Meltzer Commission (2000). The task force report of the Council on Foreign Relations (1999) advises the fund to adhere consistently to normal lending limits to redress the moral hazard problem. The reasons why East Asian financial arrangements would suffer more from the moral hazard problem than the IMF or any other regional institution have not been made clear.

The ongoing revolution in information and communication technology will no doubt accelerate financial globalization. However, it should be noted that an orderly globalization requires global governance; at present, the world economy has no system of global governance, which might include a global central bank and global regulatory authorities, and the prospects for developing one are rather remote. Global governance may appear reasonable, but in reality it is politically unacceptable and must be dismissed as quixotic.[22] As a second best alternative to a global governance system, global standards and codes of conduct on banking, corporate governance, management of monetary and fiscal policies, and many other matters have been proposed by emerging market economies and developing countries. However, questions have been raised about whether one-size-fits-all codes and standards should be imposed on EMEs and developing countries, and if so, whether they could be enforced. If regional differences matter in devising standards and codes and harmonizing institutions, it could be argued that some public goods for finance could be produced more efficiently at the regional level.

The Chiang Mai Initiative (CMI)

The 1997 Asian financial crisis set in motion two interrelated financial developments in East Asia. The first was that most of the East Asian countries, including the crisis-hit ones, increased the pace and scope of domestic financial reform to liberalize and open their financial markets and also to improve soundness, corporate governance, and risk management at financial institutions. The second was the regional movement for financial cooperation and integration that culminated in the Chiang Mai Initiative (CMI) and the Asian Bond Market Initiative (ABMI).

When the financial crisis in Thailand became contagious, spreading to other East Asian countries in the second half of 1997, Japan proposed to create an Asian monetary fund (AMF) as a framework for financial cooperation and policy coordination in the region, in particular as a means for creating lending facilities, in addition to those of the IMF, as a safeguard against future financial crises in East Asia. Although the proposal was well received throughout the region, it was shelved in the face of objections from the United States, the European Union, and the IMF.

The AMF idea was revived again when the finance ministers of ASEAN, China, Japan, and the Republic of Korea (ASEAN+3) agreed on May 6, 2000, in

22. Eichengreen (2000).

Chiang Mai, Thailand, to establish a system of bilateral currency swap arrangements among the ASEAN+3 countries under what has come to be known as the Chiang Mai Initiative. The eight countries participating in the CMI have also institutionalized regular meetings of finance ministers (the ASEAN+3 Finance Ministers' Meeting, AFMM+3) and deputy ministers (the ASEAN+3 Finance and Central Bank Deputies' Meeting, AFDM+3) for policy dialogue and coordination, as well as the annual ASEAN+3 summit.[23] As a sequel to the CMI for regional financial integration, ASEAN+3 launched the ABMI to develop regional bond markets in Asia. A regional financial arrangement for economic cooperation and policy coordination in general comprises: (1) a mechanism of short-term liquidity support, such as the CMI, for members experiencing balance-of-payments deficits; (2) a mechanism of surveillance for monitoring economic and policy developments in member countries and for imposing policy conditionality on those countries receiving financial support; and (3) a regional collective exchange rate system designed to stabilize the bilateral exchange rates of member countries. The ASEAN+3 states are working on a plan to establish a surveillance system for the CMI network. So far, there has been no serious discussion on developing a collective exchange rate system for the region as a whole. The ABMI will complement the CMI by integrating the bond markets of individual countries in East Asia.[24]

The financial cooperation structure conceived by the architects of the CMI covers only the basic principles and operational procedures for bilateral swap transactions. For the initiative to serve as a full-fledged regional financial mechanism comparable to the European Monetary System, for example, further organizational and operational details on surveillance and exchange rate policy coordination will have to be worked out.

Questions have also been raised as to the significance and viability of regional financial integration in a world economy that has seen financial globalization advance at a fast pace. In order to integrate financial markets into a single unified regional market, individual countries will have to open their financial markets. But they will then be integrating their markets into global financial markets at the same time unless they discriminate against nonregional market participants. The architects of the CMI may have been primarily interested in

23. Financial market participants have ignored the CMI as a defense mechanism against future crises because the amount of liquidity any member may draw from the system is small and, moreover, it is uncertain whether the swap borrowing could be activated in a crisis situation. Despite these criticisms and the market's disregard, ASEAN+3 has managed to close ranks to expand the scope of policy dialogue and move to the second stage of integration.

24. For additional discussion of this topic, see chapter 9 in this volume.

creating a regional liquidity support system to prevent the occurrence of financial crises. However, there is no evidence that regional financial arrangements, whatever form they may take, are effective in warding off financial crises. There is also lingering doubt about whether the CMI arrangement could avoid moral hazard in managing balance-of-payment problems in East Asia because the participating countries would not be able to impose tight conditionality on other members borrowing from the arrangement. Although these arguments raise legitimate questions, they do not mean that the creation of a regional financial arrangement in East Asia is not justified. If it were properly structured and managed, it could facilitate multilateral trade and financial liberalization, thereby contributing to global financial stability.[25]

Structure and Status of the CMI

The CMI consists of two regional financial arrangements. One is the network of bilateral swaps and repurchase agreements among eight members of ASEAN+3. The other is the expanded ASEAN swap system. The latter was created by the original five ASEAN countries, which agreed in 1977 to establish an ASEAN swap arrangement (ASA). In May 2000 the ASA was expanded to include the other five new ASEAN members, and the total amount of the facility was raised to U.S.$1 billion from the initial amount of U.S.$200 million.

The CMI network of bilateral swap arrangements (BSAs) among the eight members of ASEAN+3 provides liquidity assistance in the form of swaps of U.S. dollars for the domestic currencies of the participating countries. For each BSA, the contracting parties determine the maximum amount that can be drawn from the arrangement. The bilateral swap agreement allows an automatic disbursement of up to 10 percent of the agreed maximum amount. A country drawing more than 10 percent of the maximum from the facility is placed under an IMF macroeconomic and structural adjustment program. The BSA network is thus complementary to the IMF lending facilities. The participating countries are able to draw from their respective BSAs for a period of ninety days. The first drawing may be renewed seven times. The interest rate applicable to the drawing is the LIBOR (London interbank offered rate) plus a premium of 150 basis points for the first drawing and the first renewal. Thereafter, the premium rises by an additional 50 basis points for every two renewals, but it is not to exceed 300 basis points.

The BSAs include one-way and two-way swaps (see table 8-4). China's and Japan's initial contracts with the five Southeast Asian countries were one-way

25. Bergsten and Park (2002).

Table 8-4. Progress on the Chiang Mai Initiative

BSA[a]	Currencies	Conclusion date	Amount as of[b]	
			May 30, 2004	Feb. 24, 2006
Japan–Republic of Korea[c]	U.S.$/won (one-way)	July 4, 2001	U.S.$2 billion[d]	U.S.$15 billion
Japan–Republic of Korea	U.S.$/local[e] (two-way)	Feb. 24, 2006		U.S.$6 billion
Japan–Republic of Korea	Yen/won (two-way)	May 27, 2005		
Japan–Thailand[c]	U.S.$/baht (one-way)	July 30, 2001	U.S.$3 billion	U.S.$6 billion
Japan–Thailand	U.S.$/local (two-way)	Jan. 25, 2005		
Japan–Philippines[c]	U.S.$/peso (one-way)	Aug. 27, 2001	U.S.$3 billion	U.S.$3 billion
Japan–Philippines	U.S.$/peso (one-way)	Aug. 28, 2004		
Japan–Malaysia	U.S.$/ringgit (one-way)	Oct. 5, 2001	U.S.$1 billion[d]	U.S.$1 billion[d]
Japan–China	yen/renminbi (two-way)	Mar. 28, 2002	U.S.$6 billion	U.S.$6 billion
Japan–Indonesia[c]	U.S.$/rupiah (one-way)	Feb. 17, 2003	U.S.$3 billion	U.S.$6 billion
Japan–Indonesia	U.S.$/rupiah (one-way)	Aug. 31, 2005		
Japan–Singapore[c]	U.S.$/sing U.S.$ (one-way)	Nov. 10, 2003	U.S.$1 billion	
Japan–Singapore	U.S.$/local (two-way)	Nov. 8, 2005		
Republic of Korea–China[c]	won/renminbi (two-way)	June 24, 2002	U.S.$4 billion	U.S.$4 billion
Republic of Korea–China	won/renminbi (two-way)	May 27, 2005		U.S.$8 billion
Republic of Korea–Thailand	U.S.$/local (two-way)	June 25, 2002	U.S.$2 billion	U.S.$2 billion

Republic of Korea–Malaysia[c]	U.S.$/local (two-way)	July 26, 2002	U.S.$2 billion	
Republic of Korea–Malaysia	U.S.$/local (two-way)	Oct. 14, 2005		U.S.$3 billion
Republic of Korea–Philippines[c]	U.S.$/local (two-way)	Aug. 9, 2002	U.S.$2 billion	
Republic of Korea–Philippines	U.S.$/local (two-way)	Oct. 27, 2005		U.S.$3 billion
Republic of Korea–Indonesia	U.S.$/local (two-way)	Dec. 3, 2003	U.S.$2 billion	U.S.$2 billion
China–Thailand	U.S.$/baht (one-way)	Dec. 6, 2001	U.S.$2 billion	U.S.$2 billion
China–Malaysia	U.S.$/ringgit (one-way)	Oct. 9, 2002	U.S.$1.5 billion	U.S.$1.5 billion
China–Philippines	U.S.$/peso (one-way)	Aug. 29, 2003	U.S.$1 billion	U.S.$1 billion
China–Indonesia[c]	Rupiah/renminbi (one-way)	Dec. 30, 2003	U.S.$1 billion	
China–Indonesia	U.S.$/rupiah (one-way)	Oct. 17, 2005		U.S.$2 billion

Sources: Asian Development Bank, "Progress Report on the Chiang Mai Initiative: Current Status of the Bilateral Swap Arrangement Network as of 10 November 2004"; Japanese Ministry of Finance, "Network of Bilateral Swap Arrangements under the Chiang Mai Initiative (as of February 24, 2006)"; Japanese Ministry of Finance, "Japan's Bilateral Swap Arrangements under the Chiang Mai Initiative (as of February 24, 2006)"; and various press releases from central banks of ASEAN+3 countries.

a. Bilateral swap arrangement. The total size of a two-way BSA is double the face value of the BSA.

b. The total size of all BSAs amounted to U.S.$36.5 billion as of May 2004 and to $71.5 billion as of February 2006.

c. This contract has been replaced.

d. The U.S. dollar amounts shown do not include the amounts committed under the New Miyazawa Initiative: U.S.$5 billion for the Republic of Korea, which expired on February 24, 2006, U.S.$2.5 billion for Malaysia, and the ASEAN Swap Arrangement (U.S.$2 billion).

e. U.S.$/local (two-way) is U.S.$/yen and U.S.$/won in this case and analogous for other countries.

BSAs from which only the ASEAN five could draw. The first round of CMI implementation was completed in May 2004, with sixteen BSAs totaling U.S.$36.5 billion having been concluded. Japan participated in seven agreements, and China and the Republic of Korea took part in six each. Under these initial BSAs, the Republic of Korea, which is the largest beneficiary of the CMI, could draw a maximum of $13 billion from the system, including the resources available under the Miyazawa initiative. In the eyes of participants in the global financial market, however, the liquidity available to the Republic of Korea and other members was not enough to be of any significance in preventing future crises, and the ASEAN+3 countries therefore decided to double the total size of the CMI in 2005 (see below).

The CMI is comparable to the liquidity support arrangements that had supported the European Monetary System before the monetary union was created in 1999. However, the CMI had a different motivation from the beginning. The European facilities were created with the aim of limiting bilateral exchange rate fluctuations among regional currencies. The CMI started with high capital mobility and flexible exchange rates, although some members of ASEAN+3 have maintained a relatively fixed exchange rate regime. So far, the ASEAN+3 countries have not sought any manifest exchange rate coordination. In the absence of exchange rate coordination, incentives for mutual surveillance will be limited because a member country facing a speculative currency attack may be free to float its exchange rate against those of neighboring countries.[26]

As long as the CMI is simply a source of financial resources supplementary to the IMF, the size of the swaps does not have to be large enough to meet the potential liquidity need. Although the CMI can be managed without its own conditionality at this point, it does need to establish its own surveillance mechanism to avoid breaches of the swap contracts. Because up to 10 percent of each swap can be disbursed with only the consent of the swap-providing countries, the latter need to formulate their own assessments of the credibility and the capacity of the swap-requesting countries to honor their contracts. The current practices under the ASEAN+3 process cannot effectively resolve repayment default problems.

Most participating countries agree in principle that the CMI network needs to be supported by an independent monitoring and surveillance system that would monitor economic developments in the region, serve as an institutional framework for policy dialogue and coordination among the members, and impose structural and policy reform on the countries drawing from the BSAs.

26. Wang and Woo (2004).

However, the ASEAN+3 countries at the current stage do not seem well pre-pared to establish a policy coordination mechanism in the surveillance process, although collective efforts are being made in this regard.[27]

At the annual meeting of the Asian Development Bank (AsDB) in Jeju, Republic of Korea, in April 2004, the finance ministers of ASEAN+3 agreed to undertake a further review of the CMI to explore ways in which the scope of its operations could be further enhanced and consolidated. A working group created to conduct the review presented a report highlighting the major issues related to CMI enlargement and consolidation at the meeting of finance minis-ters held during the AsDB meeting in Istanbul in May 2005.[28] In order to develop the CMI into a more credible and effective liquidity support system, the ASEAN+3 finance ministers approved the proposal made in the report, which was intended to double the size of the existing individual bilateral swaps, with the provision that the actual increase would be decided by bilateral negotiations among the members.[29] As of February 2006, nine of the initial contracts had been replaced by ten new contracts for a total of U.S.$56 billion, more than doubling the initial amount of those contracts (U.S.$21 billion). Japan replaced the one-way contracts with the Republic of Korea, Thailand, and Singapore with two-way contracts. The maximum withdrawal for the Republic of Korea, still the largest beneficiary of the CMI, increased by U.S.$7 billion, to a total of U.S.$20 billion. The total amount of all BSAs came to U.S.$71.5 billion, which was almost double the initial amount of U.S.$36.5 billion (see table 8-4).

At this stage of development, however, there is no guarantee that the BSAs will be activated, because some of the swap-providing countries may exercise their right to opt out. Under the current CMI arrangement, any country wish-ing to obtain short-term liquidity must negotiate the activation with all swap-providing countries individually. If a large number of the members refuse to provide swaps and different swap providers demand different terms and condi-tions, then the CMI may cease to be an efficient liquidity support system. The discussion of swap activation with multiple contractual parties may take time

27. For instance, the ASEAN surveillance process is built on the basis of consensus and infor-mality in keeping with the tradition of noninterference (Manzano, 2001). East Asia, in contrast to Europe, lacks the tradition of integrationist thinking and the web of interlocking agreements that encourage monetary and financial cooperation (Eichengreen and Bayoumi, 1999). Eichengreen and Bayoumi stress that East Asia does not meet the necessary intellectual preconditions for regional integration. For this reason, they conclude that it is unrealistic to speak of pooling national sovereignties. While there is no doubt considerable work to be done in promoting policy coordination in the region, it is wrong to say that it cannot be done in East Asia.

28. ASEAN+3 (2005a).

29. ASEAN+3 (2005b).

and hence may deprive the swap-requesting country of the ability to mount an effective and prompt defense against a speculative attack. In order to avoid this inherent bias in the system, it has been proposed to create a secretariat or committee that would determine joint activation of all swap contracts of swap-requesting countries, so that swap disbursements could be made in a concerted and timely manner. At the 2005 Istanbul AsDB meeting, the finance ministers of ASEAN+3 agreed in principle to adopt a collective decisionmaking mechanism for the network of BSAs in order to ensure timely availability of liquidity from the system through the joint activation of swaps.[30] Details of the collective decisionmaking mechanism are to be worked out by the ASEAN+3 Finance and Central Bank Deputies' Meeting.

As noted earlier, the swap-requesting country can draw up to 10 percent of the contract amount without being subject to IMF conditionality with regard to policy adjustments. Several members of the CMI had previously proposed that the limit should be raised to 20 or 30 percent, and, accepting this proposal, the finance ministers of ASEAN+3 agreed to raise the limit to 20 percent at the Istanbul AsDB meeting. However, the CMI members realize that neither multilateralization of the CMI nor an increase in the drawing limit to more than 20 percent will be possible unless a more effective surveillance system is established. Creating a surveillance mechanism for the CMI has been a controversial issue, and the working group has not been able to produce a surveillance system acceptable to all members. During the Istanbul meeting, the ASEAN+3 finance ministers reaffirmed the need to enhance ASEAN+3 economic surveillance and to integrate it into the CMI, but they were not able to come to any decision on the structure, role, and location of a surveillance unit.

If the CMI members were to agree on multilateralization and on the creation of a regional surveillance unit, their agreement would be tantamount to establishing an institution similar to a regional monetary fund. Although most of the ASEAN+3 members find it premature to set up such an institution, they realize the need to create an institution that can manage and set terms and conditions for bilateral swap transactions, in addition to performing secretariat functions for policy dialogue and coordination among members. There have been several proposals for organizing an ASEAN+3 secretariat, but none has been seriously considered because the member countries have been divided on the structure and location of the secretariat. This disagreement is not likely to be resolved anytime soon.

30. ASEAN+3 (2005b).

There are two other issues concerning the enhancement of the CMI as a regional financial institution that remain unresolved. One is the enlargement of the CMI membership. Several nonmember Asian countries, including India, have expressed interest in joining the CMI. At present, there is broad consensus that enlargement should be deferred until some of the operational issues of the CMI are settled. Nevertheless, the inclusion of some of the less developed ASEAN members may be raised at future meetings of ASEAN+3.

Another issue is the coordination of exchange rate policy among the members of ASEAN+3. With the growing need to stabilize bilateral exchange rates between ASEAN+3 states, proposals have been made to strengthen the CMI network so that it might serve as an institutional base for monetary integration in East Asia in the future. Although a formal discussion of monetary integration has been put on hold, China's shift from dollar pegging to an intermediate regime in July 2005 is likely to renew the debate on the need and the modality for coordination of exchange rate policy in the region.

Barriers to Financial Cooperation and Integration

The East Asian policymakers who conceived the idea of the CMI would easily concede that the BSA system as it is currently structured has a long way to go before it can be accepted as an effective mechanism of defense against financial crises. Although at this writing six years have passed since the system was established in May 2000, the leaders of the CMI group have yet to produce an operational structure for BSAs, in particular a monitoring and surveillance mechanism. And it is highly unlikely that they will do so anytime soon since they are hindered by a number of institutional and political constraints to further expansion of the CMI.

Institutional Constraints

The most serious of these constraints is that the thirteen countries have failed to articulate the ultimate objectives of the CMI arrangement. The participating countries themselves are still unclear about whether the CMI is going to remain a regional liquidity support program or serve as a building block for the development of a full-fledged regional monetary system in East Asia. As noted in the preceding section, when bilateral swap arrangements are activated collectively and supported by a surveillance system, they constitute a de facto regional monetary fund. The CMI could thus serve as the foundation on which an elaborate system of financial cooperation and policy coordination could be built, following in the footsteps of European monetary integration.[31] At this stage of development, however, many countries in East Asia are not prepared to accept the idea of—or at least feel uneasy about—restructuring the CMI as the forerunner to an Asian monetary fund.

A second institutional constraint is related to the need to coordinate the activities of the CMI with other regional arrangements, such as the Manila framework supported by Australia, New Zealand, and the United States. Most of the CMI countries also participate in the Manila framework and in APEC. At some point in the future, the leaders of the ASEAN+3 countries may have to decide on a mode of cooperation and division of labor between these institutions and the CMI for promoting regional growth and stability. Many of the ASEAN+3 states have been engaged in policy reviews and dialogues through the APEC meetings and the Manila framework. Unless the CMI is developed into a credible financing mechanism by increasing swap amounts, it will take on a role similar to that of these other regional economic forums. The cohesion of the group will then be weakened as questions are raised about whether the thirteen countries constitute an appropriate grouping for a regional financing arrangement in East Asia.

A third impediment is that the fear of another round of financial crisis has receded, thanks to a recovery that has been faster than predicted based on previous crisis episodes. With this false perception of security, the ASEAN+3 countries have become less interested in enlarging and institutionalizing the CMI operations. Instead, their focus has shifted recently to creating free-trade areas (FTAs) in East Asia (see table 8-5).[32] The ASEAN Free Trade Area (AFTA) now includes the whole of Southeast Asia, and it continues to expand. On November 29, 2004, China and the ASEAN countries agreed to form a free-trade area by 2010, allowing for some preferential treatment for less-developed ASEAN countries. Japan has concluded a free-trade agreement with Singapore and has started

31. From the theoretical standpoint of the neofunctionalists, initial steps toward integration trigger self-sustaining economic and political dynamics, leading to further cooperation. Economic interactions create spillovers or externalities that need to be coordinated by the governments involved. Such economic policy coordination at the regional level can be seen as an inevitable response to increased economic interactions within the region. Once the integration process starts, spillovers deepen and widen integration through interest group pressure, public opinion, elite socialization, and other domestic actors and processes (George, 1985).

32. Historically, there has been much less movement toward trade regionalism in East Asia than in Europe. East Asian countries are reliant on markets in the United States and the European Union, so there has been less incentive for them to expand trade integration within the region. The first major attempt was made only in 1992, when six ASEAN countries agreed to launch a scheme for ASEAN free trade.

Table 8-5. *Progress of Major Free-Trade Agreements in East Asia, 2005*

Participants in free-trade agreements	Stages of evolution				
	Discussion	Joint study	Negotiation	Signed (year)	Implementation (year)
ASEAN					
ASEAN Free Trade Agreement					X (1993)
ASEAN–China CEC[a]					X (2005)
ASEAN–Japan CEP[b]			X		
ASEAN–India				X (2005)	
ASEAN+3		X			
ASEAN– Republic of Korea		X		X (2005)	
ASEAN–CER[c]		X			
Japan					
Japan–Singapore					X (2003)
Japan–Mexico					X (2004)
Japan–Malaysia				X (2005)	
Japan– Republic of Korea			X		
Japan–Philippines				X (2005)	
Japan–Thailand				X (2005)	
Japan–Chile		X			
Japan–India		X			
Republic of Korea					
Republic of Korea–Chile					X (2004)
Republic of Korea–Japan			X		
Republic of Korea–Mexico			X		
Republic of Korea–China	X				
Republic of Korea–Singapore				X (2005)	
Republic of Korea–Canada			X		
Republic of Korea–United States	X				

(continued)

Table 8-5. *(continued)*

Participants in free-trade agreements	*Stages of evolution*				
	Discussion	*Joint study*	*Negotiation*	*Signed (year)*	*Implementation (year)*
Republic of Korea–EFTA[d]				X (2005)	
Republic of Korea–Mercosur[e]		X			
Republic of Korea–India		X			
China					
China– Hong Kong SAR					X (2004)
China–Macao					X (2004)
China–Australia			X		
China–Brazil		X			
China–Chile				X (2005)	
China–GCC[f]		X			
China–Thailand			X		
Singapore					
Singapore–Australia					X (2003)
Singapore–New Zealand					X (2002)
Singapore–United States	Signed TIFA[g] with United States				X (2004)
Singapore–EFTA[d]					X (2003)
Singapore–Canada					X (2004)
Thailand					
Thailand–China				X	
Thailand–Australia					X (2005)
Thailand–United States	Signed TIFA[g] with United States		X		
Thailand–Japan				X	
Thailand–India					X (2004)

Source: Compiled from various sources.

a. Comprehensive Economic Cooperation.

b. Comprehensive Economic Partnership.

c. Closer Economic Relations Trade Agreement between Australia and New Zealand.

d. European Free Trade Association.

e. Southern Common Market.

f. Gulf Cooperation Council.

g. Trade and Investment Framework Agreement.

negotiations on a similar agreement with the Republic of Korea and ASEAN and with several states of ASEAN on an individual basis.

The free-trade movement is undoubtedly a desirable development, and the CMI could help further it by stabilizing bilateral exchange rates for regional currencies and minimizing the disruptive effects of financial market turbulence. The ASEAN+3 countries may thus have an incentive to broaden the scope of the CMI in parallel with negotiations on establishing free-trade areas in the region. In reality, however, it appears that free-trade discussions have rather distracted many East Asian countries from their CMI negotiations.

A regionwide East Asian FTA covering the ASEAN+3 countries is proving slow to materialize because China and Japan are seeking bilateral trade agreements rather than multilateral ones. Indeed, the current pattern of regional trade agreements in East Asia is bewildering.[33] It consists largely of a web of bilateral arrangements, many of which are still on the drawing board. There has apparently been no formal attempt to build a regional multilateral agreement like the European Common Market agreement, and bilateral agreements are unlikely to foster a collective framework.[34]

A fourth constraint is that financial deregulation and market opening have drawn East Asia away from regional financial integration. Over the past decade, a number of East Asian countries have opened up their financial markets to foreign capital by reducing restrictions on inward and outward capital flows. Financial liberalization throughout East Asia has led many countries to establish closer links with international financial centers.[35] In East Asia, there is no sign of the development of an integrated regional financial market. This relative lack of progress in regional financial integration is not surprising. Eichengreen and Park explain the various factors involved by comparing the region with Europe.[36]

According to their analysis, Europe has gone further than East Asia in the integration of product and factor markets. While the European Union has a true single market of goods and services, progress toward the creation of an Asian free-trade area remains incomplete. And while Europe has removed essentially all barriers to the free movement of capital and most barriers to the movement of labor, in East Asia limits on factor mobility remain pervasive. In Europe, regionalism is motivated in no small part by a desire for political integration that has no counterpart in East Asia. Whereas Europe has built institutions of

33. See Scollay and Gilbert (2001).
34. Wyplosz (2004).
35. Lee, Park, and Shin (2004).
36. Eichengreen and Park (2003).

transnational governance (such as the European Commission, the European Parliament, the European Court of Justice, and now the European Central Bank), East Asian integration is "weakly institutionalized." It is predicated not on transnational institutions but on intergovernmental agreements that defer to the sovereignty of the participating states. Moreover, integration in East Asia is not being driven by an alliance of key nations like France and Germany or by a single hegemonic power (the role played by the United States in the Western hemisphere); it is a more multipolar process.

As is well known, East Asia is less financially integrated than Europe. In East Asia, financial claims are all denominated in U.S. dollars and the bulk of foreign lending and borrowing are intermediated through international financial markets in New York and London. Therefore, regional financial arrangements themselves cannot effectively address the inherent structural balance-sheet problem that most East Asian emerging and developing countries are currently facing. The absence of regional financial integration is closely linked to the absence of a regional lender of last resort. In Europe, West Germany was prepared to supply a virtually unlimited amount of short-term liquidity under the European Monetary System when weak currency countries were under severe pressure from currency devaluation. In East Asia, Japan appears to play only a limited role as a regional lender of last resort.

Leadership Issues

Finally, there is a leadership problem that defies easy solution. If the thirteen countries have the more ambitious goal of developing a collective exchange rate mechanism similar to the exchange rate mechanism (ERM) in Europe, with the long-term objective of adopting a common currency, they will have to increase the number and the amounts of BSAs. As the European experience shows, such a move requires leadership that can foster cohesion among the thirteen countries by mediating the divergent interests of members.

China and Japan are expected to provide leadership in forging regional consensus for expanding and consolidating BSAs as a regional institution, but they have not been able to agree on a number of operational issues, including a surveillance mechanism. Except for Japan, no other potential swap lenders, including China, are prepared to increase the amounts of their bilateral swaps with other contracting parties. Japan could increase its swap amounts with the ASEAN states and the Republic of Korea (under the presumption that China will not borrow from Japan) to make the CMI a more credible financing scheme. However, unless Japanese authorities receive some sort of assurance that their short-term lending will be repaid, they are not likely to lead an expansion and institutionalization of the CMI. As a minimum condition for expansion of the CMI, Japan would demand the creation of an effective surveillance mechanism for the region in which it could exercise influence commensurate with its financial contribution. However, China would be unlikely to accept any arrangement in which it felt that it was playing second fiddle to Japan in a regional organization in East Asia. This concern appears to be the most serious roadblock to further development of the CMI.

China and Japan have different interests and hence different strategies for economic integration in East Asia. As far as China is concerned, economic integration with the ten ASEAN members and with the South and Central Asian countries may be more important both economically and geopolitically than financial cooperation or free trade with either Japan or the Republic of Korea. While China is a military superpower in the world and has been growing rapidly, it is still a developing economy far behind Japan in technological and industrial sophistication. These differences in the economic and military status of the two countries suggest that, even if they manage to resolve their past differences, China and Japan may find it difficult to work together as equal partners for regional integration in East Asia.

Despite slow progress in reconciliation between China and Japan, China seems to be emerging as an active player in both the international and the regional arenas. Since the mid-1990s, China has expanded the number and depth of its bilateral relationships, joined various trade and security accords, deepened its participation in key multilateral organizations, and helped address global security issues. The pinnacle of this process was the Treaty of Good-Neighborliness and Friendly Cooperation, signed by China with Russia in 2001.[37]

China borders Russia and many of the South and Central Asian countries in addition to several ASEAN members. It is therefore natural for China to seek expansion and deepening of its trade and financial relations with those neighboring countries. To that end, China has been courting ASEAN with the aim of establishing a free-trade agreement, and in November 2001 it joined the Bangkok agreement on a free-trade area that includes the Republic of Korea and the South Asian countries (Bangladesh, India, Laos, and Sri Lanka). In Central Asia, China has also taken a leading role in establishing the region's first multilateral group, the Shanghai Cooperation Organization. Founded to settle long-standing territorial disputes and to demilitarize borders, the organization now stresses counter-

37. See Medeiros and Fravel (2003).

terrorism cooperation and regional trade among Russia, Kazakhstan, Kyrgyzstan, Tajikistan, Uzbekistan, and China.[38]

In contrast, Japan has not been able to articulate its strategic interests in East Asia. While it has been at the forefront in supporting greater economic cooperation among the East Asian countries, its perspective on the geographic area of East Asia has not been altogether clear. Japan has been promoting integration among the "ASEAN+5," but which two economies are to be added to ASEAN+3 to make ASEAN+5? At times, the two economies mentioned have been Australia and New Zealand and at other times Taiwan Province of China and Hong Kong SAR.

There is also a suspicion that Japan is not interested in free trade and financial arrangements per se in East Asia for purely economic reasons. Instead, Japan is thought to be engaging in discussion of regional arrangements with other East Asian countries with the aim of maintaining its leadership role as the region's largest economy by checking and balancing China's expansion. Many analysts believe that Japan's active involvement in regional economic integration is motivated by its desire to maintain its traditional pole position.[39] Japan has also been gripped with a decade-long recession and has been unable to restructure its economy.[40] These developments, combined with its lack of a strategy for East Asian development, seem to undermine Japan's ability to pull the East Asian countries together for regional cooperation and integration.

What, then, are the likely courses of development for the regional financial architecture in East Asia? How would financial integration proceed in the region? One possible scenario is that China and Japan will come to realize that, despite the differences in their strategies, together they are the key to developing a common political will in East Asia. Sakakibara argues that the role of China and Japan in East Asia's integration process is synonymous with that of France and Germany in Europe.[41] Similarly, the Kobe Research Project report, submitted to the fourth gathering of finance ministers of the Asia-Europe Meeting

---

38. In June 2001, the presidents of six countries signed the Declaration of the Shanghai Cooperation Organization (SCO). The aim of the SCO is to strengthen mutual trust and friendly relations among member states, encouraging their further effective cooperation in the political and economic spheres and in science and technology, culture, education, energy, transportation, environmental protection, and other fields, with a view to jointly ensuring regional peace, security, and stability and creating a new international political and economic order.

39. See D. Wall, "Koizumi Trade Pitch Nests," *Japan Times,* April 21, 2002.

40. Uncertain economic prospects may make Japan unlikely to be the driver in the region's integration movement as it was in the past. China is emerging both as a strong competitor and as a promising market.

41. Sakakibara (2003).

(ASEM) held in Copenhagen in July 2002, affirms that cooperation between Japan and China, as core countries in East Asia, will be essential in leading the process of economic and financial integration in the region, just as the alliance between France and Germany played a central role in the integration and cooperation process in Europe.[42]

This realization could soften their positions and lead to compromise on an institutional setting and on augmentation of the existing financial architecture in East Asia. For instance, China might accept Japan's demand for de facto control over monitoring and surveillance in return for Japan's pledge for a substantial increase in financial assistance in the form of one-way swaps and official development assistance (ODA) to ASEAN members. China might agree to this scheme, if it were confident about concluding a free-trade agreement with the ASEAN members in the near future. A China–ASEAN free-trade pact could circumscribe Japan's influence on ASEAN affairs even though Japan is a major provider of financial resources to the region. In this process, the Republic of Korea and ASEAN could play a mediating role in the cultivation of a common political will between China and Japan.[43]

In another possible scenario, China would assume a more aggressive leadership role in regional integration. In view of the uncertain prospects for the Japanese economy, China could emerge as the region's engine of growth over the longer term if it sustains its own growth. As part of this leadership role, China might choose to negotiate both the expansion of the BSAs and a free-trade pact with ASEAN. In that case, the original CMI would become "ASEAN+1" in the sense that Japan would play second fiddle. Realizing that financial integration is an integral part of a successful free-trade area, China might indeed seriously

42. France and Germany also had a wartime legacy. Although Charles de Gaulle was a nationalist and his nationalism was popular within the country, he also appreciated that membership in the common market would benefit France economically. However, de Gaulle remained implacably opposed to any increase in the powers of the European Commission or to any other increase in supranationalism. He showed just how opposed in 1965, when he precipitated the most dramatic crisis in the history of the European Community (George, 1985). It was Chancellor Helmut Schmidt of Germany and President Giscard d'Estaing of France who restarted the stalled integration process at the end of the 1970s. The joint initiative of Chancellor Helmut Kohl and President François Mitterrand resulted in a great leap toward European monetary union in the early 1990s. The Franco-German alliance formed the core for the integration process in Europe because it was the political will of these two countries that motivated further integration.

43. Murase (2004) emphasizes the role of the Republic of Korea, pointing out that, as financial cooperation improves, the Republic of Korea will likely play a role similar to that of the Benelux countries in Europe. In the formation of a regional monetary system, it could supplement Sino-Japanese leadership while representing the interests of smaller countries in the region. In the future, the Republic of Korea, like key members of ASEAN, could be a location for the secretariat and other organizations.

consider this option. However, without Japan, ASEAN+1 would not be a viable arrangement for a regional financing scheme, simply because China is hardly in a position to commit itself to financing the balance-of-payments deficits of all ASEAN member states. It is also questionable whether ASEAN would join any regional financial arrangement in which China was the dominant member.

A third scenario is the enlargement of the CMI to include Australia and New Zealand and possibly India in South Asia. This would most likely be the route favored by Japan, which would find it easier to deal with China if there were more countries supporting Japan's strategy. However, many members of ASEAN+3 believe that, at this stage, reaching critical mass within the existing CMI should precede any enlargement discussion. Since enlargement is not likely to lead to any substantial increase in the availability of short-term financing, most ASEAN+3 members would not take the third scenario seriously.

Perhaps the most realistic scenario is that the countries participating in the CMI will simply maintain the status quo, continuing to discuss modalities of policy dialogue and debate the merits of various types of surveillance systems for the CMI and the feasibility of augmenting swap amounts—but without making any substantial progress.

Concluding Remarks

The adoption and implementation of the CMI can be counted as a major step toward strengthening financial cooperation among the thirteen East Asian countries. However, ASEAN+3 will face much tougher challenges and tasks in exploring developments beyond the CMI. The East Asian countries need to clarify for the international community what their motivations are, how they will develop an action plan, and how they believe the plan fits in with the existing global financial system.[44]

Regionalism in East Asia is taking two forms: free-trade arrangements and financial arrangements. These arrangements imply that geographically proximate countries band together to foster trade on the one hand and to promote financial and exchange rate stability on the other. The two processes reinforce each other.

The euro area pursued trade integration first, but from a theoretical point of view there is no clear reason for this. Even in Europe, trade integration slowed down whenever there were concerns about exchange rate stability among member countries, which suggests that some form of monetary integration is an important condition for trade integration.[45] Furthermore, there are many good

44. Park and Wang (2000).
45. Shin and Wang (2004).

reasons for forming a monetary union before establishing a free-trade arrangement. A monetary union can quite significantly increase trade among member countries by serving as a means of avoiding the bottlenecks that may occur in the process of negotiating and implementing a free-trade arrangement. This increased trade is likely to occur mostly within similar industries, so weakening asymmetric shocks across member countries will also decrease the costs of maintaining a monetary union. In addition, a monetary union can accelerate financial integration in the region, which might not be accomplished otherwise. Hence, a monetary union is a self-validating process.

Few East Asian policymakers would be naive enough to believe that they will be able to work out an agreement on creating an East Asian monetary fund or a common currency area in the near future. At best, monetary unification is a long-term objective, and the ASEAN+3 countries have just taken the first step toward regional integration in financial markets. However, East Asia enjoys the latecomer's advantage in promoting financial and monetary integration because it can learn from the European experience. In the end, the Western countries will have to decide whether regional financial arrangements in East Asia will contribute to global stability and welfare. The European experience suggests that they are likely to do so. It would therefore be in the interest of Europe and of the United States to support the expansion and consolidation of the CMI inasmuch as financial deepening in East Asia will support an orderly globalization of the world economy.

References

ASEAN+3. 2005a. "Report of the Review of the Chiang Mai Initiative: Ways of Enhancing Its Effectiveness." ASEAN+3 Finance Ministers Meeting, Istanbul, Turkey.

———. 2005b. Joint Ministerial Statement of the 8th ASEAN+3 Finance Ministers' Meeting, Istanbul, Turkey.

Bayoumi, T., B. Eichengreen, and P. Mauro. 1999. "On Regional Monetary Arrangements for ASEAN." Paper prepared for the ADB/CEPH/KIEP Conference on Exchange Rate Regimes in Emerging Market Economies, Tokyo, December 17–18.

Bergsten, C. Fred, and Yung Chul Park. 2002. "Toward Creating a Regional Monetary Arrangement in East Asia." ADBI Research Paper. Tokyo: Asian Development Bank Institute.

Carstens, A. 2001. "The Mexican Experience with Managing Foreign Exchange Reserves." Presentation at a seminar on foreign exchange reserve management at the IMF-World Bank Annual Meetings. Washington.

Council on Foreign Relations, Task Force Report. 1999. *Safeguarding Prosperity in a Global Financial System: The Future International Financial Architecture,* Carla A. Hills and Peter G. Peterson, chairs; Morris Goldstein, project director. Washington: Institute for International Economics.

Eichengreen, B. 2000. "Strengthening the International Financial Architecture: Where Do We Stand?" *ASEAN Economic Bulletin* 17, no 2: 175–92.

Eichengreen, B., and T. Bayoumi. 1999. "Is Asia an Optimum Currency Area? Can It Become One? Regional, Global and Historical Perspectives on Asian Monetary Relations." In *Exchange Rate Policies in Emerging Asian Countries,* edited by S. Collignon, J. Pisani-Ferry, and Yung Chul Park. London: Routledge.

Eichengreen, B., and Yung Chul Park. 2005. "Why Has There Been Less Regional Integration in East Asia than in Europe." In *A New Financial Market Structure for East Asia,* edited by Yung Chul Park, T. Ito, and Y. Wang. Cheltenham, United Kingdom: Edward Elgar.

Fischer, S. 2001. "Exchange Rate Regime: Is the Bipolar View Correct?" *Journal of Economic Perspectives* 15 (Spring): 3–24.

Frankel, J. 1999. "No Single Currency Regime Is Right for All Countries or at All Times." Working Paper 7338. Cambridge, Mass.: National Bureau of Economic Research.

Furman, J., and J. Stiglitz. 1998. "Economic Crises: Evidence and Insights from East Asia." *Brookings Papers on Economic Activity* 2.

George, S. 1985. *Politics and Policy in the European Community.* Oxford: Clarendon Press.

Glick, R., and A. Rose. 1999. "Contagion and Trade: Why Are Currency Crises Regional?" *Journal of International Money and Finance* 18: 603–17.

Griffith-Jones, S., and J. A. Ocampo. 2001. "Facing the Volatility and Concentration of Capital Flows." In *Reforming the International Financial System: Crisis Prevention and Response,* edited by J. J. Teunissen. The Hague: Forum on Debt and Development (FONDAD).

Henning, R. C. 2002. *East Asian Financial Cooperation.* Policy Analyses in International Economics. Washington: Institute for International Economics.

International Monetary Fund. 2003. "The IMF and Recent Capital Account Crises: Indonesia, Korea, Brazil." Evaluation Report. Washington.

Ito, T., E. Ogawa, and Y. Sasaki. 1999. "Establishment of the East Asian Fund." In *Stabilization of Currencies and Financial Systems in East Asia and International Financial Cooperation.* Tokyo: Institute for International Monetary Affairs.

Lawrence, R. Z. 1996. *Regionalism, Multilateralism, and Deeper Integration.* Brookings.

Lee, J.-W., Yung Chul Park, and K. Shin. 2004. "A Currency Union for East Asia." In *Monetary and Financial Integration in East Asia: The Way Ahead,* Vol. 2, edited by the Asian Development Bank. New York: Palgrave/Macmillan.

Manzano, G. 2001. "Is There Any Value-Added in the ASEAN Surveillance Process?" *ASEAN Economic Bulletin* 18: 94–102.

Medeiros, E. S., and M. T. Fravel. 2003. "China's New Diplomacy." *Foreign Affairs* 82, no. 6: 22–35.

Meltzer Commission. 2000. *Report of the International Financial Institution Advisory Commission,* Allan H. Meltzer, Chairman. Washington: U.S. Government Printing Office.

Murase, T. 2004. *A Zone of Asian Monetary Stability.* Canberra: Asia Pacific Press.

Park, Yung Chul. 2002. "Toward Creating a Regional Monetary Arrangement in East Asia." ADBI Research Paper 50. Tokyo: Asian Development Bank Institute.

Park, Yung Chul, and Y. Wang. 2000. "Reforming the International Financial System: Prospects for Regional Financial Cooperation in East Asia." In *Reforming the International Financial System: Crisis Prevention and Response,* edited by J. J. Teunissen. The Hague: FONDAD.

————. 2002. "What Kind of International Financial Architecture for an Integrated World Economy?" *Asian Economic Papers* 1, no. 1: 91–128.

Park, Yung Chul, J. H. Park, J. Leung, and K. Sangsubhan. 2004. "Asian Bond Market Development: Rationale and Strategy." Paper presented at the Conference on Regional Financial Arrangements, United Nations, New York, July 14–15.

Sakakibara, E. 2003. "Asian Cooperation and the End of Pax Americana." In *Financial Stability and Growth in Emerging Economies: The Role of the Financial Sector,* edited by J. J. Teunissen and M. Teunissen. The Hague: FONDAD.

Scollay, R., and J. Gilbert. 2001. *New Regional Trading Arrangements in the Asia Pacific.* Washington: Institute for International Economics.

Shin, K., and Y. Wang. 2004. "Trade Integration and Business Cycle Co-Movements: The Case of Korea with Other Asian Countries." *Japan and the World Economy, 2004* (Elsevier) 16, no. 2: 213–30.

Stiglitz, J. 2002. *Globalization and Its Discontents.* New York: W. W. Norton.

Wang, Y., and W. T. Woo. 2004. "A Timely Information Exchange Mechanism, an Effective Surveillance System, and an Improved Financial Architecture for East Asia." In *Monetary and Financial Integration in East Asia: The Way Ahead,* Vol. 2, edited by the Asian Development Bank. New York: Palgrave/Macmillan.

Williamson, J. 2000. "Exchange-Rate Regimes for East Asia: Reviving the Intermediate Option." Policy Analyses in International Economics 60. Washington: Institute for International Economics.

World Bank. 2001. "East Asia Regional Update: Regional Overview." Washington.

Wyplosz, C. 2004. "Regional Exchange Rate Arrangements: Lessons from Europe for East Asia." *Monetary and Financial Integration in East Asia: The Way Ahead,* Vol. 2, edited by the Asian Development Bank. New York: Palgrave/Macmillan.

9

Asian Bond Market Development: Rationale and Strategies

YUNG CHUL PARK, JAE HA PARK, JULIA LEUNG, AND KANIT SANGSUBHAN

Of all the structural weaknesses that might have caused the 1997–98 East Asian financial crisis, the absence of vibrant bond markets never fails to make the list. One year after the crisis, Donald Tsang, the financial secretary of the Hong Kong Special Administrative Region (SAR) of China at the time, cited the failure to establish a strong and robust Asian bond market as one reason for the financial turmoil in East Asia. Going further, he deploringly asked, "How is it that we in Asia have never been able to replicate the success of the Eurobond market in this part of the world?"[1] International financial institutions such as the International Monetary Fund (IMF) and the World Bank have also invariably pointed to the absence of efficient domestic bond markets as one of the major causes of the 1997 financial crisis.[2] Even before the crisis, East Asian countries were being urged to develop a domestic bond market to complement their bank-dominated financial systems.[3]

Since the crisis, the development of local bond markets has been a focus of attention as one of the major objectives of financial reforms proposed by the IMF, the World Bank, and the Asian Development Bank (AsDB) for the East

---

1. Donald Tsang, "Asian Bond Market," Asian Debt Conference, July 6, 1998, p. 1.
2. International Monetary Fund (2003).
3. See World Bank (1995).

Asian economies. In parallel, there have been repeated calls to establish regional bond markets in East Asia.[4] In response to these calls and as part of the regional efforts being made to promote financial cooperation and integration through the Chiang Mai Initiative, the Association of Southeast Asian Nations +3 SME Network (ASEAN+3) has explored possibilities and modalities for creating Asian bonds and the necessary components of market infrastructure.

There is a large and growing volume of literature on regional bond markets in East Asia.[5] Several strategies for the creation of new, and the expansion of existing, regional bond markets in East Asia have been put forward. However, some regional policymakers continue to debate the rationale for creating regional bond markets, and a full consensus has yet to be reached on the need for them.

The Rationale for Creating Asian Bond Markets

The idea of regional bond markets started with the realization that the under-development of bond markets in the region and the resulting excessive dependence on bank-intermediated financing and foreign short-term financing were major causes of the Asian financial crisis of 1997–98. The development of local currency bond markets is therefore one of the most important policy goals in the region.

The disadvantages of not having a full-fledged bond market were made evident during the Asian financial crisis of 1997–98. An efficient and mature bond market can play an important role during times when the other channels of financial intermediation—banks and equity markets—falter or fail. Most important, the existence of an alternative source of funding would reduce the corporate sector's over-reliance on short-term foreign-currency loans. A sound and healthy corporate sector contributes directly to macroeconomic and financial stability, and improved financial intermediation brings such microeconomic benefits as efficiency gains and diversification of tools for both borrowers and savers. The absence of a developed bond market in the region was one of the main factors behind the extreme volatility that precipitated the Asian financial crisis. The crisis itself spurred governments in the region to focus on promoting domestic bond markets.

Although considerable progress has been made in developing bond markets since the crisis, the breadth and depth of the Asian bond markets still lag behind those of the developed economies. With a market value of less than 50 percent of gross domestic product (GDP), the many Asian domestic bond markets are still smaller than those of the United States and Japan, where domestic bond markets are equivalent to 100 percent of GDP (see table 9-1). In addition, bond

4. See Yoshitomi and Shirai (2001).
5. See, for example, Park and Park (2003) and Oh and Park (2003).

Table 9-1. *Volume of Different Types of Financing in Asian Economies and Selected Countries, 2003*

| Country | GDP ($ Billion) | Bank loans[a] | | Stock market capitalization | | Bond market[b] | | Of which | | | |
| | | | | | | | | Public-sector bonds[c] | | Private-sector bonds[d] | |
		$ Billion	Percent	$ Billion	Percent	$ Billion	Percent	$ Billion	Percent	$ Billion	Percent
Hong Kong SAR	159.1	239.3	150.4	714.6	449.3	71.8	45.2	22.8	31.7	49.1	68.3
Indonesia	212.2	45.7	21.5	54.7	25.8	6.2	2.9	4.6	74.0	1.6	26.0
Republic of Korea	605.1	571.3	94.4	298.2	49.3	380.0	62.8	201.8	53.1	178.2	46.9
Malaysia	103.2	104.6	101.4	168.4	163.2	78.9	76.5	36.4	46.1	42.5	53.9
Philippines	78.5	23.5	29.9	23.2	29.5	2.3	3.0	1.5	64.6	0.8	35.4
Singapore	93.6	101.6	108.5	148.5	158.6	62.6	66.9	39.3	62.7	23.4	37.3
Taiwan Province of China	290.0	374.5	129.2	379.0	130.7	126.8	43.7	76.2	60.1	50.6	39.9
Thailand	149.9	113.5	75.7	119.0	79.4	63.6	42.4	48.2	75.9	15.3	24.1
Average	211.4	196.8	93.1	238.2	112.7	99.0	46.8	53.8	54.4	45.2	45.6
United States	11,262.0	8,321.4	73.9	14,173.1	125.8	20,137.1	178.8	12,003.6	59.6	8,133.5	40.4
United Kingdom	1,965.2	2,792.0	142.1	2,425.8	123.4	1,030.9	52.5	582.6	56.5	448.3	43.5
Japan	4,650.4	4,533.2	97.5	2,953.1	63.5	5,981.2	128.6	4,988.8	83.4	992.4	16.6
Average	5,959.2	5,215.5	87.5	6,517.4	109.4	9,049.7	151.9	5,858.3	64.7	3,191.4	35.3

Sources: International Monetary Fund International Financial Statistics, International Federation of Stock Exchanges, Japan Securities Dealers Association, International Financial Corporation (IFC) bond database, Thai Bond Dealing Centre, Thomson Financial, CEIC, and various central banks.

a. The term "bank loans" refers to domestic credit extended to the private sector. Except for the case of Taiwan Province of China, all bank loan data are taken from line 32 of International Financial Statistics (for table 9-1 only, September 2003).

b. All data on outstanding bonds are as of December 31, 2003, except as follows: data for Japan and Singapore (December 31, 2002), Indonesia (December 31, 2000), and the Philippines (December 31, 1999). Figures are expressed in debt denominated in local currency. Bond figures for Hong Kong SAR, Republic of Korea, Malaysia, Taiwan Province of China, the United States, the United Kingdom, and Japan are from their respective central banks. Figures for Indonesia and the Philippines are from IFC Emerging Markets Information Centre bond database. Figures for Thailand are from the Thai Bond Dealing Centre. Figures for Singapore are estimates based on data from the Monetary Authority of Singapore (MAS) and Thomson Financial.

c. The term "public-sector" refers to government and quasi-government bodies.

d. The term "private-sector" refers to the nonpublic sector and includes financial institutions, corporations, and overseas institutions.

Table 9-2. *Financing Structure of Asian Economies and Selected Countries, 1995 and 2003*

Percentage of total financing (rounded)—total outstanding bank loans, stocks, and bonds

Country	December 31, 1995			December 31, 2003		
	Bank loans[a]	Stock market	Bond market	Bank loans	Stock market	Bond market[b]
Hong Kong SAR	39.6	55.6	4.8	23.3	69.7	7.0
Indonesia	60.2	38.0	1.7	42.9	51.3	5.8
Republic of Korea	44.6	29.4	26.1	45.7	23.9	30.4
Malaysia	22.4	65.3	12.4	29.7	47.9	22.4
Philippines	30.1	64.9	4.9	47.9	47.3	4.7
Singapore	31.5	60.0	8.4	32.5	47.5	20.0
Taiwan Province of China	62.9	31.2	5.9	42.5	43.1	14.4
Thailand	50.8	43.9	5.3	38.3	40.2	21.5
Total	45.0	44.5	10.6	36.8	44.6	18.5
United States	21.1	30.4	48.5	19.5	33.2	47.2
United Kingdom (*March 31, 1995)	42.5	44.5	13.1*	44.7	38.8	16.5
Japan	43.4	27.8	28.8	33.7	21.9	44.4
Total	30.2	30.7	39.1	25.1	31.4	43.5

Source: See Table 9-1.
Notes: See Table 9-1.

markets' share of total financing in Asia is still much smaller than it is in the United States and Japan (see table 9-2); and Asian bond markets still lack liquidity and remain quite fragmented.

In the wake of the financial crisis, other important reasons for a stronger, deeper, and broader debt market in the region have also come to the fore. The huge current account surpluses of economies in the region have led to very sizable accumulations of reserves by the public sector. Total foreign exchange reserves of the major Asian economies other than Japan nearly doubled between 2000 and 2003, rising from about U.S.$700 billion in 2000 to over U.S.$1.2 trillion in 2003.[6] This has spurred demand for investment in financial instruments, especially bonds. However, the absence of deep bond markets in the emerging Asian economies means that a substantial portion of this higher demand has been satisfied through investments in bonds denominated in major foreign currencies.

6. Included in this list are China, Hong Kong SAR, India, Indonesia, the Republic of Korea, Malaysia, the Philippines, Singapore, Taiwan Province of China, and Thailand.

Table 9-3. *Net Purchases of U.S. Bonds and Notes by Asian Economies from U.S. Residents*
Billions of U.S. dollars

Country	Treasury (A)		Agency paper (B)		Subtotal (A + B)		Corporate (C)		All bonds and notes (A + B +C)	
	2002	2003	2002	2003	2002	2003	2002	2003	2002	2003
China	24.1	30.5	29.3	30.0	53.4	60.5	6.0	4.6	59.4	65.1
Hong Kong SAR	−9.1	6.0	12.6	12.0	3.5	18.0	3.7	4.3	7.2	22.3
Indonesia	0.8	0.6	0.5	0.5	1.3	1.1	0.1	0.0	1.4	1.1
Japan	30.5	148.3	37.6	24.4	68.1	172.6	10.9	12.5	79.0	185.1
Republic of Korea	12.9	5.2	0.7	8.5	13.6	13.7	1.5	0.8	15.1	14.5
Malaysia	0.9	−0.3	1.3	−1.2	2.2	−1.5	0.1	0.0	2.3	−1.5
Philippines	0.2	0.5	0.3	0.0	0.5	0.5	0.1	0.1	0.6	0.6
Singapore	−2.6	−8.3	2.2	0.7	−0.4	−7.6	1.3	3.3	0.9	−4.3
Thailand	−1.9	−6.0	0.1	0.2	−1.8	−5.8	0.2	0.4	−1.6	−5.4
Taiwan Province of China	−0.6	9.0	10.8	9.5	10.2	18.5	1.4	1.6	11.6	20.1
Total	55.2	185.5	95.4	84.6	150.6	270.0	25.3	27.6	175.9	297.6
Percent of world total	66.3	68.1	49.8	51.7	54.8	61.9	13.9	10.1	38.5	42.0
World total	83.2	272.4	191.6	163.5	274.8	435.9	182.3	272.3	457.1	708.2

Source: United States Treasury.

According to U.S. Treasury statistics, Asian investors are leading buyers of U.S. securities. As shown in table 9-3, net purchases of U.S. Treasury and agency paper by Asian economies amounted to U.S.$270 billion in 2003, more than 60 percent of the world total. Indeed, net foreign portfolio investment by the emerging Asian economies increased sharply over the five-year period 1998–2003—from U.S.$50 billion to U.S.$225 billion. Emerging Asia as a whole is now a large net exporter of portfolio capital.

However, a closer examination of the patterns of portfolio investment flows into and out of the Asian region reveals an inherent instability. Fund flows out of Asia have mainly consisted of large bond investment funds channeled to industrialized economies owing to the higher credit ratings and the greater depth of bond markets in the United States, Japan, and Europe. Some of these funds are recycled back into the region's institutions, managed by foreign financial intermediaries. Such investment is mostly in equities and derivatives, which are more volatile instruments than bank lending or debt financing. Although the flows of foreign funds into Asia have certainly helped diversify financial intermediation channels, they are more susceptible to market vagaries. Also, foreign financial intermediaries are usually large international financial institutions with considerable market power and influence because of the volumes they can mobilize relative to the size of emerging economies' financial markets. When the market is under duress, they can push prices in a particular direction. The implications for emerging markets are market volatility, a strong tendency to overshoot, and consequently daunting challenges to maintaining monetary and financial stability.

Major Initiatives

Asian countries have attempted to meet these challenges through greater collaboration on developing regional bond markets in diverse forums such as Asia Pacific Economic Cooperation (APEC), the Executives' Meeting of East Asia–Pacific Central Banks (EMEAP), and ASEAN+3.

APEC has been trying to develop regional bond markets, particularly securitization and credit-guarantee markets, to promote greater openness, diversity, and competitiveness in regional financial markets. The need to do so was reiterated in the APEC Finance Ministers' Joint Ministerial Statement of September 2002 and in the APEC Leaders' Declaration of October 2002 in Los Cabos, Mexico. The objectives of this effort are to identify impediments to the adoption of securitization markets and the creation of the credit-guarantee markets within the APEC economies and to propose appropriate solutions to remove them. It is believed that securitization coupled with credit enhancement, to the extent that it helps reconcile credit and liquidity mismatches between issuers and investors, offers significant benefits for developing markets and can also facilitate balance-sheet restructuring.

To promote regional bond markets, the central banks of East Asia and the Pacific region also formed the Asian Bond Fund (ABF). EMEAP contributed U.S.$1 billion to the first ABF (ABF1). ABF1 was to channel investment into dollar-denominated sovereign and quasi-sovereign bonds issued by Asian entities. To further the development of regional and domestic bond markets in Asia, the central banks committed U.S.$2 billion to another fund, known as ABF2, to invest in local-currency-denominated Asian bonds.

ABF1 and ABF2 were intended to serve as low-cost mechanisms for investing in Asian bonds and as catalysts for domestic financial reforms in Asia. ABF1 has had relatively little effect on the market for East Asian sovereign dollar bonds, since non-EMEAP investors are precluded from investing in it. Moreover, ABF2, created to encourage investment in local-currency-denominated bonds, is expected to have a more significant development impact, given that the component funds of ABF2 are to be offered to other investors.

Last, the ASEAN+3 countries have discussed the development of the regional bond market—both intensively and extensively—through the Asian Bond Market Initiative (ABMI). At an informal meeting of ASEAN+3 Finance Ministry and Central Bank Deputies (AFDM+3) in Tokyo in November 2002, member countries proposed discussing the feasibility of creating new Asian bond markets and improving existing ones, under the ASEAN+3 framework. The proposal received broad support from the thirteen members. One month later, Japan introduced the ABMI, a comprehensive plan for developing regional bond markets in Asia.

On February 28, 2003, AFDM+3 delegates held an informal follow-up session in Tokyo on fostering bond markets in Asia. The Republic of Korea, Japan, Thailand, and other countries put forth various proposals to facilitate the development of bond markets in the region. The delegates agreed to study the proposals in depth so as to expedite achieving tangible results. Echoing the delegates' proposals and reflections, the member countries agreed to establish six working groups to study issues related to regional bond markets, including securitization, regional credit-rating agencies, regional clearing and settlement systems, and regional credit-guarantee agencies. Since early 2003, the working groups have discussed these issues intensively in meetings and seminars.

Progress of Existing Initiatives

APEC: Development of Securitization and Credit-Guarantee Markets

An Initiative on the Development of Securitization and Credit Guarantee Markets, cosponsored by Hong Kong SAR, China, the Republic of Korea, and Thailand, was endorsed at the Ninth APEC Finance Ministers' Meeting in Los Cabos, Mexico, in September 2002. The aim of the initiative was to promote understanding and awareness of the importance of securitization and credit guarantees for regional bond-market development and to help the APEC economies identify and take concrete steps to remove obstacles to the development of securitization and credit guarantees in bond markets.

This initiative focuses on taking action through two central components. The first component consists of policy dialogues involving both the public and private sectors to promote the understanding and sharing of views on securitization and credit-guarantee markets. The second component calls for expert panels to

Table 9-4. *Asian Bond Market Initiative (ABMI) Volunteer Working Groups*

Working group	Chair country
Creation of New Securitized Debt Instruments	Thailand
Credit Guarantee and Investment Mechanisms	Republic of Korea, China
Foreign Exchange Transactions and Settlement Issues	Malaysia
Issuance of Local-Currency-Denominated Bonds by Multilateral Development Banks, Foreign-Government Agencies and Asian Multinational Corporations	China
Rating Systems and Information Dissemination	Singapore and Japan
Technical Assistance Coordination	Indonesia, the Philippines, and Malaysia

visit and provide advice to APEC economies committed to developing domestic securitization and credit guarantees for bond markets.

Four member economies—China, Thailand, Mexico, and the Philippines—have agreed to receive expert advice. Seven economies—Japan, Australia, the United States, Thailand, the Republic of Korea, Hong Kong SAR, and China—and the World Bank have provided experts. Panels of experts were formed for the recipient economies and have visited them twice. After the first and second visits to Thailand, China, and Mexico, the panels drafted and submitted action plans and policy recommendations for removing impediments to the development of securitization and credit-guarantee markets in each economy. An interagency taskforce of the countries reviewed the plans and recommendations and discussed them during the second panel visits. In addition, the first and second high-level policy dialogues were held in Seoul in April 2003 and in Hong Kong SAR in March 2004.

ASEAN+3: ABMI

Although the ASEAN+3 ABMI was officially approved at the ASEAN+3 Finance Ministers' Meeting in Manila on August 7, 2003, informal meetings and seminars had been held on the topic since early that year. One of those meetings, organized by AFDM+3, was held in Tokyo on February 28, 2003. Member countries tabled various proposals on how to foster bond markets in the region. The delegates agreed on the need to study the proposals and ideas in greater depth to achieve tangible results as soon as possible. The various views, suggestions, and proposals of the delegates were incorporated through the establishment of six working groups of volunteers who were to conduct in-depth studies on various aspects of bond market development. The six working groups and chair countries are listed in table 9-4. The working groups examine these issues through two perspectives: facilitating market access through a broad variety of mechanisms; and improving market infrastructure to foster bond markets in Asia. The market-access issues include: (1) sovereign bond issuance by Asian governments to establish benchmarks; (2) bond issuance by Asian government financial institutions to promote domestic private enterprises; (3) the creation of asset-backed securities markets, including collateralized debt obligations; (4) bond issuance in the region by multilateral financial institutions and government agencies; (5) bond issuance to fund foreign direct investment in Asian countries; and (6) the issuance of bonds denominated in a broader range of currencies and the introduction of currency-basket bonds. In turn, the issues related to creating market infrastructure to foster bond markets in Asia are: (1) providing credit guarantees through the active use of existing guarantors and the possible creation of an Asian regional guarantee facility; (2) strengthening the rating system by enhancing the role of domestic rating agencies and possibly establishing an Asian credit-rating board; (3) establishing a mechanism for disseminating information on issuers and credit-rating agencies; (4) facilitating foreign-exchange transactions and addressing settlement issues on cross-border transactions; (5) enhancing capacity building through market research and technical-assistance programs to promote policy dialogue and human-resource development among member countries; and (6) examining the components of the legal and institutional infrastructure, such as laws governing companies and corporations, securities transactions, and taxes.

Each group has subsequently organized several seminars and symposiums to facilitate the exchange of views among academics, think tanks, and private sector representatives. In addition, ASEAN+3 officials regularly hold separate meetings. The working groups' activities made officials of ASEAN+3 governments aware of obstacles to efficient coordination. Therefore, at the November 2003 informal meeting of AFDM+3 in Seoul, the ASEAN+3 countries agreed to establish a focal group to coordinate the working groups. The focal group's main role is to monitor the progress of the six ABMI working groups and to coordinate their future action plans. This includes: (1) submitting a summary progress report of ABM1 to the ASEAN+3 Finance Ministry and Central Bank Deputies' meeting; (2) providing a progress update on each working group; (3) coordinating the meeting schedules of the six working groups; and (4) reporting each group's plans to the other groups. The focal group meetings are to be held twice a year, before the AFDM+3 meetings. The six working groups were later reorganized into four groups; of the two remaining groups, the one chaired by China completed its tasks, and the other was transformed into the Technical Assistance Coordination Team (TACT).

Figure 9-1. *Yen-Denominated Collateralized Bond Obligation (CBO) Scheme of the Republic of Korea and Japan*

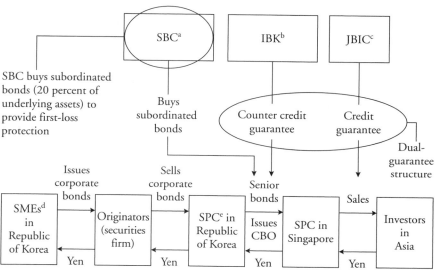

a. Small Business Corporation.
b. Industrial Bank of Korea.
c. Japan Bank for International Cooperation.
d. Small and medium-sized enterprises.
e. Special Purpose Corporation.

Three years after its December 2002 inauguration, ABMI could point to many concrete achievements. These accomplishments included issuance by the AsDB of ringgit-denominated bonds in Malaysia and the securing of permission for multilateral development banks to issue local-currency-denominated bonds in Thailand and China, the creation of a new scheme of cross-boundary primary collateralized bond obligations (CBOs) by the Republic of Korea and Japan, the provision of credit guarantees by the Japan Bank for International Cooperation (JBIC) and Nippon Export and Investment Insurance for bonds issued by Asian multilateral companies, and the launch of the AsianBondsOnline website.[7]

Most notably, in December 2004 the governments of Japan and the Republic of Korea announced the finalization of an agreement for the introduction of cross-boundary, yen-denominated CBOs by the Republic of Korea ("Korean CBOs") so as to provide much-needed financing to small and medium-sized enterprises (SMEs) in the latter country (see figure 9-1). The issue of CBOs in

7. *Asian Bonds Online,* published by the Asian Development Bank (www.asianbondsonline.org).

the Republic of Korea was all the more important in that it was structured for placement outside of the country. The implementation of an innovative, dual-guarantee structure made Korean CBOs attractive to the Asian investor base, injecting badly needed liquidity into the SME sector in the Republic of Korea through lending at an extremely competitive rate.

The size of the issue is 10 billion yen, and the underlying portfolio is composed of a pool of forty-six SME bonds. In line with other domestic CBOs in the Republic of Korea, the issue consists of senior and subordinated bonds issued by the Small Business Corporation (SBC) of Korea. To ensure that the issue would appeal to a broad spectrum of investors in Asia, the Industrial Bank of Korea (IBK) extended a fully backed credit facility to support the timely payment of the senior obligations under the senior bonds.

In preparation for such initiatives in developing regional bond markets, Japan's Ministry of Finance had amended the "Ministerial Notification" that governs the JBIC guarantee policies. This allowed the JBIC to justify taking a more proactive role in guarantee operations for appropriately structured credit-enhanced debt instruments within the region. Following this amendment, the JBIC began deliberating proposals to guarantee the initial launch of Korean CBOs.

The efforts by both countries in this pioneering initiative reflect the increased economic collaboration and harmonization between them. It is hoped that the provision of credit enhancement measures by quasi-sovereign institutions to back appropriately structured transactions within Asia will correct the—at least perceived—risk-return imbalance in regional markets and at the same time serve as a catalyst of growth in the regional bond markets. At the first Republic of Korea–Japan Dialogue, on February 4, 2006, the finance ministers of the two countries agreed to continue their joint efforts in this field, recognizing that the first issue of this pan-Asia bond had promoted bond market development in the region, and specifically in their two countries.

In addition, the Regional Multicurrency Bond (RMCB) project was created to explore the possibility of issuing regional multicurrency bonds or currency-basket bonds. The final report on this project proposed practical steps for issuing RMCBs, in the following order: (1) issuing reverse dual-currency bonds, (2) issuing asset-backed securities or collateralized bond obligations, and (3) issuing synthetic currency bonds. The working group members later agreed to launch phase II of RMCB through a research project named "Developing Asian Currency-Basket Bond Markets" that would explore the possibility of developing asset-backed-securities-type Asian currency-basket bond markets in the region.

Many issues related to the creation of infrastructure have also been discussed. Realizing the importance of this, AsDB conducted an in-depth study on the regional settlement and clearing mechanism Asia Link. The findings can be sum-marized as follows: First, although current settlement arrangements do not sig-nificantly impede cross-border transactions, there is an important degree of compliance with and convergence among market practices across the region, particularly regarding legal certainty, delivery versus payment, and support for repo and securities lending (including legal certainty on tax treatment). Sec-ond, although the establishment of a regional central security depository would be useful, there is no private sector support for such a measure, owing to the low volume of cross-border market transactions. Third, four suggestions for improving regional settlement systems were put forth: ensuring greater trans-parency, enhancing compliance with international standards, promoting greater regional cooperation, and reducing risk even further.

In addition, a proposal was recently made in favor of linking East Asia's cen-tral banks with its national clearing and settlement systems, for them to jointly serve as the clearing and settlement system for the region's bond markets.[8] At the November 7, 2004, working group meeting, it was suggested that future efforts to harmonize standards and procedures related to payment and settlement for cross-border bond transactions should take advantage of relevant studies by other forums such as ASEAN and EMEAP. This would avoid the duplication of the efforts already being made by other working groups. In this regard, the EMEAP working group is now evaluating the recommendations of the Committee on Payments and Settlement Systems of the Bank for International Settlement and the International Organization of Securities Commissions.

The long-term solution for regional credit rating is to strengthen the rule of law and enhance the quality of information disclosure by building up social cap-ital and promoting institution building. In the short run, EMEAP could con-sider establishing East Asian rating agencies, either through independent ABFs or in conjunction with ASEAN+3. EMEAP could also promote regional schemes to encourage cooperation with global rating agencies on devising sepa-rate firm-level ratings based solely on firm-specific risks.

Finally, in-depth research was conducted on the establishment of credit guar-antee mechanisms. Such mechanisms are important for developing regional bond markets because they can mitigate the credit quality gap between issuers' poor ratings and investors' requirements. The final report of the study, presented in October 2005, concludes that there is sufficient business for the mechanisms and a market gap to be filled. If the introduction of these mechanisms translates into the creation of independent institutions, a contractually committed capital base

---

8. See Oh and Park (2003).

of at least U.S.$3.5 billion will be required. A mix of business products, including bond guarantees, warehouse loans, investment in financial infrastructure, and technical assistance, is advisable in the initial stages. A number of organizational choices could be considered, such as: (1) new independent multilateral development institution (MDI) structured on a stand-alone basis; (2) an MDI structured as a subsidiary or affiliate of the AsDB; (3) the expansion of existing AsDB facilities; (4) the consolidation of bilateral efforts; or (5) public-private partnerships. In addition, member countries could introduce regulatory improvements. Regarding the findings of the report, member countries agreed that the most important requirement was for a demand study, and that, although demand in the region is sufficient to warrant exploring new mechanisms, the actual amount of demand for the mechanism remains uncertain.

Once the ASEAN+3 Finance Ministers' Meeting gives its approval at the annual AsDB meeting to be held in May 2006, a second-stage study will be conducted to devise a business model for the mechanism and to examine the viability of the preferred organizational option. In the meantime, the cochairs will hold comprehensive talks with all the member countries to build consensus on a course of action and on a time frame for deciding on the technical and nontechnical factors that will determine the future direction of the possible mechanisms.

EMEAP: ABF1 and ABF2

The ABF is the first fund of its kind in the region. The first phase of the initiative, ABF1, was launched in June 2003 and has been fully invested in U.S.-dollar-denominated bonds in the EMEAP economies. EMEAP next prepared the second phase of the project—broadening the ABF to cover local-currency-denominated bonds. Known as ABF2, this phase was launched in December 2004.[9] The aim of both phases of the initiative is to foster the bond market by improving domestic and regional bond-market infrastructure.

ABF1: the critical first step. The establishment of ABF1 was announced in June 2003. All eleven EMEAP central banks invested in ABF1 at its launch, and it had a capitalization of some U.S.$1 billion. The fund is now fully invested in U.S.-dollar-denominated bonds issued by sovereign and quasi-sovereign entities in eight EMEAP economies (China, Hong Kong SAR, Indonesia, the Republic of Korea, the Philippines, Malaysia, Singapore, and Thailand). The boon to development provided by ABF1 consists in more than the first-round demand

9. Executives' Meeting of East Asia–Pacific Central Banks and Monetary Authorities (EMEAP), "EMEAP Central Banks Announce the Asian Bond Fund 2," press release, December 2004 (www.emeap.org); EMEAP, "EMEAP Central Banks to Launch Asian Bond Fund 2," press release, June 2003 (www.emeap.org).

effect of the central banks' U.S.$1 billion investment. Indeed, the seed money invested by the EMEAP central banks has served to attract additional private sector funding, thereby deepening and broadening market demand. The promotional effect of ABF1 is expected to kindle second-round investor and issuer interest in Asian bond markets, broadening the investor base and increasing market liquidity over time.

Furthermore, the ABF1 initiative is a milestone in cooperation among regional central banks. As noted, it is the first initiative of its kind in Asia, and its success is as symbolic as it is substantive. Not only did the launch of ABF1 send a strong message to the financial markets that the regional authorities are committed to stepping up cooperation to promote bond market development; it also paved the way for the development of ABF2. That just one year elapsed from the initial discussions to the actual commitment of funds and the launching of ABF1 testifies to the rapport and sense of ownership among EMEAP members, which have proven valuable for the development of ABF2. ABF2 involves many more complex and technical issues than did ABF1, and the precedent of ABF1 was very useful for garnering political support and commitment to face the challenges to ABF2.

ABF2: the bold new second phase. Building on the momentum generated during the development of ABF1, EMEAP proceeded to extend the ABF concept to local-currency-denominated Asian bonds. Because of the project's complexity and the decision that the funds would be opened up to private sector investment in the future, EMEAP appointed private sector financial advisers to assist with designing and structuring ABF2 as well as with constructing benchmark indexes for it.

In April 2004, EMEAP announced ABF2's basic design and the state-of-the-art ideas on which that design was based. It proposed that ABF2 should consist of two components: the Pan-Asian Bond Index Fund (PAIF) and eight single-market funds (see figure 9-2). Finally, in December of that year, there was an official announcement that ABF2, initially capitalized with U.S.$2 billion, would invest in domestic-currency bonds issued by sovereign and quasi-sovereign entities in every EMEAP economy except Australia, Japan, and New Zealand. All eleven EMEAP members were to invest in it.

The PAIF is a single-bond index fund that invests in local-currency-denominated bonds in the eight EMEAP economies. It is expected to serve as a convenient and cost-effective investment mechanism and to become a new class of asset for regional and international investors seeking to diversify their exposure in Asian bond markets.

The eight single-market funds, in turn, invest in local-currency-denominated bonds issued in the respective EMEAP economies. The single-market funds are intended to provide local investors with low-cost and index-driven options

Figure 9-2. *Asian Bond Fund 2 (ABF2) Framework*

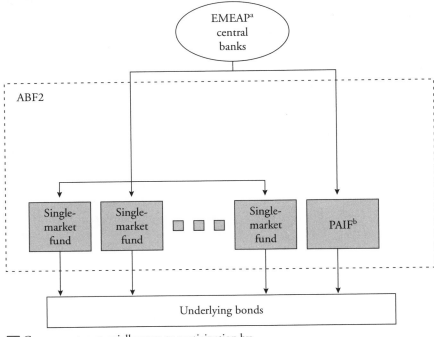

Components potentially open to participation by
other public and private sector investors.

a. Executives' Meeting of East Asia–Pacific Central Banks.
b. Pan-Asian Bond Index Fund.

while giving regional and international investors the flexibility to invest in the Asian bond markets of their choice.

The ABF2 funds are passively managed against a set of transparent and pre-determined benchmark indexes, covering local-currency bonds issued by sovereign and quasi-sovereign entities in the eight EMEAP economies. They have been designed to facilitate investment by other public and private sector parties. In 2005, the PAIF and the single-market funds of Hong Kong SAR, Malaysia, and Singapore were listed. The remaining five single-market funds will be offered to the public in the first half of 2006.

Whereas the aim of ABF1 is to attract additional money into the bond market, the objective of ABF2 goes further, seeking to have a stronger and longer-lasting positive impact on regional bond-market development. During the launch of

ABF2, individual EMEAP economies leverage the interest and momentum generated by collective investment in ABF2 to improve market infrastructure by identifying legal, regulatory, and tax hurdles in their markets and undertaking necessary reforms. Overall, ABF2 has yielded the following benefits:

—The introduction of a new class of assets: Some ABF2 funds are structured as bond exchange-traded funds (ETFs). Although new to Asia, ETFs are increasingly used in the United States and Canada. The development of bond ETFs should promote product diversification and give both retail and institutional investors a low-cost bond product with low entry thresholds.

—The removal of barriers to cross-border capital flows: ABF2 was instrumental in relaxing cross-border restrictions on participation by foreign investors in several markets. The registration of the PAIF in Hong Kong SAR, Japan, and Singapore has promoted the cross-border offering of financial products. The PAIF was also the first foreign entity to obtain permission to invest both in ETFs and in interbank traded bonds in mainland China and to enjoy flexibility in the repatriation of income. Qualified foreign institutional investors (more commonly known as QFIIs), for example, may only invest in exchange-traded renminbi-denominated bonds, in accordance with various limits on investment and repatriation. In Malaysia, foreign-exchange administration rules have been liberalized to facilitate cross-border investment, including by the PAIF. In Thailand and Malaysia, domestic bond markets now allow issues by multilateral agencies, and nonresident investors are now exempt from withholding taxes.

—The adoption of international standards: The observance of international standards would likely encourage greater foreign investment in domestic markets. The PAIF-related documents, such as its trust deed and prospectus, were carefully drafted in line with international standards and best practices and will serve as a model for other ABF2 funds. This is expected to promote the adoption of international standards in the EMEAP markets.

—Increased market transparency: Transparency improves the price discovery process, enhances market efficiency, and fosters investor confidence. Numerous studies in the United States have shown that increased transparency on trading prices has narrowed bid-ask spreads on corporate bonds.[10] Structuring some ABF2 funds as bond ETFs would enhance trading transparency, making order flows and trade information available to participants, the regulatory authorities, and the public.

—Improvement of market infrastructure: ABF2 has also improved bond-market infrastructure by introducing the iBoxx ABF family of indexes to Asia.

10. See, for example, Edwards, Harris, and Piwowar (2005).

These are a set of transparent, replicable, and credible bond-market indexes compiled by an independent index provider, the International Index Company (IIC), for the PAIF and the eight single-market funds. Although the region has several bond indexes, they are compiled by major market players in the region using proprietary data, which raises uncertainty about their impartiality. By contrast, the IIC uses multiple sources for bond valuation and adopts transparent index-construction rules to ensure that iBoxx ABF indexes are impartial, transparent, and representative. iBoxx ABF indexes are easily adopted and customized by private sector investors for other fixed-income products and derivatives.

Misconceptions regarding the ABF initiative. There has been a certain degree of confusion and misunderstanding about the ABF initiative's objectives and potential consequences. As occurs with any public sector initiative, concerns have been voiced about the potential for moral hazard—the possibility, for example, that some issuers might expect to be bailed out. Hence it should be stressed that both ABF1 and ABF2 are passively managed against predetermined benchmark indexes. Bonds are selected for inclusion in the benchmark indexes according to objective predetermined criteria. Also, the day-to-day management of ABF1 and ABF2 is carried out by third parties. These fund-management measures should help assuage any concerns over real or perceived moral hazard or the possibility that troubled bond issuers would expect relief in the event of a market collapse.

Concerns have also been raised that investments in ABF1 might crowd out existing investments in Asian bonds and that central banks' buy-and-hold strategy might deprive the market of liquidity. However, in perspective, given the large market capitalization—about U.S.$40 billion—of the sovereign and quasi-sovereign U.S.-dollar-denominated Asian bond market, the U.S.$1 billion ABF1 is unlikely to have a material impact on the smooth functioning of the markets. Moreover, any concerns about possible crowding out will be far less warranted with ABF2, not least because of the much higher total market capitalization of local currency bonds, estimated at more than U.S.$1.1 trillion, than of the U.S.-dollar-denominated Asian bonds.

Critics have argued that the long-standing health of demand for high-grade Asian bonds shows that the main reason for the underdevelopment of Asian bond markets lies in supply, not in demand. Therefore, the skeptics say, there is little to be gained from developing ABF2, which mainly addresses demand-side issues. These arguments miss the point. Note that the bulk of investor demand for local-currency-denominated Asian bonds is for those with short- to medium-term maturities. There is indeed a lack of demand and liquidity for bond issues with longer-term maturities (beyond five years), as is evidenced by the fact that the best Asian corporations have issued only a small volume of

Table 9-5. *Net Overseas Portfolio Investments of Asian Economies, 1998, 2003, and 2004*
Billions of U.S. dollars

Country	Net private sector portfolio investment (A)			Net public sector portfolio investment[a] (B)			Total (A+B)		
	1998	2003	2004	1998	2003	2004	1998	2003	2004
China	3.7	−11.4	−19.7	6.4	117.0	206.3	10.2	105.6	186.7
Hong Kong SAR	−22.1	34.0	32.3	−3.2	6.5	5.2	−25.2	40.5	37.5
Indonesia	1.9	−2.3	−3.2	6.1	4.0	0.0	8.0	1.7	−3.2
Republic of Korea	1.2	−18.3	−9.2	31.6	33.9	43.7	32.8	15.6	34.5
Malaysia	−0.3	−1.0	−8.9	4.8	10.3	21.9	4.5	9.3	12.9
Philippines	0.9	1.3	1.6	2.0	0.3	−0.5	2.9	1.6	1.1
Singapore	8.7	10.5	11.3	3.6	13.7	16.5	12.3	24.2	27.8
Thailand	−0.4	0.1	−1.5	2.6	3.0	7.6	2.3	3.1	6.1
Total	−6.3	12.9	2.7	54.0	188.8	300.6	47.4	201.7	303.4
Japan	39.2	95.1	−22.9	−4.2	202.1	170.6	35.0	297.2	147.7
Taiwan Province of China	2.4	5.9	6.2	4.8	37.1	35.1	7.2	43.0	41.3

Source: IMF International Financial Statistics database and CEIC.
a. As reflected in increased reserves.

longer-maturity, local-currency bonds. It appears that Asian companies wanting to borrow longer-term funds by issuing bonds have to turn to the global market. This, however, entails the risk of a higher cost (because of the lower foreign-currency ratings) and a possible currency mismatch (because it means issuing foreign-currency-denominated bonds). It is hoped that the ABF initiative, by stoking demand for long-term bonds, will encourage issuers to tap local bond markets for longer-term funds, thereby allowing the supply-side issue to be addressed. (On overseas investment by Asian economies, see table 9-5.)

Market-Oriented Strategy: A Road Map for Asian Bond-Market Development

Regardless of the approach ultimately chosen to foster Asian bond markets, a series of preparatory steps must also be taken. The most logical and realistic road map for developing Asian bond markets begins with deregulating and opening domestic financial systems so that more investment-grade, local-currency bonds can be issued, domestic investors can invest in foreign bonds, and foreign borrowers can issue bonds denominated in different currencies in East Asia's domestic markets.

During the early stage of development of domestic bond markets, when these markets are small and illiquid, domestic borrowers should be allowed to issue local currency bonds in regional and global bond markets. However, such liberalization should be accompanied by efforts to expand and liberalize domestic bond markets and establish a broad base of foreign and domestic investors.

Market liberalization would be the first step toward facilitating cross-border investment in bonds in Asia, which would, in turn, naturally lead to the formation of integrated Asian bond markets. In this evolutionary process, countries with a well-developed financial infrastructure and few restrictions on financial movements would emerge as regional trading centers for Asian bonds.

Market liberalization alone will not, however, lead to greater cross-border investment without a regional financial infrastructure that includes a regional clearing and settlement system, regional credit-guarantee institutions, hedging facilities, and credit-rating agencies. In addition to establishing such infrastructure, East Asian countries should also be able to join forces to harmonize their legal and regulatory systems, domestic clearing and settlement systems, market practices, and withholding taxes on bond coupon payments.

Harmonization clearly requires close cooperation within ASEAN+3 as well as leadership dedicated to East Asia's financial development and stability. However, prospects for closer cooperation among ASEAN+3 members are not promising at this stage. Many smaller member countries to which the benefits of efficient regional bond markets are rather abstract have been indifferent to the promotion of the ABMI. And it is not clear which country or group of countries has the moral authority, clout, and money to lead the regionwide financial reform and the building of regional financial infrastructure in East Asia.

In devising strategies for regional capital markets, East Asian countries can take either a market-led or a government-led approach. The market-led, or evolutionary, approach relies more on competition among countries attempting to transform their domestic capital markets into a regional market. Lack of leadership and divergent interests among ASEAN+3 members suggest that the market-oriented approach is preferable. For one thing, the thirteen countries may find it difficult to agree on any one of the several strategies for Asian bond-market development proposed by Thailand, Hong Kong SAR, Japan, and the Republic of Korea. And even if they do agree on a strategy, the chosen strategy might not see the light of day as long as some ASEAN+3 states continue to be locked in competition to transform their domestic capital markets into regional and international financial centers. This rivalry is one reason—perhaps the most important reason—the market-oriented approach would be more realistic than the government-led one.

If the market-oriented strategy were pursued, the most efficient domestic capital markets would emerge as the dominant regional capital markets. In this scenario, East Asian governments would have to work together to develop regional financial, legal, and regulatory frameworks to ensure the efficiency and stability of those regional capital markets. A more direct, government-led approach would require the active participation of East Asian governments not only in building financial and other institutional frameworks but also in offering a wide range of capital-market instruments tailored to investor preferences through, for example, schemes to guarantee principal and interest payments on private bonds, securitize bank loans, and expand credit.

Several countries have already taken steps to open their domestic bond markets to foreign borrowers and investors or to create an offshore market. The ensuing competition among these countries will lead both borrowers and investors to migrate to the markets with the most efficient payment and settlement systems, which will then become regional financial centers.

For an Asian bond market to rapidly develop, Asian currency bonds, whether sovereign or corporate, will have to be tailored to private and institutional investors' preferences in terms of maturity and credit quality. At the early stage of bond-market development, institutional investors, including various types of local currency investment funds, insurance companies, and investment banks, are likely to dictate which bonds can be issued and traded. They will also encourage healthy competition among potential regional financial centers and the building of regional financial infrastructures. Consequently, it would be desirable to bring these market participants into the planning stage of the ABMI. The public sector's role in this process will be to support the removal of impediments to market development.

If Tokyo, Hong Kong SAR, or Singapore wants to transform domestic bond markets into regional ones, or to create offshore international bond markets, they will have to attract borrowers and investors by offering low-cost lending. For these cities to become full-fledged financial centers, their respective governments will need to create a variety of market-supporting institutions and encourage the emergence of insurance and financial-derivative markets. They will also have to lead the building of a regional financial infrastructure in East Asia.

Evaluation of Current Approaches

At the current stage of Asia's development, there is no guarantee that regional efforts, even if they could be marshaled, would succeed in fostering regional capital markets as competitive as the global capital markets in North America and Europe. Furthermore, the continuing globalization of financial markets and the advances in financial technology that allow financial firms in international financial centers to reach investors and borrowers in remote corners of the world raise questions as to the need and rationale for creating regional capital markets.

It is also true, however, that given the dynamism of the East Asian economy and its enormous pool of savings, the region could accommodate large and efficient regional capital markets as competitive as global capital markets. If these markets were efficient and robust, they might improve the allocation of resources and help safeguard the region against financial crises.

ASEAN+3 has been involved primarily in building the regional infrastructure required for Asian bond markets. This includes institutions such as regional credit agencies, cross-border securities borrowing and lending mechanisms, credit enhancement and guarantee agencies, clearing and settlement systems, a centralized depository system, and exchanges and over-the-counter bond markets. In addition, the six working groups are devising plans to harmonize various financial standards, regulatory systems, and tax regimes throughout the region.

In addition to ASEAN+3, another regional forum, Asian Cooperation Dialogue (ACD), has been promoting Asian bond markets. The twenty-eight-member ACD was established following Thailand's initiative for multilateral cooperation in economic and social development in Asia.[11] While actively participating in the ASEAN+3 working groups, Thailand has been seeking the support of other Asian countries for the expansion of the ACD's activities. Prime Minister Thaksin of Thailand first proposed the creation of a regional forum for Asia-wide cooperation in September 2000, and the first ACD ministerial meeting was held in June 2002 in Cha-Am, Thailand. It was initially created as an informal noninstitutional forum in which Asian foreign ministers could exchange views on issues of mutual interest.

Unlike ASEAN+3, ACD has rather broad objectives that include cooperation in trade, finance, science and technology, information technology, energy, and the environment. Ultimately, it envisions the formation of an Asian Community. A number of member countries have volunteered to actively promote cooperation in eighteen areas in which they have expertise and interest.

At the second ministerial meeting, in June 2003 in Chiang Mai, Prime Minister Thaksin proposed that the ACD's future actions include the development of an Asian credit-rating agency, Asian-currency-denominated bonds, and an Asian

11. The member countries are ASEAN+3 and Bahrain, Bangladesh, India, Kazakhstan, Kuwait, Oman, Pakistan, Qatar, and Sri Lanka.

fund-management agency. Thailand followed up on this initiative by establishing a working group on the development of an Asian bond market in June 2003. The second working group meeting, held on April 29–30, 2004, in Thailand, examined the creation of Asian-currency-denominated bond markets.

However, Asia's regional bond markets will not become more efficient unless these cooperative efforts are accompanied by the opening of capital markets through domestic financial reform in individual member countries. Attempts to build capital markets in East Asia have been undermined by numerous institutional weaknesses and regulatory controls. The major culprits are a lack of professional expertise in the securities industry; the inadequacy of financial and legal infrastructure, including regulatory systems; low accounting and auditing standards; and opaque corporate governance. Unfortunately, ASEAN+3's six working groups are unlikely to take a stand on the urgent need for domestic reform because they are not allowed to address issues related to individual members' internal affairs.

In the end, ASEAN+3's inability to organize a joint program for domestic financial reform will likely frustrate its efforts to create robust Asian bond markets: without domestic financial market deregulation and capital account liberalization, Asian borrowers and investors will be unable to take advantage of regional bond markets since cross-border lending and investment will be restricted.

Observers of the proposals and debates taking place at the numerous ABMI workshops and conferences often become so engrossed in the details of competing plans that they lose sight of what ASEAN+3 is collectively trying to accomplish by supporting the ABI. Moreover, ABMI advocates frequently forget to ask several fundamental questions about the need and rationale for creating Asian bond markets.

One issue ABMI proponents overlook is whether existing regional bond markets are sufficiently large and efficient to meet the bond-financing needs of Asian governments and corporations. While there has been a chorus of proposals to construct regional capital markets and stock exchanges in East Asia, the fact that several bond markets already exist in the region is often ignored. In theory, East Asian corporations could also turn to stock markets in other countries of the region for their equity financing. East Asian corporations and financial institutions can also raise funds through Samurai bonds denominated in yen or Shogun bonds denominated in a foreign currency and issued in Japan, though both the Samurai and Shogun bond markets have been moribund.

Singapore has actively sought to develop a corporate bond market to allow foreign entities to issue Singapore-dollar-denominated bonds. Hong Kong SAR has taken the lead in organizing an Asian clearing and settlement network by linking its system with those of other countries in the region and thereby strengthening its status as a regional financial center. As East Asian economies continue to open their financial markets, some of their domestic bond markets will become accessible to foreign investors and borrowers and hence may eventually assume the characteristics of regional or international bond markets.

Any regional capital-market development strategy could therefore benefit from a study of why existing capital markets have been unable to serve as alternative sources of local or global financing. In particular, Tokyo was once, and perhaps still is, a logical place to establish a regional bond-trading center. But it has never gained any credibility as a regional financial center and has been unable to transform itself into a regional capital market simply because borrowing from regional markets has been more expensive than borrowing from global markets.

Also unanswered is how the proposed Asian bond markets are to be structured—that is, whether they will be distinct from domestic bond markets on the one hand, and from global bond markets on the other. In an increasingly globalized financial system, domestic and regional markets will eventually have to be integrated into the global bond markets. Therefore, in principle it can be argued that East Asian economies may be better off integrating their domestic bond markets with global markets from the beginning rather than going the roundabout way of creating regional bond markets. However, such integration might not be possible, for a number of reasons. Moreover, if direct integration indeed proves unviable, then ABMI advocates should be able to explain why that is so and at the same time whether or not the proposed regional bond markets will be building blocks for a truly integrated global financial system.

There is a general perception that global bond markets such as the Euro and Yankee markets have not been and will not be able to meet the bond financing needs of Asian governments and corporations. Indeed, it is true that global bond markets could have done more to discover more creditworthy East Asian borrowers and help them issue local- as well as foreign-currency-denominated global bonds.

Nonetheless, it must be pointed out that domestic restrictions on bond issuance and trading have seriously limited the access of many East Asian borrowers to the global bond markets and of global investors to East Asian domestic and regional bond markets. And these restrictions are also largely responsible for the narrowness, shallowness, and illiquidity of East Asia's domestic and regional bond markets. More fundamentally, ABMI advocates do not convincingly explain why East Asian borrowers whose low credit ratings preclude them from issuing investment-grade bonds denominated in their own currencies in the global bond markets would be able to do so in regional bond markets, unless they are proposing the construction of high-yield Asian bond markets.

These questions about the viability of the ABMI suggest that its objectives should be clarified in advance in order to help determine the structure and characteristics of the proposed Asian bond markets. One of the most often-heard objectives for robust Asian bond markets is to keep at least part of Asian savings in Asia, rather than sending them to other countries, in particular to the United States, which uses these funds to finance its current account deficits. Another objective is for deep and liquid Asian bond markets to help East Asian economies guard more effectively against future crises, which should allow them to raise more funds in their own currencies in regional bond markets and thereby avoid currency-mismatch problems.

A third reason for building Asian bond markets stresses the importance of pressing forward with the financial reforms that began after the 1997 crisis, especially because of recent signs of regression. A number of recent studies show that reform efforts in the region are stalled, with several countries in fact relapsing into old practices for managing financial institutions and outmoded financial policies. Many ABMI advocates rightly argue that the initiative will exert peer pressure on and generate incentives for Asian countries to move forward with financial reform.

The second of these objectives appears to be the least important. Though efficient bond markets offer a wider range of financing sources and savings instruments, and thereby facilitate the diversification of the financial system, they are no substitute for sound macroeconomic policy. Moreover, a review of the events that led up to the 1997 crisis suggests that currency mismatch may have been overstated as a cause of the crisis.

As for the first objective, the frequently heard argument that the channeling of practically all official reserves from Asia to developed markets was both a consequence and, albeit to a lesser degree, a cause of the underdevelopment of the Asian bond markets is untenable. The ASEAN+3 collectively holds nearly U.S.$1.5 trillion in reserves, the bulk of which is invested in U.S. short-term Treasury and agency securities. There is no criterion of optimum reserve holding according to which the ASEAN+3 can be claimed to have accumulated more reserves than necessary, even in light of the ASEAN+3 countries' need to build up substantial war chests to ward off future speculative attacks.

Many ABMI advocates are quick to point out that at least some reserves could be used to finance additional Asian investment. Moreover, the huge dollar-denominated holdings also entail large losses, since they earn a low return while East Asian borrowers pay a much higher interest rate on their foreign loans. The losses result from the pattern of capital flows between East Asia and the advanced countries, which is often described as East Asia exporting risky assets in exchange for importing safe ones.

Keeping East Asian savings in East Asia is certainly one of the reasons for creating ABF1 and ABF2. However, it is incorrect to claim that East Asian economies invest less than they save because of the absence of regional or domestic bond markets or the inefficiency of existing ones. Before the 1997 crisis, when they had smaller and less liquid bond markets than they do now, East Asian economies invested much more than they have in subsequent years.

Suppose East Asian countries were to unload a substantial portion—say 5 percent—of their total holdings of U.S.-dollar reserves to acquire Asian bonds. Such a portfolio substitution would certainly strengthen East Asian currencies against the United States dollar. However, when the consequences of currency appreciation are factored in, the purchase of Asian bonds might not lead to more investment in East Asia. The large holdings of foreign-exchange reserves are the result of the sterilization of surpluses the East Asian economies have generated in their current and capital accounts since the 1997 crisis. And the East Asian countries are not prepared to let their dollar exchange rates appreciate by refraining from intervening in foreign-exchange markets.

Concluding Remarks

The promotion of bond markets in Asia has recently emerged as a leading policy goal. Efforts to develop such markets have been made on numerous fronts and through many forums, such as APEC, EMEAP, and ASEAN+3. Several constructive and interesting strategies for and ways of developing regional bond markets in East Asia have been put forth.

Although these forums have all endeavored to reach the common goal of fostering Asian bond markets, their approaches are different, as are the countries and institutions participating in them. Most notably, APEC has followed a country-specific approach, trying to develop domestic bond markets in selected countries and focusing on securitization and credit guarantees. EMEAP basically relies on a demand-side approach, forming funds to invest in bonds issued by Asian entities. Finally, ASEAN+3 has taken a comprehensive approach, including providing quality bonds in Asia and building infrastructure. In this respect, the initiatives complement one another, rather than overlapping or competing. Therefore, the establishment of a mechanism or forum to coordinate and harmonize the activities of these separate initiatives and to foster regional bond markets needs to be considered.

This chapter first examined the economic tenets that justify the creation of regional bond markets in a climate characterized by bank-dominated financial structures, an overriding need to recycle Asian savings back into industrialized markets in the region, and volatile foreign-capital inflows. Next, diverse efforts and initiatives to promote regional bond markets through multilateral cooperation were reviewed in detail. The authors now propose a road map for Asian bond market development, taking into account all aspects of this policy issue and the varying stages of development of the region's financial markets.

The most expedient way to begin developing Asian bond markets is for each country to develop its own domestic bond market and then open it to foreign investors—that is, for Asian countries to open up their domestic bond markets and enable Asian issuers to sell bonds in any country, while allowing investors to buy bonds in any country's domestic market. However, East Asian bond markets are at greatly different stages of development. Some are much more liberalized than others, and the different markets have different types of capital controls. Most Asian countries do not even have the economies of scale to support all the elements of bond-market infrastructure, such as a settlement and depository system, a primary dealer system, and credit-rating, bond-pricing, and credit-guarantee agencies, all of which are required for the emergence of domestic bond markets. Therefore, without substantial political pressure in favor of such an initiative, it is unrealistic to expect each Asian country to develop and open up its domestic bond markets in the near future.

The last issue this chapter addresses relates to the building of infrastructure for the Asian bond markets, such as the establishment of a regional clearing and settlement system, regional credit-rating agencies, and regional credit-guarantee mechanisms. Relatively little research has been conducted on a clearing and settlement institution, although its importance is widely recognized by policymakers and market practitioners. The authors suggest that a regional version of the International Central Securities Depository (ICSD) be created, which could be named "AsiaSettle." It would link each country's central bank and national central securities depository (CSD).

The emergence of Asian bond markets also requires a common credit-rating system or standard among Asian countries. However, unlike a clearing and settlement system, the establishment of a regional credit-rating agency should not depend on government support. Instead, harmonization could be gradually brought about through the coordination of local and global credit-rating agencies, which should encourage a common credit-rating system. The Association of Credit Rating Agencies in Asia is currently working on such harmonization.

A new and more adequate guarantee institution, able to meet Asian bond markets' current needs, is also needed. None of the many existing guarantee institutions, including multilateral institutions and private guarantee companies, is in a position to satisfy the demand for guarantees in Asia, which is already high and expected to grow over time. In the light of lessons from the experience with the now defunct ASIA Ltd., the new institution would have a better chance of success if it were heavily capitalized and its expected return on capital were lower. The creation of a regional credit-guarantee institution would also entail a stronger capital-injection commitment from participating countries during periods of uncertainty. Thus the institution should initially be public, although commercially viable.

Arguments for building a regional institution—whether for a credit-rating or a settlement agency—are mistakenly seen as veiled attempts to introduce market protection. The building of regional infrastructure should be viewed instead as a catalyst for opening underdeveloped Asian bond markets and easing local regulations to promote international bond markets in Asia.

References

Asia-Pacific Economic Cooperation (APEC). 2003. "Summary Record of the 16th APEC Finance Ministers' Technical Working Group Meeting." Hua Hin, Thailand. www.apec.org [July].

Edwards, A. K., L. S. Harris, and M. S. Piwowar. 2005. "Corporate Bond Market Transparency and Transaction Costs." Washington: United States Securities and Exchange Commission.

International Monetary Fund (IMF). 2003. "The IMF and Recent Capital Account Crises: Indonesia, Korea, Brazil." Independent Evaluation Office Reports, July 28.

Oh, G., and J.-H. Park. 2003. "Developing the Asian Bond Markets Using Securitization and Credit Guarantee." *KIF Financial Economic Series* 2003–04. Seoul: Korean Institute of Finance.

Park, Y. C., and D. Park. 2003. "Creating Regional Bond Markets in East Asia: Rationale and Strategy." Paper presented at the Second Finance Forum of the Pacific Economic Cooperation Council, Hua Hin, Thailand, July 7–10.

World Bank 1995. "The Emerging Asian Bond Market." Working Paper, June.

Yoshitomi, M., and S. Shirai. 2001. "Designing a Financial Market Structure in Post-Crisis Asia: How to Develop Corporate Bond Markets." ADB Institute Working Paper and Tokyo: Asian Development Bank Institute.

10

The Arab Experience

GEORGES CORM

The Arab region has a rich and diversified experience of regional economic cooperation, beginning in 1944 with the creation of the League of Arab States (Arab League). The league was among the first official regional institutions to be created after World War II. The aim of the league was to develop cooperation between Arab countries in all fields, including trade, finance, and defense.

Unfortunately, the league was not very successful in securing a common Arab position in international affairs, owing to various political and economic factors that are not studied here. It also failed in a number of endeavors to develop Arab economic integration. Although some Arab subregional economic cooperation and integration agreements were signed, only the Gulf Cooperation Council (GCC), created in 1981 by the oil-rich Arabian Peninsula countries of Saudi Arabia, Kuwait, Oman, the United Arab Emirates, Bahrain, and Qatar, was successful. The Union of Arab Maghreb, which was created in 1989 by Tunisia, Algeria, Morocco, Libya, and Mauritania, has been weakened by political tensions between some of its member countries, while the Arab Cooperation Council, founded the same year by Egypt, Jordan, Iraq, and Yemen, was dissolved in 1991.

While many inter-Arab agreements on economic and financial arrangements have been signed by Arab League member countries, the implementation of these agreements has been very limited. Since the early 1970s, however, substantial progress has been made in the field of regional financial cooperation through the creation of various financial institutions to provide needy Arab countries with low-cost official regional lending. This successful experience was quickly extended to countries outside the region through the creation in 1974 of both the Islamic Development Bank (IsDB) and the Arab Bank for Economic Development in Africa (BADEA), together with the Special Arab Aid Fund for Africa (SAAFA).

Low-cost official financing was also made available to Arab and non-Arab countries in the developing world by national financial institutions created by the Arab oil-exporting countries. As this chapter describes, much of the financing originating from the region has come from pan-Arab institutions and the Islamic Development Bank, and has been made available primarily to Arab countries, but also to developing countries belonging to the Organization of the Islamic Conference and others.

In fact, since the oil-price boom of the 1970s, financial institutions in the Arab region have mushroomed, including large commercial banking and finance institutions created by Arab governments or Arab government–owned banks (Arab Banking Corporation [ABC]; Gulf Investment Bank [GIB]; Arab Investment Company [AIC]; and Gulf Investment Corporation [GIC]), in addition to numerous private Islamic banking and financial institutions.

Banking institutions were also created as consortium banks by the main Arab banks (private and government) and large banks in Europe or in other countries (Union of French and Arab Banks and Banque Arabe et Internationale d'Investissement in Paris; European Arab Bank in Brussels; Arab Malaysian Bank in Kuala Lumpur).[1] Some of these banks are no longer in existence, like some other large consortium banks that were created on international capital markets during the 1970s.

This chapter is concerned only with official financial institutions and arrangements in the Arab region that supply concessional financing or facilities and grants. Owing to particular regional economic and financial circumstances, most of these institutions provide development finance facilities to countries outside the region. Another specific feature of these institutions is that none of their shareholders are member countries of the Organization for Economic Cooperation and Development (OECD), and none tap international financial markets or domestic Arab capital markets to finance their operations. Their activities are funded exclusively from the contributions of shareholder countries, with

---

1. See Mattione (1985).

the bulk of such contributions coming from the Arab Peninsula oil-exporting countries.

In fact, Arab regional official funding flourished in the highly specific circumstances of the oil-price boom in the early 1970s. It survived the sharp downturn in oil prices during the 1980s and 1990s, and operations continued, albeit at lower levels than in the 1970s. Although the sharp upturn in oil prices beginning in 2000 led to an increase in funding, funding did not return to the levels of the second half of the 1970s and early 1980s. Today a large pool of expertise in development finance has accumulated in the region, and most institutions have geared their operations to their countries' emerging needs (equity investment, microcredit, aid to small and medium-sized enterprises (SMEs), technical assistance grants, and others). However, available resources are still being used primarily to finance infrastructure.

Available statistical aggregates are not always sufficiently detailed or are not presented in a way that facilitates proper analysis. However, the annual reports produced by some of these institutions are quite detailed. Aggregate figures from Arab sources differ from the statistics in the Development Assistance Committee (DAC) annual report. Although OECD statistics do not seem to adequately cover all Arab institutions and financial arrangements, both statistical sources are used to analyze the different official development assistance (ODA) flows originating from the region, in which Arab countries play a major role.

It is also worth noting that the region's institutional setup suffers from the fact that, as defined by the United Nations system, the Arab countries, as well as other Middle Eastern countries, belong to different regions. The UN system recognizes no Arab region as such. Thus the Economic and Social Commission for Western Asia (ESCWA) includes only some of the Arab countries (Arabian Peninsula countries, as well as Iraq, Jordan, Egypt, Lebanon, Syria, and Palestine); other Arab countries in Africa (Morocco, Algeria, Mauritania, Tunisia, Libya, and Sudan, in addition to Egypt, which is a member of both commissions) are members of the United Nations Economic Commission for Africa (ECA). Turkey belongs to the United Nations Economic Commission for Europe (ECE).

Large multilateral funding institutions, such as the World Bank and the International Monetary Fund (IMF), also do not recognize an Arab region, but rather a Middle East and North Africa (MENA) region that includes all the Arab countries except Sudan and Mauritania, together with Iran, Afghanistan, and Pakistan. The United Nations and other sister institutions always include Turkey in European regional groups, even though it is a key Middle Eastern country. This designation represents an additional complication when one looks at the Arab region.

Economic and Political Background to the Creation and Development of Arab Development Agencies

Since its creation, the Arab League has promoted a number of schemes to induce member countries to develop regional economic integration.[2] The basis of this cooperation was the Treaty of Common Defense and Economic Cooperation signed by Arab League member countries in 1950. Two collective bodies were successively created to promote economic cooperation and integration: first, in 1953, the Economic Council (which became the Economic and Social Council in 1977); then, in 1957, the Council for Arab Economic Unity, which was joined by Iraq, Yemen, Kuwait, and Egypt but was not implemented until 1964. In 1964 this council decided to create an Arab Common Market, which again only a few Arab countries joined. In 1996 the Greater Arab Free Trade Area (GAFTA) was created, which seventeen of the twenty-one Arab countries have now joined. Tariff reductions on goods attained 60 percent at the end of 2003. The GCC member countries signed a customs union in the same year, setting a common tariff ceiling of 5 percent.

Since 1991, Lebanon and Syria have signed various economic cooperation treaties, including an agreement to abolish customs duties for trade in goods. More recently, Egypt, Jordan, Morocco, and Tunisia signed an agreement called the "Aghadeer Declaration," launching a free-trade area among the four countries, which will be implemented fully by the end of 2012.

Arab League members signed many other specific agreements during the 1950s and 1960s in the field of customs harmonization, facilitation of trade and transit, and facilitation of payments and capital movements.[3] In spite of these efforts, inter-Arab trade has not developed, remaining at a level of between 6 and 8 percent of total Arab foreign trade.

Although this chapter does not discuss the problems undermining progress in Arab regional economic integration, it is worth noting that economic cooperation between Arab countries has grown substantially over the past twenty years in the area of inter-Arab private investment and official development assistance, on both a bilateral and a regional level.

This growth in cooperation can be attributed to the sudden increase in oil receipts by Arab oil-exporting countries when oil prices exploded during the 1970s. At that time, these countries' domestic economies did not have the capacity to absorb the new financial flows that were accruing to them. Some of

2. For more details see Al Imam (2004); Arab Thought Forum (2002); and Arab Monetary Fund (2005).

3. See Al Iman (2004).

these countries with small populations (Kuwait, the United Arab Emirates, Qatar, Oman, and Libya) could not find enough domestic needs to absorb the enormous financial surpluses that began to accumulate from the oil sector. In contrast, many Arab non-oil-exporting countries had very large populations (Egypt, Yemen, Syria, Sudan, and Morocco) with rather low per capita income and pressing needs for more state spending on infrastructure. Other small Arab economies, such as Lebanon, Jordan, and Tunisia, also had a major financial need to increase state investment in infrastructure, health, and education.

Because official efforts by the Arab League to promote economic cooperation and regional integration were unsuccessful, and a small group of Arab countries became very rich financially, a consensus emerged that priority should be given to building regional financial institutions to provide the poorer Arab countries with concessional loans and grants. In fact, this had begun at the end of the 1960s, when the Arab Fund for Economic and Social Development (AFESD) was created on paper in 1968, although it did not become operational until 1972. This effort accelerated when oil prices started to rise in 1971.

Another factor contributing to the building of Arab economic cooperation was of a more political nature. It is linked with the Arab-Israeli war of 1967, when Arab Gulf countries that did not participate in the war but were beginning to become richer as a result of rising oil production, agreed to extend financial assistance to the countries that participated in the war and had suffered heavy economic losses (Jordan, Egypt, and Syria). Bilateral loans or grants were provided to these three countries to rebuild their armies and help to compensate them for their economic losses.[4]

The trend was reinforced as the Arab oil-exporting countries became richer in the wake of the fourfold increase in oil prices and the 1973 Arab-Israeli war. During this period, "rich" Arab countries were encouraged to promote Arab regional financial agencies and to supply them with adequate resources to enable them to reduce the bilateral lending that was now being provided not only to other Arab countries, but also to other developing countries that were suffering from the rise in oil prices. This was also the rationale behind the creation of the Islamic Development Bank in 1974, another big financial institution whose geographic scope extends beyond the Arab world. The same could be said of the Arab Bank for Economic Development in Africa, created in 1972.[5]

Other pan-Arab institutions were created in the same economic context, such as the Arab Monetary Fund (AMF), the Arab Petroleum Investments Corporation

4. On this aspect of Arab financial cooperation, see Corm (1988).
5. See Shihata (1982).

(APICORP), the Arab Authority for Agricultural Investment and Development (AAAID), and the Inter-Arab Investment Guarantee Corporation (IAIGC).

In 1972, Arab oil-exporting countries created an organization of their own, called the Organization of Arab Petroleum Exporting Countries (OAPEC). This organization was not intended to be a substitute for the Organization of Petroleum Exporting Countries (OPEC), covering Arab and non-Arab oil exporters, but rather to act as a forum in which Arab oil-exporting countries could discuss and study the development of Arab oil policies and arrive at a common position within OPEC or in relations between OPEC and consumer countries.

Another important point is that the Arab oil-exporting countries were strong promoters and founders, with very sizable financial contributions from other lending institutions created in the same period as the International Fund for Agricultural Development (IFAD) and the OPEC Development Fund.

The oil-exporting countries also created national lending agencies to provide soft loans and grants to Arab countries and to other developing countries. Saudi Arabia, the United Arab Emirates, Kuwait, and Iraq created national agencies (called funds) to grant soft loans to Arab and non-Arab developing countries. During the same period, the Bolivarian Republic of Venezuela, then Venezuela, also created the Venezuelan External Fund to supply soft loans to developing countries.

This was at a time when developing countries began to be classified into two categories: oil-exporting and non-oil-exporting countries. Arab development agencies (ADAs) also divided Arab countries into the same categories. As regional ADAs and national external funds became operational, bilateral lending and grants from Arab oil-exporting countries began to decline, although they were again used more extensively during the first Gulf War (for Morocco, Egypt, and Syria, which participated in the coalition to liberate Kuwait from Iraqi occupation).

In fact, since the mid-1970s, Arab oil-exporting countries have devoted a substantial percentage of their GDP to foreign aid, and both ADAs and the IsDB have developed in-depth expertise in development lending and support to the public and private sectors. The amounts of ODA provided by Arab oil-exporting countries, either bilaterally or by funding regional institutions, were dependent on oil prices, with aid increasing when prices rose and decreasing when prices fell. However, the level of aid provided by Arab region oil-exporting countries, inside and outside the region, is still fairly substantial and is higher in relation to GDP than aid from OECD members of the Development Assistance Committee.

All Arab regional institutions meet each year to review policies and programs and to discuss progress in Arab economic cooperation. Ministers of finance or economic affairs sitting on the boards of these institutions regularly attend this important yearly gathering in Kuwait, where the head offices of many of these institutions are housed in the same building. In addition, Arab central governors meet annually during the AMF General Assembly.

As noted earlier, the analysis in this chapter is restricted to official Arab institutions or official institutions based in the Arab world (such as the Islamic Development Bank) that are responsible for supplying various forms of development finance and grants. The chapter also reviews existing official financial facilities to encourage trade development within the region or between the Islamic countries that these institutions cover.

An Analysis of Regional Financial Institutions and Their Activities: The Global View

It is not easy to analyze available statistics on Arab institutional aid. Although this paper is mainly concerned with regional development lending institutions, it is useful to look at the main channels through which official aid is disbursed. The following four main channels have been identified:

—bilateral official aid to Arab and non-Arab developing countries;

—aid from national aid funds to Arab and non-Arab developing countries;

—aid from regional Arab lending institutions to Arab countries; and

—aid from multilateral lending institutions with geographic specialization, namely the Islamic Development Bank and the Arab Bank for Economic Development in Africa.

The main statistical data concerning these channels are gathered by AFESD and published each year in the *Arab Unified Economic Report* (AUER). This report is prepared by AFESD but published jointly by the General Secretariat of the Arab League, AFESD, the Arab Monetary Fund, and OAPEC.

The tables and figures in this section of the chapter are based on data from either the latest annual AUER or the OECD online electronic database on ODA flows to developing countries.

Aggregated Arab ODA

According to the 2005 annual AUER, global Arab official development assistance totaled U.S.$123.8 billion for the period 1970–2004, as shown in table 10-1. However, the OECD online database on ODA flows reports a total of U.S.$96.02 billion for the same period, as shown in table 10-2. The difference might stem from the fact that AUER coverage is wider than OECD coverage. As the table shows, aid is supplied predominantly by the GCC countries (table 10-1, 94 percent). Although other Arab oil-exporting countries have also been donors, their contribution ceased after the first Gulf War. Iraq's contribution stopped even earlier, owing to the war with Iran, which depleted its financial resources.

Table 10-1. *Global Official Development Assistance from Arab Countries, 1970–2004*

Millions of U.S. dollars, unless otherwise noted

	1970– 74	1975– 79	1980– 84	1985– 89	1990– 94	1995– 99	2000	2001	2002	2003	2004	Total	Percent
United Arab Emirates	923	4,857	2,768	272	1,957	482	376	398	558	130	9	12,730	10.28
Saudi Arabia	4,013	18,515	21,503	12,253	8,698	4,359	2,505	2,455	2,674	2,803	1,902	81,680	65.96
Oman			6	198	189	77	24	24	6	10	9	543	0.44
Qatar	279	1,076	692	28	44	187	94	129	73	23	73	2,698	2.18
Kuwait	1,396	4,682	5,481	2,080	2,302	1,706	228	259	577	16	421	19,148	15.46
Total Gulf Cooperation Council	6,611	29,130	30,450	14,831	13,190	6,811	3,227	3,265	3,888	2,982	2,414	116,799	94.32
Algeria	73	449	354	262	45							1,183	0.96
Iraq	453	1,577	1,091	–76	76							3,121	2.52
Libya	559	714	846	498	118							2,735	2.21
Total other Arab countries	1,085	2,740	2,291	684	239							7,039	5.68
Total Arab region	7,696	31,870	32,741	15,515	13,429	6,811	3,227	3,265	3,888	2,982	2,414	123,838	100

Source: Arab League and others, *Arab Unified Economic Report* (2005).

Table 10-2. *Amount of ODA as a Percentage of Arab Donors' GDP, 1985–2004*

	1985	1990	1991	1992	1993	1994	1995	1996	1997	1998	1999	2000	2001	2002	2003	2004
United Arab Emirates	0.5	2.7	1.7	0.5	0.7	0.3	0.1	0.1	0.1	0.3	0.3	0.5	0.6	0.3	0.1	0.01
Saudi Arabia	2.9	4.2	1.5	0.7	0.7	0.5	0.5	0.4	0.3	0.7	1.0	1.3	1.3	1.4	1.3	0.8
Kuwait	3.0	5.0	2.4	0.8	1.4	0.1	1.6	1.1	0.6	0.8	1.1	0.5	0.7	1.5	0.04	0.8
Total Gulf Cooperation Council	2.5	4.0	1.6	0.7	0.8	0.4	0.6	0.4	0.3	0.5	0.7	0.9	1.0	1.1	0.8	0.5

Source: Arab League and others, *Arab Unified Economic Report* (2005).

Saudi Arabia is by far the largest donor among the GCC countries (66 percent of the total), followed by Kuwait (15.5 percent), and the United Arab Emirates (10.3 percent). Other GCC donors are marginal.

Aid soared from U.S.$7.7 billion in the period 1970–74 to a peak of U.S.$32.7 billion in the 1980–84 period. With the fall in oil prices, it declined to a low of U.S.$6.8 billion during the 1995–99 period. However, with the upturn in oil prices since 1999, the amounts disbursed increased substantially (2000–04), to reach U.S.$15.8 billion.

Table 10-2 shows the scale of Arab assistance in relation to the GDP of the donor countries over the past sixteen years. After peaking at a sizable 4 percent in 1990, the percentage of GDP earmarked by the GCC countries for ODA declined to 0.3 percent in 1997. Although it rose again to 1.1 percent in 2002, it declined once more to 0.5 percent in 2004 despite the further rise in oil prices.

Trend in the Arab Share of ODA from All Donors

The OECD online database allows us to compare the trend in ODA from DAC member countries and from Arab donors; it also allows us to make the same comparison between total ODA from multilateral agencies and from Arab agencies. ODA from Arab development agencies appears to be underestimated in the OECD statistical system.

According to the OECD database, Arab ODA was 7.3 percent of total ODA (DAC and non-DAC) between 1970 and 2004, but represented 95.9 percent of non-DAC ODA. During the oil boom years (1974–81), the share of Arab ODA as a percentage of total ODA fluctuated between 22 percent and 26 percent. Figure 10-1 shows the yearly trend in the Arab countries' share of total ODA since 1970. It reveals that the first peak in the share of Arab ODA in the 1974–84 period was linked with the oil-price increase, while the second peak in 1991–92 was linked with assistance provided in the context of the first Gulf War. The new increase since 2002 was again linked with an oil-price rise.

Arab Donors' Share of Total Bilateral ODA to Arab Countries

Table 10-3 reports the Arab donor countries' share as a percentage of total ODA to Arab countries, according to the OECD database. The Arab share of total ODA to Arab beneficiaries reached 26.7 percent in the period from 1970 to 2004. For certain Arab countries, this share was as high as 94.8 percent (Bahrain), 45.4 percent (Jordan), 36.9 percent (Lebanon), 79.1 percent (Oman), 76.6 percent (Syria), and 35.7 percent (Yemen). Thus almost all ODA granted to GCC countries is of Arab origin, while a very substantial part of ODA to countries suf-

Figure 10-1. *Evolution of the Share of Total ODA Provided by Arab Countries to Developing Countries, 1970–2004*

Percent

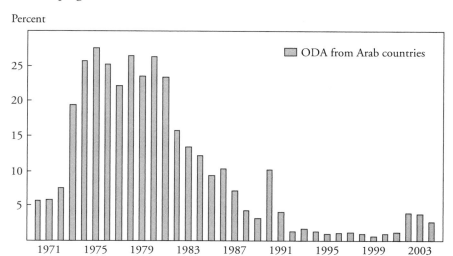

Source: Based on OECD online database: www1.oecd.org/scripts/cde/members/DACAuthenticate.asp.

fering from the Arab-Israeli conflict (Lebanon, Jordan, and Syria) came from Arab donors (between 40 percent and 80 percent).

Arab agencies provide a 10.6 percent share of the ODA supplied to the Arab region by all multilateral institutions. However, the OECD database seems to restrict coverage of Arab agencies to the two main exclusively Arab institutions, and probably excludes national funds (which may be included in bilateral aid), as well as the Islamic Development Bank and the Arab Bank for Economic Development in Africa. ODA to the Arab region has concentrated on a few countries (Egypt, Jordan, Morocco, and Syria). Bilateral Arab ODA has been more evenly distributed, although Egypt, Syria, Jordan, and Morocco have also been major beneficiaries of Arab aid.

Thus, according to the OECD database on aid flow and the main ODA aggregate shown in table 10-4, Arab ODA represents an important share of resource flows to developing countries. During the period 1970–2004, it disbursed 7 percent of total ODA, although during the oil boom years this share rose to almost 30 percent. In fact, ODA from Arab countries represented 95 percent of ODA from non-DAC countries, while the Arab donors' share totaled 58 percent of all ODA disbursed to Arab countries. According to the same OECD statistics, Arab

Table 10-3. *Distribution of Aid to Arab Countries by Different Donors, 1970–2004*

Millions of U.S. dollars

Recipient	All donors	Beneficiary country as a percentage of total	DAC countries	Non-DAC bilateral donors	Arab countries	Arab donors as a percentage of all donors	Multilateral agencies	Arab agencies	Arab agencies as a percentage of multilateral agencies
Algeria	6,731	3.2	4,803	586	544	8.1	1,343	37	2.8
Bahrain	2,388	1.1	39	2,267	2,262	94.8	81	48	58.7
Djibouti	2,621	1.2	1,698	376	374	14.3	547	30	5.6
Egypt	63,521	30.2	45,045	11,121	11,085	17.5	7,354	2,130	29.0
Iraq	10,087	4.8	8,659	362	114	1.1	1,066	38	3.5
Jordan	19,300	9.2	7,912	8,811	8,770	45.4	2,577	113	4.4
Kuwait	94	0.0	54			0.0	40	3	7.3
Lebanon	5,585	2.7	1,956	2,062	2,059	36.9	1,567	63	4.0
Libya	276	0.1	121	1	0	0.0	154	3	2.0
Mauritania	6,614	3.1	2,744	969	965	14.6	2,900	212	7.3
Morocco	18,425	8.8	9,894	4,921	4,899	26.6	3,611	383	10.6
Oman	2,258	1.1	370	1,789	1,785	79.1	99	35	35.3
Palestinian administered areas	8,645	4.1	3,718	1,389	1,362	15.8	3,538	44	1.2
Qatar	38	0.0	20	0		0.0	18		0.0
Saudi Arabia	816	0.4	442	20	5	0.6	354	1	0.3
Somalia	9,486	4.5	5,333	1,070	1,064	11.2	3,083	141	4.6
Sudan	16,772	8.0	8,126	2,917	2,912	17.4	5,729	295	5.2
Syria	17,538	8.3	2,604	13,468	13,433	76.6	1,466	166	11.3
Tunisia	7,878	3.7	5,280	466	442	5.6	2,132	233	10.9
United Arab Emirates	197	0.1	112	53	53	26.9	32	0	0.5
Yemen	11,254	5.3	3,681	4,067	4,019	35.7	3,506	407	11.6
Grand total	210,523	100	112,612	56,714	56,148	26.7	41,197	4,382	10.6

Source: Based on the OECD online database: www1.oecd.org/scripts/cde/members/DACAuthenticate.asp.

Table 10-4. *Arab Share in the Distribution of ODA, 1970–2004*

	Amount (billions of U.S. dollars)	Share (percent)
DAC countries' ODA	921	66
Multilateral agencies	368	27
Non-DAC ODA	101	7
Arab donors' ODA	96	7
Arab donors' share of non-DAC ODA		95
Total aid from all donors to Arab countries	210	15
Total aid from all donors	1,390	100
Arab donors' share of ODA to Arab countries	51	27
Arab countries' share of total Arab ODA		58

Source: Based on the OECD online database: www1.oecd.org/scripts/cde/members/ DACAuthenticate.asp.

agencies disbursed 10.6 percent of the total ODA provided by multilateral institutions worldwide. The following section, based on statistics from the main Arab official sources, gives a different picture of the size of Arab funding from the various regional institutions.

ODA from Arab Development Lending Institutions

According to AUER estimates, the amounts disbursed via national, regional, and multilateral lending institutions with a majority Arab shareholding were U.S.$72.4 billion for the 1970–2004 period, as shown in table 10-5, rather than the U.S.$6.7 billion cited in the OECD database shown in appendix table 10A-4. This represents 58.5 percent of total ODA disbursed by Arab donors since 1970, amounting to U.S.$123.8 billion, as shown in table 10-1.

Table 10-5 also illustrates the geographic distribution of aid from these various institutions. The table shows that the largest loan and aid portfolio is held by multilateral Arab institutions, or institutions that are not exclusively Arab. This portfolio represents 39 percent of total aid disbursed by all institutions. The Islamic Development Bank is by far the most active institution in this group (28.3 percent of total lending by all institutions); however 49 percent of its lending goes to the Arab region. The Arab region receives 39 percent of total lending by this group of institutions.

National institutions are the second largest distributors of development assistance (33 percent of the total). However, only 55.2 percent of their lending goes to the Arab region, while purely regional Arab institutions provide 27.9 percent of all loans. Their operations focus exclusively on Arab countries.

Table 10-5. *Total Arab-Based National, Regional, and Multilateral ODA,
Provided from Creation until December 12, 2004*[a]

Millions of U.S. dollars, unless otherwise noted

Donor	Total aid provided since creation	Arab region	Africa	Asia	Latin America	Other countries	Share of each institution (percent)
Regional Arab institutions							
Arab Fund (AFESD)	15,923	15,923	0	0	0	0	22.0
Arab Monetary Fund	4,293	4,293	0	0	0	0	5.9
Subtotal	20,216	20,216	0	0	0	0	27.9
National ODA institutions							
Abu Dhabi Fund	3,317	2,596	147	567	0	7	4.6
Saudi Fund	7,637	3,675	1,441	2,368	60	94	10.5
Kuwait Fund	13,014	6,965	2,281	3,196	303	270	18.0
Subtotal	23,968	13,235	3,868	6,131	362	371	33.1
Share of each beneficiary region (percent)	100	55.2	16.1	25.6	1.5	1.5	
Not exclusively Arab institutions							
Islamic Bank	20,528	10,049	2,015	8,423	18	24	28.3
Arab Bank for Economic Development in Africa	2,348	10	2,338	0	0	0	3.2
OPEC Fund	5,371	955	2,174	1,547	641	54	7.4
Subtotal	28,247	11,014	6,527	9,970	659	78	39.0
Share of each beneficiary region (percent)	100	39.0	23.1	35.3	2.3	0.3	
Total Arab and associated funds	72,432	44,466	10,395	16,101	1,021	449	100
Total share of each beneficiary region	100	61.4	14.3	22.2	1.4	0.6	

Source: Arab League and others, *Arab Unified Economic Report* (2005).

a. The Kuwait Fund was started 1962, others between 1974 and 1978.

The table also shows that the Arab region is the largest beneficiary of assistance from all these institutions (61.4 percent of the total). However, non-
Arab Asia (22.2 percent) and sub-Saharan Africa (14.4 percent) were also
beneficiaries. The Latin American region is only a marginal beneficiary (1.4 percent). Existing AUER statistics do not identify individual beneficiary countries
of total ODA.

Distribution of ODA by Economic Sector

Statistics from AUER can be used to analyze the distribution of Arab ODA to different economic sectors. Table 10-6 shows the cumulative distribution up to 2004. Assistance focuses on two main sectors: power, and transport and communication. In the Arab region, more than 47 percent of lending was provided to these two sectors. In Africa the transport and communication sector received up to 37.7 percent of all lending. In spite of enormous agriculture and livestock requirements, this sector has been allocated only 13.5 percent of total assistance.

The same trends are apparent in the annual statistics on the sectoral distribution of assistance for 2004. Energy, transport, and communication still represent 49.3 percent of commitments, while agriculture and livestock has declined to 4.1 percent. However, water and water drainage is on a rising trend (14.1 percent).

Unfortunately, there are no details regarding the item "other." Support to social sectors (such as health and education) is included under this miscellaneous heading. It is to be hoped that, in the future, Arab ODA will concentrate more on key sectors where the problems of the Arab economies appear to be linked increasingly with certain social issues, as described in the recently published UNDP Arab Human Development Reports.

In fact, substantial financial resources are not yet being allocated to some of the key issues identified for economic and social reforms. A major concern is the persistently large pockets of illiteracy and extreme poverty in some Arab countries and the general lack of competitive production capacity, which contributes to the Arab economies' marginal position in a globalized world economy despite their huge energy resources.[6]

Main Conclusions

The network of Arab or Arab-based regional financial institutions is complex, and there is a duplication of functions among national, regional (Arab-focused), and multilateral institutions specializing in certain Muslim or African countries. In addition, the amount of funding made available for Arab ODA has varied widely over the past thirty years. Three main issues need to be tackled in the future to increase the efficiency of institutions providing ODA.

The first relates to the heavy reliance of these institutions' activities on oil prices. The data reviewed in this section show that the amounts disbursed by these institutions are highly dependent on the price of oil. These institutions should try to diversify their funding sources to reduce their exposure to fluctuations in the financial wealth of the rich Gulf oil-exporting countries.

6. On this point see Corm (2003) and World Economic Forum (2003).

Table 10-6. *Distribution of Cumulative ODA by Economic Sector and Region, as of December 31, 2004*
Millions of U.S. dollars, unless otherwise noted

Sector	Arab countries	Sector share (percent)	African countries	Sector share (percent)	Asian countries	Sector share (percent)	Latin American countries	Sector share (percent)	Other countries	Total	Sector share all regions (percent)
Transport and communication	7,864.6	17.7	3,918.7	37.7	2,861.4	17.8	347.2	34.0	157.9	15,149.8	20.9
Power (electricity, oil, gas)	11,457.6	25.8	1,318.2	12.7	5,902.5	36.7	121.3	11.9	40.0	18,839.6	26.0
Water and water drainage	3,979.9	9.0	881.5	8.5	599.0	3.7	85.7	8.4	82.6	5,628.7	7.8
Agriculture and livestock	6,154.0	13.8	1,804.3	17.4	1,705.6	10.6	126.2	12.4	58.9	9,849.0	13.6
Industry and metallurgy	6,293.3	14.2	583.3	5.6	3,003.4	18.7	0.0	0.0	8.0	9,888.0	13.7
Other	8,716.5	19.6	1,888.8	18.2	2,029.0	12.6	340.5	33.4	101.9	13,076.7	18.1
Total	44,465.9	100	10,394.8	100	16,100.9	100	1,020.9	100	449.3	72,431.8	100
Share of each region (percent)	61.4		14.4		22.2		1.4		0.6	100	

Source: Arab League and others, *Arab Unified Economic Report* (2005).

The second issue concerns the very broad geographic mandate of some of the largest institutions. Changes in circumstances make it necessary to reshape the network created in the early 1970s. The period when the fourfold increase in oil prices created major hardships for non-oil-producing developing countries is now well past, although it remains to be seen what impact recent oil-price increases will have on the least-developed countries. Unlike in the 1970s, today there are no longer the same international pressures on rich Arab oil-exporting countries to contribute major grant aid to less-developed countries affected by sharp oil-price increases. Some of these exporting countries have themselves become borrowers on their domestic markets or on international markets.

As more resources are made available through other regional and multilateral institutions, is there still a need for Arab-based institutions to provide development funding to non-Arab countries? This is of course a question of international policy by the rich Arab oil-exporting countries, which their governments could usefully examine. Policies to gain friends in the international arena could be pursued through direct bilateral aid or their national agencies, and not necessarily through official regional funding institutions.

The third issue is the need to focus more on strategic bottlenecks affecting the performance of Arab economies. Although there is an increasing trend to commit and disburse more aid to small and medium-sized enterprises or to increase funding for the health and education sectors, as well as to support various types of institutional reform for promoting governance and sustainable development, the trend of lending to traditional infrastructure sectors still predominates.

Description of the Main Arab Regional and Multilateral Institutions

The lending conditions of the most relevant regional Arab institutions and Arab-based multilateral institutions are similar to those of the United States Agency for International Development (USAID) with regard to the loan term. Interest rates charged to borrowers vary from a minimum of 1 percent to a maximum of 4.5 to 5 percent (except by one institution, which may charge as much as 6 percent). The appendix tables provide the main lending conditions of the institutions described in this chapter.

There have also been several debt relief operations between oil-rich countries and Arab beneficiary states. However, no statistics are available because such operations were bilateral and took place within a specific political context (such as the 1991 Gulf War). World Bank statistics indicate that official debt relief operations affected only Egypt (for a substantial amount of more than U.S.$13 billion in 1991) and, very marginally, Jordan, after signing a peace treaty with Israel in 1994. Other countries, including Yemen, Morocco, Algeria, and Jordan, benefited from a number of debt rescheduling operations through the Paris Club.

Although national funds for assisting Arab and other developing economies (such as the Kuwait Fund, the Saudi Fund, and the Abu-Dhabi Fund) play an important role in providing financial assistance to the region, this chapter discusses only those institutions for which capital and resources are provided by more than one state. However, national entities are included in the appendix tables, which give details of the operations of all Arab or Arab-based development assistance institutions.

Arab Fund for Economic and Social Development (AFESD)[7]

The AFESD is the oldest institution created by the Arab countries. Although the Economic and Social Council of the League of Arab States decided to create the fund in 1968, the first meeting of the Board of Governors was not convened until three years later, in February 1972, and the fund came into operation only at the beginning of 1974. The fund is located in Kuwait, the country that created the first national fund back in 1962. The fund's basic activities are to provide soft lending to Arab League countries for infrastructure projects.

AFESD members include all twenty-one Arab countries in the League of Arab States: Algeria, Bahrain, Djibouti, Egypt, Iraq, Jordan, Kuwait, Lebanon, Libya, Mauritania, Morocco, Oman, Palestine, Qatar, Saudi Arabia, Somalia, Sudan, Syria, Tunisia, the United Arab Emirates, and Yemen. Many prominent Arab economists have been staff members or heads of the fund. Most of these economists also played a role in their own country at a later stage as ministers of economic affairs or prime ministers.

The fund's total loan commitments from the start of operations until the end of 2004 totaled 4,770 million Kuwaiti dinars (KD) (or U.S.$15.7 billion).[8] The cumulative disbursement amounted to KD2.973 million (or U.S.$9.8 billion) at the end of 2004. The fund's resources consist of its share capital of KD663 million (authorized KD800 million) and reserves of KD1.6 billion at the end of 2004.

In recent years, the fund has greatly expanded technical assistance activities in the form of grants. Either such grants are used to support inter-Arab activities (Arab research, training, and education centers, support for pan-Arab seminars on economic and social issues, and feasibility studies), or they are specifically earmarked for assisting member countries. The cumulative amount of grants for

7. www.arabfund.org. All data in this section are taken from this website.
8. www.arabfund.org/OPERATNS.htm.

supporting inter-Arab activities totaled KD37 million at the end of 2004, while national grants totaled KD68.2 million.[9]

The fund places special emphasis on supporting regional projects. During the period 1974–2004, it provided sixty-five pan-Arab loans for a total value of KD322.1 million to assist in implementing twenty-nine regional infrastructure projects.[10] In particular, it has been successful in promoting the inter-Arab grid to connect national electricity systems. In recent years, the fund has developed activities to support the private sector through loans or equity holdings. However, private sector loans represented only 2.6 percent of total loans extended in 2004.

Arab Monetary Fund (AMF) and Arab Trade Financing Program (ATFP)[11]

The AMF was created in 1976 by the Arab central banks. It began operations in 1978. The fund's capital is denominated in Arab accounting dinars (AAD),[12] equivalent to three special drawing rights (SDRs) and different from the Islamic dinar (ID). The paid-up capital in convertible currencies is AAD318.8 million. AMF annual operations are similar to IMF operations. However, the conditions are much less strict than those of the IMF and are tailored to each beneficiary's specific economic status. At the end of 2004 the number of loans extended by the fund since the start of its activities totaled 131, with a value equivalent to U.S.\$4.8 billion (AAD1,037.2 million). The balance of outstanding loans totaled AAD252.7 million at the end of the same year.

Technical assistance grants disbursed in 2004 were equivalent to AAD994,000; 4,080 trainees participated in the 119 training courses and twelve workshops organized by the fund in the period 1981–2004.

The fund takes deposits from Arab central banks and monetary agencies. Such deposits amounted to U.S.\$1,544 million at the end of 2004. The fund also supports the development of Arab capital markets via its database and the publication of a specialized quarterly bulletin. In addition, the fund manages a very successful funding program (ATFP) to stimulate inter-Arab trade. The program was established in 1989 with paid-up capital of U.S.\$500 million contributed by forty-four shareholders, including Arab banking and financial

9. www.arabfund.org/TECHASST.htm.

10. www.arabfund.org/LOANS.htm.

11. Arab Monetary Fund (2004).

12. The value of this unit should have been determined not by a fixed parity between it and the unit of Special Drawing Rights (SDR), but by a basket that included all Arab currencies weighted according to the GDP and external trade of the respective Arab countries. However, member countries never adopted the basket as defined by a special technical committee of which this chapter's author was a member.

institutions, as well as Arab central banks. Between its inception in 1991 and 2004, it provided 342 credit lines to banks in member countries, worth a total of U.S.$3.5 billion. However, the fund does not actively promote an inter-bank Arab market for official or banking deposits, and neither does it provide swap facilities with Arab central banks.

Islamic Development Bank (IsDB)

The IsDB is by far the largest multilateral Arab-Muslim country financial institution. Total cumulative approved operations at the end of the 2004–05 financial year (from January 1, 1976, to February 9, 2005) were equivalent to U.S.$38.3 billion. Up to 61 percent of this amount was used to finance trade,[13] while 37 percent went to project and technical assistance and 2 percent to special assistance operations.[14]

The bank's capital was subscribed in a new account currency, the Islamic dinar (ID).[15] Fifty-five countries contributed to it, including twenty-one Arab countries, representing 69.21 percent of the capital. The largest contributor by far was Saudi Arabia, with 27.33 percent, followed by Libya (10.96 percent), Egypt (9.48 percent), and the United Arab Emirates (7.76 percent).

The bank's initial capital was ID2 billion. As of February 9, 2005, it stood at ID15 billion (authorized) and ID8.1 billion (disbursed). Between the start of its activities in 1976 and February 9, 2005, the IsDB approved 1,397 financing operations (excluding trade financing and special assistance operations), and technical assistance grants totaled U.S.$189 million and trade financing U.S.$23.3 billion. Until February 21, 2004, its ten largest beneficiaries in cumulative project financing were the following countries: Turkey (U.S.$756 million); Iran (U.S.$731.2 million); Algeria (U.S.$695.9 million); Egypt (U.S.$601.8 million); Lebanon (U.S.$571.6 million); Pakistan (U.S.$559.1 million); Jordan (U.S.$540.3 million); Indonesia (U.S.$526.4 million); Oman (U.S.$515.7 million); and Malaysia (U.S.$503.8 million).[16]

The bank has a variety of operations and activities, some of which have been decentralized to specialized affiliate institutions, namely:

—the IsDB Infrastructure Fund to help to raise private capital for financing infrastructure development in its member countries. Committed investments amount to U.S.$980.5 million;

13. Trade between the bank's member countries accounted for only 11 percent of total exports and 14 percent of total imports in 2001. However, the level is higher than between Arab countries (6 to 8 percent, as already mentioned).

14. See Islamic Development Bank (2005).

15. One Islamic dinar is equivalent to one SDR.

16. See Islamic Development Bank (2004).

—the World Waqf Foundation[17] (and the Awkaf Properties investment fund that develops and invests Awquaf real estate properties, the beneficiaries of which are the needy, orphans, and others);

—the Islamic Corporation for the Development of the Private Sector, established in 1999 with capital of U.S.$1 billion; since it started, forty-seven projects valued at U.S.$270.2 million have been approved;

—the Islamic Corporation for Insurance of Investment and Export Credit (ICIEC);

—the Islamic Research and Training Institute.

The IsDB is also encouraging the development of other Islamic financial institutions and the promotion of funding techniques consistent with the principles of Islamic law. This is why, in 1989, it also created the Unit Investment Fund to provide private or public Islamic institutions with a vehicle through which to invest resources according to Islamic principles. The bank provides funding according to Islamic economic principles, which prohibit the charging of interest but allow various types of profit-sharing schemes or the leasing of capital goods and receipt of rent from the borrower.

OPEC Fund

Although not a purely Arab regional institution, the OPEC Fund can be considered a multilateral financial institution that is funded largely by the contributions of the rich Arab oil-exporting OPEC members. The OPEC Fund was established in 1976 as an expression of South-South solidarity. All non-OPEC developing countries are eligible for fund assistance. It provides concessional loans for projects, programs, and balance-of-payments support, as well as grants for technical assistance, food aid, and other types of assistance. In addition, in the past few years it has participated in the financing of private sector activities.

Between its creation and the end of December 2005, 119 countries benefited from the fund. Cumulatively, it has committed U.S.$7,906.5 million in development assistance and disbursed U.S.$5,187.5 million. Least developed countries (LDCs) receive the biggest share of fund resources (56 percent of the fund's public sector lending commitments by the end of 2003).

The fund has extended 1,064 loans to the public sector with a value of U.S.$6,168.10 million, of which 79 percent went to project financing and 12 percent to balance-of-payments support; it has participated in eighty-three financing operations in favor of the private sector, totaling U.S.$417.9 million,[18] and has

17. The term "Waqf" applies to properties placed in trust for charitable purposes according to Islamic law. In Islamic and Arab countries, waqfs are important economic institutions.
18. www.opecfund.org/about/about.aspx.

provided 773 grants with a value of U.S.$348.6 million, of which 32 percent was extended to technical assistance, 15 percent to emergency relief, 10 percent to the AIDS Fund special account, 6 percent to the Food Aid Special Account, and so on.[19] Funding worth U.S.$861.1 million has been channeled to IFAD and U.S.$110.7 million to the IMF Trust Fund.[20] By the end of 2005, contributions pledged by member countries amounted to U.S.$3,435 million and reserves stood at U.S.$2,249 million.

Arab Bank for Economic Development in Africa

BADEA cumulative disbursements from 1974 to 2003 totaled U.S.$1.4 billion, in addition to Special Arab Aid Fund for Africa commitments of U.S.$214.2 million.[21] There has been an upward trend in annual commitments in recent years, rising from U.S.$95.6 million in 1997 to U.S.$140 million in 2003. Its lending has concentrated on infrastructure (51.7 percent), agricultural and rural development (28.4 percent), and to a lesser extent, energy (6.9 percent) and other sectors.

Arab Authority for Agricultural Investment and Development (AAAID) and Arab Organization for Agricultural Development (AOAD)

The Arab League has created two specialized agricultural institutions. AAAID was founded in 1974, with the aim of promoting investment in the agricultural sector. Its paid-up capital at the end of 2003 is U.S.$340 million. It has invested U.S.$383 million in the sector, comprising U.S.$157 million in loans and U.S.$226 million in equity participation.[22] AOAD was created in 1972. Its mission is to provide technical assistance, database information, and scientific knowledge on Arab agricultural sectors.

Inter-Arab Investment Guarantee Corporation (IAIGC)

The decision to create this institution was taken in 1970, but it did not come into operation until 1975. Its paid-up capital at the end of 2004 was U.S.$122.5 million, with reserves of U.S.$178.8 million.[23] The institution provides insurance cover for inter-Arab investment and export credits. In spite of its limited resources, the institution is quite efficient.

By 2004, the IAIGC had signed forty-seven guarantee contracts with a total value of U.S.$134.6 million. It had a portfolio of current contracts worth

19. For the full breakdown of disbursements, see www.opecfund.org/projects_operations/grant_operations.aspx.
20. www.opecfund.org/about/about.aspx.
21. OPEC Fund for International Development (2004).
22. www.aaaid.org/english/financial_situations.htm.
23. www.iaigc.org/index_e.html.

U.S.$266.1 million at the end of 2004, 36.3 percent of which was for investment guarantees and 63.7 percent for export credit guarantees.[24]

It produces several annual publications, including an annual report entitled "Investment Climate in the Arab Countries." This report contains a detailed review of investment trends in each Arab country and of any new legal or institutional change beneficial or detrimental to the investment climate. It also monitors inter-Arab investments.

Arab Gulf Program for United Nations Development Organizations (AGFUND)

This very special regional institution was created by Prince Talal Bin Abdul Aziz Al Saud in 1981, with the support of the leaders of the Arab Gulf states, who are its members and contribute its budget. AGFUND supports sustainable development efforts of every type, targeting the neediest groups in all developing countries. Support beneficiaries are NGOs, which receive their funding through projects arranged with UN specialized institutions: the United Nations Development Programme (UNDP), the United Nations Children's Fund (UNICEF), the United Nations High Commissioner for Refugees (UNHCR), the United Nations Development Fund for Women (UNIFEM), the United Nations Population Fund (UNFPA), and others.

Cumulative commitments totaled U.S.$237.8 million at the end of 2003, and cumulative disbursements totaled U.S.$198 million for 925 projects in 131 different countries. Health projects represented 23.5 percent of total assistance; capacity building, 36.3 percent; education, 15 percent; and special development, 25.2 percent.[25]

Other Pan-Arab Regional Financial Institutions

Three major official financial regional institutions promote private and equity investment. The mandates of these institutions differ in their geographic and sectoral focus. The Arab Investment Company is a pan-Arab joint stock company founded in 1974 and owned by seventeen Arab states, and more than 55 percent of its U.S.$450 million paid-up capital has been subscribed by the Gulf oil-exporting countries. It has been established to take equity holdings in economically viable projects in any Arab country.[26]

The Gulf Investment Corporation was founded in 1983 with authorized capital of U.S.$2.1 billion, subscribed by the six GCC member states. Disbursed

24. Inter-Arab Investment Guarantee Corporation (2005).
25. OPEC Fund for International Development (2004).
26. www.taic.com/company.htm.

capital and shareholder equity is U.S.$1 billion. GIC has established a diversified portfolio of equity holdings in different companies in its member countries.[27]

In 1975 the Arab Petroleum Investments Corporation (APICORP) was also created as an inter-Arab joint stock company with capital contributed by the Arab oil-exporting countries in the Organization of Arab Petroleum Exporting Countries. APICORP has been set up to support hydrocarbon and energy-related industries in Arab countries by means of equity financing or medium-term loans. Its authorized capital is U.S.$1.2 billion, and its disbursed capital is U.S.$550 million.[28]

In addition, two regional financial institutions play an important technical role that should be enhanced in the future to serve as a catalyst for developing Arab financial markets. One is the Union of Arab Banks, created in 1977, with its headquarters in Beirut, Lebanon, and a membership that includes all major Arab banks. The union organizes technical seminars on all banking-related topics (Cooke ratio, combating money laundering, electronic banking, credit cards, and others). The other is the more recently created Union of Arab Stock Exchanges, with a mandate to promote links between the various Arab stock markets. Its headquarters is also in Beirut, and it organizes seminars and workshops on technical issues.

Conclusion: Increasing the Efficiency of Regional Arab Arrangements and Institutions

There is no lack of arrangements and institutions in the Arab region to promote regional cooperation and support greater efficiency in the Arab economies within the globalization context. Rather, efforts have been scattered among a plethora of different institutions with overlapping mandates of varying regional scope. This was the result of the highly specific economic and political circumstances that affected the region. The level of funding provided by the various institutions has also been heavily dependent on fluctuations in oil prices, and it is crucial to find additional funding sources to reduce this dependency in the future.

In spite of all the regional financial cooperation efforts in place, it has to be acknowledged that the region's economic performance has been weak in comparison with that in other regions in the world, in particular the Southeast Asian economies. Until recently, this weak performance stemmed in part from the steady decline in oil prices and the Arab economies' overall dependence on oil exports. It is also the result of structural economic problems affecting the region and, in particular, falling productivity deriving from increasing dependence on

27. www.gulfinvestmentcorp.com/about.htm.
28. www.apicorp-arabia.com.

the oil sector and the concentration of domestic investment on the real estate and energy-related sectors.[29]

The Arab network of regional development institutions and arrangements is striving to improve the technical and financial services it provides to the Arab and other regions. However, these institutions should be more aggressive in tackling the main obstacles described in this chapter. The following lines of action could provide a basis for future reforms of regional financial arrangements in the Arab region.

Tapping Resources from Domestic and International Financial Markets to Reduce Oil-Price Dependency and Increase Lending and Grant Assistance

The funding capacity of national and regional Arab financial institutions is highly reliant on contributions from the main rich oil-exporting countries. The level of these contributions, especially for national funds to support other Arab and developing countries, is dependent on the highly volatile oil receipts of donor countries, particularly as those receipts affect bilateral aid and country contributions to the capital of regional institutions.

To lessen this dependence and increase their capacity to fund new types of activities and reforms needed for more sustainable growth, Arab institutions should begin to tap domestic and regional financial markets. While regional development institutions in Latin America and Asia are tapping their domestic and foreign capital markets to increase their lending capacity, no Arab development institution has ever attempted to do so in domestic or foreign capital markets. This ought to be a very feasible solution, especially in view of the solvency of the main state contributors to the capital of these institutions. The positive sharp upturn in oil prices in recent years has consolidated this solvency after it was eroded by the invasion of Kuwait in 1990 and the successive years of high budget deficit in Saudi Arabia owing to decline and low oil prices during the period 1982 to 1999. The Saudi budget now has a surplus and the domestic debt has been reduced, while the state of Kuwait has been able to reconstitute the foreign assets of its Future Generation Fund.

No matter how willing "rich" Arab governments are to increase their share in the subscribed capital of these institutions, the time would seem ripe for governments sitting on the institutions' boards to introduce a legal mechanism to allow the institutions to tap financial markets, as other regional or multilateral institutions have been successful in doing.

Domestic capital markets are still in need of deepening, which they could achieve by issuing high-quality bonds. Although most Arab equity markets, mainly in the Gulf region and in a few other Arab countries, have been booming

29. On this point see Economic and Social Commission for Western Asia (2003 and 2004).

because of higher oil prices, bond markets are still very narrow and not properly institutionalized. If regional institutions were to issue prime quality bonds, it could give a very welcome boost to these markets.

In fact, Arab domestic capital markets are still very narrow in comparison with emerging markets in Asia or Latin America. In spite of the huge financial assets of individuals, private and public banks, and financial institutions, the region still has no real regional financial market. In the future, the various pan-Arab financial institutions could play a major role in deepening and enlarging capital markets in the region.

Rationalizing the Institutional Network and Improving Its Operational Efficiency

There is certainly room for merging institutions. Surely BADEA should be merged with the Islamic Development Bank in order to remove the duplication of effort between the two institutions with respect to Africa.

Another useful topic of discussion is the need to pool regional resources earmarked for the Arab region, as these are scattered among national, regional, and multilateral funds. Should all regional development lending be conducted through one institution, for example, the Arab Fund for Economic and Social Development? In this case, the IsDB could specialize in lending to non-Arab countries, while the AFESD would become the sole development lender to the Arab region. Another alternative might be for the IsDB to entrust "Arabic window" operations to the AFESD, which it would continue to fund.

Of course, these are very thorny issues, because no institution would agree lightly to have its mandate revised or its bureaucracy merged with another. However, it goes without saying that beneficiary entities in Arab countries should also become more efficient in order to make more effective and speedier use of these institutions' financial resources.

Concentrating Funding on the Most Strategic Bottlenecks

Most Arab economies could be characterized as rent economies, with oil being the main determinant of GDP growth for both oil-exporting and non-oil-exporting countries. Non-oil exporters have in fact developed a dependence on financial resources from oil exporters, either as grants and aid or as migrant remittances. For this group of countries, the amount of ODA from "rich" Arab countries and from Arab agencies, in addition to workers' remittances from oil-exporting countries, constitutes a major growth variable.

Other factors explaining the lack of productivity include the fact that the educational sector is not linked with the needs of local economies, and the unemployment rate is very high in the entire region, affecting mainly the younger generation. At the same time, Arabian Peninsula countries import a substantial number of foreign workers, while unemployment is growing among their own nationals; there are very large numbers of immigrants from the Indian subcontinent and other Arab countries.

The private sector lacks competitiveness because it does not spend on research and development (R&D) and on quality control of its products; domestic markets continue to be controlled by a few large family groups that extend their business horizontally, but not vertically. The informal sector, which is a major source of employment, is not encouraged to modernize and develop to enable it to be integrated into the modern segment of the economy by means of subcontracting, licensing, or franchising. This is why the value-added component of GDP is still very low. All this has led to a continual brain drain that undermines the productivity of Arab economies. In addition, workers' salaries in the private sector are not competitive with salaries in other regions of the world, such as Asia and Central Europe.

There is a general lack of governance and transparency in the public sector and in relations between the private and public sectors, which encourages corruption and the resultant high transaction costs. An additional stimulus to corruption is very low public sector salaries in low-income Arab countries.

A lack of productivity and innovation in the Arab economies creates more unemployment or disguised unemployment, fueling the brain drain still further. This creates a vicious circle that is not easy to break without substantial changes in economic policies.

While these interlinked bottlenecks persist, no sharp increase in intraregional trade is likely. If the network of Arab and Arab-based official financial institutions can be reshaped to make it more efficient, it will be easier to clear the main economic bottlenecks. The focus should be on the need for more financial support for R&D, economic innovation, human resource training, linkages between the educational system and the private sector, and other ways to improve productivity in Arab economies and increase private sector competitive capacity on both domestic and international markets.

The trend to supply SMEs with sufficient funding and improve the capacity of the informal sector should be given a substantial boost. More collective efforts are needed from the various national, regional, and multilateral institutions based in the Arab region to curb the severe brain drain that is undermining the region.

The governors of the institutions that meet every year should review current lending operations to set new priorities and new orientations for the development assistance provided by the national and pan-Arab development institutions within the region.

Table 10A-1. *Activities and Lending Conditions of Arab and Arab-Based Agencies*

Financial development funds	Loans				Maximum contribution to the project cost	Forms of assistance	Beneficiaries	Sectors
	Maturity (years)	Grace period (years)	Interest rate (percent)					
Abu Dhabi Fund for Development (ADFD)	8–20	3–8	3–6		50 percent of total project cost and up to 10 percent of fund capital	Loans, grants, equity participation, issuing guarantees, technical assistance	Governments, public institutions, private enterprises	Social and economic projects (infrastructure, agriculture, power, transport, mining, manufacturing)
Arab Authority for Agricultural Investment and Development (AAAID)					50 percent of total project cost	Loans, equity participation	Governments, private sector	Agriculture (plant and animal production, agricultural research and development)
Arab Bank for Economic Development in Africa (BADEA)	18–30	4–10	1–4		60 percent of the project cost and up to U.S.$18 million (in exceptional cases)	Concessional loans, line of credit, technical assistance	Governments, private sector	Agriculture, rural development, infrastructure, industry, energy, health, education, environment, trade

Institution				Type of assistance	Recipients	Sectors
Arab Fund for Economic and Social Development (AFESD)	22–30	4–7	3–4.5	Loans, guarantees, loan syndication, lines of credit, equity participation, leasing, underwriting of securities, and others; grants for technical assistance, training advisory services	Governments, public enterprises and corporations, private sector	Economic and social projects (infrastructure, agriculture, industry, housing, energy, etc.)
Arab Gulf Program for United Nations Development (AGFUND)			Up to 25 percent of total cost of a project	Grants, training personnel, and teachers	Nongovernmental organizations (NGOs)	Humanitarian projects (education, health, nutrition, water, sanitation, etc.)
Arab Monetary Fund (AMF)	3–7 (can be provided)	4–5	Up to 475 percent of paid subscription of a member country	Concessional short- and medium-term loans, technical assistance, training	Government, private sector (banking and monetary institutions)	Monetary (economic reforms, correcting balance of payments, exchange rate stability, capital market development, etc.), trade

(continued)

Table 10A-1. *(continued)*

| Financial development funds | Loans | | | | Forms of assistance | Beneficiaries | Sectors |
	Maturity (years)	Grace period (years)	Interest rate (percent)	Maximum contribution to the project cost			
Arab Petroleum Investments Corporation (Apicorp)					Loans, equity participation, debt financing	Government, public and private sector	Petroleum industry
Kuwait Fund for Arab Economic Development (KFAED)	22–30	2–10	1.5–4	50 percent of total project cost (in exceptional cases)	Direct loans, participation in the project capital, guarantees, grants, technical, and other support assistance	Governments, development institutions, private corporations that have a development impact	Agriculture, transport, energy, industry, water, sewage
Arab Trade Financing Program (ATFP)	6 months to 5 years (depends on the goods)		2.5 points above 6-month LIBOR		Credit lines (pre-export credit, postshipment credit, buyer credit, import credit, etc.) Providing trade data and information	Exporters and importers of Arab-origin commodities	Promoting trade in goods of Arab origin

Institution				Instruments	Beneficiaries	Objectives/Coverage
Inter-Arab Investment Guarantee Corporation (IAIGC)				Guarantee contracts	Private sector (investors, exporters, contractors, and others)	Insurance coverage for inter-Arab investment, export credits, promoting investment opportunities, providing information
Islamic Development Bank (IsDB)[a]	15–25	3–7	0	Loans, leasing, equity participation, technical assistance, profit sharing, etc.	Governments, private institutions	Social and economic projects (agriculture, infrastructure, trade, education, health, and others)
Organization of Petroleum Exporting Countries Fund for International Development (OPEC FUND)	1–2.75			Concessional loans, grants (for technical assistance, food aid, research, etc.)	Governments, public and private sectors	Social and economic projects, programs, balance of payments

(continued)

Table 10A-1. (continued)

Financial development funds	Loans				Forms of assistance	Beneficiaries	Sectors
	Maturity (years)	Grace period (years)	Interest rate (percent)	Maximum contribution to the project cost			
Saudi Fund for Development (SFD)	15–50	5–10	1–2.5	50 percent of total project cost and less than 5 percent of the fund capital	Concessional loans, grants, export credit, and insurance	Governments, organizations in LDCs, private sector	Social and economic welfare (transport, social, infrastructure, communication, agriculture, industry power, mining, etc.) Non-oil exports
Arab Organization for Agricultural Development (AOAD)					Technical assistance, providing sector's database and information		Agriculture

Arab Investment Company (AIC)	Equity participation, providing banking services	Public and private sectors	Agriculture, industry, service projects
Gulf Investment Corporation (GIC)	Equity participation, financial advisory services, Gulf equity products, marketing selected international equity, etc. Treasury	Governments, quasi-governmental institutions, corporate investors in the Gulf region	Developing private enterprises and economic growth

a. The IsDB provides finance under different legal schemes in conformity with the Sharia, which prohibits charging interest.

Table 10A-2. *Main Activity Indicators of Selected Arab and Arab-Based Agencies, 2003*

Millions of U.S. dollars

	Capital at end of 2003		Cumulative to end of 2003	
Agency	Subscribed	Paid-up	Commitments	Disbursements
Arab Gulf Program for United Nations Development (AGFUND)[a]	251	251	238	198
Abu Dhabi Fund for Development (ADFD)	1,089	580	3,384	2,061
Arab Bank for Economic Development in Africa (BADEA)	1,500	1,500	2,197	1,387
Arab Fund for Economic and Social Development (AFESD)	2,714	2,280	15,492	9,502
Kuwait Fund for Arab Economic Development (KFAED)	6,600	6,600	12,400	9,836
OPEC Fund for International Development (OPEC Fund)	3,435	2,920	6,896	4,588
Arab Trade Financing Program (ATFP)	500	500	3,984[b]	3,505[b]
Islamic Development Bank (IsDB)	9,912	4,050	34,244	23,784
Saudi Fund for Development (SFD)	8,267	8,267	6,473.80	5,276.86

Source: *Arab National and Regional Development Institutions 2004,* OPEC Fund for International Development. For Arab Trade Financing Program (ATFP), see www.Atfp.Org.Ae/English/Report/Eng2004.Pdf.

a. Paid-in capital + reserves.

b. In 2004.

Table 10A-3. *Evolution of Arab-Based National, Regional, and Multilateral Official Development Assistance (ODA), 1998–2004*

Millions of U.S. dollars, unless otherwise noted

Agency	1998	1999	1998–99 (percent)	2000	1999–2000 (percent)	2001	2000–01 (percent)	2002	2001–02 (percent)	2003	2002–03 (percent)	2004	2003–04 (percent)
Regional Arab institutions													
Arab Fund (AFESD)	844.0	869.0	3	913.0	5	926.7	2	963.1	4	1,037.5	8	1,041.6	0.4
Arab Monetary Fund	64.0	66.0	3	158.0	139	261.3	65	146.0	−44	296.9	103	180.8	−39
Subtotal	908.0	935.0	3	1,071.0	15	1,188.0	11	1,109.1	−7	1,334.4	20	1,222.4	−8
National ODA institutions													
Abu Dhabi Fund	169.0	218.0	29	120.0	−45	384.0	220	496.0	29	177.4	−64	10.0	−94
Saudi Fund	61.0	83.0	36	71.0	−14	292.5	312	189.0	−35	224.3	19	191.4	−15
Kuwait Fund	459.0	492.0	7	357.3	−27	386.5	8	720.4	86	283.6	−61	487.4	72
Subtotal	689.0	793.0	15	548.3	−31	1,063.0	94	1,405.4	32	685.3	−51	688.8	0.5
Not exclusively Arab institutions													
Islamic Bank	654.0	703.0	7	1,528.5	117	1,587.2	4	888.6	−44	2,437.8	174	913.8	−63
Arab Bank for Economic Development in Africa	110.0	114.0	4	130.0	14	157.2	21	134.9	−14	88.4	−34	181.6	105
OPEC Fund	196.0	197.0	1	250.4	27	167.9	−33	487.0	190	268.7	−45	279.8	4
Subtotal	960.0	1,014.0	6	1,908.9	88	1,912.3	0	1,510.5	−21	2,794.9	85	1,375.2	−51
Total Arab and associated funds	2,557.0	2,742.0	7	3,528.2	29	4,163.3	18	4,025.0	−3	4,814.6	20	3,286.4	−32

Source: Arab League and others, *Arab Unified Economic Report* (1999, 2000, 2001, 2002, 2003, 2004, 2005).

Table 10A-4. *Arab Donors' and Arab Agencies' Share of Total ODA to Developing Countries, 1970–2004*
Millions of U.S. dollars, unless otherwise noted

Year	All donors	Arab agencies	Arab countries	DAC countries	Multilateral donors	Non-DAC bilateral donors	Arab countries to DAC countries (percent)	Arab countries to all donors (percent)	Arab agencies to multilateral donors (percent)	Arab countries to non-DAC bilateral donors (percent)
1970	6,869		382	5,421	1,067	382	7.0	5.6		100
1971	7,765		436	6,034	1,295	436	7.2	5.6		100
1972	8,224		604	6,247	1,373	604	9.7	7.3		100
1973	10,686		2,058	6,675	1,953	2,058	30.8	19.3		100
1974	14,234	117	3,641	7,784	2,808	3,641	46.8	25.6	4.2	100
1975	17,908	159	4,904	9,180	3,792	4,936	53.4	27.4	4.2	99.3
1976	16,884	412	4,231	8,779	3,842	4,263	48.2	25.1	10.7	99.3
1977	18,099	1,101	3,978	9,276	4,824	3,999	42.9	22.0	22.8	99.5
1978	24,756	963	6,505	12,238	5,985	6,532	53.2	26.3	16.1	99.6
1979	28,136	256	6,572	15,305	6,229	6,602	42.9	23.4	4.1	99.5
1980	33,594	280	8,808	16,979	7,766	8,849	51.9	26.2	3.6	99.5
1981	32,675	400	7,576	17,198	7,895	7,582	44.1	23.2	5.1	99.9
1982	29,850	388	4,652	17,625	7,570	4,655	26.4	15.6	5.1	99.9
1983	29,080	313	3,863	17,780	7,435	3,865	21.7	13.3	4.2	100
1984	30,286	146	3,654	19,041	7,586	3,658	19.2	12.1	1.9	99.9

1985	32,262	127	2,975	21,185	8,083	2,994	14.0	9.2	1.6	99.4
1986	37,830	143	3,855	25,210	8,749	3,872	15.3	10.2	1.6	99.6
1987	41,686	72	2,931	28,877	9,866	2,943	10.2	7.0	0.7	99.6
1988	45,005	60	1,889	31,946	11,124	1,935	5.9	4.2	0.5	97.6
1989	46,814	138	1,440	32,923	12,401	1,490	4.4	3.1	1.1	96.7
1990	57,629	75	5,833	38,462	13,292	5,876	15.2	10.1	0.6	99.3
1991	61,529	153	2,406	42,991	15,905	2,632	5.6	3.9	1.0	91.4
1992	61,070	283	774	42,773	17,238	1,059	1.8	1.3	1.6	73.1
1993	56,560	184	910	39,018	16,279	1,263	2.3	1.6	1.1	72.0
1994	60,490	257	764	40,970	18,583	937	1.9	1.3	1.4	81.5
1995	59,697	−21	527	40,481	18,455	761	1.3	0.9	−0.1	69.3
1996	56,636	−36	573	39,088	16,709	839	1.5	1.0	−0.2	68.2
1997	48,686	−37	549	32,394	15,435	857	1.7	1.1	−0.2	64.0
1998	51,106	−8	434	35,207	15,170	728	1.2	0.8	−0.1	59.6
1999	52,677	37	238	37,830	14,311	535	0.6	0.5	0.3	44.4
2000	50,327	35	443	36,064	13,479	783	1.2	0.9	0.3	56.6
2001	52,153	145	595	35,124	16,120	909	1.7	1.1	0.9	65.5
2002	60,825	139	2,321	40,752	17,362	2,712	5.7	3.8	0.8	85.6
2003	70,608	44	2,642	49,755	17,720	3,133	5.3	3.7	0.2	84.3
2004	78,308	379	2,057	54,836	21,048	2,875	3.8	2.6	1.8	71.5
Grand total	1,390,942	6,704	96,022	921,446	368,748	101,197	10.4	6.9	1.8	94.9

Source: OECD online database: www1.oecd.org/scripts/cde/members/DACAuthenticate.asp.

References

Al Imam, M. M. 2004. *International Experiences in Economic Integration and Lessons for Arab Integration* (in Arabic). Beirut: Center for Arab Unity Studies.

Arab League, Arab Fund for Economic and Social Development (AFESD), Arab Monetary Fund, and the Organization of Arab Petroleum Exporting Countries (OAPEC). 1999–2005. *Arab Unified Economic Report.* Abu Dhabi, United Arab Emirates.

Arab Monetary Fund. 2003 and 2004. *Annual Report.* Abu Dhabi.

———. 2005. *Arab Economic Integration: Challenges and Horizons* (in Arabic). Abu Dhabi.

Arab Thought Forum. 2002. *Arab Cooperation Horizons between Regionalism and Globalization* (in Arabic). Amman.

Corm, G. 1988. *The Fragmentation of the Middle East.* London: Unwin Hyman-Hutchinson.

———. 2003a. "Challenges for Human Development in the Arab Region" (in Arabic). Paper presented at the First Arab Conference on Human Development, held by the Arab League in Cairo, February 24–26, 2003.

———. 2003b. *Cooperation and Mobilization of Financial Resources for Sustainable Development in the Mediterranean Region.* United Nations Environment Program (UNEP), Blue Plan, Regional Activity Center, Sophia Antipolis, France. www.planbleu.org.

———. 2003c. "The Private Sector's Role in the Development of Mashreq Countries" (in Arabic). Paper presented at a seminar on the private sector's role in the development of Arab economies, held by the Islamic Development Bank in Cairo, May 2003.

Economic and Social Commission for Western Asia (ESCWA). 2003. *Analysis of Performances and Assessment of Growth and Productivity in the ESCWA Region.* First Issue. New York.

———. 2004. *Analysis of Performances and Assessment of Growth and Productivity in the ESCWA Region.* Second Issue. New York.

Inter-Arab Investment Guarantee Corporation. 2005. *Annual Report 2004.* Kuwait.

Islamic Development Bank. 2004. *Annual Report for Year 1424 H (2003–2004).* Jeddah, Saudi Arabia.

———. 2005. *Thirty-One Years in the Service of Development.* Economic Policy and Strategic Planning Department, Islamic Fund Report, June.

Mattione, R. P. 1985. *OPEC's Investments and the International Financial System.* Brookings.

OPEC Fund for International Development. 2004. *Arab National and Regional Development Institutions, 2004 (and 2003): A Profile.* Vienna.

Organization for Economic Cooperation and Development (OECD). *Geographical Distribution of Financial Flows to Developing Countries.* www.oecd.org/cad/stats/sdienligne.

Shihata, I. F. I. 1982. *The Other Face of OPEC: Financial Assistance to the Third World.* London: Longman.

World Economic Forum. 2003. *The Arab World Competitiveness Report, 2002–2003.* Oxford University Press.

11

An Analysis of Financial and Monetary Cooperation in Africa

ERNEST ARYEETEY

Since the early 1990s there has been renewed interest among African nations in developing financial and monetary cooperation arrangements that help to strengthen their own financial institutions and complement their efforts to reach out to a rapidly globalizing world. The new arrangements are intended to help improve not only the mobilization of resources, both domestic and foreign, but also the regulation of institutions in order to avert crises in financial and exchange rate systems. The realization that strong financial systems are important in providing access to greater financial resources from more varied sources, particularly as countries pursue macroeconomic reforms, is certainly now more widespread.

This new interest is not surprising, considering that one of the most significant developments in global finance has been the growth in capital flows between industrialized and developing economies, although this has eluded Africa. Africa's share of the significantly expanded private capital flows to developing countries averaged only 1.6 percent in the period 1992–2002. There are also indications that private capital flow to Africa slowed down in the wake of the East Asian crisis, even though this was considered to be far less significant than the slowdown in East Asia (see figures 11-1 and 11-2). These developments

I appreciate the valuable research assistance from Edna Kwami and Christian Ahortor.

Figure 11-1. *Net Private Capital Flows, 1970–2003*

Percent of GDP (constant 2000 U.S. dollars)

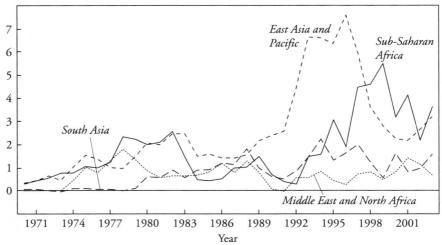

Source: Generated from World Bank (2005, CD-ROM).

Figure 11-2. *Net Foreign Direct Investment Inflows to Developing Countries, 1970–2002*

Billions of U.S. dollars

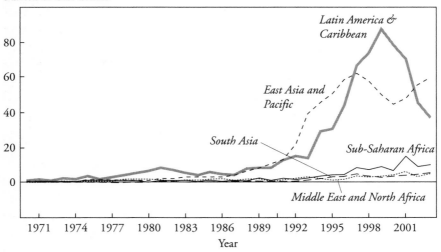

Source: Generated from World Bank (2005, CD-ROM).

have been partially blamed on the fragility of financial markets in the region, despite financial sector reforms in many countries.[1]

The interest in greater financial and monetary cooperation for the purpose of enhancing resource flows and regulating such flows is partially linked to the turmoil that the world saw in the 1990s, resulting from the financial crises in Asia and other parts of the world. The crises led to discussions on a new international financial architecture, based on strengthening the surveillance of financial markets through requirements for greater transparency and information flow; strengthening financial regulation and supervision; assisting countries to overcome difficulties in implementing international standards and regulations through capacity building; improving liability management by borrowers; discouraging dogma in exchange rate determination; sharing responsibility for crisis resolution among private creditors, the international community, and debtor authorities; and finally a number of measures for dealing with emergencies, including the imposition of reserve requirements on short-term capital flows, withholding taxes on such short-term inflows, and expanding country reserves. The new architecture also calls for greater transparency in the functions of international financial institutions. While the new measures are generally regarded as essential for bringing sanity to the operations of financial markets and limiting the occurrence of crises, it is not clear whether such measures necessarily attract and sustain private capital.

The emergence of European Monetary Union (EMU) has raised considerable interest in the development of similar arrangements in parts of Africa.[2] Thus, beyond the issue of finding their proper place in the international financial architecture, subregional integration bodies have considered financial cooperation as part of a broader framework for achieving greater regional integration, including greater monetary cooperation. In West Africa, for example, the medium- to long-term aim of the monetary cooperation program, adopted in 1987 by the Economic Community of West African States (ECOWAS), was to achieve convertibility of West African currencies and create a single currency by the year 2000. What has been achieved so far is much more modest. The West African Clearing House (WACH) has been transformed into the West African Monetary Agency (WAMA); a credit-guarantee fund for the WAMA clearing and payments mechanism has been introduced; and West African travelers' checks have been issued since late 1998. Further progress in achieving a common currency has been constrained by the severe macroeconomic conditions in member states.

---

1. See Aryeetey and Senbet (1999).
2. Honohan and Lane (2000).

One objective of the newly established East African Cooperation Agreement is to create a common market, subsequently a monetary union, and ultimately a political federation. Achieving these goals is predicated on progress in policy harmonization, macroeconomic stability, and infrastructure development. It has not moved as fast as the West African nations on the monetary cooperation front. The treaty steered clear of customs union and common market issues, having only two articles on safeguards.

Financial and monetary cooperation in southern Africa is dominated by the role of South Africa, which drives both the regional currency areas in the Common Monetary Area (CMA) and the Southern African Development Community (SADC). Indeed, there are various regional integration initiatives involving the southern African region, each with its own action program. The declaration and treaty establishing the SADC in 1992 does not specifically refer to a regional currency area. However, monetary integration is generally considered in the region to be one way in which economic integration could be furthered, culminating in the creation of a regional monetary union. For the moment, however, monetary integration in SADC may be regarded as a long-term objective, and not as urgent as in West Africa.

While different parts of Africa may be moving at different speeds toward financial and monetary cooperation, there have been a number of assessments of how such arrangements relate to similar developments in other parts of the world. Following the introduction of the euro, Honohan and Lane analyzed the prospects for greater monetary integration in Africa in the wake of European Monetary Union. They argued that, even though the structural characteristics of African economies are quite different from those of European economies, much could be gained from monetary cooperation, with the European Union acting as an external agency of restraint and to promote stability in the financial sector. They conceded, however, that one should not expect too much from such arrangements. They observed that there was little evidence of contagious attacks on African currencies requiring the coordination of exchange rate policies. Also, economies of scale in the prudential regulation of financial systems could be achieved through international cooperation, without the need for a common currency. They also suggested that the same was true of enhanced risk-pooling through the financial system. Finally, their study concludes that though the European Monetary Union has only a marginal impact on the net benefits of monetary cooperation, the euro would be a natural anchor for any African monetary union, especially if the United Kingdom and the pound sterling were to join the European Monetary Union, strongly promoting the idea that "the most likely route to new monetary cooperation in Africa is through a common peg to the euro."[3]

Considering the various pressures and dynamics for financial and monetary cooperation in Africa, this chapter discusses the scope of such moves and the experiences of different parts of the region. The aim is to draw attention to factors underlying current initiatives in the region and to assess their prospects for achieving set objectives. The next section discusses various expectations of regional financial cooperation arrangements. The chapter then discusses African experiences of regional financial and monetary cooperation; this review looks at the different types of cooperation arrangements and how they are linked to the structure of financial markets. Finally, the chapter assesses the outcomes of cooperation efforts and looks at the potential for enhanced financial and monetary cooperation in parts of Africa.

Expectations of Financial and Monetary Cooperation in Africa

The discussion of financial and monetary cooperation may be linked to the concept of optimal currency areas, even though it is possible to achieve considerable cooperation in the absence of such a union. The literature on optimal currency areas is relevant because African countries' search for additional financial resources from global sources and the need to protect themselves against any adverse side effects makes it important to bolster confidence in their currencies. In the past, the search for confidence boosters often led them to align their currencies with one of the major world currencies, usually the U.S. dollar. However, current understanding of the short- and long-term consequences of monetary and exchange rate policies has grown remarkably, while there has been a trend toward greater independence among monetary authorities around the world. This has improved confidence in many currencies, to the extent that the decision on which currency a country should align with is becoming less influenced by concerns about confidence. In the absence of concerns about confidence, the thinking regarding currency alignments revolves around the fundamental economic natures of the different economies. The old saying that "birds of a feather flock together" is today reflected in many of the financial and monetary cooperation attempts being made throughout Africa. How can countries with similar interests support one another? What figure 11-3 shows is that the flow of private

---

3. Honohan and Lane (2002, p. 1).

Figure 11-3. *Net Private Capital Flows, 1980–2001*

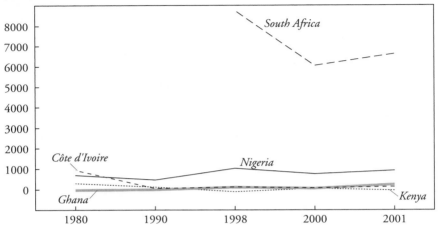

Source: Generated from World Bank (2003, CD-ROM).

capital to African countries was patchy in the 1990s, hence the search for a more level playing field.

In light of the above expectations, cooperation within a currency union can be considered from four main angles, depending on the extent to which:

—the cooperation arrangement fosters the development of an agency of restraint to the government;

—the arrangement deepens the financial system;

—the arrangement reduces the probability of speculative pressures;

—the arrangement leads to the international integration of economies.

The issue of developing an agency of restraint for African countries first gained prominence following the work of Collier and Gunning, who suggested that many of the past ills of African economies were caused by bad policies resulting from unrestrained fiscal programs in many countries, and by the fact that no internal agencies existed to restrain governments. They then argued that an integration arrangement with Northern partners would generate broad gains from global liberalization. Such a union is also expected to enhance the credibility of African economic liberalization and generate the desired investment inflows. They further argued that integration with the North has incorporated effective sanctions, which current African regional arrangements have not. This

Table 11-1. *Money and Quasi Money (M2) as a Percentage of Gross Domestic Product, 1980–2001*

Country	1980	1990	2000	2001
Benin	17	24	29.9	31.0
Botswana	26	26	26.8	31.7
Cameroon	21	23	17.3	18.3
Côte d'Ivoire	27	29	21.8	24.1
Ethiopia	n.a.	37	41.3	45.2
Ghana	16	13	26.8	17.4
Kenya	30	27	43.1	39.3
Malawi	18	18	16.8	15.5
Mozambique	n.a.	40	30.4	30.7
Nigeria	24	19	24.8	28.6
Senegal	27	23	25.4	26.5
South Africa	50	54	56.2	59.7
Tanzania	n.a.	19	19.2	20.0
Uganda	13	6	16.9	16.5
Zambia	28	20	24.1	21.0
Zimbabwe	31	28	24.8	36.4

Source: World Bank (1998, 2003).
n.a. Not available.

is because they guard against policy reversals.[4] In this arrangement, the European Union acts as the agency of restraint for African economies. Thus, the discussion has focused largely on external agencies of restraint that may not have similar structural characteristics but may have a common interest. This is certainly quite different from an external agency of restraint built around a collective of similar economies.

Regarding the deepening of financial systems, Senbet points to the increasing need for and interest in linking financial institutions on a regional basis. The lack of depth in financial systems is shown in table 11-1. Senbet has argued that one way to address the thinness and illiquidity of African capital markets is for the various countries to pool resources for regional cooperation in banking and capital market development. Properly functioning markets can position a country competitively in markets for global capital. This promotes the inflow of international capital and subjects a country to international discipline. Furthermore, accessing global markets for capital reduces reliance on foreign aid. The regionalization of African stock markets is expected to enhance mobilization of both domestic and global financial resources to fund regional companies, while

4. See Collier and Gunning (1995).

injecting more liquidity into the markets.[5] For this to work, the tax treatment of investments must be harmonized, since tax policy is an important incentive or disincentive for both issuers and investors. Ultimately, regulations and accounting reporting systems, along with clearance, settlement, and depository systems, should conform to international standards. The establishment of regional securities and exchange commissions, regional self-regulatory organizations, regional committees to promote the harmonization of legal and regulatory schemes, and coordinated monetary arrangements (for example, via currency zones) are some of the mechanisms for such financial integration.

Honohan and Lane suggest that the regionalization of banking could offer some potential for risk reduction through "better international diversification of loan portfolios."[6] The internationalization of the banking sector is seen as an effective way of minimizing vulnerability to financial crises, as multicountry banks are perceived to be more diversified and less vulnerable to a downturn in any one country.

With respect to containing speculative pressures, it is the view of Honohan and Lane that, as African economies are not on the radar of the world's holders of private capital, they are not in much danger of being swamped by speculative attacks. They point out that one reason why African countries may suffer from contagion is that the financial system is largely dependent on European banks, a fact that ensures that the banks are likely to view different countries in the same way and that may lead to countries' being treated similarly even when this is unnecessary. Nevertheless, there is little evidence of exchange rates' being the subject of contagion. Were the likelihood of contagion to be high, a monetary cooperation arrangement could be expected to have both negative and positive effects.

There is also little evidence that the creation of monetary cooperation arrangements will eventually lead to greater economic and political integration. While a number of African countries appear to be pursuing greater degrees of financial and monetary cooperation, particularly in West Africa, with a view to accelerating the process of regional integration, the experience of other areas tends to be the reverse, as in the European Union.

While expectations differ on how much cooperation arrangements may achieve, there have been only a few technical analyses of the likely outcomes of such arrangements. In analyzing the cost and benefit of the common monetary area in South Africa, Grandes applied a two-step econometric approach based on the theory of generalized purchasing power parity (G-PPP).[7] This study empha-

5. Senbet (1998).
6. Honohan and Lane (2000, p. 14).
7. See Grandes (2003).

sized two aspects of the monetary integration process in southern Africa in the light of G-PPP theory and determined whether the monetary area, including Botswana, constituted an optimal currency area in the classic sense. He concluded that the area formed an optimal currency area, given the existence of common long-term trends in their bilateral real exchange rates. He also observed that further macro efficiency gains could be made if the countries went all the way and developed a full monetary union. This was because there was evidence of similar production structures, higher output correlation, and risk-hedging possibilities, and peripheral countries were able to resort to South Africa's capital markets and overdraft facilities at the reserve bank. However, the difficulties that had to be overcome were: a degree of divergence in terms-of-trade shocks, lack of export diversification, and the predominance of interindustrial trade patterns.

Other relevant works on optimal currency areas for Africa include a paper by Anyanwu.[8] He estimated the macroeconomic effect of monetary unions on trade and output and suggested that a monetary union is beneficial to bilateral trade and economic growth. In his study, he used panel economic indicators for individual West Africa Economic and Monetary Union (WAEMU) members, as well as non-WAEMU ECOWAS counterparts, to determine whether monetary union brought price, output, fiscal, and trade stabilization during the period 1990–2001. The panel data contained both a time component and a cross-sectional component, in a bid to determine the magnitude of expected change in one country as a result of a unit change in any variable. The results suggested that economic growth stability was greater in WAEMU countries than in non-WAEMU countries during the analysis period, but the same was not observed for inflation. Inflation instability in the WAEMU region was greater than in the non-WAEMU region. He suggested that more work needed to be done in the areas of price stability, fiscal discipline, and intraregional trade to make union meaningful. He also suggested that important benefits from monetary union could come through central bank credibility.

African Financial and Monetary Cooperation Experiences

In view of continuing difficulty with financial management in a number of countries, despite reform, it is not surprising that countries should seek refuge in supranational arrangements. Indeed, arrangements for achieving financial and monetary cooperation among different countries in Africa date back as far as colonial days. These cooperation arrangements were widespread in both the

8. Anyanwu (2003).

French and British colonies, and much of what we see today is derived from those early experiences.

Financial and Monetary Cooperation in West Africa

Financial and monetary cooperation among many ECOWAS countries started long before postindependence economic integration efforts began in the sub-region.[9] Because the arrangements were originally driven by administrative convenience and seigniorage considerations,[10] exchange rate policy and fiscal restraint were not an issue. An essential component of colonial economic arrangements was the institution of an orderly financial and monetary system. In British West Africa, following legislation that effectively established a common currency,[11] the monetary policy of the four colonies was administered by the West African Currency Board (WACB), which was established in 1912 and had its headquarters in London. The currency board was established among others to provide for and to control the supply of currency in the British West African Colonies, Protectorates and Trust Territories. In practice, however, WACB was no more than an automatic money-exchange organization issuing as much local currency as the banks wanted to buy for sterling, and vice versa. It definitely did not function as a monetary authority, and its effectiveness as a currency board has been questioned.[12] Uche also argued that the prime motivation for its creation was to facilitate greater efficiency in the management of the financial affairs of the colonies: "It made economic sense to administer these geographically proximate colonies through one currency board which was headquartered in London. Inter colony integration therefore could only have been an incidental benefit of the currency board system and not its objective."[13]

Commercial banking in British West Africa was also developed along regional cooperative lines, cutting across country borders. This led to the establishment of the Bank of British West Africa as the first bank in the region. The bank

9. ECOWAS embraces over 200 million people in all fifteen states of West Africa, ten of which have parallel allegiances to other groupings, and (until 1999) Mauritania. Thus the now dormant Mano River Union (MRU) embraced Guinea, Liberia, and Sierra Leone; the erstwhile West African Economic Community (WAEC) comprised Benin, Burkina Faso, Côte d'Ivoire, Mali, Mauritania, Niger, and Senegal; and the remaining six ECOWAS states (Cape Verde, Gambia, Ghana, Guinea-Bissau, Nigeria, and Togo) belonged to no other grouping until Guinea-Bissau and Togo joined other French-speaking countries and the members of the Mano River Union to establish WAEMU in 1994.

10. Honohan and Lane (2000, p. 6).

11. The British colonial currency was pegged to, and fully backed by, the pound sterling, and the currency board was modeled on the currency arrangements in the British Bank Act of 1844.

12. Honohan and Lane (2000).

13. Uche (2001, p. 6).

maintained offices in all four colonies, where it adopted similar administrative and operational policies. Uche argues that the fact that only modest economic exchanges occurred in these colonies is an indicator that the subregional institutions were not designed for this purpose.

With political independence in the 1950s and 1960s, the role of the WACB system began to change. Governments adopted a more interventionist and nationalistic ideology, and having a national currency became a symbol of sovereignty. This led most participants to abandon the currency board arrangement. Various countries began to establish their own central banks. The first to pull out was Ghana in 1957, followed by Nigeria in 1959. Sierra Leone and Gambia, however, operated their own currency board–type arrangement for a few more years, and in 1971 Gambia was the last African country to abandon the sterling peg. Honohan and Lane have documented the extensive use of national central banks to finance government budgets in the early postindependence years, completely unrestrained by the usual regulations of central banks.[14]

More recent integration efforts in the English-speaking part of the subregion have been driven by the ECOWAS agenda. Thus, as in other parts of Africa, West Africa's experience with formal regional integration has been largely driven by the desire to overcome the constraint of small economic size, which was hampering their ability to industrialize efficiently, by extending the logic of protected and state-led economic development to a larger number of countries. Indeed, the preamble to the 1975 ECOWAS Treaty noted that the community was being created in view of the overriding need to accelerate, foster, and encourage the economic and social development of member states in order to improve the living standards of their peoples.[15] ECOWAS saw regional integration as a multistep process eventually leading to a customs union and later to a common market integrating states in the West African subregion politically and culturally. Both the original treaty and the subsequently revised 1992 version (complemented by more than thirty protocols and supplementary protocols) include initiatives to promote cooperation and development in industry, transport, telecommunications and energy, agriculture, natural resources, commerce, and monetary and financial matters, as well as social and cultural affairs. The principal areas of operation have been:

—expanding the regional market;

—harmonizing agricultural and industrial policies through production integration;

14. Honohan and Lane (2000).
15. ECOWAS (1975).

—ensuring the harmonious integration of physical infrastructure;

—promoting monetary and financial integration to facilitate trade;

—maintaining regional peace, stability, and security; and

—ensuring free movement of persons, including rights of residence and establishment.

Although the creation of a West African Monetary Union has been high on the ECOWAS agenda since its inception in 1975, owing to the length of time required to achieve that objective, some West African countries have considered forming a second monetary zone, the West African Monetary Zone (WAMZ) under the umbrella of ECOWAS. The creation of WAMZ is seen as a possible means of accelerating the formation of a unified West African Monetary Union. Monetary cooperation is very important to ECOWAS members that are not in the CFA franc (le franc des Colonies Françaises d'Afrique) zone because their French-speaking counterparts with a common currency are perceived to be relatively stable and intraregional trade in that region is also seen to be more extensive than in the rest of the ECOWAS region.

A timetable was set for a group of countries—Gambia, Ghana, Nigeria, Guinea, and Sierra Leone—to meet the policy convergence criteria set for the union. These conditions are economic stability, budgetary discipline, an inflation rate of no more than 5 percent, and a healthy foreign exchange reserve; once these were met, it was anticipated that monetary union would be introduced by July 2005. There are also ongoing efforts to set up institutions, such as the convergence council, technical committees, and the West African Monetary Institute.

While some believed that the varying socioeconomic conditions that exist in the different countries will make it difficult for the member countries to attain an inflation level of under 5 percent and also to build enough foreign exchange reserves, others thought that these could be achieved by the end of 2004, thus paving the way for a common currency (the eco) to be introduced. Table 11-2 shows the status of the convergence criteria at the start of the endeavor. All of the countries in the second monetary zone satisfied the criterion of central bank financing of the budget deficit at the end of 2000, and all of the countries except Ghana met the inflation conditions. For many, the budget deficit/GDP ratio and the gross foreign currency reserve conditions were difficult to meet. Only Nigeria succeeded. The countries also found it more difficult to meet the more stringent secondary convergence criteria. By 2004, the countries' ability to achieve the convergence criteria had worsened significantly. Ogunkola suggested that, even if all the convergence criteria were met, it was still doubtful that a sta-

Table 11-2. *The State of Primary Convergence Criteria, 2000*

Country	Budget deficit/ GDP ratio, excluding grants (percent)	Inflation rate (percent)	Central bank financing of budget deficit/ year-1 tax revenue (percent)	Gross reserves/ annual imports in months	Number of criteria satisfied
Benchmark	≤5 percent	<10 percent	≤10 percent	≥3 months	
Gambia	3.84	0.80	0.00	2.94	3
Ghana	10.74	40.50	8.20	0.53	1
Guinea	5.99	7.20	6.20	1.15	2
Nigeria	1.88	6.90	0.00	4.30	4
Sierra Leone	17.30	−2.75	1.87	1.26	2

Source: West African Monetary Institute.

ble regional currency area would be achieved, given that economic restructuring was a long-term endeavor.[16]

Interestingly, even though the planned single currency for the zone is to serve the interests of local people and the business community, there is little public education on the subject. The current flurry of activity to speed up implementation of a common currency for West Africa suggests that this may be an area in which policymakers are prepared to relax their opposition to the "variable geometry" approach suggested by Collier and Gunning.[17] Opposition to the approach was based on the belief that it ran counter to the principles and ideals of the African Economic Community, namely equality of nations and shared purpose in integration. The fear was that variable geometry could lead to the exclusion of some countries and to the division of the continent into subregions dominated by external influences. The creation of WAEMU was seen as one such example. While supporters have referred to it as an attempt to quicken the pace of monetary union, opponents consider it more as a tool to serve sectional interests.[18]

Trends in the CFA franc zone. The early experience of French-speaking West African countries was not too different from that of their English-speaking counterparts. Under French colonial rule, the colonies were organized under one colonial administration into a federation. France issued currencies in each colony, and these were firmly pegged to the French franc. The currencies were later consolidated into the CFA franc, issued by the Central Bank for Overseas

16. Ogunkola (2002).
17. Collier and Gunning (1995).
18. See, for example, Lavergne and Daddieh (1997).

France (Caisse Centrale de la France d'Outre Mer). In setting up the franc zone in western Africa, the objectives of the monetary authorities included achieving: convertibility into French francs at a fixed parity; free capital mobility throughout the zone; pooling of most foreign exchange reserves at the French Treasury; the establishment of a common trade and financial policy toward the rest of the world; and guaranteed convertibility by France through the establishment of "operations accounts" for each colonial central bank with the French Treasury.[19]

For most of the pre-independence period, many of these colonies remained only marginally autonomous within a French West African federation. The degree of economic integration among them remained somewhat higher than among English-speaking countries in the same region. With political independence in 1960, however, some barriers to trade and to the movement of factors of production began to emerge. Manu has argued that several attempts to form a pan-francophone body in the region failed largely because France opposed the formation of a strong federation in the region over which it had little influence.[20]

In the view of Uche, it was "not surprising that all the regional bodies that emerged in the post-independence francophone zone of the 1960s were either loose affiliations or simply non-functional."[21] These included the political association called Union Africaine et Malgache (UAM), which was established in 1961, and later became the Organisation Commune Africaine et Malgache (OCAM). Membership was open to all French-speaking African countries that had signed cooperation agreements with France. Uche also describes the Union Douaniere des Etats de l'Afrique Occidentale (UDAO) as ineffective.[22] This customs union comprised Côte d'Ivoire, Benin, Burkina Faso, Niger, Senegal, Mali, and Mauritania. Their objective was to redistribute the customs duties that the coastal states collected on transit trade with landlocked members.[23] Uche, and also Honohan and Lane, have argued that France was not particularly interested in promoting intraregional trade among French-speaking West African countries, and therefore did nothing to facilitate it: "It was more interested in promoting its own trade with the various francophone countries in the region."[24] And this is seen as having motivated France to support the establishment of the Central Bank of West African States (Banque Central des Etats de

19. Boughton (1991, pp. 1–2).
20. See Manu (1989).
21. Uche (2001, p. 10).
22. Uche (1999).
23. See Bach (1983).
24. Uche (2001, p. 10); see also Honohan and Lane (2000).

l'Afrique de l'Ouest, BCEAO) in 1962. The creation of BCEAO eliminated currency restrictions in the trade of French-speaking countries with France.

The regional central bank for the Central African Zone is the Bank for Central African States (Banque des Etats de l'Afrique Centrale, BEAC). It was established in 1972 with the sole purpose of issuing currency. Like BCEAO (the central bank for the eight West African countries), BEAC was to maintain a fixed exchange rate with the French franc and manage monetary policy, consisting of credit controls, while currency convertibility was, and still is, guaranteed through an "operations account" with the French Treasury.

Strikingly, all three integration organizations in West Africa (English- and French-speaking) have promoted quite similar projects to advance their objectives, including the establishment of institutions for human development, agricultural and industrial development, and monetary cooperation. Despite a certain commonality of purpose—liberalizing intra-area trade and achieving other forms of cooperation—there has been very little effective coordination among them. Considering the significant overlap in both goals and activities, it is surprising that member countries found it necessary to maintain a multiplicity of institutions. Explanations include the "French factor" (that is, the desire of successive Paris governments to support organizations that grouped their former colonies in the region), as well as a lack of confidence by individual countries in the capacity of such institutions to protect their interests.[25] In a sense, it has been a case of seeking double assurance without paying a higher premium.

In fact, recent developments in financial and monetary cooperation are an outcome of recent trade integration experiences. In the 1980s, the survival of CEAO as a regional trade body had come under serious threat, largely as a consequence of the malfunctioning of existing trade arrangements. The institution of a preferential regional cooperation tax on manufactured exports from member countries worked largely to the advantage of Côte d'Ivoire and Senegal. Since the compensation mechanism did not work properly, the loss of revenue from member states was considered to be a serious setback to the integration effort. The absence of complementary industrial structures ensured that the number of industrial products registered under the regional cooperation tax hardly changed. The poor functioning of the system of preferences and the inherent loss of revenue to several members led to difficult fiscal situations in those states. By 1991, arrears to the secretariat and to the compensation fund amounted to 45.5 billion CFA francs, which was four times as much as the institutions' combined budgets.[26]

25. Bundu (1997).
26. Bach (1997, p. 87).

Governments used the banking system to finance these deficits. By the mid-1980s, the banking system had almost ground to a halt owing to the nature of its institutional mechanisms. Most of the banks were joint ventures between national governments and one of four major banks based in France. Key senior management was provided by French nationals seconded from the parent banks in France. Although deposit mobilization has been low in the franc zone, funds were secured from the two central banks, the Central Bank of West African States and the Bank for Central African States. For years, governments in several member states directly or indirectly pushed the banks into lending to state-owned enterprises, or to regional and political groupings, or to some of the governments' own suppliers, who never paid. Although the central banks were freed by statute from any fiscal pressure, they were forced to lend through commercial banks to relieve fiscal needs. The two central banks acted as though they were agents of the fiscal authorities and refinanced politically directed or government-inspired bank lending that was never paid back. The majority of commercial banks failed because they issued bad loans, although some were rescued later. These and other problems contributed to the banking crises in the CFA zone in the 1980s. Thus, by 1993 almost all of the countries in the zone were in deep recession. Capital movements were blocked, and it became difficult to effect current international payments.

The fiscal problems of member states continued, alongside growing pressure from international financial institutions to carry out macroeconomic reforms in the early 1990s and forge a joint program of activities to address the economic crises without necessarily having to devalue the CFA franc. The resulting programs for budgetary and fiscal policy harmonization led to the institution of several arrangements for regional banking commissions and the harmonization of legislative and regulatory frameworks to govern economic and social activities, including social insurance and business law. The plan was to go further and develop a single financial market, a regional stock exchange, and a free-trade zone. Thus the preparatory work for launching WAEMU took place between 1991 and 1994. By 1994 a number of the institutions that had been agreed to in Ouagadougou in 1991 had been established and had become operational, but the idea of avoiding devaluation had to be abandoned in view of continuing economic crises and increasing pressure from multilateral development agencies. Thus, the 50 percent devaluation announcement was made on the eve of the member states' meeting, in Dakar in January 1994, to formalize into a treaty institutional developments over the previous three years.

A regional financial market was created under the auspices of WAEMU to comply with two main objectives: all actors in the regional financial market must have equal opportunities where they are located; and international standards with respect to the settlement/delivery schedule, simultaneity of securities/cash exchanges, and the distinction between operational, regulatory, and supervisory functions must be complied with. To address these needs, the regional stock exchange (Bourse Régionale des Valeurs Mobilières, BRVM) was established in September 1998, and its eight regional branches were interconnected to the headquarters and other institutions. Also, the Regional Savings and Capital Market Board (Conseil Regional de l'Epargne Publique et des Marché Financiers) was established and put in charge of supervising the regional stock exchange.

The regional stock exchange has two main components: a primary market that deals with financial securities and a secondary market that deals with the liquidity and mobility of securities already issued. The main products traded in the market are bonds, debts, and negotiable debt instruments. The exchange is a private limited company with a capital base of U.S.$4.84 million, 87 percent of which is owned by private businesspeople in the region and 13 percent by the member states. The regional exchange has thirty-eight listed companies transferred from the Abidjan stock exchange, with Ivorian companies dominating. The financial market project was made possible in the WAEMU region because there was already a highly integrated monetary and financial union built on harmonized monetary and banking regulations, successful restructuring of the union's financial sector, and a sustained effort to restructure the macroeconomic framework.

The formation of EMU was a significant factor in encouraging the CFA zone countries to maintain their arrangement at the time of the 1994 devaluation. The legacy of the French colonial system appears to have survived much longer after independence than the British colonial system, and two franc-based monetary unions in West Africa are still functioning, with most of the original members remaining participants. Both BEAC and BCEAO are still in existence and continue to develop their programs and instruments of monetary policy, financial sector integration, and capital market institutions. After the devaluation, monetary policy moved from direct controls to market-based instruments, taking account of all relevant domestic and macroeconomic indicators. Direct BEAC advances to governments were phased out in 2004, when the first Treasury bills by governments were issued.[27] So far, monetary policy has been effective in pushing inflation down in the subregion and interest rates are set by the central bank.

27. Zafar and Kubota (2003).

Financial and Monetary Cooperation in Eastern and Southern Africa

East Africa had a currency board very similar to the one in English-speaking West Africa. In East Africa, the three core members retained the currency board arrangement, with a common currency, until five years after independence. The old monetary cooperation group (the East Africa Community, which existed from 1960 to 1977) was made up of Kenya, Tanzania, and Uganda. In the old currency area, there was free circulation of the national currencies at par and common external capital controls, as well as free movement of capital within the union. However, the new East Africa Community was inaugurated in January 2001 to replace the one that collapsed in 1977, with the long-term objective of forming a monetary union. Articles 94 and 97 of the treaty establishing the new union relate to monetary cooperation and financial matters and maintaining the convertibility of the various currencies. The new EAC is made up of the same members as the old one, with the main objective being to establish a monetary union and a unit of account for the community, known as the East African Currency Unit.[28]

The Rand Monetary Area (RMA) dates back to 1910, when the South African Customs Union (SACU) came into being. It was not established formally until 1974, with South Africa, Lesotho, and Swaziland signing an agreement on clearing arrangements, bank supervision, and the development of a forward exchange market. Botswana withdrew from the rand zone in 1974 before the agreement was signed. The RMA was transformed into a common monetary area in 1986.

Another cooperation arrangement worthy of note is the Southern African Development Community (SADC). This regional cooperation group was formed in the 1980s by nine countries in southern Africa, with the main objective of making their economies less dependent on South Africa. Following independence, Namibia joined the union in 1990, together with South Africa, after the democratic election that led to the formation of a government of national unity in 1994. SADC objectives include poverty alleviation and the maximum utilization of regional resources.

The SADC financial and investment sector was formally established in 1995. This common currency area includes South Africa, Lesotho, Namibia, and Swaziland. South Africa was given responsibility for the management and development of financial and investment protocol. There is a council of finance ministers under the chairmanship of the South African minister of finance, which meets from time to time to give guidance to any program that will ensure closer

28. Ogunkola (2002).

financial cooperation among the participating countries. There is also a committee of treasury officials and a committee of governors of central banks and their officials with specific duties. A number of technical subcommittees and working groups are also drawn from among the officials of SADC central banks to work on specific projects. The committee of governors is required to encourage the establishment of sound and well-managed privately owned banking institutions to provide financial services in a competitive environment.

The central banks' responsibility has been restricted to the creation and maintenance of a stable financial environment conducive to sustainable economic growth and, in addition, they must protect the value of the currency. The central bank governors are required to work jointly to develop interlinkable national payments and clearing settlements systems for financial transactions compatible with national systems, so as to provide more effective cross-border settlement of interregional financial transactions. There is also a focus on capital market development in the subregion.

A statistical database for essential economic time series from the twelve SADC countries is now available at the South African Reserve Bank to help the governors gain a better understanding of the regional economic environment and learn from one another's experiences. A data bank has also been established to provide information on issues relating to legislation, relationships with governors, functions and responsibilities of management, policy objectives, monetary policy procedures and instruments, and administrative structures for each central bank. To standardize bank regulation and supervision in the region, the central banks have formed an eastern and southern African banking supervisors' group for this purpose.

Of the twelve SADC members, South Africa is the most advanced in the region. In the rand zone, Lesotho, Namibia, and Swaziland hold their currencies at par with the South African rand, and the central banks in these countries function as a currency board by issuing currencies that are backed by 100 percent foreign assets. The rand circulates alongside local currencies, thus generating seigniorage opportunities for South Africa.

The SADC cooperation system is judged to have benefited its member countries.[29] There is relative macroeconomic stability in the region, reflected by low inflation rates. In many countries, there is also clear evidence of convergence of fiscal and monetary policies.

---

29. Uche (1999).

An Assessment of Current Financial and Monetary Cooperation Arrangements

This section focuses on the experiences of the CFA zone and draws on those experiences for lessons for the rest of the region.

The CFA Zone Experience and Its Relevance for the Rest of Africa

Honohan and Lane suggest that, even though the underlying structure established for the franc zone in West and Central Africa appeared to be solid, it had problems:

> The underlying economic philosophy of the franc zone arrangements was always that of an open and competitive market. . . . The institutional arrangements are strikingly modern in appearance. In particular there have been multinational central banks (which are thus independent of any one national government), rules constraining monetary financing of fiscal deficits, an open capital account, widespread presence of foreign-owned banks and the lowest inflation rates in Africa. From some points of view the regime has looked like a precursor to EMU with its single currency, its freedom of capital movements and its multinational central bank. However, any attempt to draw conclusions for the prospects of wider African monetary unions must pause to consider the 1980s crisis of the CFA zone.[30]

It is clear that, until the mid-1980s, the economic performance of the franc zone countries was acceptable, and the fixed exchange rate with France appeared to remove macroeconomic uncertainty and encourage external investment. The relatively high growth rates that were achieved and stable CFA franc notes ensured that the subregion outshone such unstable countries as Ghana and Nigeria with inconvertible local currencies. And because some parts of the franc zone banking system appeared to function properly, the zone received substantial deposits of flight capital from its neighbors.

Honohan and Lane wrote that the inflexibility and brittle character of the system's institutional mechanisms proved to be its downfall, bringing the functioning of the banking system almost to a halt in several of the countries from the mid-1980s. This led to the deep recession that they experienced all the way through 1993. A parallel market in the CFA franc developed, and capital movements were blocked, while it became difficult to effect current international payments. As we saw earlier, a large number of the banks failed, even though

30. Honohan and Lane (2000, p. 6).

some were recapitalized: "Depositors in some banks had gone without access to their funds for years. The banks that continued to function now tended to be highly selective in their clientele, both on the deposit and on the lending side. Interbank markets were operating on a very limited basis. Having lost heavily from the collapse of debtor banks, the central banks were close to being unable to cover their operating expenses."[31]

It was these problems that eventually led to devaluation in 1994. However, much of the blame for the situation is placed on the behavior of governments, which used the banking system to finance projects in which they had an interest, albeit indirectly. It is believed that the banks agreed to make the kinds of loans that led to their collapse because of an unusual relationship that had developed between the governments and the French ownership of many of the banks:

> Most were joint ventures between the national Governments and one of four major French-based banks; sometimes the Government was the majority shareholder, sometimes not. In either case, the key senior management was provided by French nationals seconded from the parent banks in France. However, the objective of the French shareholders is unlikely to have been solely profit maximization. They had other interests, including the commercial interests in Africa of their French customers. They will not have been unaware of the wider political agenda of the French Government, which was owner of the French banks for at least part of the period, and a strong influence at all times.[32]

In the end, even though the central banks were apparently freed by statute from any fiscal pressure, they bowed to indirect pressure to lend through banks to relieve fiscal needs. Recapitalizing them through the central bank led to the eventual collapse of the system.

Honohan and Lane have argued that this particular rules-based system did not guarantee sound policy since it encouraged a false sense of security. The rules did not guarantee the correct incentives, and their rigidity induced a banking practice that subordinated both commercial and central banking to fiscal pressures. The three rules that they judged to be problematic were:

—the exchange rate rule, which "could not cope with the procyclical public sector wage policy and the optimistic policy of ratcheting official purchasing prices for the all-important cash crops (especially coffee and cocoa) to the highest figures attained to date";

31. Honohan and Lane (2000, p. 7).
32. Honohan and Lane (2000, p. 8).

—the rule that the banking sector could not lend the government more than a fraction of its annual revenue needs because it "merely diverted the pressures into indirect borrowing through public enterprises and other associated bodies and through government payments arrears";

—The rule that each national government was responsible to the central bank for the debts of any insolvent bank because it encouraged "insouciant lending by the central bank to unsound banks."[33]

It is apparent that the rules could not operate within a political environment that was not being adapted quickly enough for the rigid arrangements. The need to ensure consistency of macroeconomic and financial fundamentals with a fixed exchange rate system was not given the appropriate importance: "This sorry story of implosion of the CFA zone financial system, culminating in the major devaluation of January 1994, serves as a cautionary tale for fans of monetary unions and, indeed, of rules-based monetary systems in general. The limitations of such rules must be recognized whether they be the specific rules adopted in the CFA zone, or those of a currency board."[34]

The CFA zone is reckoned to have recovered substantially from the troubles of the 1980s, following the devaluation and a restructuring of the zone's regulatory arrangements. Following the banking crisis in the zone, some of the new institutional arrangements adopted include the centralization of responsibility for bank supervision in two regional banking control commissions. This provides a new multinational "agency of restraint" that fills a gap in the previous institutional arrangements, in contrast to European Monetary Union, where national central banks are still responsible for regulating commercial banks.

The CFA is now pegged to the euro, and this is seen as providing greater nominal and real exchange rate stability. Honohan and Lane are not certain that there are obvious lessons to be drawn from the current arrangements for other African countries. They query whether EMU, together with the new focus on the use of a common currency as an insulator against contagious or correlated capital movements and on the use of regional financial authorities as a quasi-external discipline on national financial policy, points to any increased likelihood of additional cooperative arrangements.

Scope for Developing African Monetary Unions

There is no doubt that EMU has inspired a lot of discussion concerning the creation of monetary unions among groups of African countries. What is not yet

33. Honohan and Lane (2000, p. 9).
34. Honohan and Lane (2000, p. 10).

clear is the extent to which they will seek to develop external agencies of restraint, as the current CFA franc zone has done. Honohan and Lane suggest that monetary union may be viewed in a number of ways: as an agency of restraint on governments; as a bulwark against contagious speculation; as a way of achieving economies of scale in the financial sector; and, finally, in a traditional role as an optimum currency area (OCA), involving arguments relating to the pattern of trade and to the degree of factor mobility.

Monetary union as an external agency of restraint. There are two elements to this issue: political considerations and seigniorage. While, for many years, there has been little interest in delegating the conduct of monetary policy to an external agency, there is a clear indication from West Africa that countries are now more willing to entrust that role to a supranational body.

The creation of the second monetary zone and the agreement on convergence criteria both point to renewed interest in developing an external agency of restraint. However, Ogunkola does not consider the various elements for successful optimal currency areas to be present, particularly in view of wide divergences in production outcomes and potential. There is presumed to be little interdependence among the nations, and they face large common and idiosyncratic shocks. And it is this that will make it difficult for individual countries to entrust the preparation of monetary and exchange rate policies to external agencies, particularly in the face of mounting adverse shocks to their economies. Ogunkola sees the fact that countries are struggling to attain the convergence criteria as evidence of that difficulty.[35]

However, Honohan and Lane suggest that "the record of macroeconomic mismanagement in many African countries means that there is a strong case for delegation of monetary policy, if a suitable supranational monetary authority exists. Put differently, since policymaking resources are scarce in Africa, it may make sense to 'outsource' monetary policy as one possible resolution to the search for 'agencies of restraint.'"[36]

The major problem remains that a supranational monetary authority may require some degree of political integration if it is to be accepted as democratically accountable. Political integration may also be desirable to minimize the "hold-up" problem in setting monetary policy. And that is missing in the region at present, making it difficult to be very optimistic about the outcomes. The current initiative is to use monetary union to spearhead regional economic cooperation within a region where economic cooperation has so far been limited.

35. Ogunkola (2002).
36. Honohan and Lane (2000, p. 11).

Honohan and Lane suggest that, if there were enough resources to support monetary union, it might lead slowly to greater political integration: "This political and administrative process would likely be a more potent force for economic integration than the direct effect of achieving exchange rate stability across African borders."[37]

On the question of seigniorage, it is the fear of loss of seigniorage revenue that might deter countries from abdicating responsibility for monetary policy. And many African countries rely extensively on seigniorage, amounting to an average of around 1.5 percent of the region's GDP. It is obvious that the countries will have to work out appropriate alternatives to high seigniorage and find ways of distributing these equitably.

Deepening financial sectors and fighting contagion. There are opportunities for improving the poorly developed banking and financial sectors. A fundamental concern for countries contemplating membership of a monetary union or a currency area is whether it leads to greater financial resources for development. This is linked to the extent to which it makes available the rest of the world's resources, namely the benefits of globalization. As seen earlier, Africa has been left out of the massive international capital that flowed to developing economies when the world economy opened up in the 1980s. The good news is that it was also bypassed by the global financial crisis associated with such massive capital flows. In its global marginalization, Africa stands to lose out on the potential benefits of globalization, although it is presumed to escape the risks of globalization.

Successful globalization is characterized by mutual gains for both global investors and emerging economies in Africa. While benefiting from globalization, Africa should also contribute to improving the global risk-reward ratio faced by global investors. Those international investors must evaluate their investment portfolios on the basis of the global risk-reward ratio. In this regard, the benefits from globalization include the following:

—Diversification benefits: Africa's competitiveness in attracting international capital depends on its role in improving the global risk-reward ratio faced by international investors. The potential benefits from international portfolio diversification stem fundamentally from diversity in countries' economic cycles. For instance, a combined strategy of investment in both non–United States equities and the U.S. market generally dominates investment in the U.S. market alone. Can Africa contribute to the emerging markets portfolio, and ultimately to the global portfolio? To the extent that Africa's economies do not move in tandem with those of the advanced economies, there are opportunities for inter-

37. Honohan and Lane (2000, p. 12).

national investors to benefit from the inclusion of African financial markets in the global portfolio.

—Bargains in Africa and stock return potential: Indicators point to gross undercapitalization of Africa, suggesting potential bargains. Very low price-earnings multiples are currently observed in African stock markets, suggesting that there is significant undervaluation, given an acceptable range of emerging market risks. Also, the recent performance of African stock markets is encouraging and indicative of the potential for high returns.[38]

There are considerable benefits to Africa as a recipient of global capital, with integration into the global economy, or both and these include the following:

—Access to a diversified source of external finance: Access to a *diversified* source of external capital lessens heavy reliance on sovereign debt and its attendant crisis, and on official flows, which are already shrinking.

—Reduction in the cost of capital: Globalization allows for local securities market risks to be shared internationally. Global risk sharing leads to a reduction in the local cost of capital.[39] In other words, greater risk sharing by international investors leads to a reduction in the cost of capital for local firms, since risks of local shares are shared globally.

—Discipline and exposure to best practices: Globalization enhances the credibility of domestic capital market institutions, as foreign investors demand world-class services. Governments will be under greater pressure to strengthen the rule of law, enforce contracts, and increase the growth of available information in response to international investor demands.

—Reversal of flight capital: Evidence from other regions, such as Latin America and East Asia, suggests that globalization of local markets leads to large reversals of flight capital. Given that Africa stands within the top tier of regions in terms of flight capital stock per GDP, there is potential for a significant reversal of flight capital if the region is sufficiently integrated into the global economy.

The other side of the coin is that globalization engenders considerable risks, with the associated crisis, as witnessed in East Asia. The global risks stemming from volatility in global financial markets, the large unfavorable fluctuations in international exchange rates, and large unfavorable swings in international interest rates manifest themselves in large unfavorable swings in international capital flows. For instance, countries that experienced large capital flows suffered commensurately large and sudden outflows. The sudden and massive collapse of

38. Senbet (1998).
39. Errunza, Senbet, and Hogan (1998).

capital inflows can be enormously costly. Not only will there be sudden with-drawals of deposits, leading to a credit crunch in the economy; in addition, creditors will be unwilling to supply short-term credit even for a liquidity crisis, and there will be default and *contagion* of the type experienced in East Asia (and earlier in Mexico). The damage associated with the financial crisis was evident in the dramatic declines in the asset and currency values of East Asia.

Capital markets are relatively new to most of Africa. In West Africa, for example, with the exception of Nigeria and Côte d'Ivoire, other stock markets were set up only in the past few years. They may be seen as a natural outgrowth of the financial reforms that have taken place in these countries.[40] International investors have begun paying attention to Africa, and a total of eighteen special-ized investment funds have been established since 1993, which are now trading in New York and Europe. Regionalization is emerging as a way of addressing the thinness and scarce liquidity problem of African capital markets. In particu-lar, the Abidjan stock market has emerged as an anchor for the CFA countries, with an increased potential to serve other countries in West Africa. This effort has encouraged discussion between Ghana and Nigeria on setting up another subregional exchange for English-speaking West Africa. The Nigerian Stock Exchange and the Ghana Stock Exchange signed a memorandum of under-standing in 1999 to ascertain the feasibility of a regionalized exchange. Ironi-cally, however, while this discussion is taking place, a new effort is under way to start a second Nigerian exchange in Abuja. The establishment of regional securi-ties and exchange commissions, self-regulatory organizations, and committees to promote harmonization of legal and regulatory schemes are among the mech-anisms under discussion. The tax treatment of investments has to be harmo-nized, since tax policy is an important incentive or disincentive for both issuers and investors. Ultimately, regulations and accounting reporting systems, along with clearance, settlement, and depository systems, should conform to inter-national standards.

Summary and Concluding Remarks

There is no doubt that there is still a long way to go before financial and mone-tary cooperation can be firmly established in Africa. Since the introduction of the euro, the perceived pressure on African governments to set up similar arrange-ments has increased, despite the fact that institutional and other structural con-ditions are quite different. In parts of Africa, there is certainly a tendency to

40. See Jefferis and Mbekewani (2001).

view financial and monetary integration as the best possibility for bringing about faster political integration

The current struggles of the West African Monetary Zone to achieve convergence give ample indication of the difficulties facing the region as it seeks to achieve financial and monetary cooperation. On the other hand, the fact that the CFA franc appears to have achieved some stability since the implementation of reforms and pegging to the euro suggests that having an external anchor might help. In any case, this experience raises question as to the prospects for using an externally based peg to achieve financial cooperation among any group of African countries.

References

Anyanwu, J. C. 2003. "Estimating the Macroeconomic Effects of Monetary Unions: The Case of Trade and Output." *African Development Review* 15, nos. 2–3: 126–45.

Aryeetey, E., and L. Senbet. 1999. "Essential Financial Market Reforms in Africa." Background Paper for "Can Africa Claim the 21st Century?" Washington: World Bank.

Bach, D. C. 1983. "The Politics of West African Economic Co-Operation: C.E.A.O. and E.C.O.W.A.S." *Journal of Modern African Studies* 21, no. 4: 605–23.

———. 1997. "Institutional Crisis and the Search for New Models." In *Regional Integration and Cooperation in West Africa, A Multidimensional Perspective,* edited by R. Lavergne. Ottawa: Africa World Press and International Development Research Centre.

Badiane, O. 1997. "National Policies as Impediments to Regional Economic Integration." In *Regional Integration and Cooperation in West Africa, A Multidimensional* Perspective, edited by R. Lavergne. Ottawa: Africa World Press and International Development Research Centre.

Boughton, J. M. 1991. "The CFA Franc Zone: Currency Union and Monetary Standard." Working Paper WP/91/133. Washington: International Monetary Fund.

Bundu, A. 1997. "ECOWAS and the Future of Regional Integration in West Africa." In *Regional Integration and Cooperation in West Africa, A Multidimensional Perspective,* edited by R. Lavergne. Ottawa: Africa World Press and International Development Research Centre.

Collier, P., and J. W. Gunning. 1995. "Trade Policy and Regional Integration: Implications for the Relations between Europe and Africa." *World Economy* 18, no. 3: 387–409.

Economic Community of West African States (ECOWAS). 1975. *Treaty of the Economic Community of West African States.* Lagos.

Errunza, V., L. W. Senbet, and K. Hogan. 1998. "The Pricing of Country Funds from Emerging Markets: Theory and Evidence." *International Journal of Theoretical and Applied Finance* 1, no.1: 111–43.

Grandes, M. 2003. "South Africa's Monetary Area: An Optimum Currency Area: What Costs, Which Benefits?" DELTA Working Paper. Paris: Ecole des Hautes Etudes en Sciences Sociales/Ecole Normale Supérieure.

Honohan, P., and P. R. Lane. 2000. "Will the Euro Trigger More Monetary Union in Africa?" UNU WIDER Working Paper 176. Helsinki.

Jefferis, K., and K. Mbekewani. 2001. "Laws, Institutions and Capital Markets Integration in Sub-Saharan Africa." Technical Paper. Paris: OECD Development Centre.

Lavergne, R., and C. K. Daddieh. 1997. "Donor Perspectives." In *Regional Integration and Cooperation in West Africa, A Multidimensional Perspective,* edited by R. Lavergne. Ottawa: Africa World Press and International Development Research Centre.

Manu, M. 1989. "The Future of ECOWAS." Nigerian Institute of International Affairs Lecture Series 49. Lagos.

Ogunkola, E. O. 2002. "The Second Monetary Zone in West Africa and the Future of a Single Monetary Zone in Sub-Saharan Africa." Department of Economics, University of Lesotho.

Senbet, L. W. 1998. "Globalization of African Financial Markets." Paper prepared for the United Nations University and AERC conference "Africa and Asia in the Global Economy." Tokyo, August.

Uche, C. U. 1999. "Foreign Banks, Africans and Credit in Colonial Nigeria, c.1890–1912." *Economic History Review* 52, no. 4: 669–91.

———. 2001. "The Politics of Monetary Sector Cooperation among the Economic Community of West African States' Members." Department of Banking and Finance, University of Nigeria, Enugu.

World Bank, 1998, 2003, 2005. *World Development Indicators.* Washington.

Zafar, A., and K. Kubota. 2003. "Regional Integration in Central Africa: Key Issues." Africa Region Working Paper Series 52. World Bank.

Contributors

ERNEST ARYEETEY
University of Ghana

GEORGES CORM
Saint Joseph University, Beirut

ROY CULPEPER
North-South Institute, Ottawa

ANA TERESA FUZZO DE LIMA
Institute of Development Studies,
University of Sussex

STEPHANY GRIFFITH-JONES
Institute of Development Studies,
University of Sussex

JULIA LEUNG
Hong Kong Monetary Authority

JOSÉ LUIS MACHINEA
ECLAC

JOSÉ ANTONIO OCAMPO,
Department of Economic
and Social Affairs, United Nations

JAE HA PARK
Korea Institute of Finance

YUNG CHUL PARK
Korea University

FERNANDO PRADA
FORO Nacional/Internacional, Lima

GUILLERMO ROZENWURCEL
National University of San Martín,
Argentina

FRANCISCO SAGASTI
*FORO Nacional/Internacional,
Programa Agenda: Peru*

KANIT SANGSUBHAN
*Fiscal Policy Research Institute
of Thailand*

ALFRED STEINHERR
*European Investment Bank,
Luxembourg and Free University
of Bozen-Bolzano*

DANIEL TITELMAN
ECLAC

CHARLES WYPLOSZ
*Graduate Institute of International
Studies, Geneva, and Center
for Economic Policy Research*

Index

AAAID. *See* Arab Authority for Agricultural
Investment and Development
ABEDA. *See* Arab Bank for Economic
Development in Africa
ABF. *See* Asian Bond Fund
ABMI. *See* Asian Bond Market Initiative
AC. *See* Andean Community
ACD (Asian Cooperative Dialogue), 284
ADC. *See* Andean Development
Corporation
AfDB. *See* African Development Bank
AfDF. *See* African Development Fund
AFDM+3. *See* ASEAN+3
AFESD. *See* Arab Fund for Economic and
Social Development
Africa: aid projections for, 41; Arab develop-
ment financing for, 14, 80, 292, 295,
304, 305, 312; and colonialism, 11,
338–39, 341–43, 345; cooperation
arrangements in, 348–54; creditworthy
countries, lack of, 53–54; EIB lending
to, 160; expectations of cooperation in,
333–37; external agencies of restraint

on, 335; financial and monetary cooperation in, 329–56; globalization's effect
on, 352–54; least developed countries,
prevalence of, 51–52; lessons from,
54–58, 337–47; monetary union, development of, 350–54; political integration in, 351–52; regional cooperation,
challenges confronting, 53–54; risk
reduction from regionalized banking,
336; tax policy, need to harmonize, 336;
trade integration, 12. *See also specific
countries, regions, and institutions*
African Development Bank (AfDB): allocation of resources by, 102; concessional
lending of, 16, 80; financial standing of,
90, 93; graduation policies of, 86–88;
history of, 12–13, 35, 44; industrial
country membership in, 44; influence of
Nigeria, 98; infrastructure operations of,
20, 85; loan conditions and costs, 94;
social sector operations, 84; transport,
energy, and environment programs, 85
African Development Bank Group, 54